The Making of Visual News

The Making of Visual News

A History of Photography in the Press

Thierry Gervais

in collaboration with Gaëlle Morel

Translated by John Tittenson

B L O O M S B U R Y
LONDON • OXFORD • NEW YORK • NEW DELHI • SYDNEY

Bloomsbury Academic
An imprint of Bloomsbury Publishing Plc

50 Bedford Square
London
WC1B 3DP
UK

1385 Broadway
New York
NY 10018
USA

www.bloomsbury.com

BLOOMSBURY and the Diana logo are trademarks of Bloomsbury Publishing Plc

First published in French in 2015

British Library Cataloguing-in-Publication Data
A catalogue record for this book is available from the British Library.

ISBN: HB: 978-1-4742-9520-8
PB: 978-1-4742-9519-2
ePDF: 978-1-4742-9523-9
ePub: 978-1-4742-9521-5

Library of Congress Cataloging-in-Publication Data
A catalog record for this book is available from the Library of Congress.

Cover design by Irene Martinez Costa
Cover image: Miss Paris, 1934. Melle Élisabeth Argal élue la veille, achetant des journaux sur lesquels figure son visage © Keystone

Typeset by RefineCatch Limited, Bungay, Suffolk
Printed and bound in India

For **Gabriel**.

Contents

List of figures

Acknowledgements

Our sincerest thanks go to Émilie Bernard, Sylvain Besson, Robert Burley, Marta Braun, Clément Chéroux, François Cheval, Elisa Julia Gilmour, Peter Higdon, Anna Jedrzejowski, Cordula Lebeck, Robert Lebeck, Paige Lindsay, Rachel Lobo, Olivier Lugon, Jean-Michel Morel, Cécile Nédélec, Doina Popescu and Paul Roth.

Research for this project was supported with funding from the Faculty of Communication and Design, Ryerson University, Toronto, Canada.

The English translation of the text was supported by the Ryerson Image Centre, Toronto.

About the Authors

Dr. Thierry Gervais is associate professor at Ryerson University and Head of Research of the Ryerson Image Centre (RIC), Toronto. He was the Editor in Chief of *Études photographiques* from 2007 to 2013 and is the author of numerous articles on photojournalism in peer-reviewed journals and scholarly publications. He was the curator of the exhibition *Dispatch: War Photographs in Print, 1854–2008* (RIC, Fall 2014) and the co-curator of the exhibitions *Views from Above* (Centre Pompidou-Metz, Spring 2013), *Léon Gimpel (1873–1948), The Audacious Work of a Photographer* (Musée d'Orsay, Paris, Spring 2008), and *L'Événement: Les images comme acteurs de l'histoire* (Jeu de Paume, Paris, Winter 2007). At the RIC, he organized the symposia "The 'Public Life' of Photographs" (2013), "Collecting and Curating Photographs: Between Private and Public Collections" (2014), and "Photography Historians: A New Generation?" (2015). In the Fall 2016, he edited *The "Public" Life of Photographs*, the first volume of the academic "RIC Book" series published in partnership with the Ryerson Image Centre and MIT Press.

Dr. Gaëlle Morel is Exhibitions Curator at the Ryerson Image Centre (Toronto). She received her PhD in the History of Contemporary Photography from Université Paris 1 Panthéon-Sorbonne. In 2009, Dr. Morel served as the guest curator of the Mois de la Photo in Montreal on the theme of *The Spaces of the Image* and edited the accompanying catalogue. In 2012, Dr. Morel curated the Berenice Abbott exhibition at the Jeu de Paume in Paris and the Art Gallery of Ontario in Toronto, as well as edited the accompanying publication. Most recently, she curated of *Robert Burley: The Disappearance of Darkness*, an exhibition produced by the Ryerson Image Centre which toured to the National Gallery of Canada and the Nicéphore-Niépce Museum in Chalon-sur-Saône, France. She has also taught the history of contemporary art and the history of photography at the university level in both France and Canada. She co-teaches the Exhibition and Publication of Photographs course in the Film + Photography Preservation Collections Management Master's program at the School of Image Arts, Ryerson University. Her research deals with the artistic and cultural recognition of photography from the 1970s, and photographic modernism in the 1930s. She has written essays that have appeared in a number of magazines and books.

Introduction

The earliest uses of photography in the press date from the 1840s, with the first caption including the words "from a photograph" appearing in the French weekly *L'Illustration* of August 26, 1843.[1] At the time photographs were used as models by engravers, who copied them onto boxwood blocks, which were then combined with type as the pages were composed. From the very infancy of the illustrated press, photography's role was tied to a rhetoric of image-legitimation that encouraged press ventures whose emphasis, in contrast with that of the press generally, was on information at the expense of opinion.[2] Thus in 1845 the fourth volume of *L'Illustration* was introduced as follows: "*L'Illustration* is not a political forum; its sole ambition in this respect is to reflect, as in a truthful mirror, the men and events of its time, in the interests of its present readers and for the instruction of those who, later on, will take the trouble to consult its written pages, driven solely by a passion for truth."[3] While photographs took on the aspect of engravings once they were reproduced in the press, their mechanical mode of production fueled the pro-image discourse and gave credibility to this new journalistic approach. In 1850 the journalist Adolphe Joanne drew on the supposed objectivity of the photographic process as a way of persuading his readership: "In order to convince the most resolute skeptics, we are supporting our contention with irrefutable evidence: we are reproducing as faithfully as possible six daguerreotypes expressly commissioned for *L'Illustration* . . . Would a denial of the daguerreotype not be a denial of light itself? Show me the man foolish enough not to believe in the sun and its works!"[4] This faith in photography's mechanical character was regularly invoked by journalists and press publishers to explain their choice of images. In 1886 Thomas Grimm described Nadar's photographic interview with the scientist Eugène Chevreul in *Le Journal illustré* as an interpretation-free method of producing "a document of absolute exactitude."[5] Fifty years later, when *Picture Post* ran Robert Capa's photographs of the Battle of Rio Segre, between Spanish Republicans and Franco's forces in the autumn of 1938, the article's header called the images "simply a record of modern war

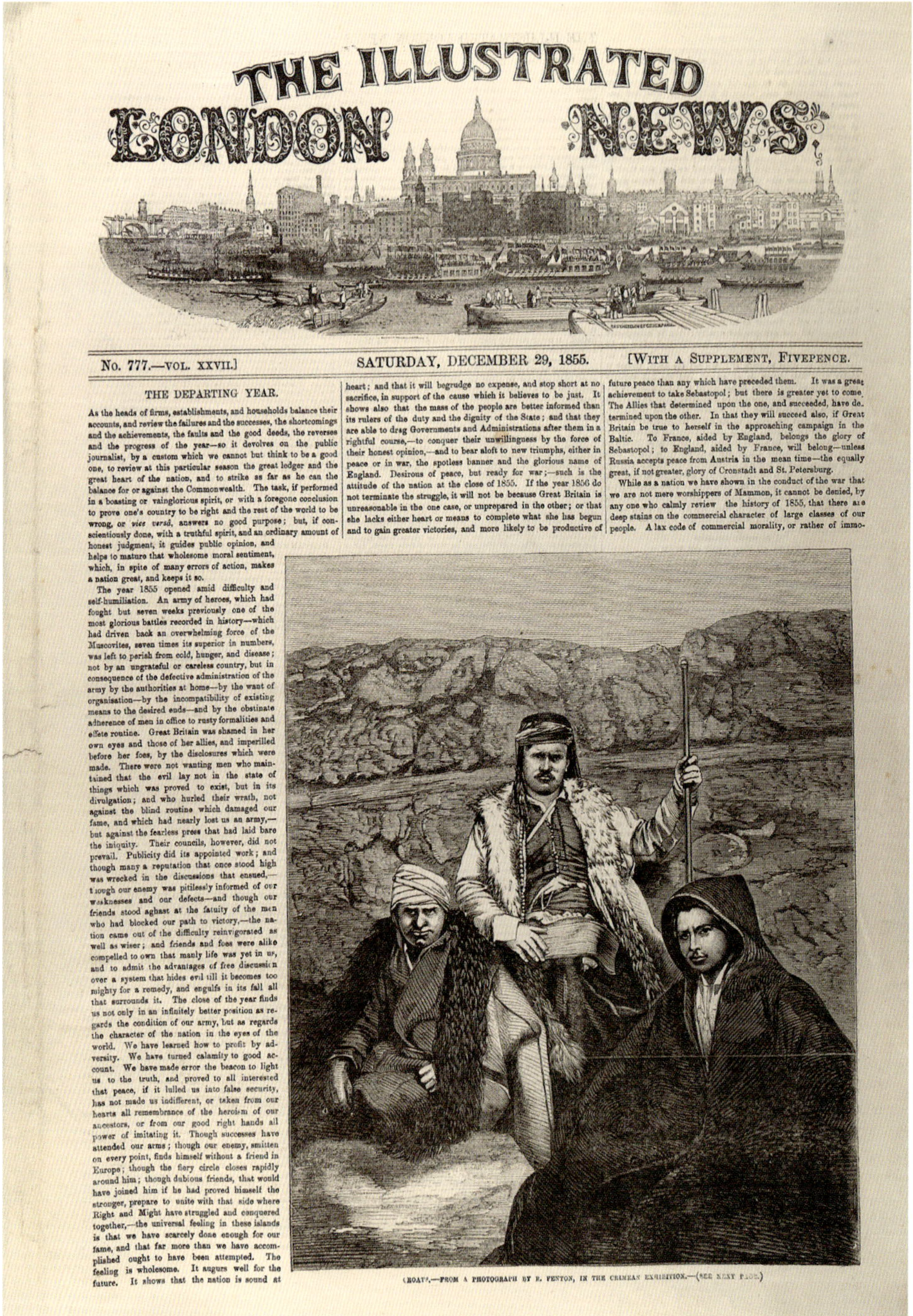

THE ILLUSTRATED LONDON NEWS.

No. 777.—VOL. XXVII.] SATURDAY, DECEMBER 29, 1855. [WITH A SUPPLEMENT, FIVEPENCE.

THE DEPARTING YEAR.

As the heads of firms, establishments, and households balance their accounts, and review the failures and the successes, the shortcomings and the achievements, the faults and the good deeds, the reverses and the progress of the year—so it devolves on the public journalist, by a custom which we cannot but think to be a good one, to review at this particular season the great ledger and the great heart of the nation, and to strike as far as he can the balance for or against the Commonwealth. The task, if performed in a boasting or vainglorious spirit, or with a foregone conclusion to prove one's country to be right and the rest of the world to be wrong, or *vice versâ*, answers no good purpose; but, if conscientiously done, with a truthful spirit, and an ordinary amount of honest judgment, it guides public opinion, and helps to mature that wholesome moral sentiment, which, in spite of many errors of action, makes a nation great, and keeps it so.

The year 1855 opened amid difficulty and self-humiliation. An army of heroes, which had fought but seven weeks previously one of the most glorious battles recorded in history—which had driven back an overwhelming force of the Muscovites, seven times its superior in numbers, was left to perish from cold, hunger, and disease; not by an ungrateful or careless country, but in consequence of the defective administration of the army by the authorities at home—by the want of organisation—by the incompatibility of existing means to the desired ends—and by the obstinate adherence of men in office to rusty formalities and effete routine. Great Britain was shamed in her own eyes and those of her allies, and imperilled before her foes, by the disclosures which were made. There were not wanting men who maintained that the evil lay not in the state of things which was proved to exist, but in its divulgation; and who hurled their wrath, not against the blind routine which damaged our fame, and which had nearly lost us an army,—but against the fearless press that had laid bare the iniquity. Their councils, however, did not prevail. Publicity did its appointed work; and though many a reputation that once stood high was wrecked in the discussions that ensued,—though our enemy was pitilessly informed of our weaknesses and our defects—and though our friends stood aghast at the fatuity of the men who had blocked our path to victory,—the nation came out of the difficulty reinvigorated as well as wiser; and friends and foes were alike compelled to own that manly life was yet in us, and to admit the advantages of free discussion over a system that hides evil till it becomes too mighty for a remedy, and engulfs in its fall all that surrounds it. The close of the year finds us not only in an infinitely better position as regards the condition of our army, but as regards the character of the nation in the eyes of the world. We have learned how to profit by adversity. We have turned calamity to good account. We have made error the beacon to light us to the truth, and proved to all interested that peace, if it lulled us into false security, has not made us indifferent, or taken from our hearts all remembrance of the heroism of our ancestors, or from our good right hands all power of imitating it. Though successes have attended our arms; though our enemy, smitten on every point, finds himself without a friend in Europe; though the fiery circle closes rapidly around him; though dubious friends, that would have joined him if he had proved himself the stronger, prepare to unite with that side where Right and Might have struggled and conquered together,—the universal feeling in these islands is that we have scarcely done enough for our fame, and that far more than we have accomplished ought to have been attempted. The feeling is wholesome. It augurs well for the future. It shows that the nation is sound at heart; and that it will begrudge no expense, and stop short at no sacrifice, in support of the cause which it believes to be just. It shows also that the mass of the people are better informed than its rulers of the duty and the dignity of the State; and that they are able to drag Governments and Administrations after them in a rightful course,—to conquer their unwillingness by the force of their honest opinion,—and to bear aloft to new triumphs, either in peace or in war, the spotless banner and the glorious name of England. Desirous of peace, but ready for war;—such is the attitude of the nation at the close of 1855. If the year 1856 do not terminate the struggle, it will not be because Great Britain is unreasonable in the one case, or unprepared in the other; or that she lacks either heart or means to complete what she has begun and to gain greater victories, and more likely to be productive of future peace than any which have preceded them. It was a great achievement to take Sebastopol; but there is greater yet to come. The Allies that determined upon the one, and succeeded, have determined upon the other. In that they will succeed also, if Great Britain be true to herself in the approaching campaign in the Baltic. To France, aided by England, belongs the glory of Sebastopol; to England, aided by France, will belong—unless Russia accepts peace from Austria in the mean time—the equally great, if not greater, glory of Cronstadt and St. Petersburg.

While as a nation we have shown in the conduct of the war that we are not mere worshippers of Mammon, it cannot be denied, by any one who calmly review the history of 1855, that there are deep stains on the commercial character of large classes of our people. A lax code of commercial morality, or rather of immo-

CROATS.—FROM A PHOTOGRAPH BY R. FENTON, IN THE CRIMEAN EXHIBITION.—(SEE NEXT PAGE.)

Figure 0.1 *The Illustrated London News*, December 29, 1855, cover, engraving from a photograph by Roger Fenton.

seen from the inside."[6] In this context the camera was recurrently described as an entity in its own right, functioning independently of the human hand in the service of a magazine. In the early twentieth century, when photography became the main vehicle for visual information, the French weekly *La Vie au grand air* captioned a series of photographs of the Paris Grand Prix, "The Race as seen by photography: what the lenses of our seven photographers saw." Thus was the role of the photographer played down.[7] In December 1938 *Life* also recounted the Battle of Rio Segre, publishing the same photographs by Capa, but ignoring the photographer himself: "*Life*'s camera gets closer to Spanish War than any camera has ever got before."[8] Occurring in articles, editorials, headlines and captions, turns of phrase like these were part of a discourse that attributed and promoted an authenticity legitimated by the mechanical nature of photography. Even so, the images have very little in common visually. Joanne's daguerreotypes had been translated into black hatching by the engraver; Nadar staged scenes in his studio; the Paris Grand Prix horses had been photographed at full gallop, in postures invisible to the naked eye; and two of the four Capa photographs chosen by the *Life* editors were out of focus. These formal characteristics, which revealed opposed photographic procedures (pose versus snapshot), contrasting means of reproduction (engraving versus photomechanical printing) and different modes of representation (drawing versus photography), did not enter into a rationale that concentrated on the modalities of the picture-taking process. In 1961, when magazines like *Life* and *Paris Match* were achieving record circulations,[9] semiologist Roland Barthes looked into the structure of photography in the press: "The photograph professing to be a mechanical analogue of reality, its first-order message in some sort completely fills its substance."[10] He went on to assert that "in the light of common sense . . . the description of a photograph is literally impossible."[11] Photography in general, and photojournalism in particular, was considered not as a representation springing from formal shaping, but as a reality hotline.

In the early 1970s the rhetoric pumped out by credibility-seeking media corporations became the cornerstone of the first histories of photojournalism, by Tim Gidal and Gisèle Freund: respectively *Modern Photojournalism: Origin and Evolution, 1910–1933* (1973) and *Photography and Society* (1974), of which the latter includes a long analysis of press photography.[12] In addition to their mutual contemporaneity and Germanic origins, both these authors worked in the illustrated press in the 1920s–1930s. Photojournalist Tim Gidal was close to Stefan Lorant, who edited the *Münchner Illustrierte Presse* in Germany before fleeing the Nazi threat in 1934 and taking refuge in England, where he founded *Lilliput* and then *Picture Post*.[13] Gisèle Freund, in parallel with an academic career that culminated in 1936 in a PhD in sociology at the Sorbonne—her dissertation was titled *La Photographie en France au XIXe siècle* (Photography in France in the 19th century)—was having her pictures published regularly in the magazines *VU* and *Life*.[14] From the outset both authors address photography as the faithful reflection of reality, in accordance with the line laid down by the profession. Gidal reminds the reader that "while the painter *interprets* events and happenings, the photographer is able to *reflect* them in a precise and accurate form."[15] Freund, for her part, declares that "photography opened a window, as it were."[16] Once this guiding principle is established, both books proffer a history focused on the work of photographers and their relationship with events: "genuinely committed" for Gidal[17] and working "with a concern with objectivity that makes [their] material remarkably valuable" for Freund,[18] photographers display responsibility and develop a professional ethic.[19] Those who had covered wars, like Roger Fenton (Crimean War, 1853–1856) and Timothy O'Sullivan (American Civil War, 1861–1865), and those who, like Jacob Riis and Lewis Hine, portrayed social conditions in North America at the turn of the twentieth century, are presented as the pioneers of a practice that came to maturity in Germany in the late 1920s. The advent of the new Leica and Rolleiflex-type cameras, together with discretion on the part of photographers and publication of their series in the *Berliner Illustrirte Zeitung*—and more especially the *Münchner Illustrierte Presse*—inaugurated photojournalism's modern era. In this context Erich Salomon, with his involvement in political debate and aristocratic soirées, or Felix H. Man, concerned with the everyday aspect of current events, embodied a new generation of photographers seen as a community of respectable gentlemen, in contrast with the lowlife camera-wielders of the past. Both Salomon and Man rejected the theatricality of official poses and the irritating use of the magnesium flash in favor of snapshots taken unbeknownst to their subjects. According to Gidal and Freund, then, modern photojournalistic images were the work of photographers using a low profile to provide a truer account of things. The ideal lines and forms of press photography were invisible, and at the same time masked the presence of the photographer.

Paradoxically, both the men of the press and the historians were simultaneously developing a narrative in which the photographer, far from disappearing, played the leading role. War photographers like James H. Hare, who covered the Russo–Japanese conflict in 1904, Robert Capa, who followed the Republicans during the Spanish Civil War from 1936 to 1938, and Gilles Caron, who went to Chad in 1970 to report on the war between the regular army and the rebel forces, were presented as active participants in the events they were photographing. Hare is seen giving first aid to a wounded man in a sequence published in *L'Illustration*; a full-page portrait of Capa in *Picture Post* is accompanied by a short text explaining how his physical appearance lets him blend in with the Republicans; and the *Paris Match* cover of March 7, 1970, devoted to "The reporters who got out of Chad alive," features not only Caron, but Raymond Depardon, Michel Honorin and Robert Pledge as well.[20] Commitment and courage on the part of photographers became newsworthy and were recounted in ways that helped shape a

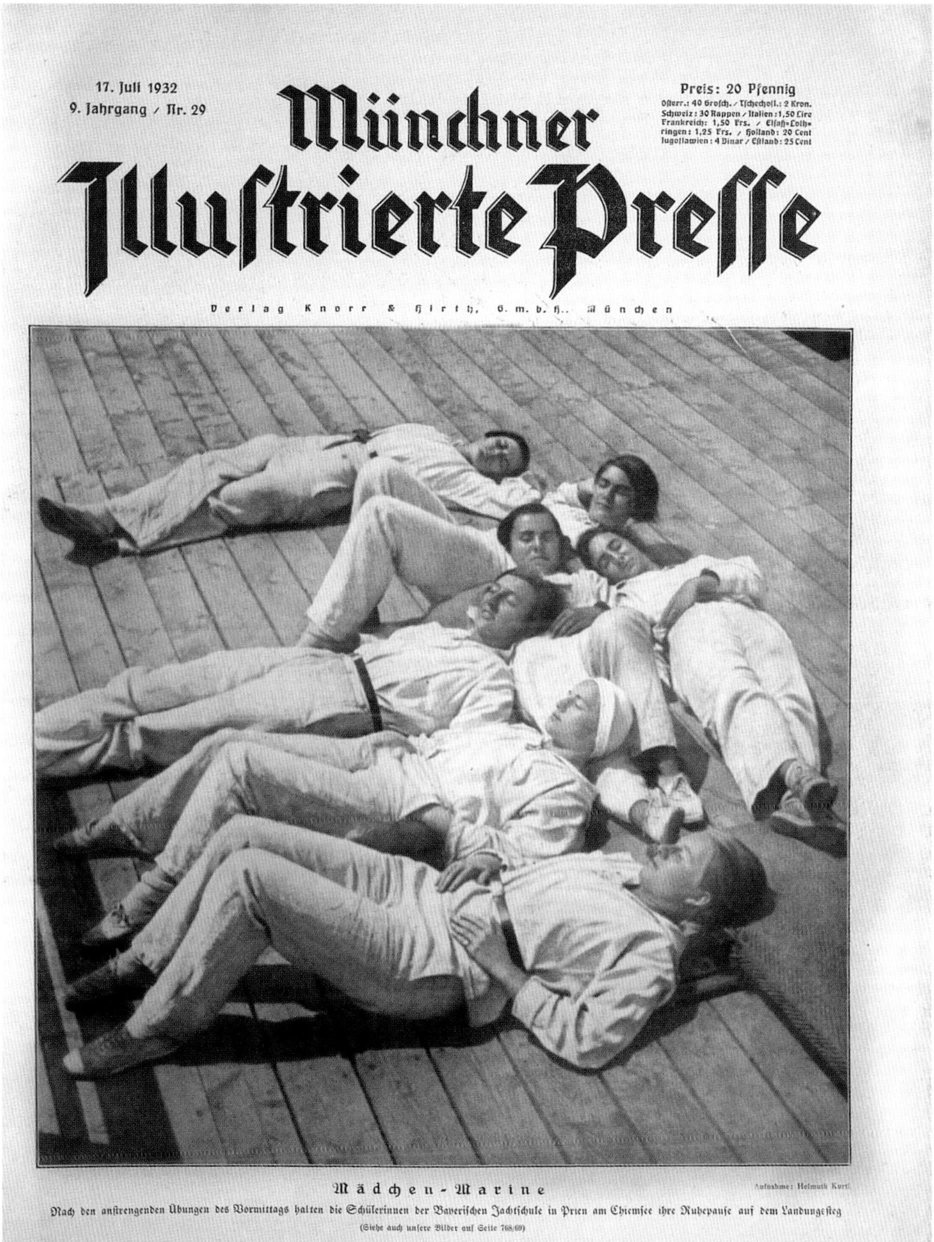

Figure 0.2 *Münchner Illustrierte Presse*, July 17, 1932, cover, photograph by Felix H. Man (Dephot).

mythology of the photographer-hero as a "modern-day knight"[21] risking his life for the journalistic cause. No longer a mere observer whose camera holds up a mirror to reality, the photographer was now an actor whose path crossed that of his subjects. He was also presented as an observer with something to say about current events. John Heartfield's photomontages in the German and French Communist press in the 1920s and 1930s are the most visible expression of this handling of news.[22] The definition of the photographic essay that appeared in *Life* in April 1937 and the launch, a few months later, of the "Photographic Essay" feature in the pages of the magazine, also testify to the go-between function attributed to the photographer in the general press.[23] Here the photographer was likened to an essayist whose style enhances our perception of events. In the course of the 1950s Eugene Smith and Henri Cartier-Bresson brought out photographic essays bearing their personal stylistic imprint, and the close attention given to their images by press publishers was evidence of authorial recognition.[24] The defense of author's rights undertaken by Magnum Photos, founded in 1947, and the institutionalization of photojournalism that took place during the 1970s, also acknowledged and underscored the photographer's role.[25] In this changed frame of reference press photography was marked by a visible aesthetic evident in a concern with composition, play on light and shade, and out-of-focus effects that allowed the photographer to express himself visually.

The new section on photojournalism in the most recent edition of Beaumont Newhall's *The History of Photography* (1982) and the many chapters on news photography in *A New History of Photography*, edited by Michel Frizot (1998), point up this tension between the mechanical objectivity of the camera and the subjectivity of choice of the photographer.[26] Newhall describes the development of photomechanical reproduction processes as a long striving for authenticity of form; yet he also compares Eugene Smith's *The Thread Maker*—taken from the "Spanish Village" essay published in *Life* in 1951—to a "Michelangelo drawing."[27] Similarly *A New History of Photography* extols the Leica cameras developed in Germany in the 1920s as the vital tools for a photojournalist trying to get as close to events as possible, but also foregrounds them as the favorites of the "masters,"[28] among whom are mentioned Henri Cartier-Bresson and André Kertész.

The tricky part played by the picture editors and art directors at the magazines added to the confusion of the narratives resulting from this tension. Few were the texts that failed to mention Stefan Lorant's work at the *Münchner Illustrierte Presse* in the interwar years and Wilson Hicks's contributions to *Life* between 1937 and 1950. Tim Gidal describes at length his mentor's close involvement with the work of his photographers and the way, as he [Gidal] sees it, this process of interchange gave rise to series that were the genesis of modern photojournalism. Driven by a quest for historical legitimacy, Gidal's book generated a chronology for modern photojournalism that has been widely reproduced and rarely challenged.[29] Wilson Hicks theorized his own role in *Words and Pictures* (1952), in which

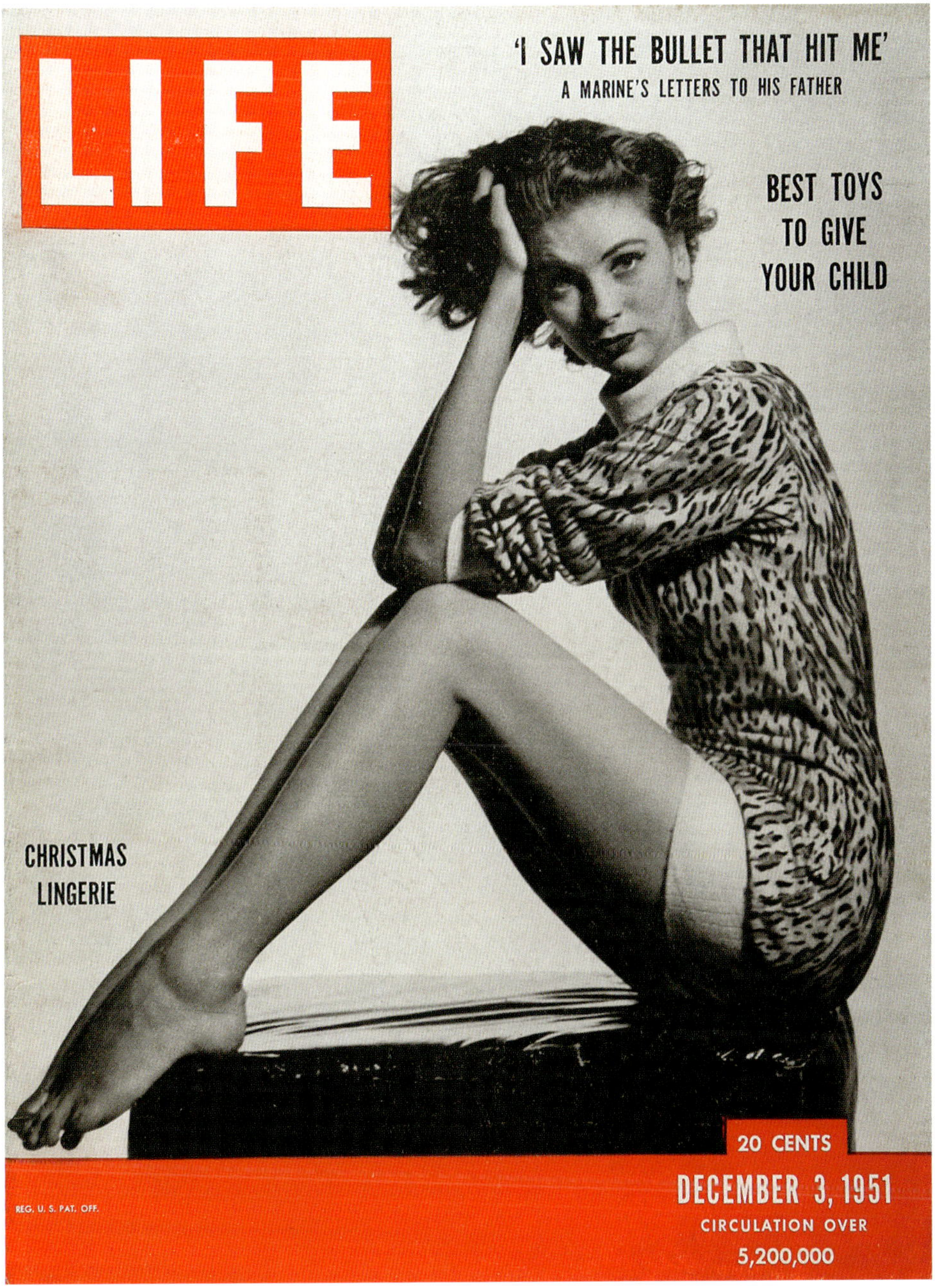

Figure 0.3 *Life*, December 3, 1951, cover, photograph by Gerald Sharland.

he explains the protracted preliminaries to the publication of photographs in *Life*.[30] Because of his position of power at the magazine, relations were strained between Hicks, who claims to have looked at 350,000 images a year—of which only 10,000 were published—and his photographers.[31] "He was often unpopular with them," notes Gisèle Freund, "because of his brusque carrot-and-stick manner: but those who worked with him had the deepest respect for his knowledge of photojournalism and for his rich imagination."[32] John Morris, who was Hicks's assistant for the first half of 1941, recalls that "he was the one who had to make the tough decisions: which stories to cover and which *not* to . . . It was no wonder that he was generally disliked. Nobody loves a naysayer."[33] Thus the picture editors emerge as instigators of reportages and mentors for young photographers, but also as decision makers whose wielding of authority could be embittering.[34] They functioned above all as an additional voice in the visual information machinery, while underscoring its collective side.

The most recent histories of photojournalism, by Bodo von Dewitz and Robert Lebeck (2001), and Mary Panzer and Christian Caujolle (2005), both mention at the outset the collegial underpinning of press photography publication.[35] To emphasize the numerous implications of this situation and to illustrate their point, these authors pass over the original prints in favor of reproductions in illustrated newspapers and magazines. From the engravings "from a photograph" published in the *Illustrirte Zeitung* in 1845 to the snapshots in *Paris Match* of holidaymakers caught unawares by the 2005 tsunami, these two books show the different types of photographs that play a part in representing current events, the diversity of the layouts proposed by art directors, and the changes in the text/image balance decided by the editors. Published images have since been subjected to academic research exploring the construction of visual information from multiple points of view—such as Jason E. Hill and Vanessa R. Schwartz edited volume *Getting the Picture: the Visual Culture of the News*.[36]

This book reflects this view of photography as an essential part of the presentation of current events, while considering each published image as a representation produced by a photographer and then selected by a picture editor largely on the basis of formal criteria. In giving rise to new methodologies and shifting the focus of the considerations driving this field of research since the 1970s, aesthetic analysis is producing a consistent account of the role of photography in the press. Visual study of news photographs involves an emphasis on images at the expense of text, or at least a measurement and analysis of the disparity between publishers' statements of intent and the actual use of images in periodicals. In the nineteenth century the press published declarations vaunting the supposed authenticity of photographs, when in fact, once reproduced, they could not be distinguished from other kinds of images.[37] Conversely, while *Life* compares the style of a photographer to that of an essayist, the pictures favored by the magazine are informed by an aesthetics of transparency which minimizes the photographer's role.[38] A fresh look at press objects with a view to understanding the uses of images also enables a clear distinction between an illustrated newspaper and a magazine according to the space given to photography, as well as a more extensive chronology. This history covers the photography-centered magazines that first appeared in the late nineteenth century and considers the interwar period much more as a new phase than as a beginning. Making press photography aesthetics the focal point of this study historicizes the information value of the images and enhances our understanding of the belief systems exploited by press publishers. The visual effects aimed at masking—or on the contrary, calling attention to—the photographer's presence, functioned as guarantees of credibility in separate historical periods. The same is true of periodicals' constant adaptation of layout and graphics which, according to the context, served a visual narrative or urged contemplation of an individual image.

Lastly, this approach calls for detachment from images' mere information value in the interests of assessing their seduction potential. The astonishing graphic compositions of Lucien Faure, appointed art director of *La Vie au grand air* in 1899; Léon Gimpel's high-angle shots in *L'Illustration* during the Belle Époque; the photomontages attacking Hitler's rise to power on the cover of the *Arbeiter Illustrierte Zeitung*; and the sophisticated photographs of luxury items in *Fortune* and of unclothed women on the covers of *Stern* in the 1970s—these were all reminders of the published images' power to seduce. The specialist and general press had in common the creation of products that had to beguile readers if they were to make their way on a competitive market. The success of these press ventures hinged on finding a balance between form and content that would meet a given public's expectations.

The history of press photography in this book is that of a use involving technical, economic and cultural parameters. A use that gave rise to the magazine form, encouraged the professionalization of photojournalists, shaped twentieth-century news, and generated press objects whose cultural influence and impact are still with us today. This story began with the launch of the first magazines in the late nineteenth century, and closed with the end of the reign of the great general weeklies, the diversification of the uses of the press image, and the institutional recognition photography which was accorded in the 1970s. The corpus under scrutiny includes such famous news magazines as *VU*, *Life*, *Picture Post* and *Paris Match*, other lesser-known ones such as *Collier's Weekly*, *Voilà* and *Illustrated*, and political publications like *Arbeiter Illustrierte Zeitung* and *USSR in Construction*. The choice of a long timeline and problems of access have forced us to concentrate on the Western press. Access to private collections like Robert Lebeck's and recent advances in research possibilities—notably thanks to the online availability of all issues of *Life*, and the digitization and indexing of the collection of periodicals at the

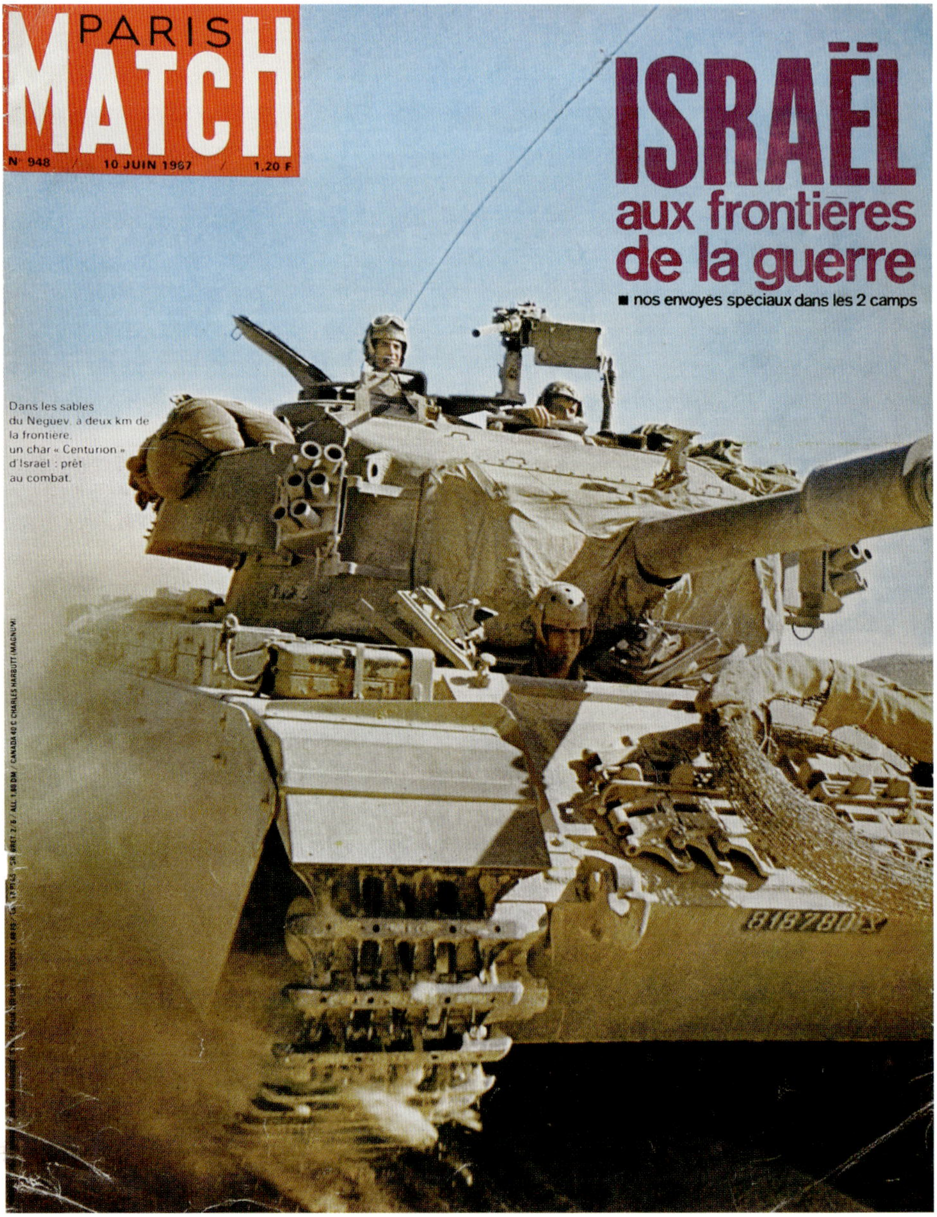

Figure 0.4 *Paris Match*, June 10, 1967, cover, photograph by Charles Harbutt (Magnum). © *Paris Match / Scoop*.

Musée Nicéphore Niépce in Chalon-sur-Saône, France—have allowed us to address extensive corpuses and consult thousands of pages and images.[39] Our study was limited to photography-centered magazines, which meant excluding the daily and specialist press. The importance of publications like *Détective*, *Excelsior*, *Fortune*, *Elle*, *Libération*, *Paris-Soir*, *PM*, *Rolling Stone* and *Vogue* made this a difficult choice: we can only plead a concern for consistency.

Chapter 1
The Invention of the Magazine (1843–1918)

The first uses of photography in the press date from the 1840s, but it was not until the late nineteenth century that illustrated weeklies in the West abandoned drawings for photographs in their news coverage.[1] This major shift in the making of visual news hinged on technical, economic and cultural factors. The advent of portable cameras using glass plates or film sensitive enough to enable snapshots triggered a whole new generation of enthusiasts; more numerous than before, liberated from the technical constraints of old, and bent on recording what was happening around them, they turned out a vast repository of invaluable images. At the same time the high-quality halftone screens perfected by the Levy company in Philadelphia enabled the process to be used cheaply and on a massive scale for reproduction in the press; and with movie theaters now specializing in newsreels, photography gradually took hold in the weeklies as a way of attracting readers and covering current affairs. In the course of the 1890s the historic illustrated newspapers—*The Illustrated London News* (1842–1971), *L'Illustration* (1843–1944), and *Illustrirte Zeitung* (1843–1944)—gradually moved toward the photography-halftone illustration tandem, although a form of visual hierarchy persisted: drawings reproduced by engravers still loomed large, with publications seeking to preserve their identity and not lose a loyal readership built up over decades. Concurrently, new periodicals—*The Illustrated American* (1890–1899), *Collier's Weekly* (1895–1957) and *La Vie au grand air* (1898–1914/1916–1922) were appearing and targeting a new public via massive recourse to images, mostly taken from photographs and all reproduced in halftone. Photography was thus becoming the main conduit for news, but differences in use from one publication to another defined the two main types of periodical coexisting during the Belle Époque: illustrated weeklies as envisaged and designed in the mid-nineteenth century; and magazines, whose form and structure were then taking shape and would continue to evolve as the twentieth century advanced.

From a photograph

Photography had become a tool in the news illustration process well before the development of halftone.[2] The earliest recorded use dates from August 26, 1843, when the French weekly *L'Illustration* published an engraving "from a daguerreotype"[3] of the Fort of San Juan of Ulúa, in Veracruz. Nothing distinguishes this illustration visually from the others on the same page, apart from the specific mention of its photographic origin. *L'Illustration* began publication in Paris in March 1843, a year after *The Illustrated London News* and four months before the *Illustrirte Zeitung* in Leipzig; all three used woodcuts to illustrate current events and propose a new kind of press entity. At the time woodcuts were the sole means of producing images in relief that could be associated with type in the composing of a newspaper page. Whatever their provenance—drawing, painting, engraving, photograph—all the images offered to the editors of these weeklies had to pass through the hands of an engraver if they were to appear. Regularly, then, although not as a matter of course, the photographic halftones of landscapes, cityscapes, public celebrations and above all, portraits, were translated into black hatching by wood engravers. Along with numerous unknowns, a few famous photographers saw their images leave the studio and go into circulation in various periodicals: thus daguerreotypes by the Frenchman Charles François Thibault showing the barricades during the uprising in Paris in June 1848 were published in *L'Illustration*;[4] eight photographs of the Crimean War by Englishman Roger Fenton (1819–1869) appeared in *The Illustrated London News* over the period 1854–1855;[5] and many images of the American Civil War, by Mathew Brady (1823/24–1896) and Alexander Gardner (1821–1882) were to be found in *Harper's Weekly* (1857–1916) and *Frank Leslie's Illustrated Newspaper* (1855–1922) between 1861 and 1865.[6] For the technical reasons mentioned earlier all these images had lost their tonal subtleties during the engraving process required by publication, but comparison of the originals with their published avatars also reveals additions and modifications undertaken by the engravers for cultural reasons. The daguerreotype's exposure time of a few seconds allowed Thibault to catch only ghostly silhouettes of the soldiers seizing control of Rue du Faubourg-du-Temple[7]; but this strictly photographic incongruity was not let through by *L'Illustration*'s engraver, who reworked each individual figure so as to provide the standard degree of picturesqueness (see Figures 1.1 and 1.2).[8] A similar fate awaited Fenton's photograph of General Bosquet and Captain Dampierre outside their tent near Malakoff: in the engraving published in *The Illustrated London News* (see

Figures 1.3 and 1.4) the fuzzy background and blank white sky were respectively enhanced with chatting soldiers and clouds.[9]

Two features emerge from this early use of photography in the press: first, the medium aroused no great enthusiasm on the part of nineteenth-century publishers, with the wording "from a photograph" occurring only rarely in illustration captions; and second, photography's specific visual characteristics were addressed as flaws to be rectified in the light of prevailing illustrative standards. Many photographs contributed to the illustration process by providing raw material for draftsmen and engravers, but at the cost of both their identity and their content.

The famous image of the gatekeeper that appeared in *L'Illustration* of July 25, 1891 is clear testimony to the role accorded photography at the time.[10] To illustrate the railroad workers' strike Ernest Clair-Guyot (1856–1938) focused on the different occupations involved, and for the gatekeeper he resorted to a montage of photographs and drawings. To save time he cut out photographs of the train and the figure and glued them onto an ink and gouache landscape painted by himself. The montage was then photographically reproduced on a coated woodblock, so that rather than interpreting the lines of the illustration, the engraver could follow them directly with his chisel. In the course of the nineteenth century, then, photography most certainly became a tool for news illustration, but unobtrusively so, without its formal qualities upsetting the long-established representational pecking order: as published the gatekeeper illustration had been stripped of its photographic attributes and was no different from the other images in the French weekly. Thus the press developed a mix of photography and drawing whose hybrid outcome was concealed by the engraver's work of reproduction.

The archives of *L'Illustration* testify to this covert use of photography and the circumstances of its contribution to news coverage during the period 1880–1890. Photography modified and brought new vitality to the illustration process, but in return it had to submit to the standards governing publication in the press. Some photographic portraits from the period had not been retouched by the draftsman before being handed on to the engraver, because they bore the stamp of iconographic norms that had been in force for decades. Almost all the surviving photographs have been retouched in ways that cast doubt on their origin: visible marks that suggest that they did not meet the prerequisites for publication and had to be adapted by a draftsman in order to become acceptable as illustrations. Cropping was the commonest of the modifications effected by the draftsman before engraving, the upshot being a new spatial organization of the visual components.[11] Another frequent form of intervention consisted in changing the emphasis within a photograph with the aid of a translucent white paint that played down the importance of certain elements by reducing their visibility.[12] Illustrators likewise continued to rectify what were still seen as the flaws of photography: the absence of clouds in the sky, blur due to

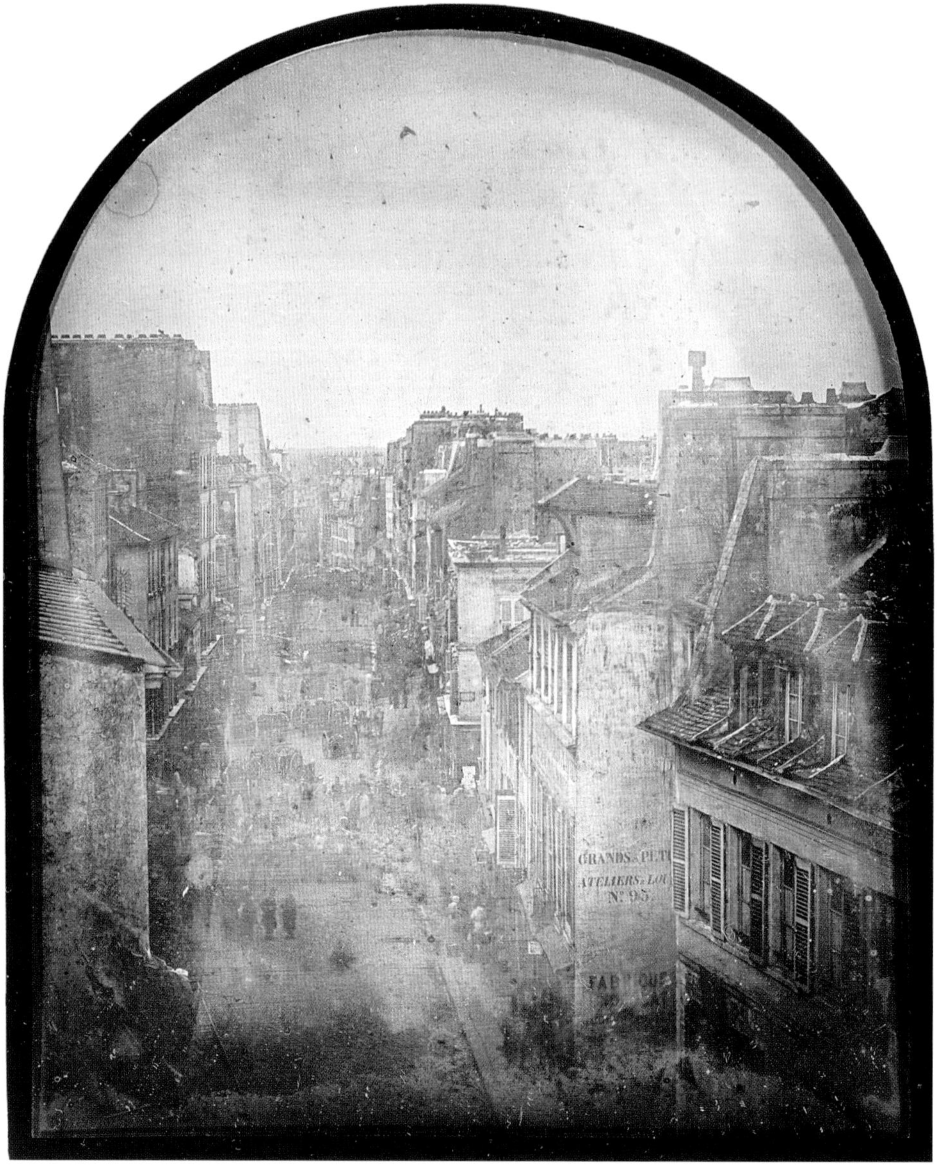

Figure 1.1 Charles François Thibault, 'The barricade of rue Saint-Maur [du Faubourg-du-Temple] after the attack by General Lamoricière's troops,' daguerreotype, 12.7 x 10.4 cm, 1848. © RMN / H. Lewandowski.

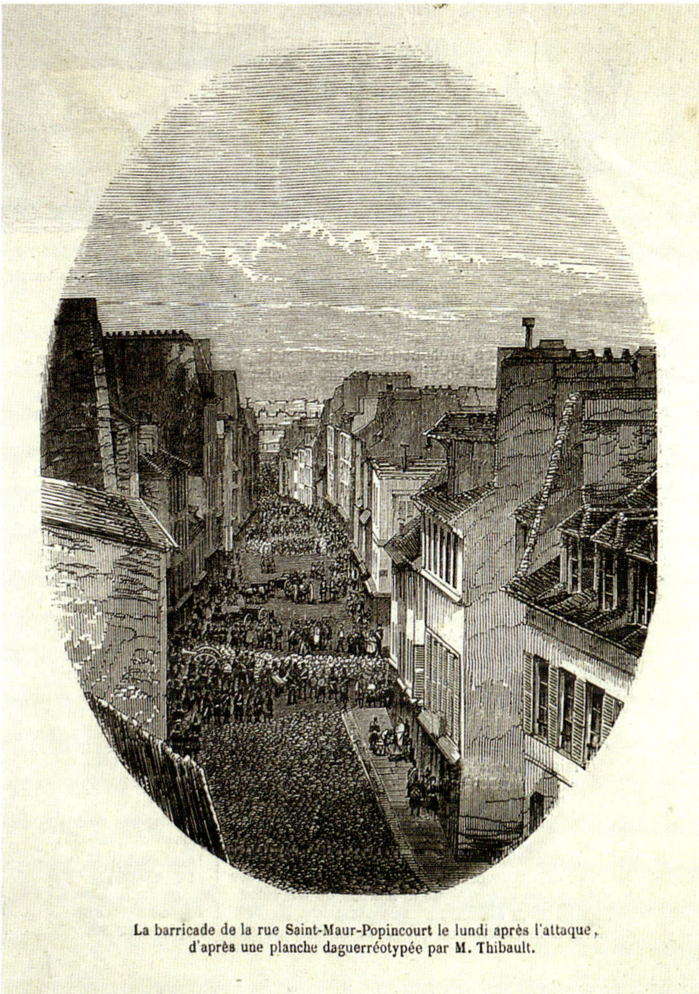

Figure 1.2 *L'Illustration*, July 1–8, 1848, p. 276 (detail). From a photograph by Charles François Thibault.

camera shake, and lack of contrast.[13] Thus photographs were treated as illustrative material whose descriptive qualities were at the service of the final composition. Within this system, once they had been cropped and retouched, they gained time for the illustrator without interfering with the work process or, even, the form of the published image. After the alterations carried out by the illustrator, the remaining photographic elements were manually masked by a second, technical procedure: the translation by the engraver of halftones into black and white hatching.

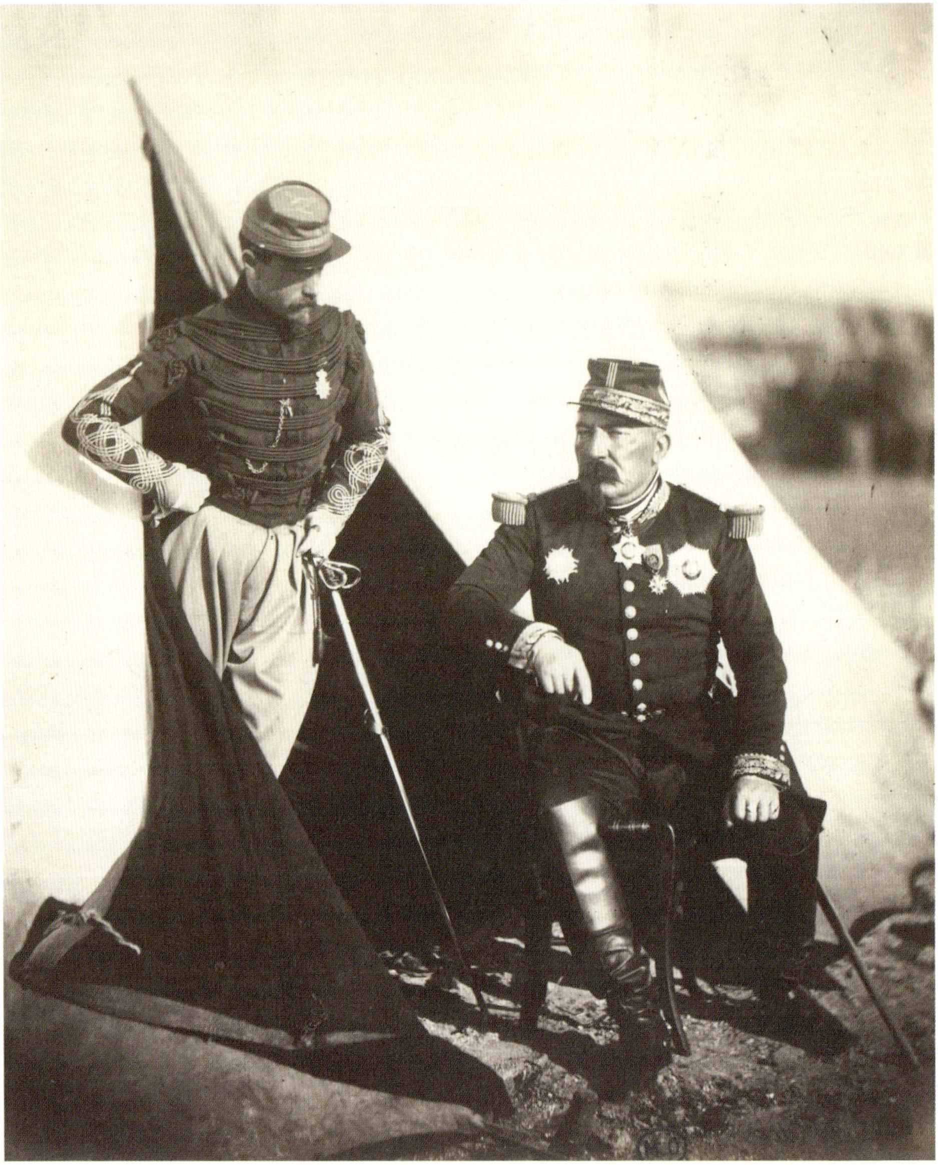

Figure 1.3 Roger Fenton, 'Général Bosquet and Capitaine Dampierre. Incidents of Camp Life – Photographs Taken in the Crimea,' salted paper print, 18.3 x 15.2 cm, 1855. © Musée d'Orsay, distributed by RMN Grand Palais / Patrice Schmidt.

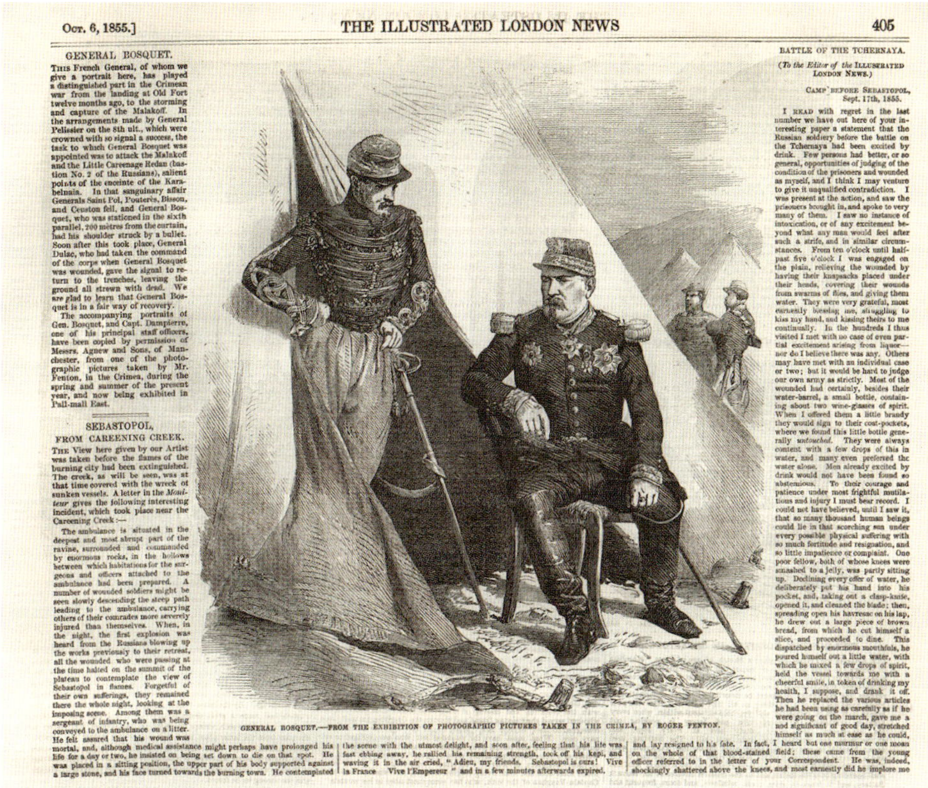

Oct. 6, 1855.] THE ILLUSTRATED LONDON NEWS 405

GENERAL BOSQUET.

This French General, of whom we give a portrait here, has played a distinguished part in the Crimean war from the landing at Old Fort twelve months ago, to the storming and capture of the Malakoff. In the arrangements made by General Pelissier on the 8th ult., which were crowned with so signal a success, the task to which General Bosquet was appointed was to attack the Malakoff and the Little Careenage Redan (bastion No. 2 of the Russians), salient points of the enceinte of the Karabelnaia. In that sanguinary affair Generals Saint Pol, Pouterès, Bisson, and Ceuston fell, and General Bosquet, who was stationed in the sixth parallel, 200 mètres from the curtain, had his shoulder struck by a bullet. Soon after this took place, General Dulac, who had taken the command of the corps when General Bosquet was wounded, gave the signal to return to the trenches, leaving the ground all strewn with dead. We are glad to learn that General Bosquet is in a fair way of recovery.

The accompanying portraits of Gen. Bosquet, and Capt. Dampierre, one of his principal staff officers, have been copied by permission of Messrs. Agnew and Sons, of Manchester, from one of the photographic pictures taken by Mr. Fenton, in the Crimea, during the spring and summer of the present year, and now being exhibited in Pall-mall East.

SEBASTOPOL, FROM CAREENING CREEK.

The View here given by our Artist was taken before the flames of the burning city had been extinguished. The creek, as will be seen, was at that time covered with the wreck of sunken vessels. A letter in the *Moniteur* gives the following interesting incident, which took place near the Careening Creek:—

The ambulance is situated in the deepest and most abrupt part of the ravine, surrounded and commanded by enormous rocks, in the hollows between which habitations for the surgeons and officers attached to the ambulance had been prepared. A number of wounded soldiers might be seen slowly descending the steep path leading to the ambulance, carrying others of their comrades more severely injured than themselves. When, in the night, the first explosion was heard from the Russians blowing up the works previously to their retreat, all the wounded who were passing at the time halted on the summit of the plateau to contemplate the view of Sebastopol in flames. Forgetful of their own sufferings, they remained there the whole night, looking at the imposing scene. Among them was a sergeant of infantry, who was being conveyed to the ambulance on a litter. He felt assured that his wound was mortal, and, although medical assistance might perhaps have prolonged his life for a day or two, he insisted on being set down to die on that spot. He was placed in a sitting position, the upper part of his body supported against a large stone, and his face turned towards the burning town. He contemplated the scene with the utmost delight, and soon after, feeling that his life was fast ebbing away, he rallied his remaining strength, took off his kepi, and waving it in the air cried, "Adieu, my friends. Sebastopol is ours! Vive la France. Vive l'Empereur!" and in a few minutes afterwards expired.

GENERAL BOSQUET.—FROM THE EXHIBITION OF PHOTOGRAPHIC PICTURES TAKEN IN THE CRIMEA, BY ROGER FENTON.

BATTLE OF THE TCHERNAYA.

(*To the Editor of the* Illustrated London News.)

Camp before Sebastopol, Sept. 17th, 1855.

I read with regret in the last number we have out here of your interesting paper a statement that the Russian soldiery before the battle on the Tchernaya had been excited by drink. Few persons had better, or so general, opportunities of judging of the condition of the prisoners and wounded as myself, and I think I may venture to give it unqualified contradiction. I was present at the action, and saw the prisoners brought in, and spoke to very many of them. I saw no instance of intoxication, or of any excitement beyond what any man would feel after such a strife, and in similar circumstances. From ten o'clock until half-past five o'clock I was engaged on the plain, relieving the wounded by having their knapsacks placed under their heads, covering their wounds from swarms of flies, and giving them water. They were very grateful, most earnestly blessing me, struggling to kiss my hand, and kissing theirs to me continually. In the hundreds I thus visited I met with no case of even partial excitement arising from liquor—nor do I believe there was any. Others may have met with an individual case or two; but it would be hard to judge our own army as strictly. Most of the wounded had certainly, besides their water-barrel, a small bottle, containing about two wine-glasses of spirit. When I offered them a little brandy they would sign to their coat-pockets, where we found this little bottle generally *untouched*. They were always content with a few drops of this in water, and many even preferred the water alone. Men already excited by drink would not have been found so abstemious. To their courage and patience under most frightful mutilations and injury I must bear record. I could not have believed, until I saw it, that so many thousand human beings could lie in that scorching sun under every possible physical suffering with so much fortitude and resignation, and so little impatience or complaint. One poor fellow, both of whose knees were smashed to a jelly, was partly sitting up. Declining every offer of water, he deliberately put his hand into his pocket, and, taking out a clasp-knife, opened it, and cleaned the blade; then, spreading open his havresac on his lap, he drew out a large piece of brown bread, from which he cut himself a slice, and proceeded to dine. This dispatched by enormous mouthfuls, he poured himself out a little water, with which he mixed a few drops of spirit, held the vessel towards me with a cheerful smile, in token of drinking my health, I suppose, and drank it off. Then he replaced the various articles he had been using as carefully as if he were going on the march, gave me a nod significant of good day, stretched himself as much at ease as he could, and lay resigned to his fate. In fact, I heard but one murmur or one moan on the whole of that blood-stained field; these came from the young officer referred to in the letter of your Correspondent. He was, indeed, shockingly shattered above the knees, and most earnestly did he implore me

Figure 1.4 *The Illustrated London News*, October 6, 1855, p. 405. From a photograph by Roger Fenton.

Photography, then, became a significant contributing factor in the illustrations of the period, but without being considered an informational plus. While captions sometimes specified an image's photographic origin, the forms of the illustration signaled a manual process. With their meshing of photography and drawing, these hybrid images—part art (as indicated by their authors' signatures) and part information (as indicated by the publication context)—made up the bulk of *L'Illustration*'s iconographic corpus for the 1880s and 1890s. The coming-together of the press and photography was not self-evident and for technical and cultural reasons was not even especially sought after. It was in this context that the first halftone reproduction processes were developed—a context in no way favorable to photographic news coverage at the expense of drawing.

The halftone age

The invention of the photomechanical reproduction process generally known as halftone is often referred to as the long-awaited technological event that would put an end to press publishers' dependency on engravers and finally enable them to reproduce photographs faithfully. While this idea is not completely wide of the mark, it is not completely true either: as the photographic interview with Eugène Chevreul carried out by Paul Nadar (1820–1910) in 1886 demonstrates, technical parameters alone cannot explain the choice of photography over drawing. For the scientist's centenary Nadar had drawn up a photographic and stenographic recording protocol specifically aimed at the following goal: "For the first time the reader is going to be the spectator, as if he were actually present."[14] Published in the *Journal illustré* of September 5, 1886, the interview comprises thirteen photographs using Stanislas Krakow's halftone method (see Figures 1.5 and 1.6) to remarkable effect: although the *Journal illustré* was printed on poor quality paper, the images are reproduced with a subtlety that does justice to their photographic values and forms. However, when the interview was published none of those involved drew attention to Krakow's contribution, even continuing to speak of "engravings"[15] and "drawings"[16] in reference to the halftone reproductions.[17] Krakow's method used photography to obtain a matrix in relief, but was initially seen by its inventor as a means of enlarging or reducing drawings for publishing purposes: it enabled reproduction of photographic tones, but was meant to solve layout problems by adapting engravings to the space intended for them on the page.

To achieve his goal Nadar created a visual narrative providing each image with a number and a brief caption as a guide for *Journal illustré* readers. Drawing on three separate interviews with Chevreul—and disregarding their chronology when necessary—Nadar produced highly effective visual associations and homed in on subjects that enthused him, such as aerial navigation and the role of images in the science field. The caption for the final image reads, "I haven't told you everything. But telling is not enough, one has to prove, one has to *show*! I have to *make you see*! You have to *see*! *I want to show, because it's when I see that I believe!!!*": an appropriate summing up of Chevreul's method and a vindication of the image/word association in the weekly in question. Thus the scientist and the journalist are working hand in hand, both seeking to provide proof; and to do this they want to see, then show, so that we as their readers and spectators can believe them. The photographic interview with Chevreul is marked by an unprecedented modernity brought to bear not on the man of letters but on the man of science. This was an avant-garde journalistic breakthrough in which photography played a decisive part, but one which neither photographers nor printers—nor even readers—would endorse before the late years of the nineteenth century. Only *Le Figaro* repeated the venture when it published a photographic interview with General Boulanger in 1889, with photographs by Paul Nadar in halftone reproductions by Krakow.[18]

It was only in the 1890s that halftone became a serious rival for engravers in European and American periodicals.[19] The technical principle was simple: a fine screen was interposed between the photograph and the zinc plate to be used by the printer. The function of the screen was to convert the photographic shadings into a network of black dots of varying sizes, which could then be etched in relief on the plate. The idea first appeared in the 1850s, notably in a process patented by the Englishman William Henry Fox Talbot in 1852, which was taken up, developed and adapted in the following decades by the Frenchmen Charles-Guillaume Petit and Stanislas Krakow, the American Frederic Ives and the German Georg Meisenbach, who took out their own patents between 1878 and 1884.[20] All of them, however, were confronted with the same problem, which explains the gap between the dates of the patents (the 1880s) and the utilization of the method by periodicals (in the 1890s): namely that none of them succeeded in producing a screen at once sufficiently fine and sufficiently tough for industrial use.

It was in the early 1890s that the Levy brothers in Philadelphia solved the problem with their "almost universally used standard screen."[21] It was only then that halftone became a major competitor for wood-engravers and that press publishers were gradually won over and ingrained cultural prejudices overcome: halftone gave results whose "monotony"[22] attracted unfavorable comment and whose grayness lacked engraving's appealing contrasts. On the other hand, for publishers it meant savings in terms of time and money—a half to a tenth of the cost[23]—and greater flexibility in terms of layout. These benefits ultimately led to full acceptance by the press.

To a certain extent the big European illustrateds shared these misgivings about halftone in the 1890s. In 1893 photographs began to appear on the front page of the *Illustrirte Zeitung*, but only very sporadically until the closing years of the century.[24] As halftone took over from engraving, publishers used it to reproduce drawings as well as photographs, and called on their engravers to retouch the plates so as to eliminate details seen as superfluous or to add contrast to the gray of a sky. Thus they maintained the hybrid approach dating back to the early engravings taken from photographs, as a gesture toward readers' visual habits. In the case of *L'Illustration*, in France, it was not until 1904 that photographs numerically outstripped illustrations.[25] This shift was the outcome not of technical progress, but of a decision taken by the periodical's newly appointed director, René Baschet: declining sales led Baschet to broaden the editorial line to include not only foreign and domestic politics, but also illustrated coverage of topical events; a change of emphasis that was complemented by a fresh approach to illustration involving increased resort to photographs. This meant savings on the cost of images and improved the

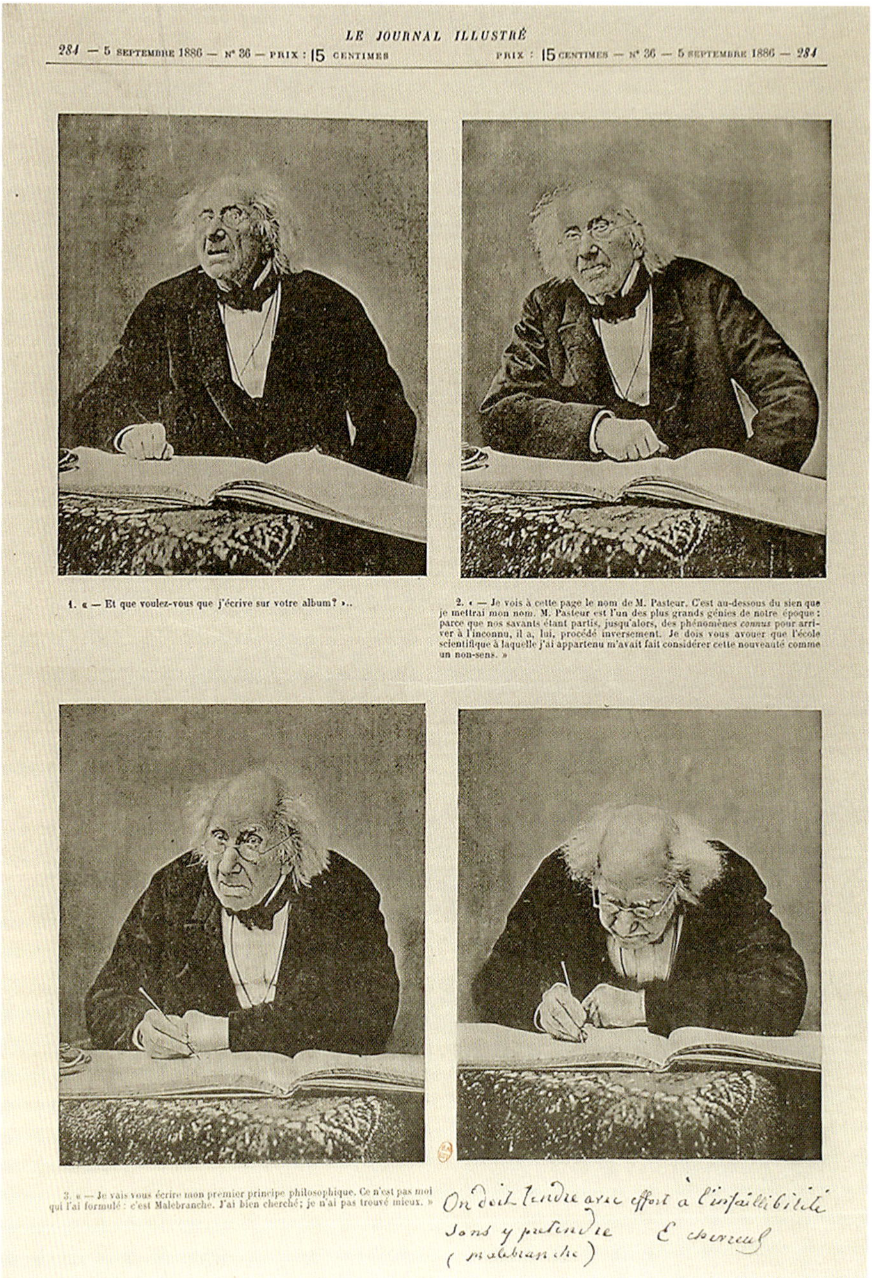

LE JOURNAL ILLUSTRÉ

284 — 5 SEPTEMBRE 1886 — N° 36 — PRIX : 15 CENTIMES PRIX : 15 CENTIMES — N° 36 — 5 SEPTEMBRE 1886 — 284

1. « — Et que voulez-vous que j'écrive sur votre album? »..

2. « — Je vois à cette page le nom de M. Pasteur. C'est au-dessous du sien que je mettrai mon nom. M. Pasteur est l'un des plus grands génies de notre époque : parce que nos savants étant partis, jusqu'alors, des phénomènes *connus* pour arriver à l'inconnu, il a, lui, procédé inversement. Je dois vous avouer que l'école scientifique à laquelle j'ai appartenu m'avait fait considérer cette nouveauté comme un non-sens. »

3. « — Je vais vous écrire mon premier principe philosophique. Ce n'est pas moi qui l'ai formulé : c'est Malebranche. J'ai bien cherché; je n'ai pas trouvé mieux. »

On doit tendre avec effort à l'infaillibilité sans y prétendre (Malebranche) E. Chevreul

Figures 1.5 and 1.6 *Le Journal illustré*, September 5, 1886, pp. 284 and 288. Photographs by Paul Nadar.

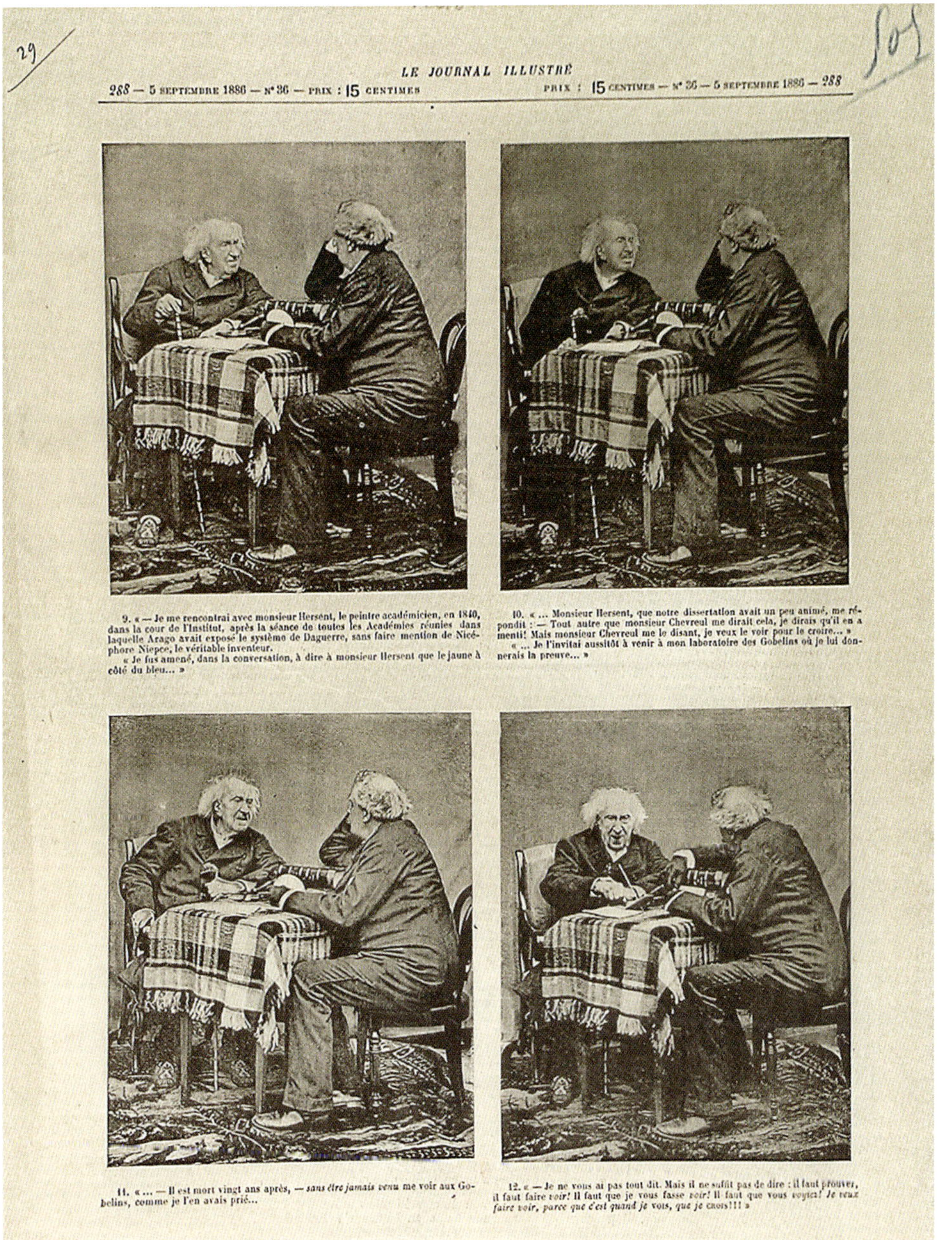

LE JOURNAL ILLUSTRÉ

288 — 5 SEPTEMBRE 1886 — N° 36 — PRIX : 15 CENTIMES

PRIX : 15 CENTIMES — N° 36 — 5 SEPTEMBRE 1886 — 288

9. « — Je me rencontrai avec monsieur Hersent, le peintre académicien, en 1840, dans la cour de l'Institut, après la séance de toutes les Académies réunies dans laquelle Arago avait exposé le système de Daguerre, sans faire mention de Nicéphore Niepce, le véritable inventeur.

« Je fus amené, dans la conversation, à dire à monsieur Hersent que le jaune à côté du bleu... »

10. « ... Monsieur Hersent, que notre dissertation avait un peu animé, me répondit : — Tout autre que monsieur Chevreul me dirait cela, je dirais qu'il en a menti! Mais monsieur Chevreul me le disant, je veux le voir pour le croire... »

« ... Je l'invitai aussitôt à venir à mon laboratoire des Gobelins où je lui donnerais la preuve... »

11. « ... — Il est mort vingt ans après, — *sans être jamais venu* me voir aux Gobelins, comme je l'en avais prié...

12. « — Je ne vous ai pas tout dit. Mais il ne suffit pas de dire : il faut prouver, il faut faire *voir!* Il faut que je vous fasse *voir!* Il faut que vous *voyiez! Je veux faire voir, parce que c'est quand je vois, que je crois!!!* »

paper's competitiveness with regard to the new-style periodicals that had appeared in the late nineteenth century and used the potential of photography and halftone to create innovative forms of print media. Thus Baschet's choices drew on a tried and true reproduction technique (halftone using the Levy brothers' screens); economic considerations (for the same price he could publish fifty percent more photographs); and a cultural shift that saw readers beguiled by a constant stream of images (the previous drawback of the "show-through" effect, which prevented recto–verso printing of images, no longer applied).

American periodicals like *Frank Leslie's Illustrated Weekly* were quicker to respond to photography and by 1890 some of them revolved entirely around halftone reproduction. From the outset *The Illustrated American* predominantly used photographs for its coverage of the theater and politics, and became famed for such striking visual compositions as those devoted to immigrant life on the streets of New York (see Figure 1.7). Made up of unattributed snapshots bordered in different ways and meticulously arranged, these pages of images offered fresh presentations of news that made the most of halftone and the developments in photography itself that were a feature of the period.[26]

The advent of the gelatin silver process in the late 1880s made photography more accessible and attracted a host of new, curious practitioners.[27] More light-sensitive that its predecessors, the gelatin silver process offered a dry medium that could be mass-produced. It also involved such major technical innovations as the shutter, which enabled the capturing of fractions of a second—out of the question for a hand removing and replacing a lens cap—and thus made the snapshot possible. In addition the camera became small enough to be portable and the photographer could venture out unencumbered by a view camera. Taken up on an industrial scale, these changes led to an overall simplification of the process summed up by the famous Kodak slogan of 1888, "You press the button, we do the rest." Gone were the days when a photographer had to be a combined chemistry/technology whiz, and the new method was eagerly seized on by the middle classes in search of a useful spare time activity. Thus more and more photographs were being taken by a generation of amateurs recording the private and public aspects of everyday life. Some of them, like Jacques Henri Lartigue, played with the medium and delighted in the visual souvenirs they created, while others, like Léon Gimpel, turned into relentless experimenters, joining photographers' clubs and striving to force the technology to yield the images they were dreaming of.[28] In some cases they became the darlings of press editors who saw this amateur output as an invaluable source of supply for their image needs.

In Europe and the United States ambitious publishers were increasingly out to transform the illustrated weekly and enhance their market shares through technological, economic

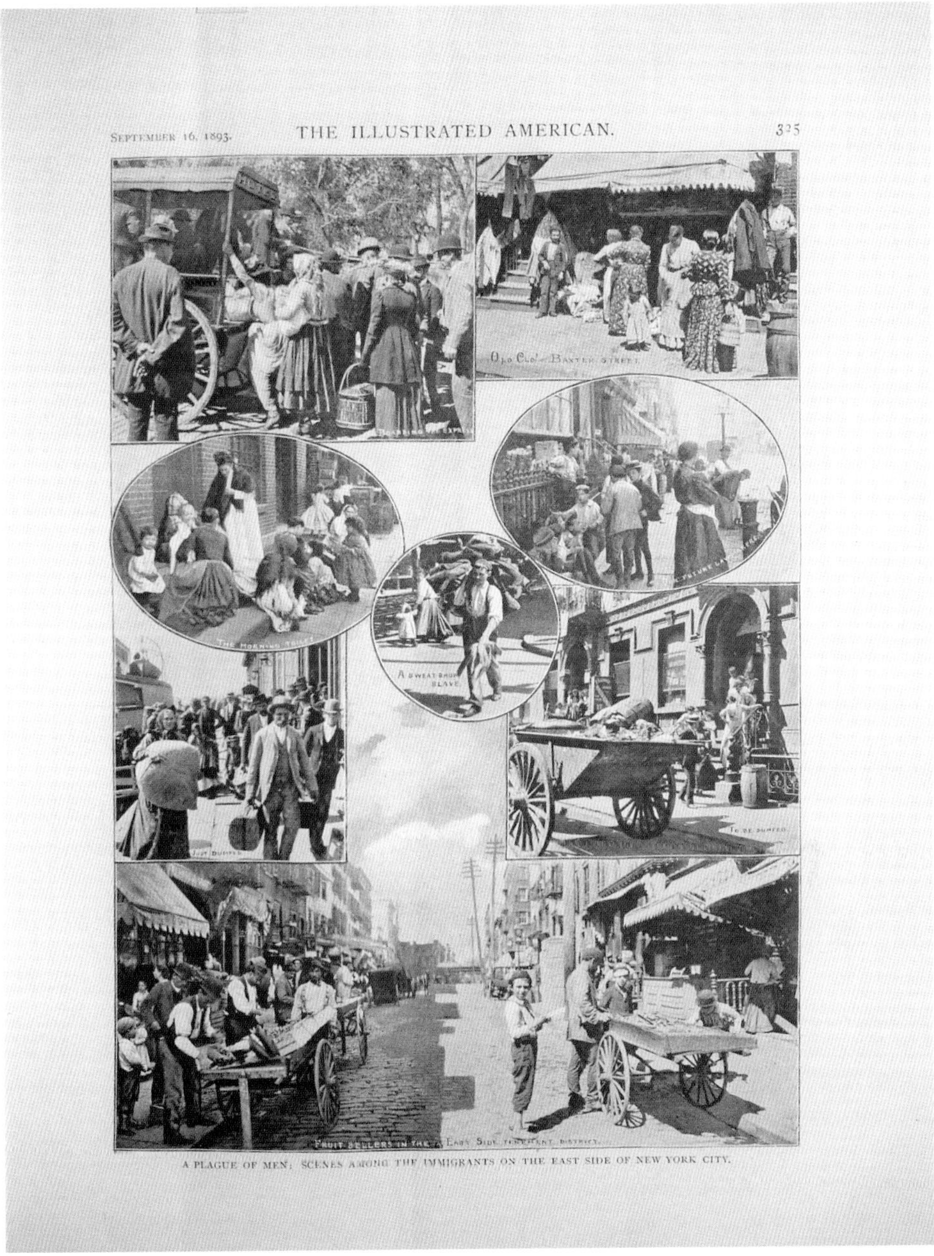

Figure 1.7 *The Illustrated American*, September 16, 1893, p. 325.

and cultural innovation. Launched in New York in 1888, *Once a Week* would become *Collier's Weekly* in 1895. In 1894, Leopold Ullstein bought the *Berliner Illustrirte Zeitung* (1892–1945), and in France in 1898 *La Vie au grand air* and *La Vie illustrée* began publication within a few months of each other. All these periodicals opted for photography for their news coverage.

Press photographers

These editorial and illustrative approaches generated a high level of demand for news photographs, and various organizations set out to meet it. In the United States Underwood & Underwood (1881) and Keystone (1892), distributors of a vast range of stereoscopic images—including such topical material as the Boer War in South Africa (1899–1902)—became major press suppliers. In France Maurice Branger and Marcel Rol founded their press photography agencies in 1904, offering general news coverage of the Paris scene. Their organization enabled broader and faster circulation of the photographs, as well as the setting-up of image banks the press could draw on when necessary. Newspapers relied above all, though, on amateurs who sent in their eyewitness pictures, and it was not uncommon for the weeklies to include inserts giving photographers instructions on how to provide publishable material.

Léon Gimpel (1873–1948) belonged to this generation of photographers who became press correspondents.[29] In March 1904 he photographed Count Henry de La Vaulx's stabilization experiments with a spherical balloon in Cannes harbor, and on an impulse sent his pictures to *La Vie au grand air*, *La Vie illustrée* and *L'Illustration*.[30] All three weeklies accepted them, and for Gimpel this marked the beginning of an association with *L'Illustration* that would last over thirty years. In his memoirs Gimpel mentions that "by a curious turn of events, [his] initial collaboration with *L'Illustration* coincided with the beginning of Monsieur René Baschet's reign as director."[31] Far from being a coincidence, this was the outcome of Baschet's new illustration policy and highlighted, interestingly, publishers' concerns with the aesthetic aspect of photography. When covering visits to Paris by foreign dignitaries, and the aeronautic exploits that so enthused the Belle Époque, Gimpel was hampered by competition from agencies which had at their disposal not only entire teams of photographers, but also communication channels that meant quicker connection with potential publishers. An experienced, technically accomplished photographer, Gimpel was as skilled in color as in black and white, in both indoor and outdoor settings; this, combined with his visual daring, gave him a distinct edge on his competitors. Notably he photographed the king and queen of Denmark in color only a few weeks after the Autochrome process came onto the market in June 1907, together with views of the lights of Paris and the passing of a Voisin biplane in an overhead shot whose visual play with differences of level is disconcerting in the extreme (see Figure 1.8).[32]

What Gimpel offered was a different formal category within the range of published images: all his photographs refer to news items, but above all they embody a photographic event tailored to appeal to publishers. It would seem, then, that the reporting of news hinged not only on factuality, but equally on the aesthetics and even the spectacular aspect of the accompanying images. All Gimpel's photographs were conserved as lantern slides that he grouped and sequenced for screenings for the photographers' associations that proliferated during the Belle Époque. Facing the screen in a darkened room, audiences took in the slideshow and Gimpel's narrative, with his technical feats adding to the spectacle of the news (see Figure 1.9).

The last category of press photographers comprised those actually employed by the weeklies, among them Ernest Clair-Guyot, who added photography to his output as an illustrator at *L'Illustration*,[33] and James H. (Jimmy) Hare (1856–1946), whose long career in the United States saw him with *The Illustrated American*, *Collier's Weekly* and *Leslie's Illustrated Weekly*, and whose war photographs were published internationally. Hare's work at the turn of the century signaled the inception of a new profession—that of photojournalist—together with new ways of using images in the press. The photography/halftone tandem boosted the impression of authenticity, but raised representational issues for publishers. The numerous photographs submitted to the weeklies did not match the illustrative canons; this was notably the case of Jimmy Hare's war images, which had to be justified to the readership and demanded the designing of new layouts.[34]

In 1898, after working the New York scene for *The Illustrated American*, Hare offered to go to Cuba and cover the Spanish–American War for *Collier's Weekly*. In late June the American army disembarked on the island and the battle of San Juan, which played a decisive part in the outcome of the war, took place in early July. However, in contrast with the kind of news Hare had been photographing so far, the battles were highly unpredictable, lasted several days, lacked pre-planned high points, and took place in harsh conditions that made the ideal point of view hard to find and often dangerous. In other words, photographing the war was a complicated exercise whose results were a poor fit with traditional depictions of battle. As Hare's biographer, Cecil Carnes explains in his account of this episode:

> His idea of war was founded on old-time formal paintings of dignified battle scenes. He had grown up in the 'Gentlemen of the Guard, fire first!' tradition. Incredible as it must seem, he confidently expected, when he reached the front line, to find the American and Spanish infantry drawn up face to face in serried ranks and picking each other off at a distance of fifty paces or so.[35]

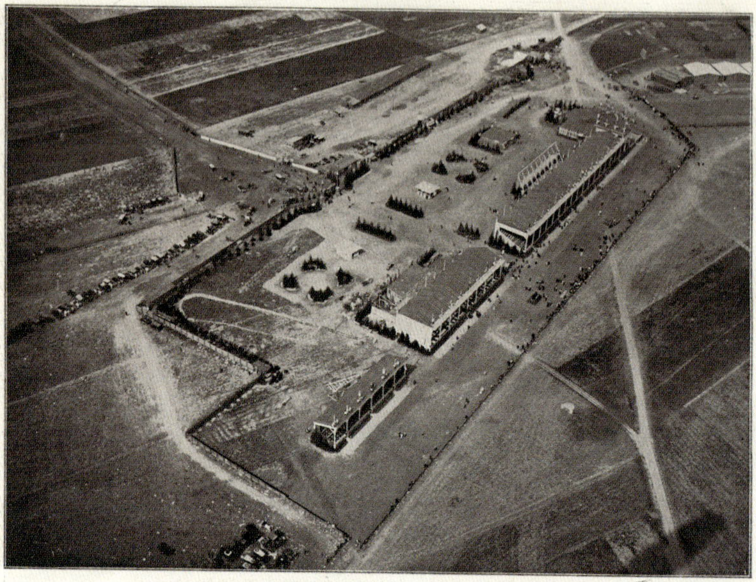

Les tribunes de Bétheny, comme les voyait Hubert Latham, quand il volait à 150 mètres d'altitude.

A l'angle inférieur droit, on distingue une partie de l'ombre du *Zodiac III*, à bord duquel opérait notre photographe, M. Gimpel.

sérieux progrès dans la mise au point de plusieurs types de moteurs.

Un de ces moteurs, après avoir amusé le public par son fonctionnement original, fut le point de départ d'un incident dont la solution ne paraît point définitive. Grâce à un dispositif dont la description sortirait de notre cadre, le *gnome*, qui comprend sept cylindres rayonnants, tourne en même temps que l'hélice qu'il actionne. Il agit ainsi comme volant régulateur du couple et se refroidit directement au contact de l'air sans intervention d'ailettes ou de circulation d'eau.

Au dernier moment, Farman, profitant de l'autorisation signée par un commissaire, remplaçait par un *gnome* le moteur spécifié dans son engagement. La réclamation de ses concurrents a été repoussée par les commissaires de Bétheny.

***

Les dirigeables eurent un rôle secondaire ; l'épreuve de distance réservée aux aéronats ne réunit que deux concurrents : le *Colonel-Renard*, cubant 4.000 mètres cubes, qui couvrit les 50 kilomètres en 1 h. 19 min. 49 sec., et le *Zodiac III*, de 1.400 mètres cubes seulement, qui, retardé quelques instants par une panne de moteur, se laissa distancer de moins de 5 minutes.

L'un et l'autre se montrèrent à plusieurs reprises, manœuvrant avec une égale habileté. Aussi, quand, dimanche matin, le *Zodiac III* vint flâner dans le ciel de Bétheny, les habitués des tribunes qui, les jours précédents, avaient admiré la souplesse et la rapidité de ses évolutions, furent stupéfaits de le voir zigzaguer avec une lenteur et des hésitations inaccoutumées. Les plus malins en concluaient que le comte de La Vaulx avait confié la barre à un de ses élèves.

Il n'en était rien : M. de La Vaulx donnait, au contraire, une nouvelle preuve de maîtrise, en se prêtant aux moindres caprices du photographe de *L'Illustration*, M. Gimpel, qu'il avait eu l'amabilité de prendre à bord. M. Schelcher, collaborateur de M. de La Vaulx à la Société Zodiac et l'un des recordmen de la photographie en ballon, dont nos lecteurs connaissent les magnifiques clichés.

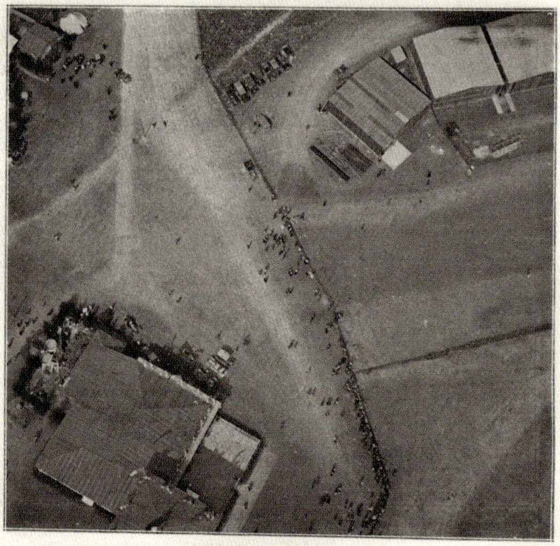

BÉTHENY VU DE LA PASSERELLE DU « ZODIAC III ». — L'angle de la grande tribune et l'entrée du parc des aéroplanes.

L'Illustration, *avec sa rapidité coutumière, a pu mettre sous les yeux de ses lecteurs, dès la semaine dernière, des photographies dessins montrant, dans le ciel mouvementé de Bétheny, les plus beaux vols de Latham, de Paulhan, de Blériot, de Curtiss. Nous somm heureux d'être à même de publier aujourd'hui une nouvelle série de documents photographiques d'un intérêt inédit. Après la vision des aér*

Figure 1.8 *L'Illustration*, September 4, 1909, pp. 162–3. Photographs by Léon Gimpel.

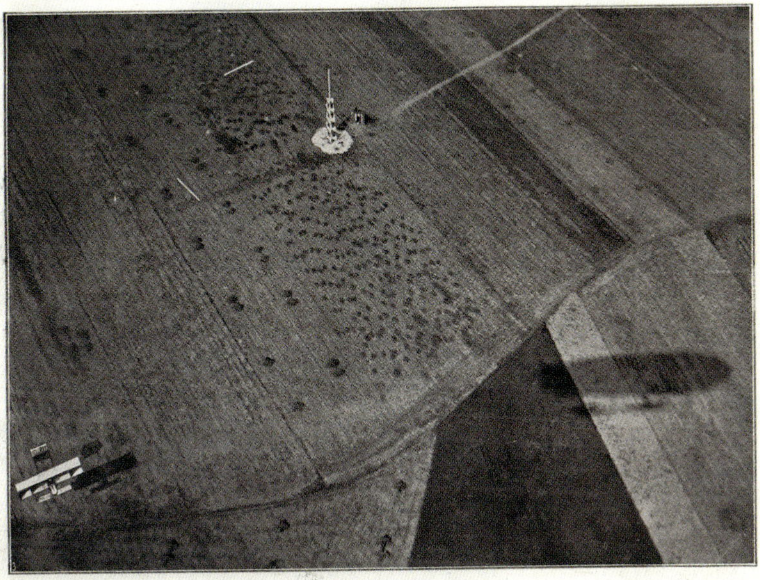

Au-dessus d'un biplan "Voisin" qui vient de virer au large d'un pylône.

Près du pylône, deux bandes de calicot blanc fixées sur le sol indiquent aux aviateurs l'angle du virage ; à droite du biplan et sous lui, son ombre ; à l'angle droit de la photographie, l'ombre du *Zodiac III*.

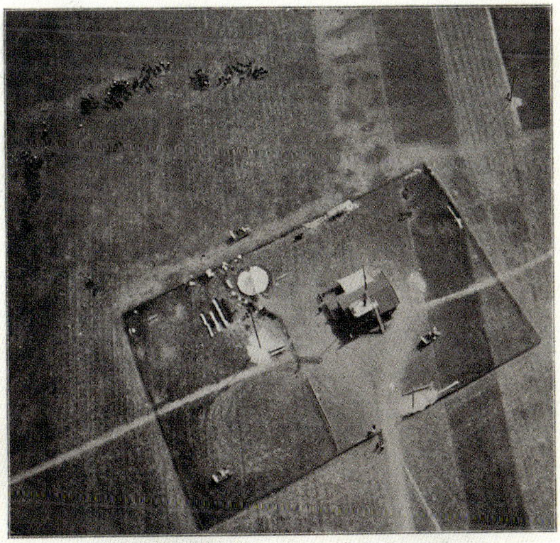

L'enceinte officielle, en face des tribunes, avec le poste du comité, le mât des signaux, la cabine des chronométreurs, çà et là des automobiles, et, en arrière, un peloton de dragons à cheval.

se trouvait retenu à terre par ses fonctions de commissaire sportif.

Dans les tribunes de Bétheny, sur la pelouse, tous ceux qui ne sont pas encore montés en aéroplane — et ils sont nombreux — se demandaient ce que Latham ou Paulhan pouvaient bien voir, quand, à une centaine de mètres en l'air, ils daignaient abaisser leurs regards sur les terriens. Nos photographies satisferont cette légitime curiosité.

A l'heure où elles furent prises, il y avait peu d'aéroplanes en l'air et peu de spectateurs. Néanmoins, ces baraques de toutes formes plantées au milieu des champs, les pelotons de dragons, le vol d'un biplan que, seul, le déplacement de son ombre faisait paraître au-dessus du sol, formaient un ensemble amusant, que l'on contemplait et photographiait dans des conditions de confortable étonnantes, évidemment supérieures à celles qu'offrent les aéroplanes. Le bruit et la trépidation du moteur sont insensibles sur la passerelle où circule une brise délicieuse, inconnue dans les ballons libres dépourvus de vitesse propre.

Cette ascension présentait un autre intérêt : elle nous a permis de juger pratiquement la facilité avec laquelle on peut aujourd'hui se promener en dirigeable. On commande un *Zodiac*, comme on loue un yacht ou une auto. Et l'on arriverait presque à le loger dans sa malle. MM. le comte de La Vaulx et Schelcher avaient apporté leur aéronat dans l'express qui les amenait à Reims.

Le *Zodiac III* est plus grand que ses aînés, dont nous avons parlé il y a quelques mois. La nacelle, longue de 20 mètres sur 1 m. 50 de hauteur et 80 centimètres de largeur, se divise en quatre travées de 5 mètres que l'on assemble au moyen de quelques boulons. L'enveloppe pliée se transporte comme une pièce d'étoffe. Le montage et le gonflement, qui demandent un jour et demi avec un personnel restreint, s'achèvent en quatre ou cinq heures si l'on dispose d'une compagnie d'aérostiers.

* * *

Si beaucoup regrettèrent de ne pouvoir s'offrir un tour sur la passerelle du *Zodiac*, un plus grand

planes tels qu'ils apparaissaient aux spectateurs, il était curieux de fixer la vision inverse, celle qui s'offrait aux aviateurs eux-mêmes, quand ils planaient au-dessus de la piste, autour des pylônes de virage. C'est ce résultat qu'a obtenu notre collaborateur M. Gimpel en allant prendre, de la nacelle du petit dirigeable Zodiac III, *compagnon d'altitude de Latham, des photographies «à vol d'oiseau» des champs de Bétheny*

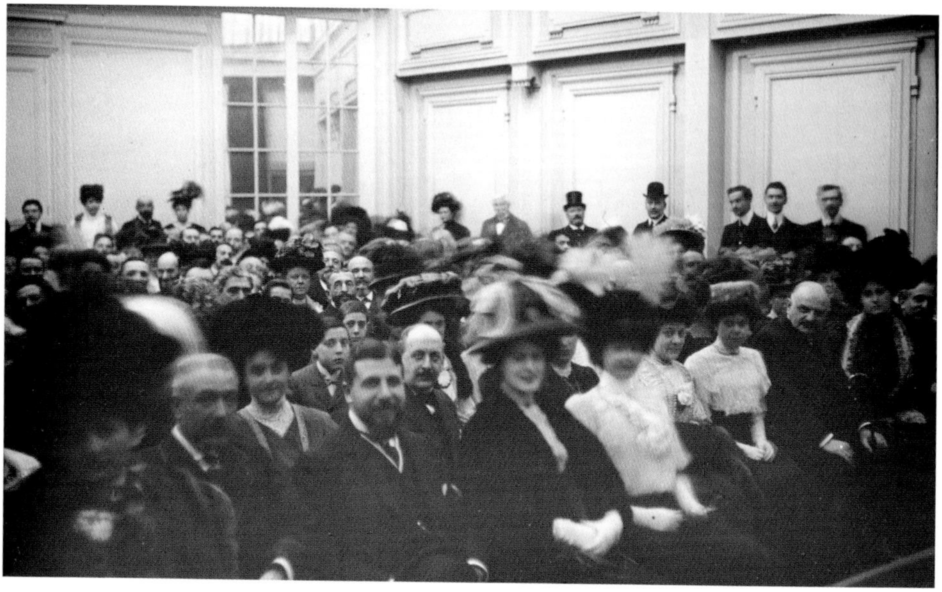

Figure 1.9 Léon Gimpel, 'Projection of color photographs at the Societé française de photographie,' lantern slide, 9 x 12 cm, February 4, 1908. From the collection of the Societé française de photographie, Paris.

Obviously such was not the case. Hare brought lots of photographs back from his ventures onto the battlefield, where he followed the successes and reversals of the American troops, but none of them reflected the standards of his personal visual grounding. Nonetheless they showed soldiers on the march, lying camouflaged in long grass, and sheltering from enemy fire behind an embankment; and covered actual operations, with observation of enemy movements through binoculars or from the nacelle of a tethered balloon, batteries of cannon firing from amidst clouds of smoke, and the bringing in and treatment of the wounded. As documentation these images were precise and invaluable, but they did not fit with the traditional representations of war as still governed by the rules of history painting.[36]

The photographs from the front reached New York in the second half of July, and appeared in *Collier's Weekly* on July 30. In the meantime the editors boosted the "From the Front" segment with archival images and had illustrators come up with battle scenes such as the final American infantry charge at El Caney, with soldiers running—and dying—in lines, in a chaos of action and smoke, on their way to taking the fort visible in the background: a straightforward composition that could only be the work of an artist's imagination in its orderly conveying of the courage—and inevitable success—of the American army.[37] Hare's photographs, with their less dramatic subjects and profusion of confused detail, did not possess the same narrative effectiveness and could not be published in the same way. And so the task of narrating and illustrating the war fell to the editors—not yet called "picture editors"—who would sort, crop, sequence, and caption the photographs so as to ensure their meaning and their impact. Thirty-seven of Hare's pictures were chosen and grouped together page by page to illustrate different episodes in the war in the July 30 issue of the magazine. Series of photographs were published edge to edge, underscored with brief captions and evocative titles: "At the Front, near Santiago, July 1 and 2," "In Front of San Juan, July 1 and 2" (see Figure 1.10), "The Exodus from Santiago, after Notice of Bombardment Had Been Given," and "After the Battle, Caring for the Disabled Soldiers."[38] Graphically speaking, this thematic arrangement seemed the best suited to the quantity of photographs received and to a page-by-page recounting of the different phases of the conflict.

When relations between Japan and Russia became tense early in 1904, it became apparent that war was a big issue at *Collier's Weekly*, which sent a whole team—including Jimmy Hare—to Asia. His photographs were published in *Collier's Weekly* and in Europe as well, in illustrated weeklies like the *Berliner Illustrirte Zeitung* and *Die Woche* (1899–1944) in Germany, and in *L'Illustration* and even the daily *Le Matin* (1884–1944) in France.[39] This kind of circulation testifies to the interest the images generated, even if the publishers still insisted on justifying, and even excusing, their formal presentation. *L'Illustration* had always defended photography as an authenticating enhancement of journalistic credibility,[40] but in presenting Jimmy Hare to its readers the weekly still felt obliged to highlight the element of danger: "Not to speak of the serious risks run by a war correspondent, photographer, or journalist, when we know the circumstances behind these results—the rudimentary facilities, the delicacy of handling required by the art of photography—we can only express surprise and would not dream of stinting on our respect and admiration for our bold, inventive contributors." In the description that follows of the way the photojournalist works we see the figure of the sorely tested hero beginning to emerge. Having to be on the spot to record the facts valorizes the photographer's work and so can justify the form of the published images: "Think of all the courage this represents . . . and do not be too severe if from time to time we show you an image that is slightly less than perfect"[41] (see Figure 1.11). The retouching of the accompanying photograph provides a demonstration: at the very least the prints sent from the front had to be corrected with gouache to soften contours and adjust certain shadows. Even before publication the images of the Japanese army were being defended in terms of the journalistic approach they exemplified, and further legitimated by the journalist's commitment and willingness to put his own life in danger.

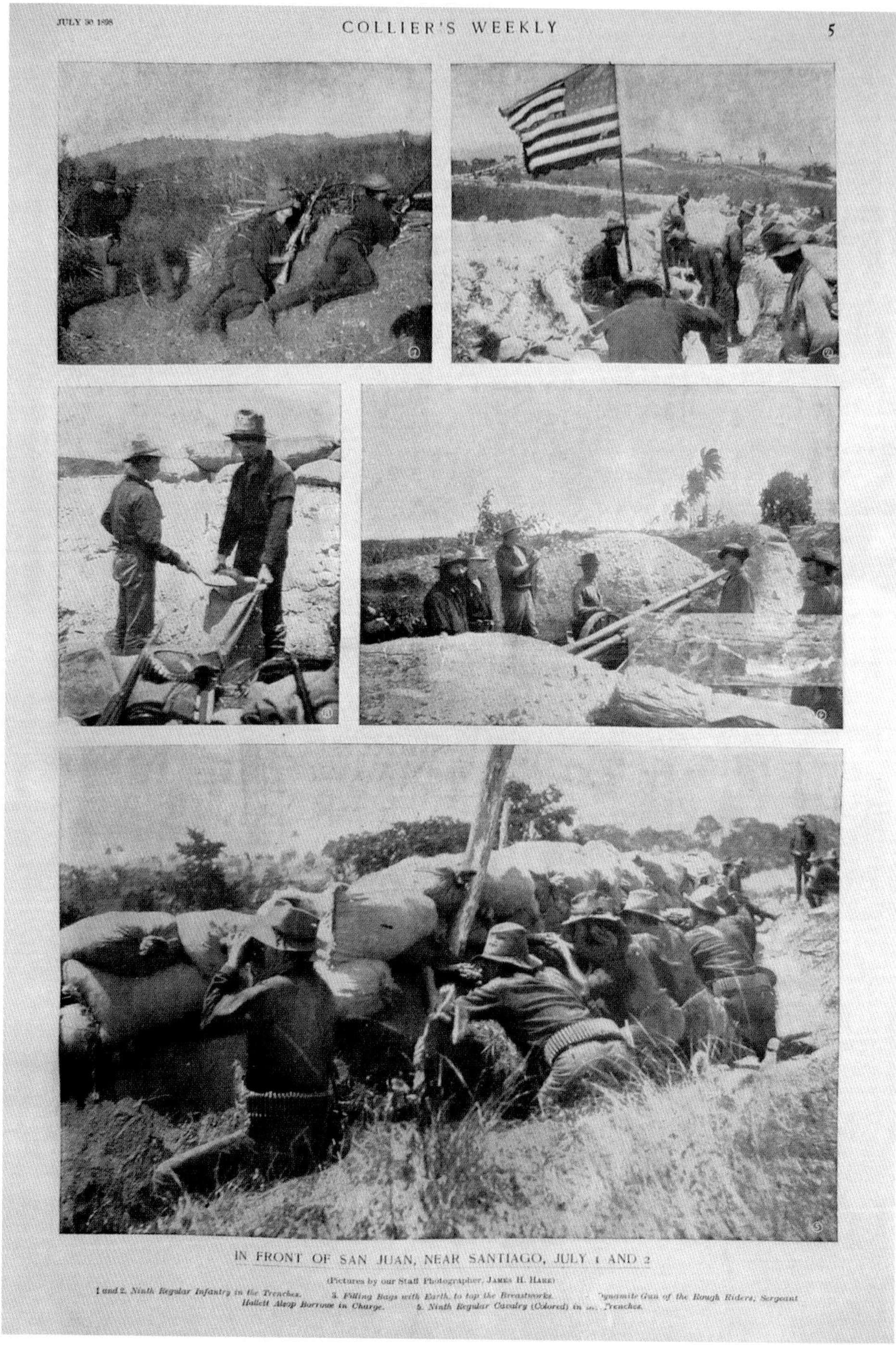
JULY 30 1898 COLLIER'S WEEKLY 5

IN FRONT OF SAN JUAN, NEAR SANTIAGO, JULY 1 AND 2

(Pictures by our Staff Photographer, JAMES H. HARE)

1 and 2. Ninth Regular Infantry in the Trenches. 3. Filling Bags with Earth to top the Breastworks. [illegible]ynamite Gun of the Rough Riders; Sergeant Hallett Alsop Borrowe in Charge. 5. Ninth Regular Cavalry (Colored) in [illegible] Trenches.

Figure 1.10 *Collier's Weekly*, July 30, 1898, p. 5. Photographs by James H. Hare.

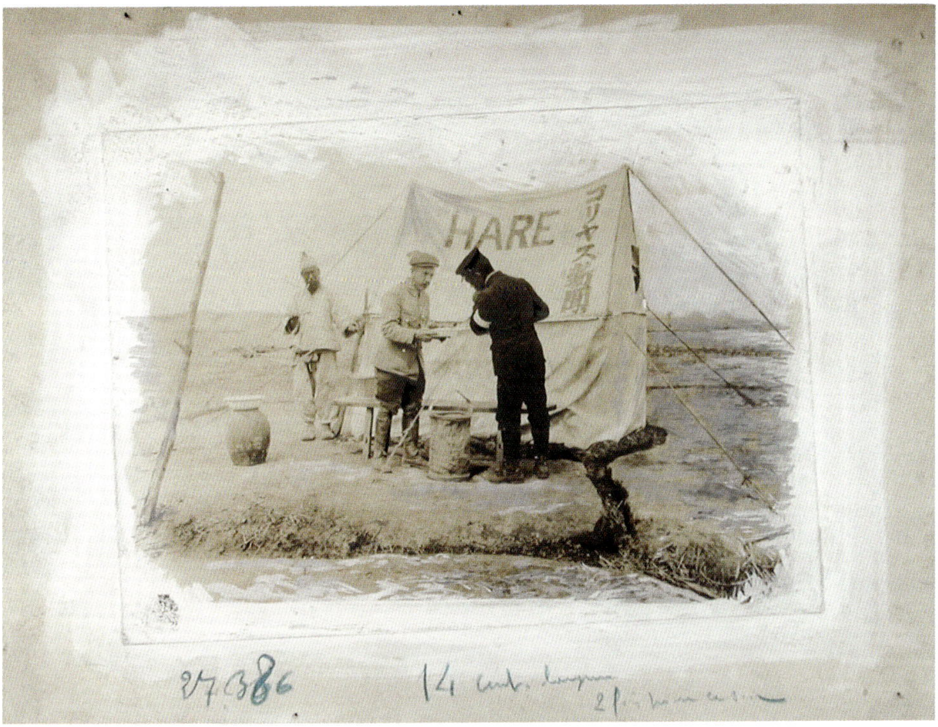

Figure 1.11 Anonymous, 'Jimmy Hare's tent, American photographer, *Collier's Weekly* and *L'Illustration* correspondent, on the banks of the Yalu River,' gelatin silver print mounted on cardboard and retouched with white gouache, 18 x 24 cm, 1904. From the collection of *L'Illustration* / BnF, Paris.

In both *Collier's Weekly* and *L'Illustration* photographs sometimes took up an entire page, but more usually were part of a careful layout. The opening sentences of the article accompanying the seven pictures skillfully arranged on a double page in *L'Illustration* of August 27, 1904 provide an explanation: "From among all the photographs we have received from the war zone these last few days, we have chosen a series focusing on episodes from everyday campaign life on the Japanese side and showing the Japanese soldier busying himself at his various duties"[42] (see Figure 1.12).

For the editors the illustration process now involved a new task. Where once they had required their illustrators to produce the images they needed, they now had to make do with what came in. Pictures were no longer made after the event, but while it was actually taking place. Moreover they came in quantity, and the editors had to learn to sort, select and arrange them on the page in order to get the desired information across. From among the

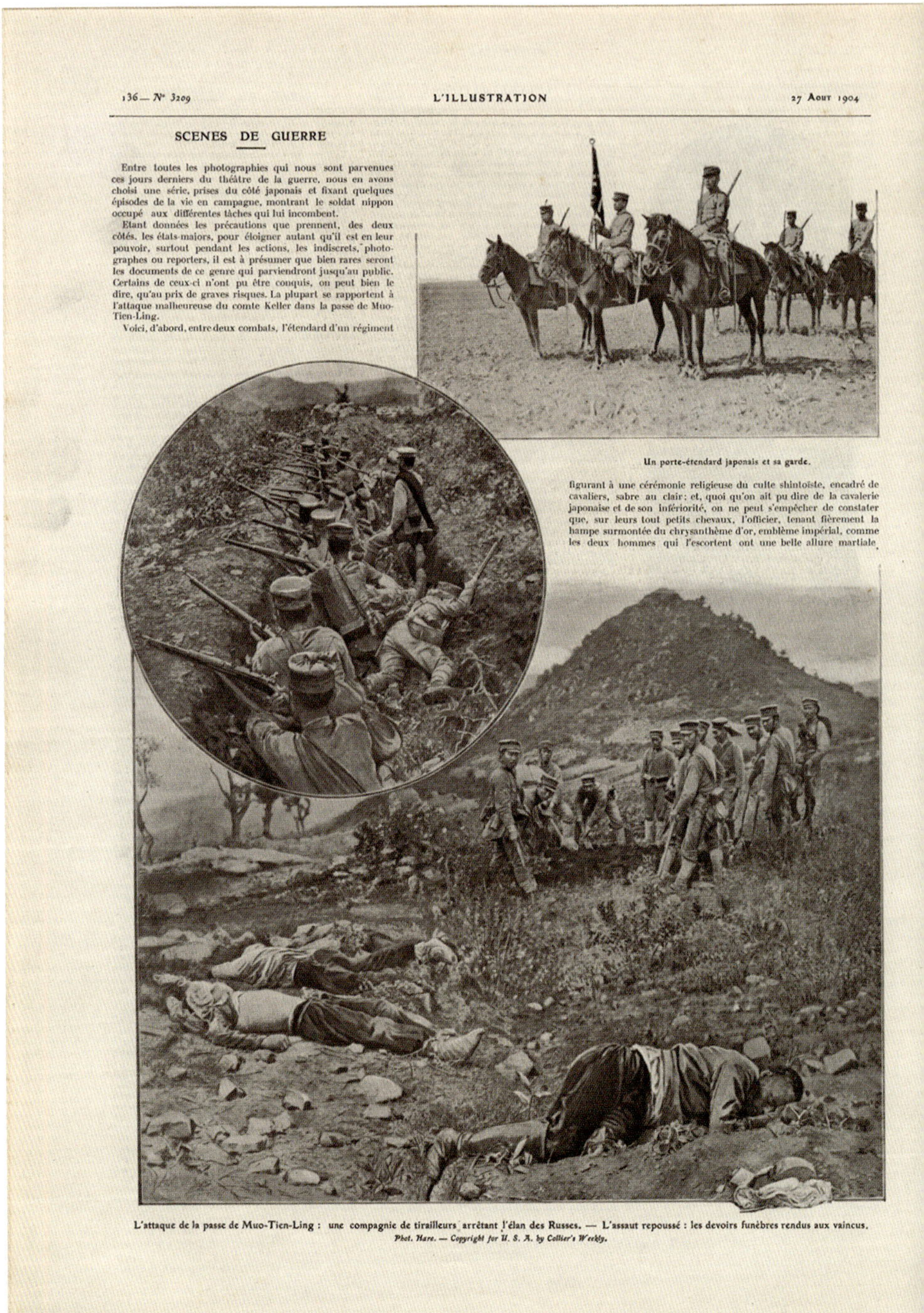

136 — N° 3209 L'ILLUSTRATION 27 Aout 1904

SCENES DE GUERRE

Entre toutes les photographies qui nous sont parvenues ces jours derniers du théâtre de la guerre, nous en avons choisi une série, prises du côté japonais et fixant quelques épisodes de la vie en campagne, montrant le soldat nippon occupé aux différentes tâches qui lui incombent.

Etant données les précautions que prennent, des deux côtés, les états-majors, pour éloigner autant qu'il est en leur pouvoir, surtout pendant les actions, les indiscrets, photographes ou reporters, il est à présumer que bien rares seront les documents de ce genre qui parviendront jusqu'au public. Certains de ceux-ci n'ont pu être conquis, on peut bien le dire, qu'au prix de graves risques. La plupart se rapportent à l'attaque malheureuse du comte Keller dans la passe de Muo-Tien-Ling.

Voici, d'abord, entre deux combats, l'étendard d'un régiment figurant à une cérémonie religieuse du culte shintoïste, encadré de cavaliers, sabre au clair; et, quoi qu'on ait pu dire de la cavalerie japonaise et de son infériorité, on ne peut s'empêcher de constater que, sur leurs tout petits chevaux, l'officier, tenant fièrement la hampe surmontée du chrysanthème d'or, emblème impérial, comme les deux hommes qui l'escortent ont une belle allure martiale.

Un porte-étendard japonais et sa garde.

L'attaque de la passe de Muo-Tien-Ling : une compagnie de tirailleurs arrêtant l'élan des Russes. — L'assaut repoussé : les devoirs funèbres rendus aux vaincus.

Phot. Hare. — Copyright for U. S. A. by Collier's Weekly.

Figure 1.12 *L'Illustration*, August 27, 1904, pp. 136–7. Photographs by James H. Hare.

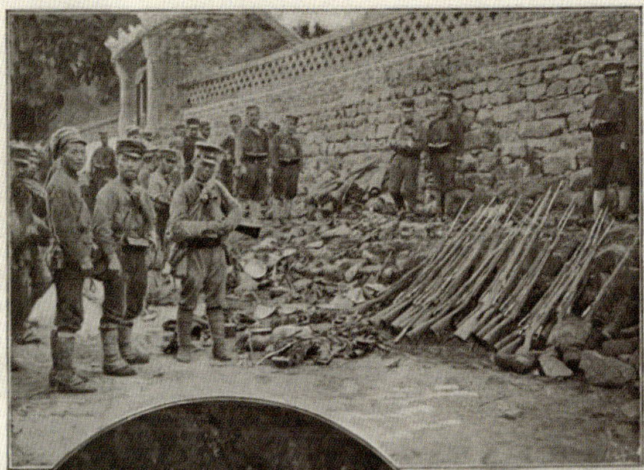

Le butin.

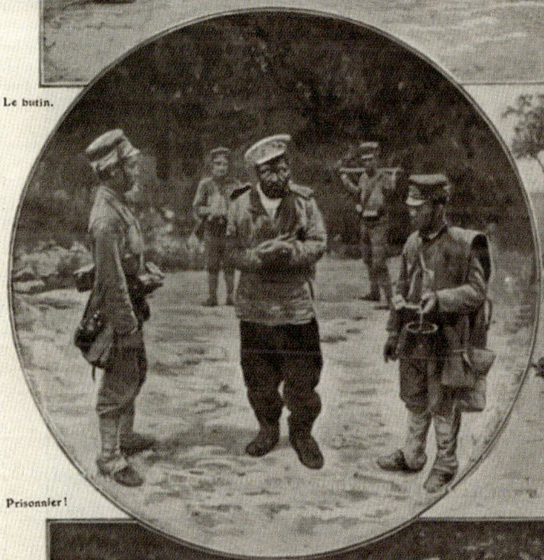

Prisonnier !

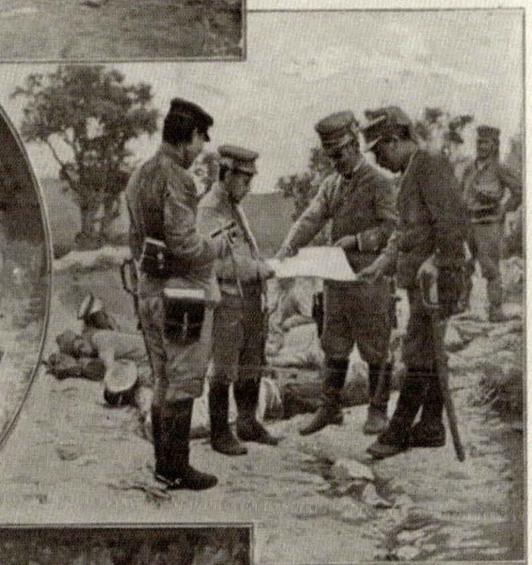

La critique des "opérations" par le major Takakusangi.

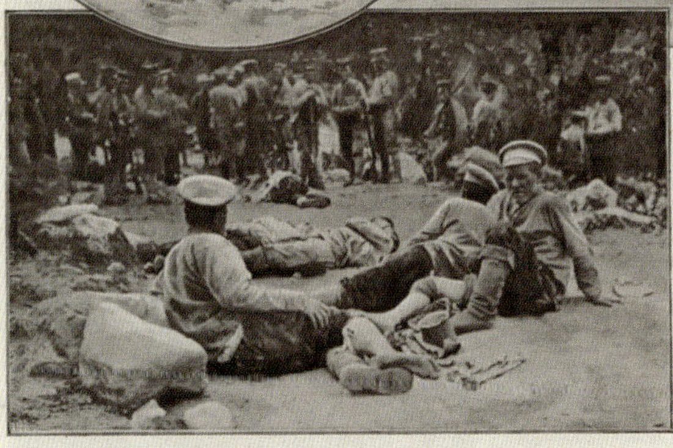

L'attaque de la passe de Muo-Tien-Ling : les blessés et les morts avant l'arrivée des civières.

Phot. Hare. — Copyright for U. S. A. by Collier's Weekly.

même dans cette circonstance pacifique·

Mais, maintenant, les Japonais sont au feu. Couchés dans la tranchée, pendant un assaut de l'ennemi, les fantassins de la première ligne, celle qui soutient tout d'abord le choc de l'assaillant, sont attentifs, l'arme au poing, le doigt à la détente, prêts à tirer, au premier signal, aussitôt que le but humain sera à « bonne portée ». Ce but, qui court à la mort, un officier, debout, le guette, plus exposé lui seul que tous les autres aux balles russes qui ont déjà abattu plus d'un défenseur de la position.

Puis ce sont quelques clichés saisis après la bataille : ici, une équipe de soldats japonais préparant une tombe aux morts, qui gisent de place en place sur la terre nue, l'un, au premier plan, tombé à côté de sa « boule de son », au moment, sans doute, où, afin de se donner des forces pour combattre, il prenait un suprême et maigre repas; là, la moisson des fusils enlevés à l'ennemi, rangés en gerbes, contre les murailles du temple de Kouan-Tu, pêle-mêle avec des débris de fourniment, des munitions, tout un fatras bizarre; plus loin, un officier japonais, le major Takakusangi, faisant à des camarades la critique du combat, à deux pas de pauvres cadavres encore sans sépulture, refroidis à peine; puis des blessés par tas, les mourants exhalant leurs derniers râles près de leurs compagnons légèrement atteints, sous l'œil des vainqueurs, sans doute émus malgré eux devant ces adversaires de tout à l'heure, maintenant réduits à l'impuissance et captifs.

Enfin, un tableau presque reposant, après ces visions pénibles : celui de deux petits soldats japonais qui, chargés de la conduite d'un lamentable Russe, grièvement blessé, le cou traversé d'une balle et se traînant cependant, mais incapable de porter son équipement, l'ont débarrassé de ce faix pour lui rendre la marche moins pénible.

Et au moment où, de part et d'autre, on se reproche violemment, d'inutiles, d'atroces cruautés, il est consolant de penser que la férocité n'est, ni dans une armée ni dans l'autre, la règle sans exceptions.

photographs filed by Jimmy Hare the team at *L'Illustration* chose a "series" to be laid out sequentially, with a beginning and an end. The reader is led from a photograph of a Japanese standard bearer to views of the trenches, plunder and prisoners, and finally of the "wounded and dead before the arrival of the stretchers." Thus the images and their orchestration make the reader a spectator as a military incident unfolds.

In the issue of December 10, 1904 this use of layout to suggest time passing reaches it high point with a series of sixteen photographs by Jimmy Hare titled "A Day's Fighting between Yen Tai and the Cha Ho, Photographed Hour by Hour"[43] (see Figure 1.13). The photographs are arranged sequentially in four lines: we begin with the Japanese general staff and then, in a series of "successive" images of the battlefield, we accompany "the photographer, Mr Hare, advancing toward the firing line." To ensure that the reader follows the photographer through the battle, *L'Illustration* numbered each image, indicating a viewing order that reflects the temporal flow of the action. Closing with a picture of Hare himself, this sequence chimes with the content of the article relating to the photographer: captioned "Mr Hare stops taking photographs to give first aid to the wounded," the picture

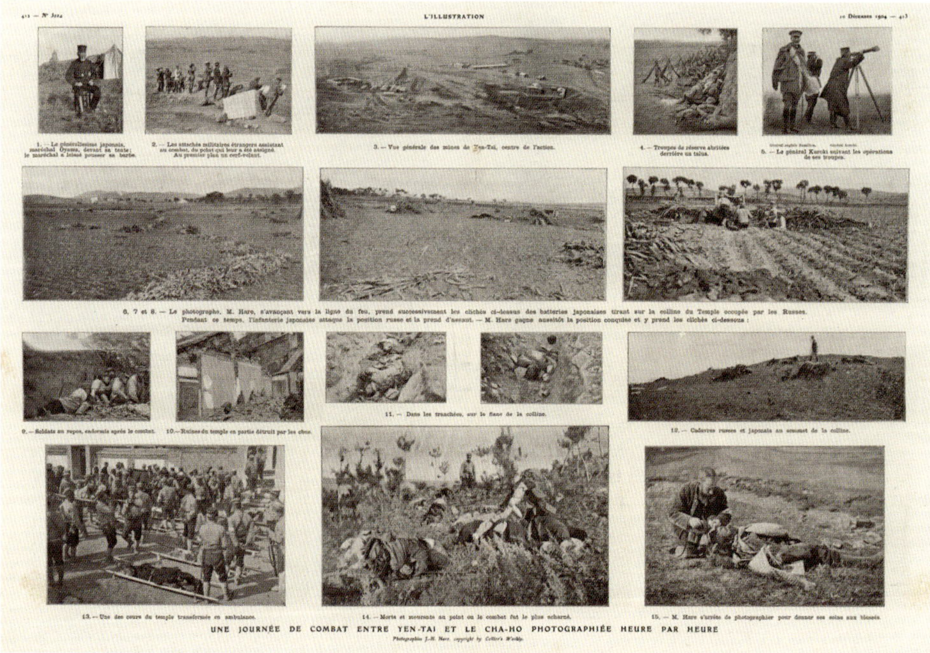

Figure 1.13 *L'Illustration*, December 10, 1904, pp. 412–13. Photographs by James H. Hare.

presents him not as a purveyor of news but as a direct participant in the conflict. Everything possible is done to give the reader/spectator the feeling of having first-hand access to the war. In this double page spread it is no longer a matter of *representing* a battle scene, but of *presenting* the actual battle, "hour by hour." Hare's photographs and their layout propose an illustration protocol which tends simultaneously to glorify the photographer and to hide the act of representation, to conceal mediatization of news, in order to guarantee its credibility.

Late in the war an article by Gustave Babin devoted to Hare's pictures and war photography in general took a look at this new kind of presentation: "No one will have failed to notice how unexpected this image of war is—so accurately captured by a lens that excludes lies or delusion—and how far removed from the epic tableaux once used to portray it."[44] In this contribution to the standard rhetoric of legitimation, the author declares, "This is war today: a few patches of smoke far away in the sky, men crawling cautiously along on their stomachs and taking shelter in every furrow in the ground. War is now made of a series of tiny, identical incidents: that is the way we see a battle in which a hundred thousand soldiers are lost." Although these small photographs did not systematically replace the great battle compositions, we can only agree with Babin that the pictures from the Russo–Japanese front had stood traditional representations of war on their head.[45] Layouts offering an analytical breakdown of events, as opposed to the grand syntheses of the illustrators, fit equally with the modernity of the Russo–Japanese conflict[46] and the change in journalistic practice. No longer concentrated in the drawing, the news narrative now unfolded across the page. Benefiting from international circulation, Hare's photographs helped *Collier's Weekly* achieve the aim it had set itself on February 13, 1904—"to set a new standard of weekly journalism"[47]—in highlighting the persona of the photojournalist. Described as an artist during the Spanish–American War, in 1914 Hare was given the ultimate accolade as "the greatest of war photographers"[48] by *Leslie's Weekly*, which sent him to cover the First World War. Opting for photography not only changed journalism, it also utterly changed the form of the illustrated periodicals.

The role of the art director

On the cover of its first issue, dated October 20, 1898, the French weekly *La Vie illustrée* (1898–1912) announced twice as many pictures as *L'Illustration* for half the price.[49] The first image was on the cover and image-quantity structured the economy of the entire issue in question.[50] Graphically speaking the cover of *L'Illustration*—simple, sparse typography and an engraving showing the magazine's attributes, that is, the writer's pen, the artist's charcoal, and the engraver's burin—still reflected its nineteenth-century roots, whereas *La Vie illustrée* used this key space for an eye-catching photograph. Initially this illustration was an oval or a circle that tallied with the curve of the printed title,[51] but then the image broke free of this constraint in the interests of the overall graphic harmony of the page. Images, tables of contents, and color began to be orchestrated in ways that would convey information and provide arresting compositions. In one example *La Vie illustrée* of July 8, 1904, reporting on the Russo–Japanese War, featured on its cover "the execution of a Koungouse in Manchuria"[52] (see Figure 1.14). The original photograph was cropped to fit the magazine's vertical format and focus attention on the executioner, holding his bloody sword in one hand and presenting the head of his victim to the crowd with the other.[53] The vivid red of the two-color printing heightened the ambience of violence by the addition of bloodstains to the sword and on the ground. On this cover the photograph does not illustrate the text, and the print is not there to serve the illustration: text and image form the abscissa and the ordinate of a composition aimed at mediation of the event on the page. The formal interest of *La Vie illustrée* here lies in this association, which makes the cover a space where seeing and reading go hand in hand. In the early twentieth century general news publications were still wary of too-modern graphics, while the sporting press found the formal renewal it needed in the exercise of greater freedom and initiative.

Pierre Lafitte and Henri de Weindel, respectively directors of *La Vie au grand air* and *La Vie illustrée* both wanted readers to *leaf through* their weeklies,[54] which meant being able to linger over something other than print. Combining the resources of photography and the potential of halftone, both periodicals offered a product whose abundant, deftly deployed images turned the reader into a spectator. In its issue of February 4, 1899 the sports magazine *La Vie au grand air* published sixty illustrations, all of them photography-derived.[55] There were very few pages given over to print alone and most often what text there was took the form of captions sprinkled over space orchestrated by illustrations. Given the quantity and variety of images, the magazine had to come up with individual design solutions for each issue, and for this it appointed an art director whose job was not only to choose the photographs, but also to decide on an editorially meaningful layout. The task of visually shaping the sporting news was entrusted to Lucien Faure. As at *La Vie illustrée* the cover became a locus of graphic construction where text and image intermingled according to the stories. Faure regularly set up a visual dynamic by creating associations between the compositional lines of a photograph and the title (see Figure 1.15), but he also composed photomontages in which he made play with photography's supposed realism. For the issue of November 3, 1904 he reproduced a close-up of the face of a stopwatch and its hands, together with cut out images of the cyclist and the long distance runner who had just broken the one-hour records[56] (see Figure 1.16). With layouts like these the art director was aiming much more at a spectator than a reader: and not just the spectator of speed records, but also the spectator of image forms calculated to catch the eye. Contact with *La Vie au grand air* came initially via the cover, which had

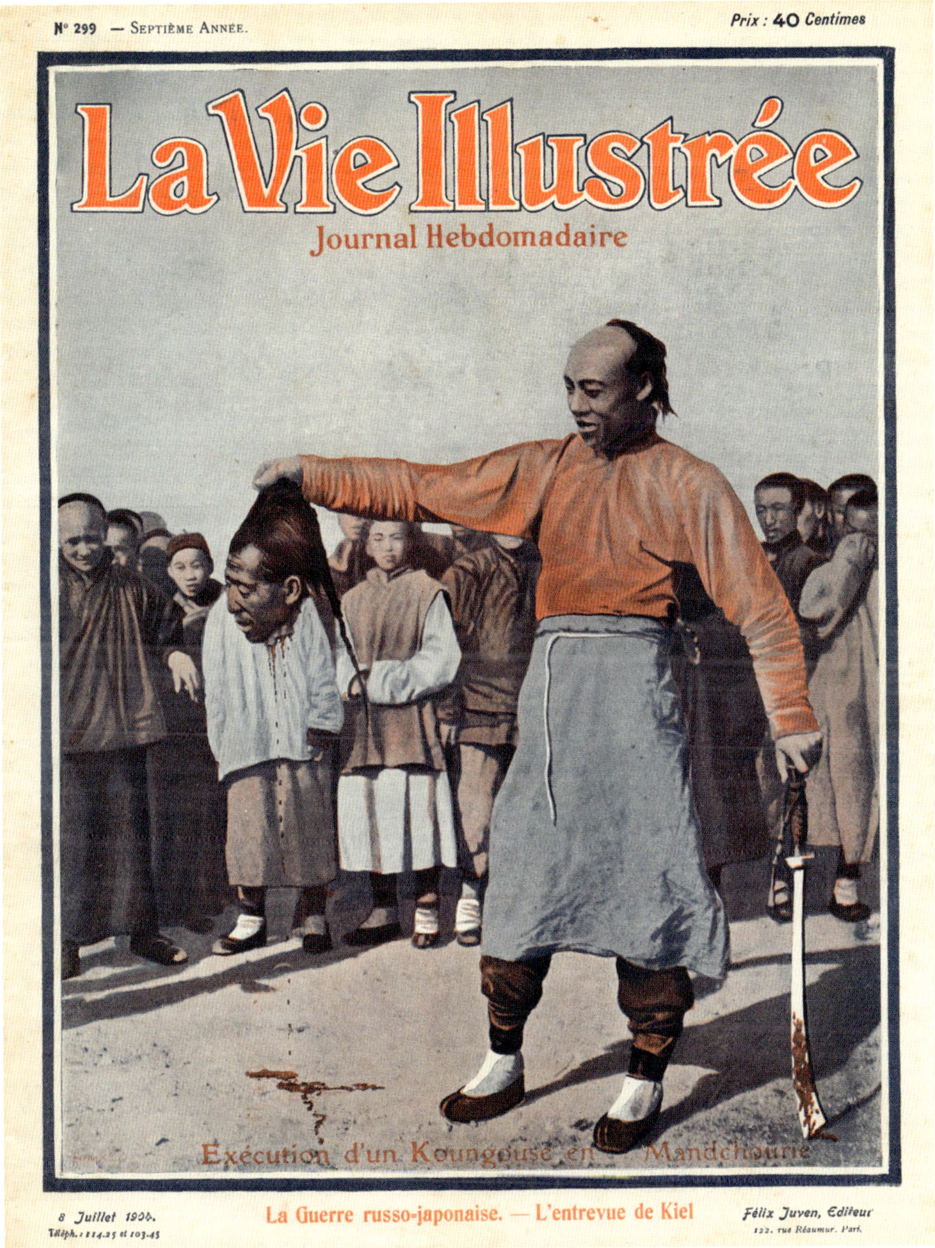

Figure 1.14 *La Vie illustrée*, July 8, 1904, cover. Photograph by George Rogers.

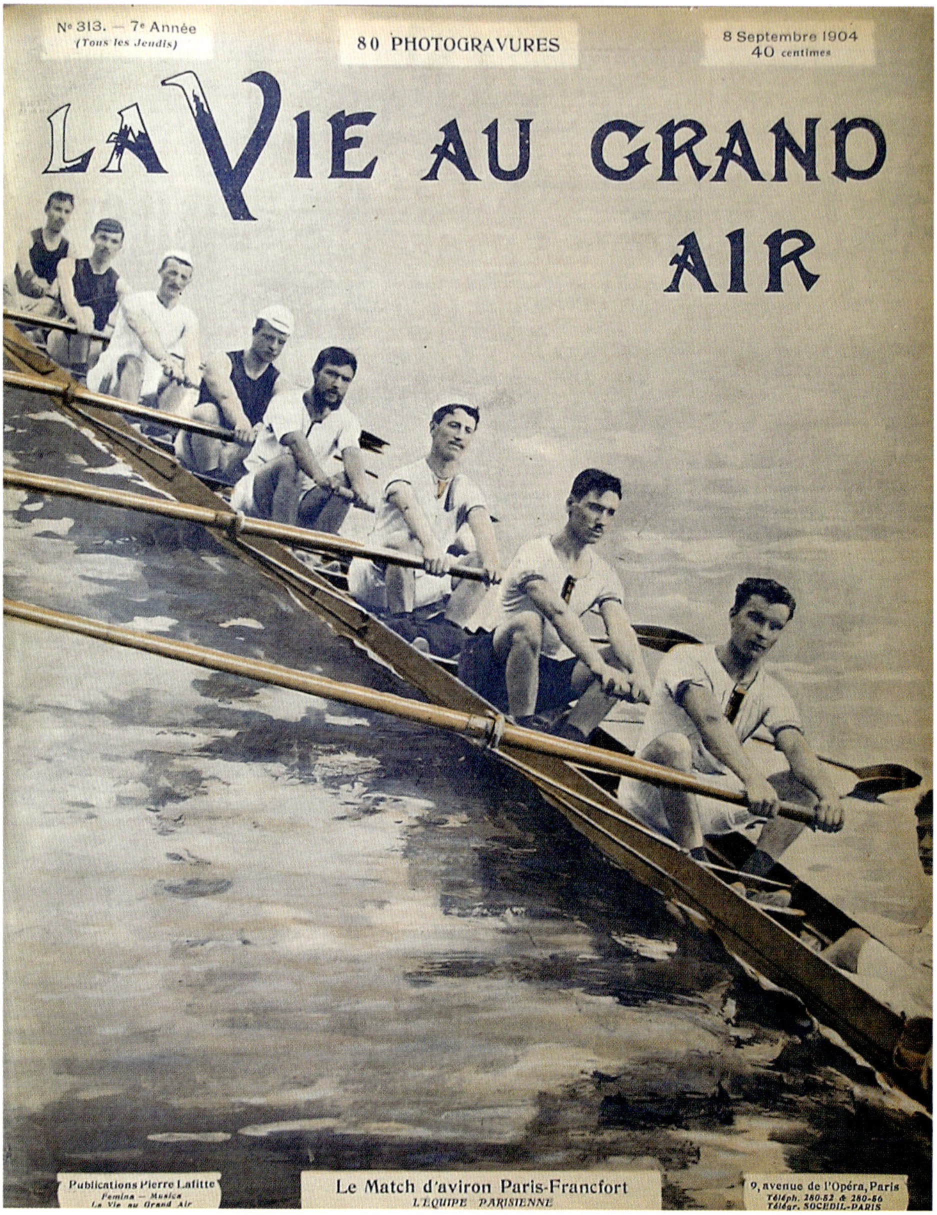

Figure 1.15 *La Vie au grand air*, September 8, 1904, cover.

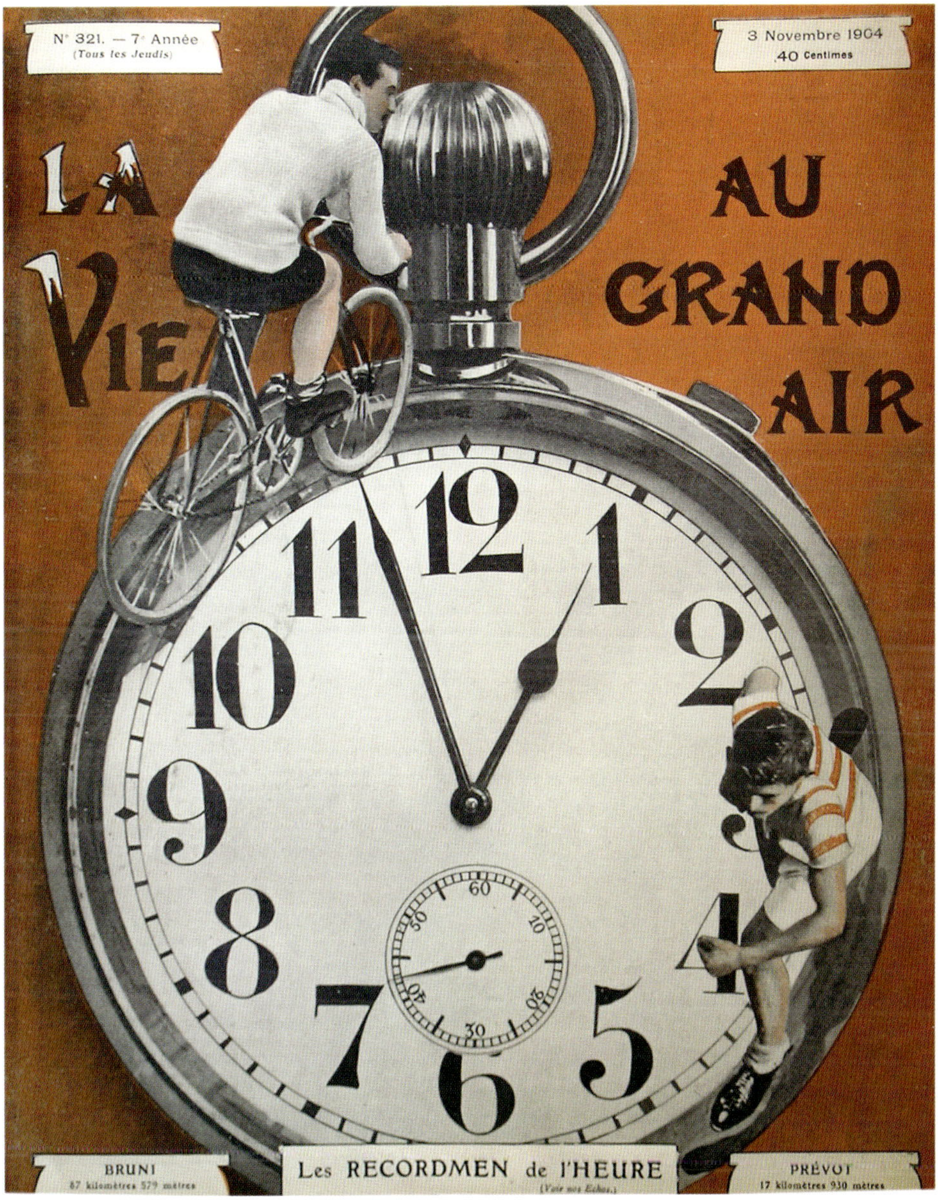

Figure 1.16 *La Vie au grand air*, November 3, 1904, cover.

to attract the reader, and then the issue was orchestrated by the layout of the full and double page spreads.[57]

Faure always had plenty of photographs to use as sports news illustrations, but those worthy of a full page were sometimes lacking. This was especially true of races or wrestling matches to come, for which he did not have images as such. In these cases he resorted to archival photographs of the venues or the personages concerned, combining rectangular or circular images set edge to edge or sometimes overlapping in complex graphic constructions like the one complementing Fioravanti's article "For Whom the Gold Belt," published on December 24, 1903[58] (see Figure 1.17). While the writer sees French wrestler Paul Pons as the likely winner, the layout revolves around a question mark formed by precise masking of eight portraits. Set centrally on the page, this dynamic arrangement spreads the text on each side of the question mark's curves, with the introductory paragraph inside the loop. Thus out of an assortment of classical, not to say monotonous images—studio portraits, in fact—Faure succeeded in producing a lively accompaniment for the news item. Developed for covers and full pages, these clever graphic ploys became tools for the kind of visual news narrative that found its full scope in the double-page spread.

The layout devoted to the London Olympics in 1908 reveals the resources and the goals of this kind of visual mediation[59] (see Figure 1.18). In a montage with the title at the top, the images in the middle, and four lines of captions at the bottom, are nine snapshots including the finish of the 100 and 200 meters, the winner of the 1500 meters, and the end of the marathon. The images are numbered from left to right and from top to bottom, with each number indicating a caption, but the narrative sequence is broken by an overlaid image of the American Francis C. Irons, who had just beaten the world long-jump record and been photographed frontally during one of his attempts. Taking up the entire height of the page and decontextualized by tight silhouetting, Irons's body partially covers some of the other photographs as it hurtles toward the reader/spectator. The sequence of the snapshots is disrupted by Irons, who astonishes not only by breaking the world record, but also by creating a spectacular visual effect.

The use of photography for news purposes brought new illustrative constraints. For the coverage of the rugby final in Paris in 1903, Faure had to call in an illustrator, a choice he explained as follows:

> Our readers should not imagine that this is what old-style illustrated journalism called a "composition." This splendid plate is a faithful reproduction of a photograph. However, the snapshot's very rapidity makes it more suited to capturing situations than to indicating movement. This is why we called on skilled draftsman Tofani to come to the aid of photography by imbuing this scene with the liveliness the camera had robbed it of.[60]

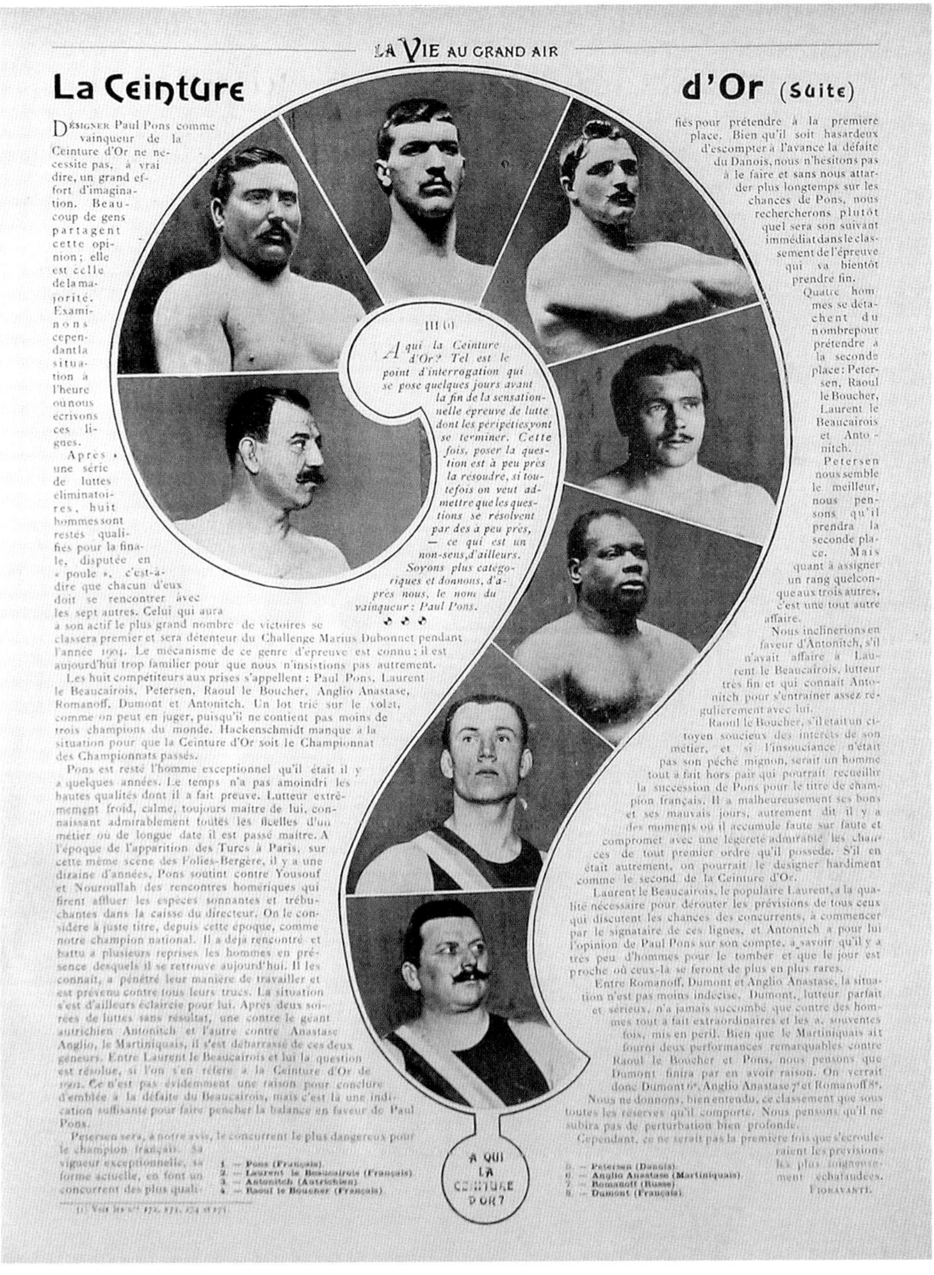

LA VIE AU GRAND AIR

La Ceinture d'Or (Suite)

DÉSIGNER Paul Pons comme vainqueur de la Ceinture d'Or ne nécessite pas, à vrai dire, un grand effort d'imagination. Beaucoup de gens partagent cette opinion; elle est celle de la majorité. Examinons cependant la situation à l'heure où nous écrivons ces lignes.

Après une série de luttes éliminatoires, huit hommes sont restés qualifiés pour la finale, disputée en « poule », c'est-à-dire que chacun d'eux doit se rencontrer avec les sept autres. Celui qui aura à son actif le plus grand nombre de victoires se classera premier et sera détenteur du Challenge Marius Dubonnet pendant l'année 1904. Le mécanisme de ce genre d'épreuve est connu; il est aujourd'hui trop familier pour que nous n'insistions pas autrement.

Les huit compétiteurs aux prises s'appellent : Paul Pons, Laurent le Beaucairois, Petersen, Raoul le Boucher, Anglio Anastase, Romanoff, Dumont et Antonitch. Un lot trié sur le volet, comme on peut en juger, puisqu'il ne contient pas moins de trois champions du monde. Hackenschmidt manque à la situation pour que la Ceinture d'Or soit le Championnat des Championnats passés.

Pons est resté l'homme exceptionnel qu'il était il y a quelques années. Le temps n'a pas amoindri les hautes qualités dont il a fait preuve. Lutteur extrêmement froid, calme, toujours maître de lui, connaissant admirablement toutes les ficelles d'un métier où de longue date il est passé maître. A l'époque de l'apparition des Turcs à Paris, sur cette même scène des Folies-Bergère, il y a une dizaine d'années, Pons soutint contre Yousouf et Nouroullah des rencontres homériques qui firent affluer les espèces sonnantes et trébuchantes dans la caisse du directeur. On le considère à juste titre, depuis cette époque, comme notre champion national. Il a déjà rencontré et battu à plusieurs reprises les hommes en présence desquels il se retrouve aujourd'hui. Il les connaît, a pénétré leur manière de travailler et est prévenu contre tous leurs trucs. La situation s'est d'ailleurs éclaircie pour lui. Après deux soirées de luttes sans résultat, une contre le géant autrichien Antonitch et l'autre contre Anastase Anglio, le Martiniquais, il s'est débarrassé de ces deux gêneurs. Entre Laurent le Beaucairois et lui la question est résolue, si l'on s'en réfère à la Ceinture d'Or de 1902. Ce n'est pas évidemment une raison pour conclure d'emblée à la défaite du Beaucairois, mais c'est là une indication suffisante pour faire pencher la balance en faveur de Paul Pons.

Petersen sera, à notre avis, le concurrent le plus dangereux pour le champion français. Sa vigueur exceptionnelle, sa forme actuelle, en font un concurrent des plus qualifiés pour prétendre à la première place. Bien qu'il soit hasardeux d'escompter à l'avance la défaite du Danois, nous n'hésitons pas à le faire et sans nous attarder plus longtemps sur les chances de Pons, nous rechercherons plutôt quel sera son suivant immédiat dans le classement de l'épreuve qui va bientôt prendre fin.

Quatre hommes se détachent du nombre pour prétendre à la seconde place : Petersen, Raoul le Boucher, Laurent le Beaucairois et Antonitch.

Petersen nous semble le meilleur, nous pensons qu'il prendra la seconde place. Mais quant à assigner un rang quelconque aux trois autres, c'est une tout autre affaire.

Nous inclinerions en faveur d'Antonitch, s'il n'avait affaire à Laurent le Beaucairois, lutteur très fin et qui connaît Antonitch pour s'entraîner assez régulièrement avec lui.

Raoul le Boucher, s'il était un citoyen soucieux des intérêts de son métier, et si l'insouciance n'était pas son péché mignon, serait un homme tout à fait hors pair qui pourrait recueillir la succession de Pons pour le titre de champion français. Il a malheureusement ses bons et ses mauvais jours, autrement dit il y a des moments où il accumule faute sur faute et compromet avec une légèreté admirable les chances de tout premier ordre qu'il possède. S'il en était autrement, on pourrait le désigner hardiment comme le second de la Ceinture d'Or.

Laurent le Beaucairois, le populaire Laurent, a la qualité nécessaire pour dérouter les prévisions de tous ceux qui discutent les chances des concurrents, à commencer par le signataire de ces lignes, et Antonitch a pour lui l'opinion de Paul Pons sur son compte, à savoir qu'il y a très peu d'hommes pour le tomber et que le jour est proche où ceux-là se feront de plus en plus rares.

Entre Romanoff, Dumont et Anglio Anastase, la situation n'est pas moins indécise. Dumont, lutteur parfait et sérieux, n'a jamais succombé que contre des hommes tout à fait extraordinaires et les a, souventes fois, mis en péril. Bien que le Martiniquais ait fourni deux performances remarquables contre Raoul le Boucher et Pons, nous pensons que Dumont finira par en avoir raison. On verrait donc Dumont 6e, Anglio Anastase 7e et Romanoff 8e.

Nous ne donnons, bien entendu, ce classement que sous toutes les réserves qu'il comporte. Nous pensons qu'il ne subira pas de perturbation bien profonde.

Cependant, ce ne serait pas la première fois que s'écrouleraient les prévisions les plus soigneusement échafaudées.

FIORAVANTI.

III (1)

A qui la Ceinture d'Or? Tel est le point d'interrogation qui se pose quelques jours avant la fin de la sensationnelle épreuve de lutte dont les péripéties vont se terminer. Cette fois, poser la question est à peu près la résoudre, si toutefois on veut admettre que les questions se résolvent par des à peu près, — ce qui est un non-sens, d'ailleurs. Soyons plus catégoriques et donnons, d'après nous, le nom du vainqueur : Paul Pons.

A QUI LA CEINTURE D'OR ?

1. — Pons (Français).
2. — Laurent le Beaucairois (Français).
3. — Antonitch (Autrichien).
4. — Raoul le Boucher (Français).
5. — Petersen (Danois).
6. — Anglio Anastase (Martiniquais).
7. — Romanoff (Russe).
8. — Dumont (Français).

(1) Voir les nos 172, 173, 174 et 175.

Figure 1.17 *La Vie au grand air*, December 24, 1903, p. 963.

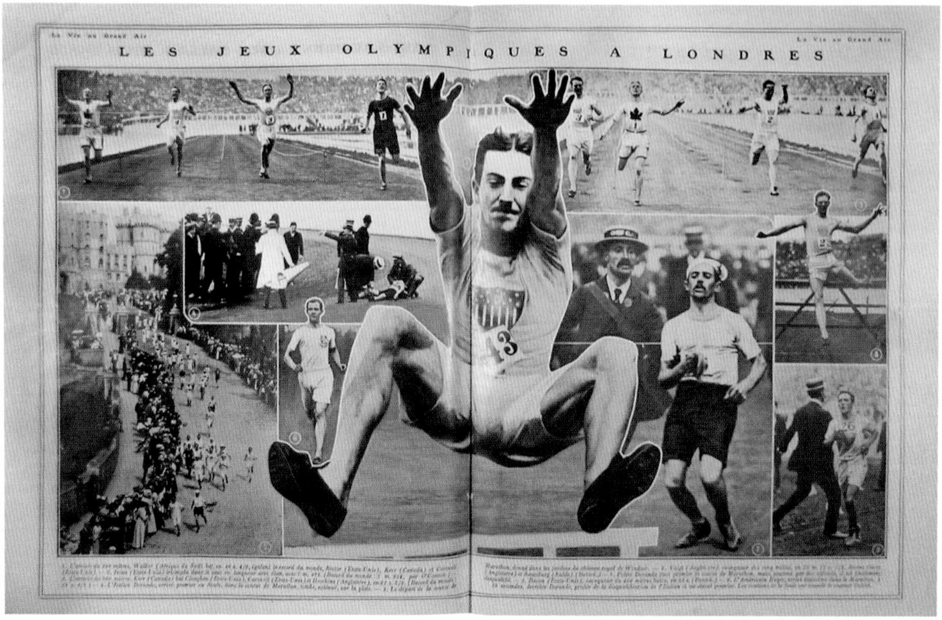

Figure 1.18 *La Vie au grand air*, August 1, 1908, pp. 88–9.

Committing to the dynamics of modern journalism, however, meant abandoning the illustrative mode in which drawing endlessly helped to compensate for the shortcomings of photography; instead there was recourse to layouts offering the reader the spectacle of sports news through modern forms of photography and montages drawing on newsreels.[61]

To illustrate the 1902 Paris Grand Prix, the magazine's center spread offered "what was seen by the lenses of *La Vie au grand air*'s six photographers," adding in a caption that these snapshots of the race gave "the reader a truly cinematic account of Kizil Kourgan's victory."[62] In addition to the Lumière brothers' shorts ("sujets actuels")[63] and Méliès's famous reconstructed newsreels,[64] screened news continued to gain ground in the Paris cinemas of the Belle Époque.[65] Pressman Pierre Lafitte was not unaware of the visual revolution in the coverage of political, social and sporting news. It was probably too early to mention the cinema when he wrote his introductory article for the new version of *La Vie au grand air* in 1899, but in 1910, in the first issue of the illustrated daily *Excelsior*, he was categorical: "*Excelsior* will be what it is setting out to be: the cinema of universal news."[66] As historians René Jeanne and Charles Ford later put it, "Under the reign of the cinema, news came differently than before."[67] Their subject here is the content of the news, but the remark could equally apply to the actual forms of the press. It was not until the interwar years and the coming of such famous magazines as *VU* and *Life* that comparisons were made between *mise en scènes* and layout:

> The little paper cinema that is the magazine has been lured . . . into making the *mise en scène* of its pages something living, then something talking—that is to say, by a simple combining of the photographic and the typographic, conveying forms of significance sufficiently "explosive" for the reader to be able to enjoy the magazine like a spectator: effortlessly.[68]

The use of images in such classical illustrated papers as *L'Illustration* and *Illustrirte Zeitung* still testified, during the Belle Époque, to a complex relationship with the fine arts model involving a tension between "difference" and "deference";[69] in the new magazines like *La Vie illustrée* and *La Vie au grand air*, by contrast, the virtually systematic use of photographs and the use of montage to highlight their quantity and variety drew directly on the cinematic model.

To let the reader "leaf through" an issue without having to stop and read, *La Vie au grand air* injected a visual dynamic into each page, one centering not only on the narrative produced by the sequencing of photographs, but also on the spectacular effect of their overlapping. Writing about early cinema, historian Tom Gunning points out that in newsreels the narrative mode often went hand in hand with that of attraction in filmic construction and that a close-up was considered an effect, a "visual moment."[70] This definition of the cinema of those early times also takes it for granted that the spectator can be absorbed in a "fictional world" and at the same time willingly submit to the appeal of an effect. Is this dual relationship not what the reader of *La Vie au grand air* was engaging in as he flipped through? And does not the double page devoted to the London Olympics effect a fit between narrative (with its numbered images) and spectacle (with the frontal cut-out of Irons, the American long jumper)?

The distinction between the illustrated nineteenth-century paper and the twentieth-century magazine lies in the shift in reading rhythms and the change in actual physical handling occasioned by the weeklies' near-exclusive use of photography. The illustrator and the engraver give way to the artistic director, who now shapes the news not within the image, but on the page. This mutation is apparent in *Collier's Weekly* and *La Vie illustrée*, but finds its most innovative expression in *La Vie au grand air*. In its addressing of an overtly diverting subject—sports—Lucien Faure's graphic structuring of text and images made full pages and double page spreads freestanding, thereby freeing the reader/spectator from the obligation of the cover-to-cover reading order. Each issue was designed in such a way as to allow a random, autonomous grasp of the news: the modern Belle Époque reader was no longer reading an illustrated weekly, he was leafing through a magazine.[71]

Reflections of the war

In the years immediately preceding the First World War, photography had become the principal conduit for visual information, as signaled in the spring of 1912 by the decision by *Le Petit Parisien* (1876–1944), one of France's four million-selling dailies, to drop its illustrated literary supplement in favor of a weekly "entirely illustrated by photography."[72] Prior to this the use of color printing had allowed its competitor *Le Petit Journal* (1863–1944) to rule the roost with its supplement for two decades, but photography would prove the trump card in the *Petit Parisien*'s revenge strategy.[73] Throughout the War *Le Miroir* (1912–1920) would devote 15 of its 16 pages to photographs of the conflict,[74] each page or double page covering a separate subject with a choice of images (1 to 8 per page), a heading, and detailed captions (see Figure 1.19). To ensure the necessary supply of images, the supplement launched a regular front page appeal, beginning on August 16, 1914: "*Le Miroir* will pay any price for especially interesting photographs of the War"[75] (see Figure 1.20). While the weekly published photographs of different provenances, including official sources, photographic agencies, and foreign newspapers, its visual identity was defined by the images of the amateurs who responded to its call.

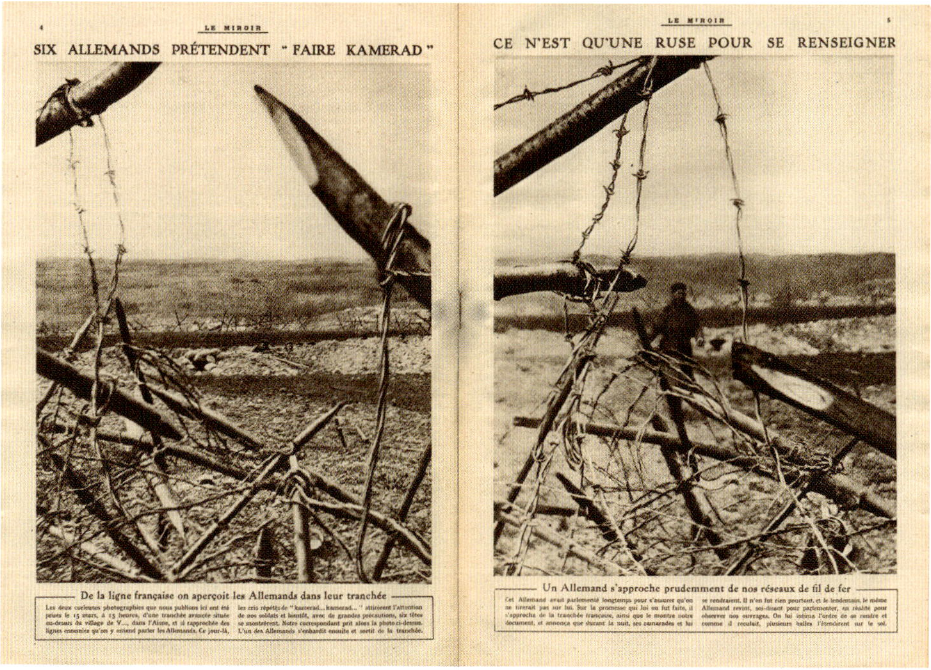
4 LE MIROIR

SIX ALLEMANDS PRÉTENDENT "FAIRE KAMERAD"

De la ligne française on aperçoit les Allemands dans leur tranchée

Les deux curieuses photographies que nous publions ici ont été prises le 15 mars, à 15 heures, d'une tranchée avancée située au-dessus du village de V..., dans l'Aisne, et si rapprochée des lignes ennemies qu'on y entend parler les Allemands. Ce jour-là, les cris répétés de "kamerad... kamerad..." attirèrent l'attention de nos soldats et bientôt, avec de grandes précautions, six têtes se montrèrent. Notre correspondant prit alors la photo ci-dessus. L'un des Allemands s'enhardit ensuite et sortit de la tranchée.

LE MIROIR 5

CE N'EST QU'UNE RUSE POUR SE RENSEIGNER

Un Allemand s'approche prudemment de nos réseaux de fil de fer

Cet Allemand avait parlementé longtemps pour s'assurer qu'on ne tirerait pas sur lui. Sur la promesse qui lui en fut faite, il s'approcha de la tranchée française, ainsi que le montre notre document, et annonça que durant la nuit, ses camarades et lui se rendraient. Il n'en fut rien pourtant, et le lendemain, le même Allemand revint, soi-disant pour parlementer, en réalité pour observer nos ouvrages. On lui intima l'ordre de se rendre et comme il reculait, plusieurs balles l'étendirent sur le sol.

Figure 1.19 *Le Miroir*, May 16, 1915, pp. 4–5.

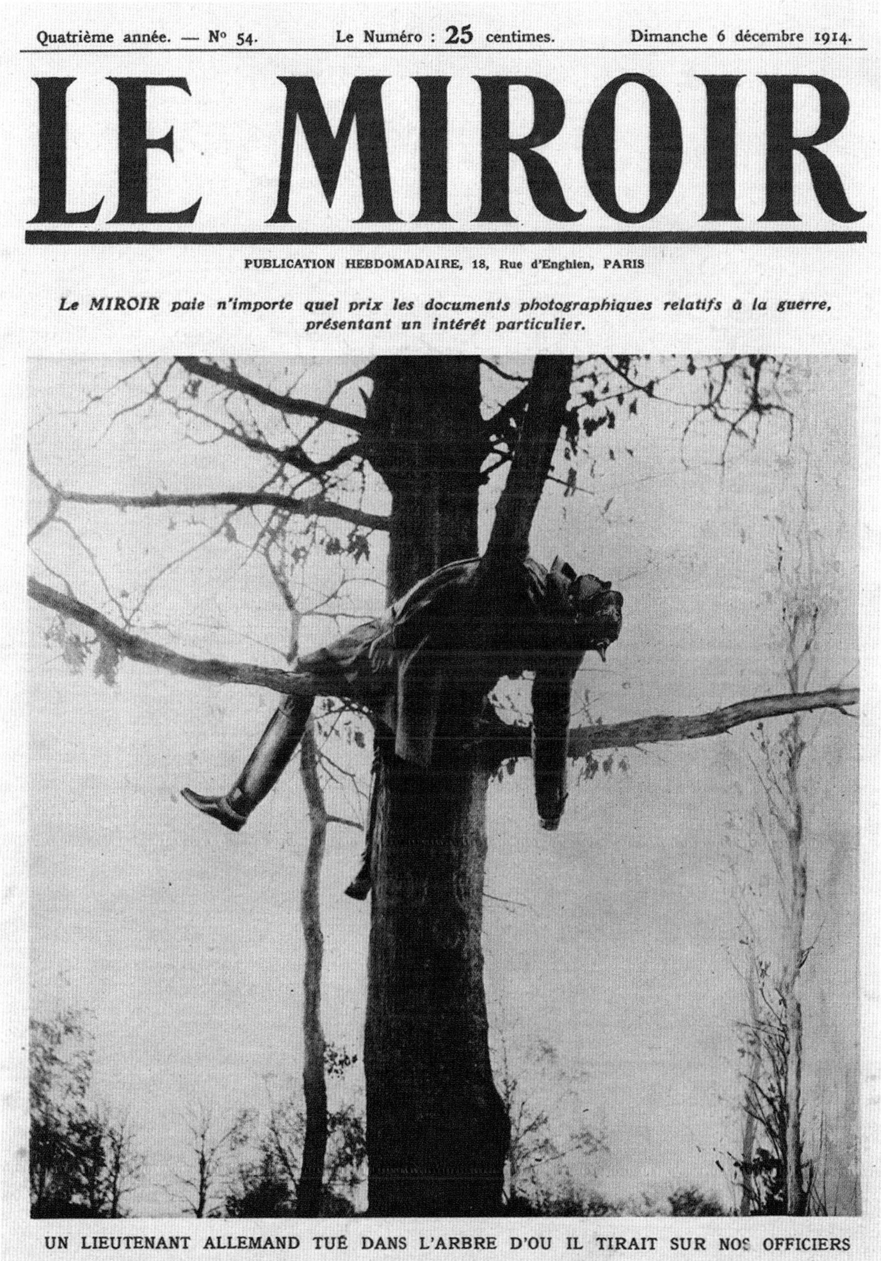

Quatrième année. — N° 54. Le Numéro : **25** centimes. Dimanche 6 décembre 1914.

LE MIROIR

PUBLICATION HEBDOMADAIRE, 18, Rue d'Enghien, PARIS

Le MIROIR paie n'importe quel prix les documents photographiques relatifs à la guerre, présentant un intérêt particulier.

UN LIEUTENANT ALLEMAND TUÉ DANS L'ARBRE D'OU IL TIRAIT SUR NOS OFFICIERS

Les meilleurs tireurs allemands ont pour mission de faire feu sur nos officiers. Celui-ci, atteint par un éclat d'obus, est resté sur son perchoir, tragique épouvantail qui n'effraie pas les corbeaux.

Figure 1.20 *Le Miroir*, December 6, 1914, cover.

Like many of its counterparts *Le Miroir* covered civilian life behind the lines, but its distinctiveness lay in illustrating life at the front with photographs sent in by soldiers who had slipped a portable camera into their packs for use not only during breathing spaces, but also during troop movements and even attacks. These images were sometimes lacking in definition and/or visual impact, but their arrangement on the page, backed up by unambiguous captions, meant the magazine could show its readers the effects of shelling, life in the trenches, the battlefields, and crimes and atrocities—all committed by the enemy. Pictures of mangled bodies scattered along trenches or hanging from the branches of trees were published with no second thoughts, illustrating initially a belligerent optimism, then the misgivings prompted by a conflict that was bogging down. To stimulate rivalry between photographers *Le Miroir* even launched a competition for the "most arresting war photographs,"[76] specifying that "set-up scenes and photographic tricks" were unacceptable. A snapshot of a shell exploding during a charge by French dragoons near Calais became a double-page spread in the issue of May 2, 1915[77] (see Figure 1.21); it was awarded a prize of 15,000 francs for the best photograph

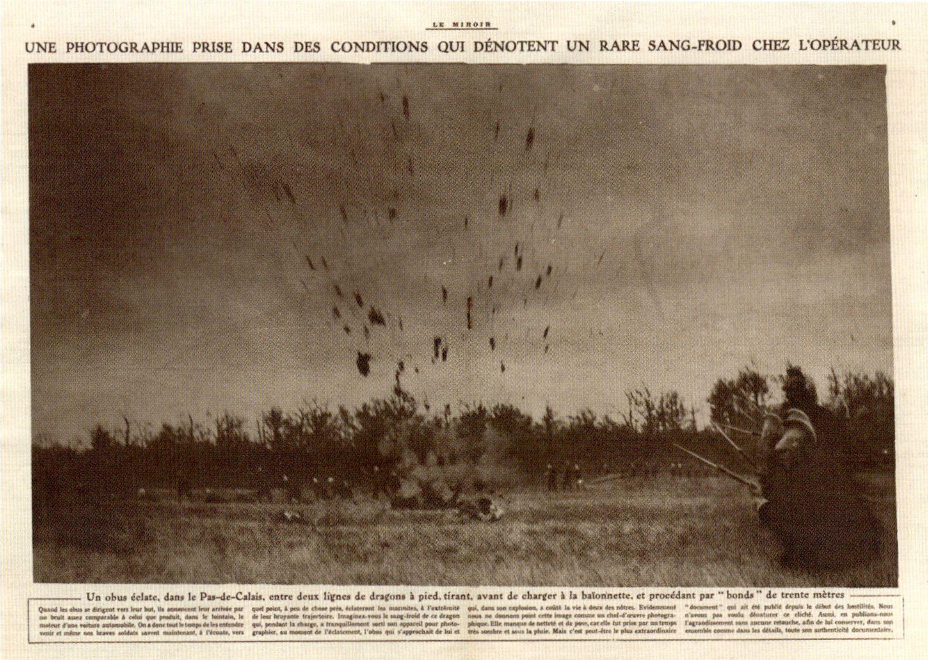

LE MIROIR

UNE PHOTOGRAPHIE PRISE DANS DES CONDITIONS QUI DÉNOTENT UN RARE SANG-FROID CHEZ L'OPÉRATEUR

Un obus éclate, dans le Pas-de-Calais, entre deux lignes de dragons à pied, tirant, avant de charger à la baïonnette, et procédant par " bonds " de trente mètres

Quand les obus se dirigent vers leur but, ils annoncent leur arrivée par un bruit assez comparable à celui que produit, dans le lointain, le moteur d'une voiture automobile. On a donc tout le temps de les entendre venir et même nos braves soldats savent maintenant, à l'écoute, vers quel point, à peu de chose près, éclateront les marmites, à l'extrémité de leur bruyante trajectoire. Imaginez-vous le sang-froid de ce dragon qui, pendant la charge, a tranquillement sorti son appareil pour photographier, au moment de l'éclatement, l'obus qui s'approchait de lui et qui, dans son explosion, a coûté la vie à deux des nôtres. Evidemment nous ne donnons point cette image comme un chef-d'œuvre photographique. Elle manque de netteté et de pose, car elle fut prise par un temps très sombre et sous la pluie. Mais c'est peut-être le plus extraordinaire "document" qui ait été publié depuis le début des hostilités. Nous n'avons pas voulu dénaturer ce cliché. Aussi, en publions-nous l'agrandissement sans aucune retouche, afin de lui conserver, dans son ensemble comme dans les détails, toute son authenticité documentaire.

Figure 1.21 *Le Miroir*, May 2, 1915, pp. 8–9.

published since the opening of the competition and was reused on April 9, 1916 under the heading "The Highest-Priced War Photograph."[78] Pictures like these, combining military and photographic interest, were rare and were usually given the plum spots, like the center spread. The use of photogravure and rotary presses enabled nuanced greys and deep blacks hitherto impossible with halftone, but the images also betray generous recourse to retouching: here a clearer outline of a canon, there a less blurred silhouette. It may seem contradictory that the editors demanded from their amateur photographers "all possible guarantees of authenticity and origin"[79] for their submissions, while these very pictures were retouched with gouache to clarify their message. It should be remembered then that the uses of photographs was part of a broader process of illustration in which illustrators and retouchers contributed to the overall visual significance. *Le Miroir*, which regularly boasted of being "the only weekly publication to have appeared without interruption" during the War, claimed to be thus building up "the most comprehensive as well as the most artistically illustrated body of documentary coverage."[80] In this context retouching was an additional means of ensuring that the images reached the target audience. And the major role *Le Miroir* accorded photography in its (highly partisan) account of the War, together with the quantity and diversity of its pictures, and the quality of its layout and printing, would make it a major source for the history both of photojournalism and of the First World War. On July 4, 1920 the magazine gave up general news in favor of a focus on sports.

Photography was initially an everyday visual reference for engravers. Between 1890 and 1920 it was accepted by press editors and became an essential tool in the making of news. Its acceptance was founded on the parallel development of halftone and amateur photography during the 1890s and on the savings these two factors brought to the illustration of current events. The compositions of illustrators did not vanish from the press, however, and for a long time they remained the yardstick for photography—until the cinema took over. It would seem, then, that the advent of photography was not expected, or even desired by publishers, and that it brought no sudden revolution to the illustrated press. The photomontages that yielded combinations of the realistic and the curious, intensive recourse to retouching in order to spell out the message, and above all the layout techniques developed by art directors to guarantee the effectiveness of the photographs, were the upshot of a pragmatic management of news that had to adapt to the forms taken by the medium. It would be a quarter of a century before photography would become the major visual vector for news, but by the end of the First World War printing technology had been tried and tested, the image producers identified, and the role of art directors defined.

Chapter 2
General News Magazines: European Know-How (1919–1936)

The interwar years are considered a crucial period in the history of press photography and are seen by many as marking the beginnings of "modern photojournalism."[1] For authors like Tim Gidal and Gisèle Freund this genesis can be specifically situated in Germany in the period 1928–1933, and can be attributed to the development of Leica cameras, with the increased mobility they allowed, the emergence of a new generation of photographers like Erich Salomon and Martin Munkácsi, and the backing of press editors like Kurt Korff and Stefan Lorant, respectively at the *Berliner Illustrirte Zeitung* and the *Münchner Illustrierte Presse*. At once logical and consistent, this view of things has been repeatedly restated since the 1970s, shaping in the process the history of a golden age in which the photojournalist figures as Modernism's knight in shining armor.[2]

The problem, however, is that the same arguments could be advanced for the pre-First World War years, which saw the advent of hand-held "detective" cameras, photographers like Jimmy Hare covering armed conflicts all over the world, and publishers like Pierre Lafitte and Robert J. Collier gambling on the resources of photography as they set out to conquer a new readership. Moreover, this version concentrates on image production, whereas visual information is the outcome of a collective process—to which the photographer contributes. So while the period is rich in achievements, it needs to be seen as a stage in the development of the illustrated press, during which recognition of photography as a journalistic medium firmed up. In both Germany and France the press expanded markedly in terms of publications and circulation, and in a context of fierce competition the snapshot, until then seemingly just a photographic genre worth publishing,[3] became an effective photojournalistic style that history would later dub "candid photography."[4] Similarly, layout designs became an identity marker and the complex overlappings of photographs that appeared in the sporting press early in the century found their way into the general news press. These developments benefited photographers, whose names were to be seen more and more often both in captions and on magazine covers. Not only were they now able to make a living, they also acquired journalist status.

Berliner Illustrirte Zeitung before the war

The first issue of the *Berliner Illustrirte Zeitung* appeared on January 4, 1892, and like *La Vie illustrée* in France and *Collier's Weekly* in the United States, took advantage of halftone to illustrate its pages with drawings and photographs. In 1894 it was acquired by Leopold Ullstein who, with his sons, built the Ullstein Verlag empire, which lasted until Hitler's coming to power in 1933 and the takeover of the company by the Nazis. Just as *La Vie illustrée* offered an alternative to *L'Illustration*, *Berliner Illustrirte Zeitung* was a competitor for *Illustrirte Zeitung*. In 1904, when the sale of single issues was authorized,[5] *Berliner Illustrirte Zeitung* began using eye-catching covers that helped street vendors catch the attention of potential buyers. This new attractiveness centered on a readily readable typeface for the title, and above all on a visually striking full-page cover photograph. Whatever the subject—national or international politics, sport, culture, new discoveries—it was ushered in on the cover, in a photograph. The picture of Japanese officers in discussion around a map (1904) references the advance of the Japanese army in Korea; the one of a swarming street (1906) introduces the business district in San Francisco; a snapshot of two galloping horses symbolizes jockey Bernard Dillon's victory in the Epsom Derby; and the portrait of Italian opera conductor Ruggero Leoncavallo (1904) signals his upcoming performance of *Der Roland von Berlin* in the German capital.[6] The portrait in all its many variants was the genre most featured: classical, meticulously lit studio versions of the head and shoulders or three-quarter view type, like the one of writer Franz Adam Beyerlein taken in Albert Meyer's Berlin studio (1904).[7] But there were more highly charged studies, too, like that of painter Franz von Lenbach (1904), gazing darkly downwards amid Pictorialist-inflected chiaroscuro (see Figure 2.1).[8] The artistic approach could not have been more different, though, in the 1911 portrait of Benno König, who had just won the first "Deutscher Rundflug" round-Germany air race, which required landings in seventeen cities before the return to Berlin.[9] Ullstein Verlag had financed the race, and the *Berliner Illustrirte Zeitung* editors chose a photograph of the aviator warmly wrapped up and enhanced by a low-angle shot whose visual modernity was in tune with the conquest of the air that Germany and France were competing for in those prewar years (see Figure 2.2).[10] *Berliner Illustrirte Zeitung* also drew

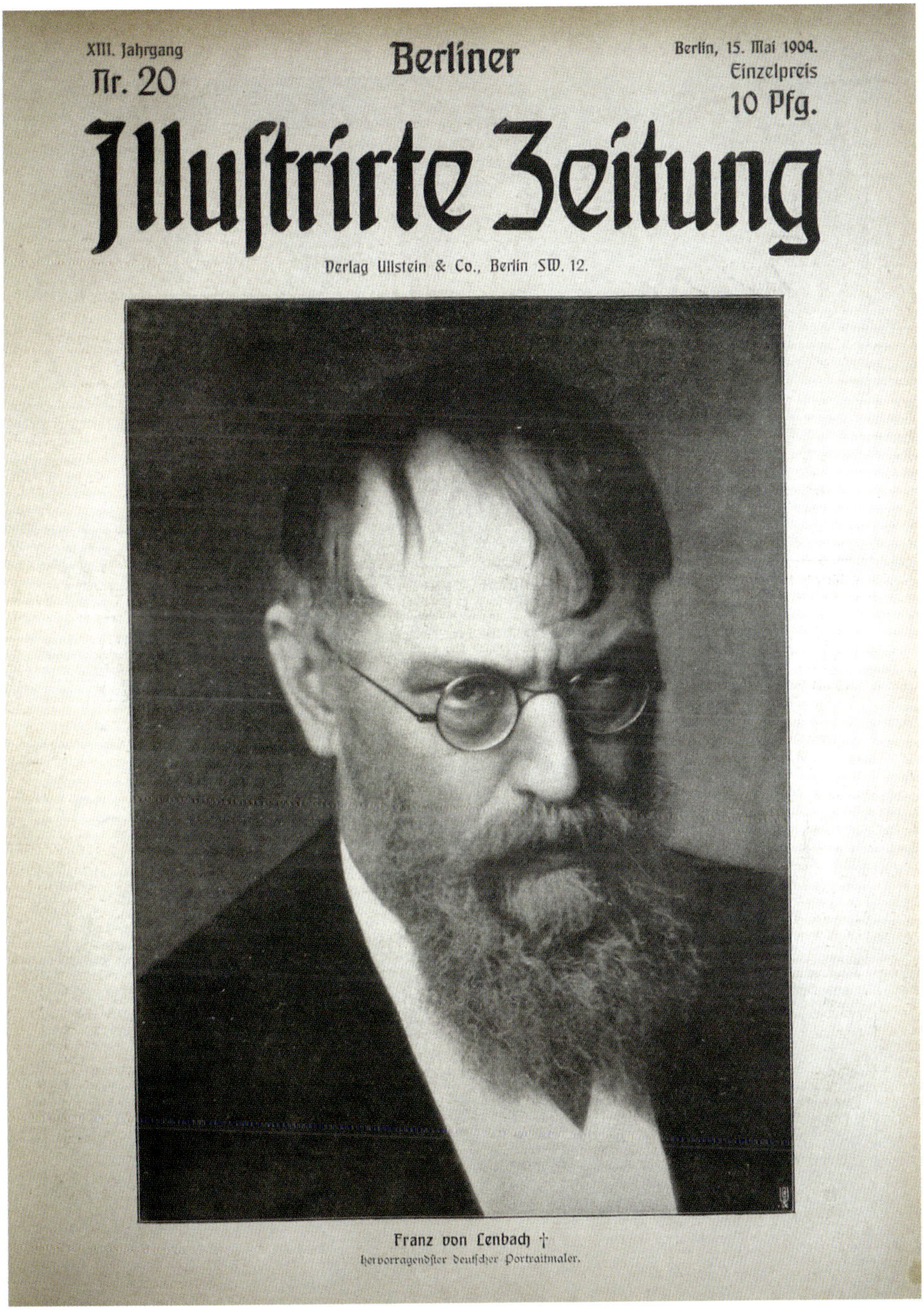
XIII. Jahrgang
Nr. 20
Berliner
Berlin, 15. Mai 1904.
Einzelpreis
10 Pfg.
Illustrirte Zeitung
Verlag Ullstein & Co., Berlin SW. 12.
Franz von Lenbach †
hervorragendster deutscher Portraitmaler.

Figure 2.1 *Berliner Illustrirte Zeitung*, May 15, 1904, cover.

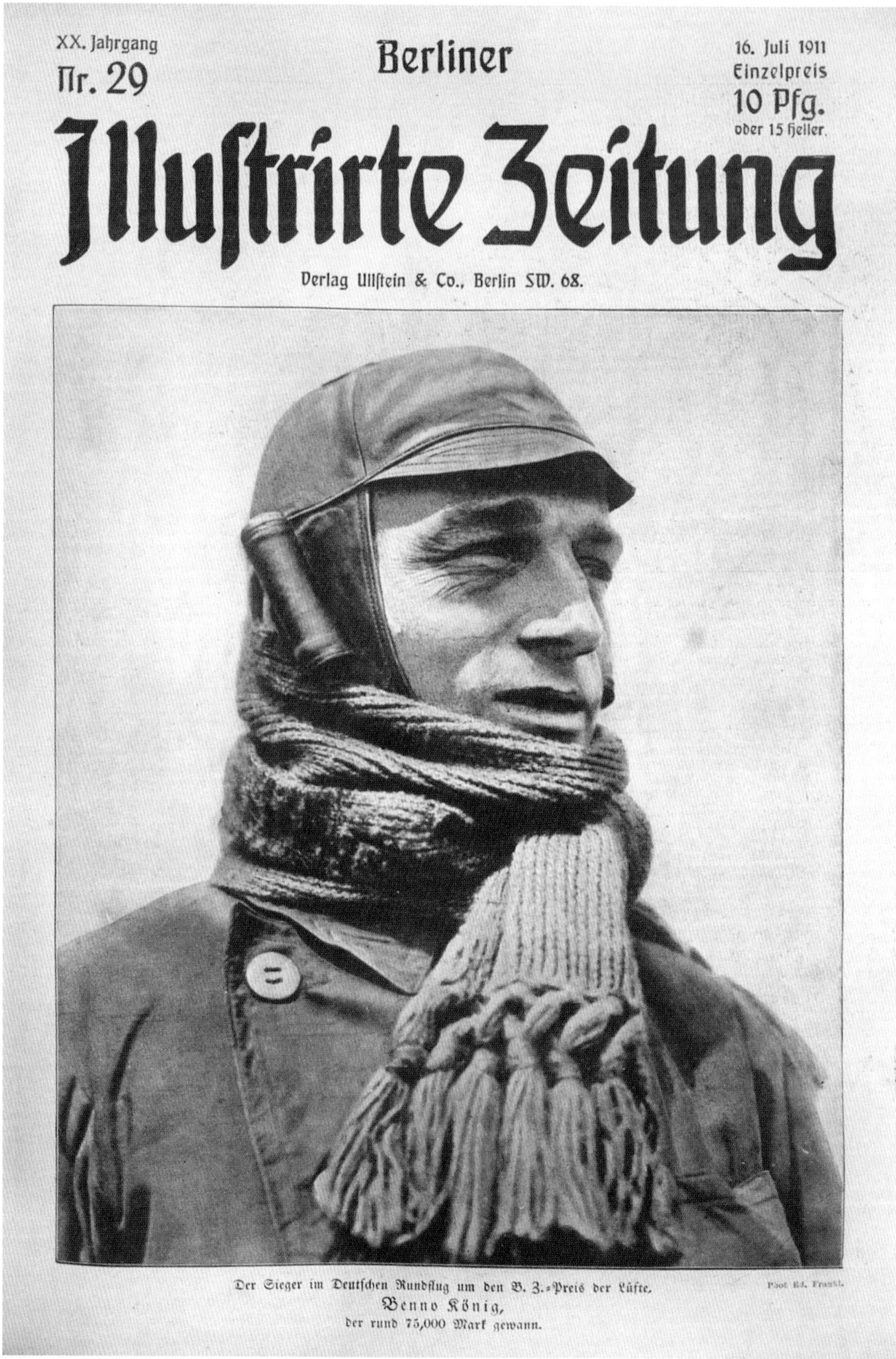

XX. Jahrgang
Nr. 29

Berliner
Illustrirte Zeitung

16. Juli 1911
Einzelpreis
10 Pfg.
oder 15 Heller.

Verlag Ullstein & Co., Berlin SW. 68.

Der Sieger im Deutschen Rundflug um den B. Z.-Preis der Lüfte,
Benno König,
der rund 75,000 Mark gewann.

Phot. Ed. Frankl.

Figure 2.2 *Berliner Illustrirte Zeitung*, July 16, 1911, cover.

aesthetically on the snapshot, made possible by new hand-held cameras loaded with gelatin silver plates and used for news pictures by the first "photographic reporters:"[11] we see the American boxer Jack Johnson shown in the ring with a referee (1910), and Theodore Roosevelt surrounded by members of his African expedition (1910).[12] Both the boxer and the former president of the United States were photographed in their professional contexts, which seems not to have been the case for the illustrators Heinrich Zille and Fritz Koch-Gotha.[13] The two are sitting on a bench outdoors, Zille slightly slumped, legs crossed, and with his elbow on the back of the seat as they smoke together and smile at the photographer, who has probably knelt to avoid a crushing high-angle shot. The natural lighting, the relaxed poses, and the smiles indicative of their trust in the photographer add up to an unaffected intimacy the reader can readily share with the winners of the Menzel Prize for the two best illustrations of the year (see Figure 2.3). This use of photography and the accompanying page design changed little in the postwar years, and lived on under the Nazis. It sometimes happened that the content of a photograph overspilled its frame, partially blocking out the title and adding an impression of depth, but the image was always bordered with white and captioned. It was this context of practices dating from before the war that gave rise to some of *Berliner Illustrirte Zeitung*'s most famous covers, like the detail of photograph by Wilhelm Steffen showing the politicians Friedrich Ebert (president of the Reich) and Gustav Noske (minister for war) standing in the Baltic Sea, hands behind their backs and wearing only swimsuits, as Josef Rieger (administrator of the PRO Foundation) pops his head out of the water and brandishes a trident draped with seaweed (see Figure 2.4).[14] Somewhere between the private snapshot and the political caricature, this incongruous image successfully turned the spotlight on the two representatives of the new Weimar Republic who, a few months earlier, had violently put down the Spartacist uprising and caused the deaths of the Marxist leaders Karl Liebknecht and Rosa Luxemburg.[15]

In an article written in 1927 for a book celebrating Ullstein's fiftieth anniversary, *Berliner Illustrirte Zeitung* editor in chief Kurt Korff said of the magazine's aims and photography's part in achieving them, "It was not the importance of the material that determined the selection and acceptance of photos, but solely the allure of the image itself."[16] Adhered to since the Belle Époque in a sports weekly like *La Vie au grand air*,[17] the photographic principle of form over content now spread to general news and became the rule in the course of the 1920s. The perceptiveness of Kurt Korff, Kurt Safranski (head of magazine publishing at Ullstein[18] and founder of the American photographic agency Black Star in 1935) and Carl Schnebel, who became art director at *Berliner Illustrirte Zeitung* in 1928, lay in spotting what could constitute the "allure" of one photograph as opposed to another, getting exclusive rights to it, and skillfully highlighting it in the layout. This was how *Berliner Illustrirte Zeitung* came to acquire the services of such soon to be famous photographers as Martin Munkácsi, Erich Salomon, Alfred Eisenstaedt, and Willi Ruge. All of them

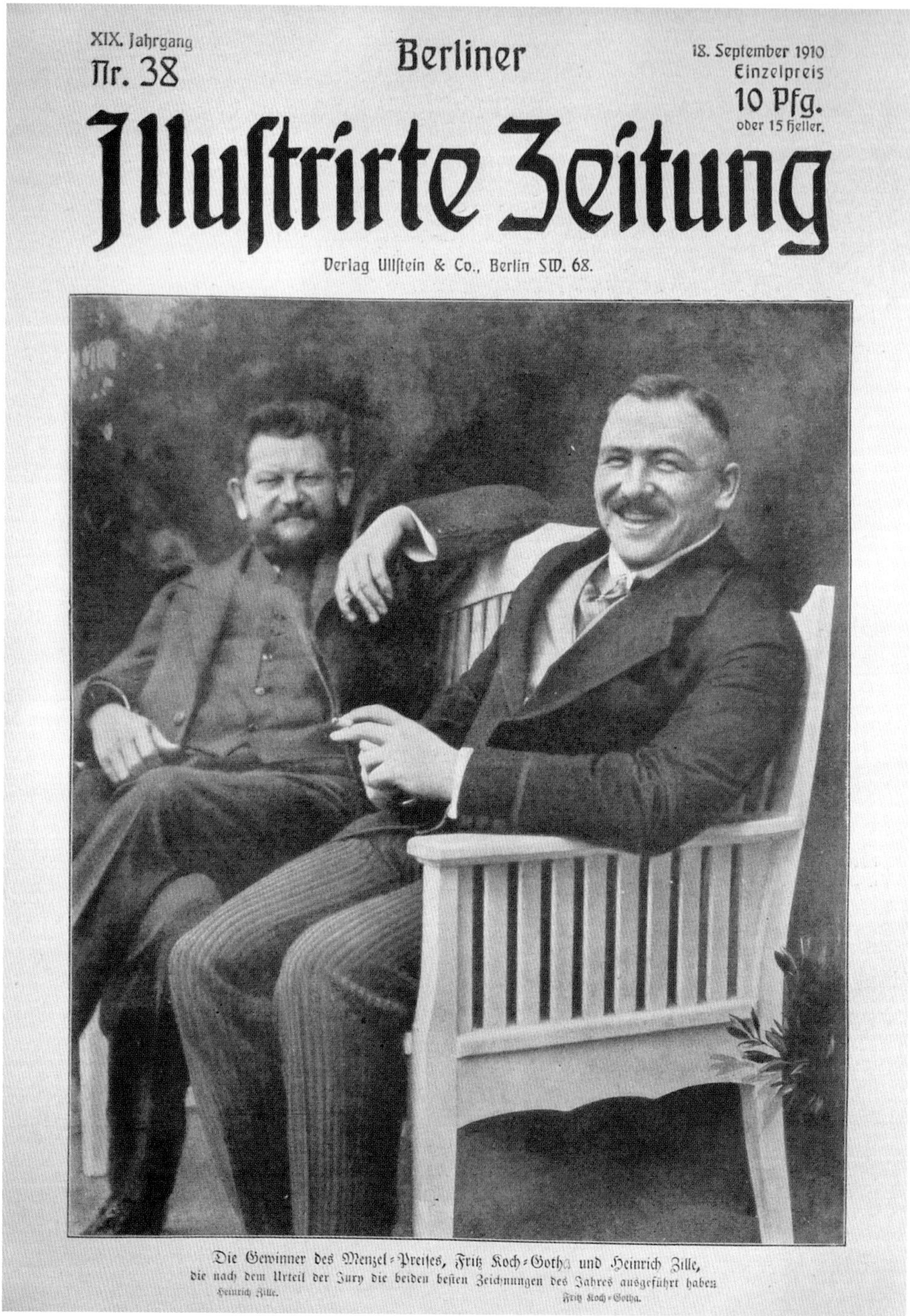

XIX. Jahrgang
Nr. 38

Berliner
Illustrirte Zeitung

18. September 1910
Einzelpreis
10 Pfg.
oder 15 Heller.

Verlag Ullstein & Co., Berlin SW. 68.

Die Gewinner des Menzel-Preises, Fritz Koch-Gotha und Heinrich Zille,
die nach dem Urteil der Jury die beiden besten Zeichnungen des Jahres ausgeführt haben
Heinrich Zille. Fritz Koch-Gotha.

Figure 2.3 *Berliner Illustrirte Zeitung*, September 18, 1910, cover. Photograph by Ed. Frankl.

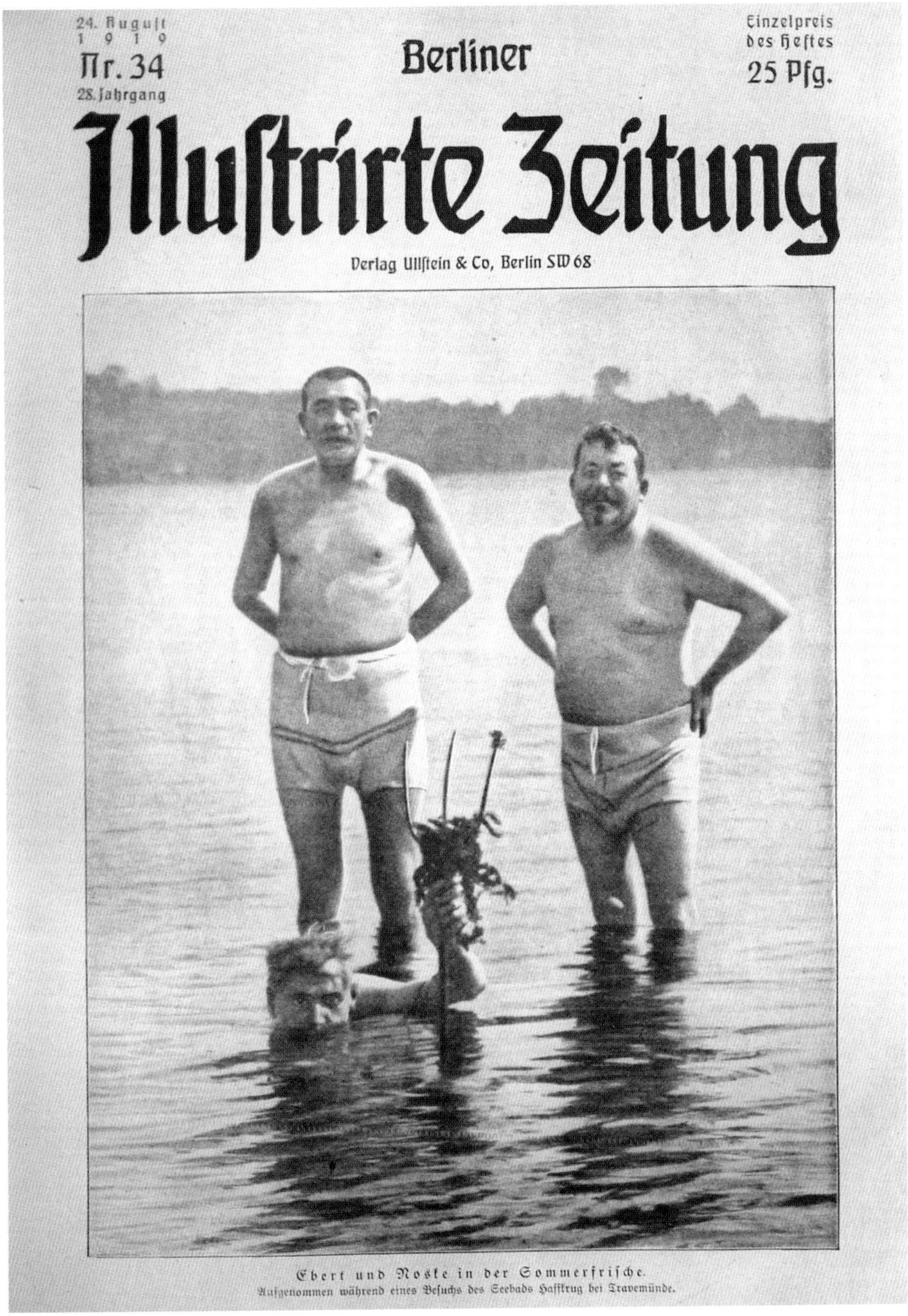

Figure 2.4 *Berliner Illustrirte Zeitung*, August 24, 1919, cover. Photograph by Wilhelm Steffen.

published frequently in the magazine, to which Ullstein gave the funding necessary to ensure special relationships with the photographers and the photographic agencies.[19]

The postwar German press: a competitive market

Between 1919 and 1932 the number of magazines published in Germany rose from 4,000 to 7,500: an increase that testified to reader interest and implied fierce competition.[20] In 1924 Ullstein launched the monthly *UHU*, whose director, Friedrich Kroner, gave photography an essential role. The last issue appeared in 1934. Snapshots, high-angle shots, anamorphic portraits, and artistic photographs, all reproduced in photogravure, were regular features, with all sorts of stylistic tricks of the trade—symmetry effects, multiple cut-outs, full bleed, sequences, overlays—deployed to enhance them and emphasize their message. This small format (24 × 18 cm) monthly also published articles on contemporary photography, among them one by Martin Munkácsi and Albert Renger-Patzsch on amateur photography,[21] one on photograms, illustrated by László Moholy-Nagy[22] (see Figure 2.5), and one on the image that contains Kurt Tucholsky's assertion: "A photograph if properly chosen, punches, boxes, whistles, grips the heart and conveys the one and only new truth."[23] Publication of images as part of the news had always been urged as a more accessible tool of communication than text,[24] and Tucholsky's emphasis on the importance of selection was reiterated by Kurt Korff in relation to *Berliner Illustrirte Zeitung*: "Not every photo conveyed an impression of the desired intensity. More than the text, the photo has to have the most intense possible concentration, has to capture a situation at its climax."[25]

At the end of the war *Berliner Illustrirte Zeitung* still looked very much like its Belle Époque version, and until 1924 it continued to seek the equilibrium that would ensure its viability. When the Deutschmark stabilized the price was set at 20 pfennigs and the number of pages increased to thirty-two (it would reach forty by the end of the decade); a considerable amount of space was granted to news photography, but also—most of all?—to a serial. Published as a centerpiece, the serial took up half the pages in each issue and formed a kind of gray area interspersed with pages of advertising. Austrian writer Vicki Baum was probably the major single factor in *Berliner Illustrirte Zeitung*'s success: her consecutively published *Stud. chem. Helene Willfüer* (Helene, 1928) and *Menschen im Hotel* (Grand Hotel, 1929) are said to have generated additional sales of 200,000.[26] With a record circulation of 1.9 million in 1931, *Berliner Illustrirte Zeitung* became Germany's top-selling publication, all categories included.[27] To the sixteen pages of the serial were added six pages of advertising, while the remaining ten pages—six at the beginning, four at the end—were given over to photographs. Grouped together on single or double pages, they were as a rule small and accompanied by a brief text; the layout, though, while meticulous, had not changed since the beginning of the century. Images were halftone, and neither the weight nor the finish of the paper worked to the advantage of the photographs, which lacked the depth and silkiness to be found in *UHU*, *Arbeiter Illustrierte Zeitung*, or the French magazine *VU*, all printed in rotogravure.

This distinctive structure was also adopted by the *Münchner Illustrierte Presse*, which became *Berliner Illustrirte Zeitung*'s main competitor, although never giving Ullstein cause for concern. At its peak in 1931 the Munich weekly had a circulation of some 700,000—less than half that of *Berliner Illustrirte Zeitung*.[28] It also featured a serial sandwiched between two groups of images, at the beginning and the end, while the cover set out to pull in readers with a photograph, the title of its serial, and the name of the author. The similarity of layout between the two was striking and even gave rise to a heated exchange of articles: the first in *Berliner Illustrirte Zeitung*, headed "Berliner 'Imitierte' Zeitung" ("The Imitation of the *Berliner Zeitung*"), to which *Münchner Illustrierte Presse* riposted with "Berliner 'Irritierte' Zeitung" (The Irritation of the *Berliner Zeitung*).[29] After its launch in Munich on December 5, 1924, *Münchner Illustrierte Presse* opened an office in Berlin to spread its editorial net wider. It was here that Stefan Lorant began working in 1928, providing the magazine with articles and news photographs until his arrest and imprisonment by the Nazis in 1933.[30] The *Berliner Illustrirte Zeitung / Münchner Illustrierte Presse* race for readers and advertisers forced Korff and Lorant to secure the best novelists and the best photographers.

For both these periodicals the work of visual mediation hinged on two considerations: coming up with a layout that set the photographs off to maximum advantage, and finding images that met—or even anticipated—reader expectations. Korff also noted in his 1927 article on *Berliner Illustrirte Zeitung*:

> [T]he major changes in the appearance of illustrated magazines, which are no longer directed by press editors who 'illustrate' their subjects, but by people who, like screen writers and directors, see life in pictures. The editors of *Berliner Illustrirte* were also, as a result, the first to take on an 'art director', someone with an artist's eye whose job it was to seek out the strongest and the best photographic solutions—not only in terms of individual pictures, but also in the *arranging* of the pictures among themselves and in their relation to the text, etc.[31]

As is often the case in this kind of self-serving article—this one was written for a book celebrating fifty years of Ullstein publishing—the author and *Berliner Illustrirte Zeitung* are credited with all sorts of innovations, including the appointment of an art director to an editorial team, which had in fact first happened at *La Vie au grand air* as early as 1899.[32]

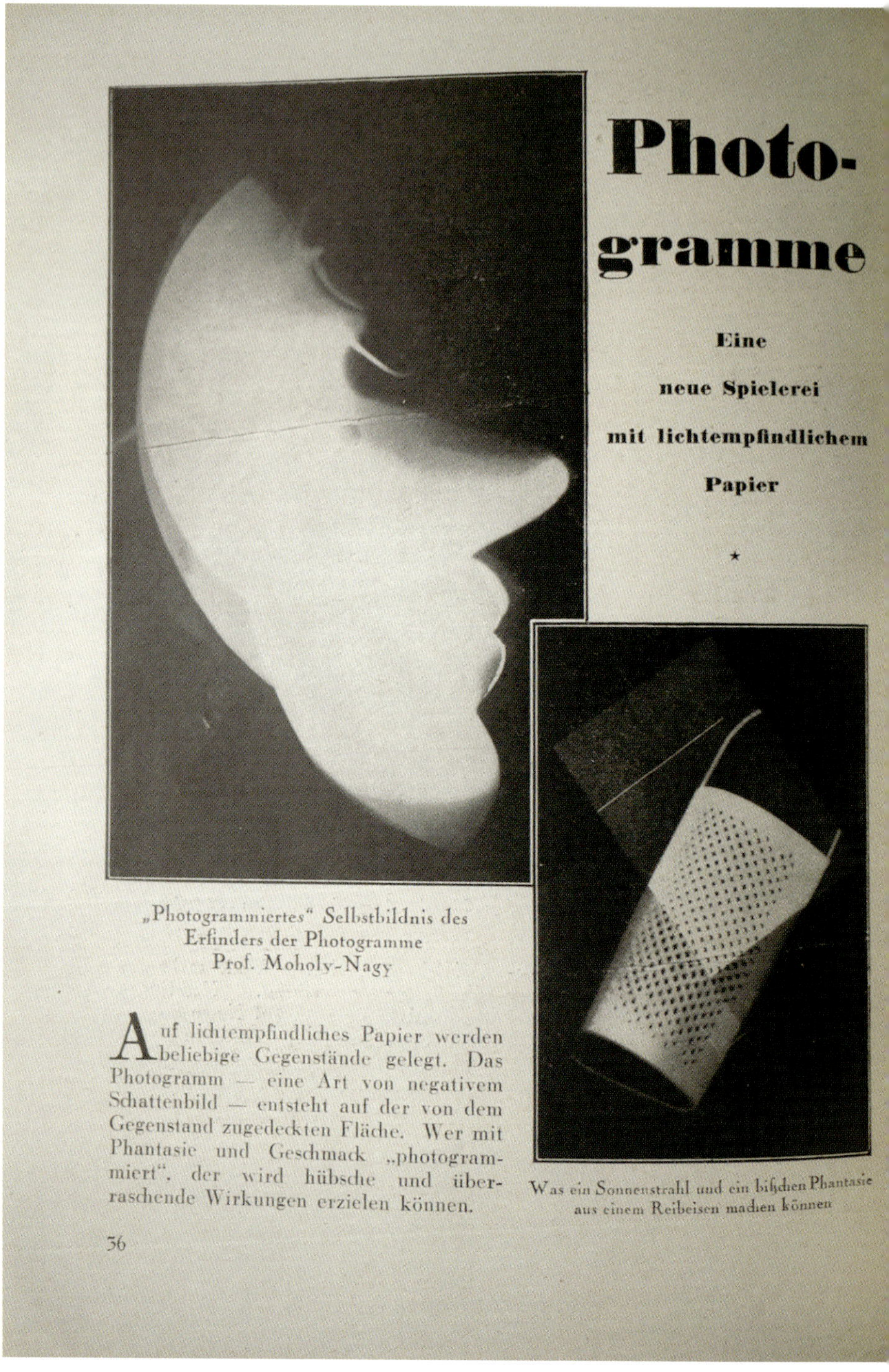

Photo-gramme

Eine neue Spielerei mit lichtempfindlichem Papier

★

„Photogrammiertes" Selbstbildnis des Erfinders der Photogramme Prof. Moholy-Nagy

Auf lichtempfindliches Papier werden beliebige Gegenstände gelegt. Das Photogramm — eine Art von negativem Schattenbild — entsteht auf der von dem Gegenstand zugedeckten Fläche. Wer mit Phantasie und Geschmack „photogrammiert", der wird hübsche und überraschende Wirkungen erzielen können.

Was ein Sonnenstrahl und ein bißchen Phantasie aus einem Reibeisen machen können

36

Figure 2.5 *UHU*, February 1928, pp. 36–7. Photographs by László Moholy-Nagy.

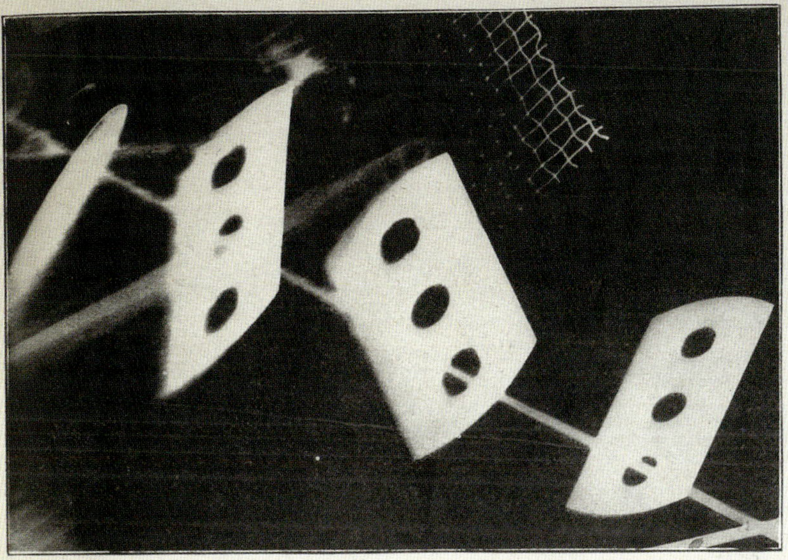

Endlich eine Verwendung für alte Rasierklingen

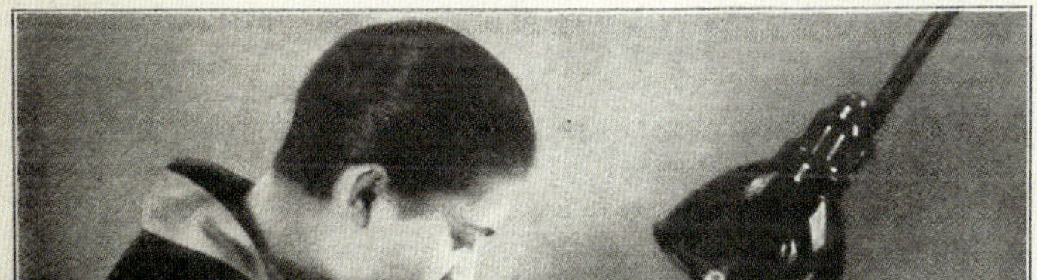

Aufnahmen Moholy-Nagy

Die Hauptsache bei Photogrammen ist die geschickte Auswahl von Gegenständen, die einfache und zugleich eigenartige Formen besitzen und auf dem Papier überraschende Wirkungen ergeben

The parallel between the journalistic ambitions of the Frenchman Pierre Lafitte and the German Kurt Korff continues in their shared references to the cinema. While Lafitte declared in 1909 that photographs and their page make-up would make *Excelsior* the "cinema of universal news,"[33] Korff was saying in 1927:

> It is no accident that the development of the cinema and the development of the *Berliner Illustrirte Zeitung* run roughly parallel. To the extent that life became more hectic, and the individual was less prepared to leaf through a magazine in a quiet moment, to that extent it became necessary to find a sharper, more efficient form of visual representation, one which did not lose its impact on the reader even if he only glanced fleetingly at the magazine page by page.[34]

For both of them photographic layout should facilitate quicker and random access to the news via simply leafing through a magazine. Kurt Safranski maintained this presentation, as did Carl Schnebel during the 1930s.

Looking at the first issues of *Berliner Illustrirte Zeitung*, though, it would seem that editorial attentiveness to images and their layout dated back to well before the First World War. In 1904 the weekly, in its treatment of the Russo–Japanese War, the vexations of winter, national politics, or sports, made effective use of combinations of impactful images, interacting or in sequence, whose framing and/or masking contributed to the composition of the page.[35] This graphic approach was pursued and adapted from year to year without ever causing the kind of sudden or too visible change that might have attracted new readers at the risk of driving away established ones. Thus the graphic embellishments gradually disappeared, but the editors never did away with the border around the single and double page spreads; sometimes it might be broken by one or more images, but this was never taken to the point of publishing full-bleed pictures.[36] As a rule *Berliner Illustrirte Zeitung*'s first pages were taken up by general and political news, while those that followed the serial focused more on culture and sports. The photographs, which were grouped on single or double pages—sometimes three consecutively, but rarely more—were always accompanied by an article covering a fifth of the page area at most. Beginning in 1929 two types of layout were used, depending on the quality of the photographs. When a subject was considered important—the Graf Zeppelin's round-the-world flight in 1929, for instance[37]—but the photographs lacked that "most intense possible concentration"[38] referred to by Korff, the layout took the form of a patchwork of small images highlighted by sophisticated effects of overlaying, difference, symmetry and masking that offset the monotony of the studio portraits, the sameness of visual documentation, and the haphazard ambiguity of snapshots (see Figure 2.6). The stylization of these layouts resembled that of *La Vie au grand air*, with narrative effects still intermingling with the spectacular. Conversely the editors had regular access to groups of images more uniform in terms of subject and formal considerations. Such was notably the case for the article on the German expedition to Central Asia, headed by Emil Trinkler and photographed by Walter Bosshard, and André Kertész's now famous account of life at the Trappist monastery at Soligny, both published in 1929[39] (see Figures 2.7 and 2.8). In both instances the number of images was reduced, to six and seven pictures respectively—half the number of the Graf Zeppelin article—while their format was widened and they were sequenced in the interests of a strictly non-spectacular narrative. The art director has superposed the corners of some of the images and used the entire space of the double page for the unfolding of the narrative, but the layouts minimize the graphic effects in order to highlight the photographs. Commissioned by the French magazine *VU* in September 1928, Kertész's report on the Cistercian community living under a vow of silence was not published until April 16, 1930.[40] Meanwhile it had been sold to Ullstein, who published the reportage not only in *Berliner Illustrirte Zeitung*, but also—somewhat deviously—in *UHU*, where it served to illustrate the confessions of a defrocked monk.[41]

A Hungarian who had moved to Paris in 1925, Kertész wasted no time in making contact with the artistic community in Montparnasse—especially its Surrealist branch—and succeeded in living off the sales of his images. His photographs of monastic life at Soligny are marked both by the uniqueness of this access to a way of life by definition reclusive, and the banality of the monks' daily existence. The compositional approach is simple but considered, making play with vanishing points and frontality, and with repetition and singularity in its depicting of the exodus from Holy Office, breakfast in the refectory, the dormitory, and keeping watch over a deceased brother. The clarity of the subjects and the soberness of their presentation chime perfectly with the characteristics of the monks' lives, and in their selection, ranking and subdued ordering over three pages, the photographs making up the *Berliner Illustrirte Zeitung* series form a precise, effective whole.

Münchner Illustrierte Presse was more predictable in terms of its layouts, which often relied on symmetry effects. Bosshard's photographs from India, a documentary account of the impact of the economic crisis in Königsberg, Felix H. Man's sociologically revealing portraits of the inhabitants of Schleswig-Holstein (see Figure 2.9), and Alfred Eisenstaedt's street-photography coverage of London's shantytowns are all similarly arranged around a central axis.[42]

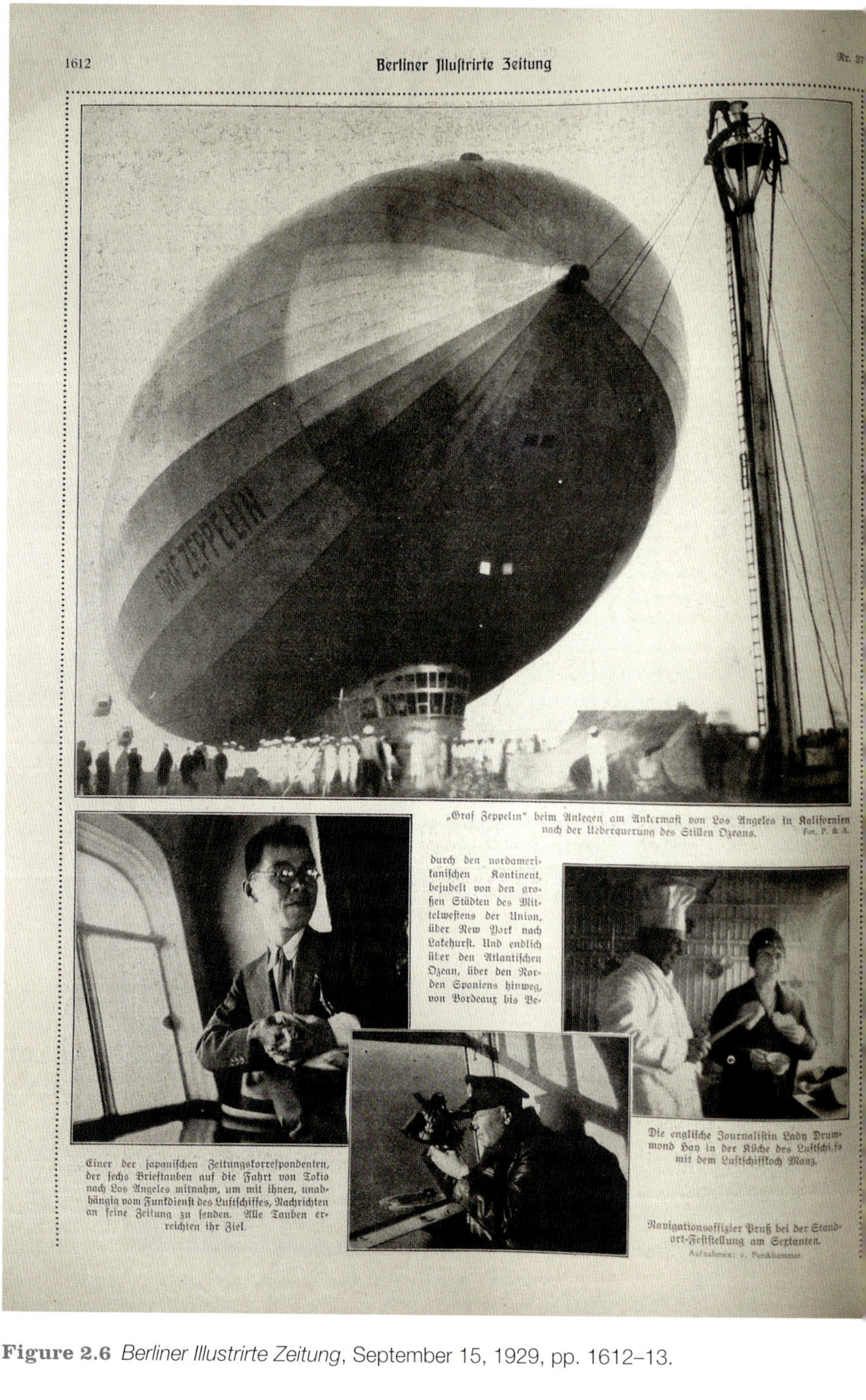

1612 Berliner Illustrirte Zeitung Nr. 37

„Graf Zeppelin" beim Anlegen am Ankermast von Los Angeles in Kalifornien nach der Ueberquerung des Stillen Ozeans. Fot. P. & A.

durch den nordamerikanischen Kontinent, bejubelt von den großen Städten des Mittelwestens der Union, über New York nach Lakehurst. Und endlich über den Atlantischen Ozean, über den Norden Spaniens hinweg, von Bordeaux bis Be-

Einer der japanischen Zeitungskorrespondenten, der sechs Brieftauben auf die Fahrt von Tokio nach Los Angeles mitnahm, um mit ihnen, unabhängig vom Funkdienst des Luftschiffes, Nachrichten an seine Zeitung zu senden. Alle Tauben erreichten ihr Ziel.

Die englische Journalistin Lady Drummond Hay in der Küche des Luftschiffs mit dem Luftschiffkoch Manz.

Navigationsoffizier Pruß bei der Standort-Feststellung am Sextanten. Aufnahmen: v. Perckhammer.

Figure 2.6 *Berliner Illustrirte Zeitung*, September 15, 1929, pp. 1612–13.

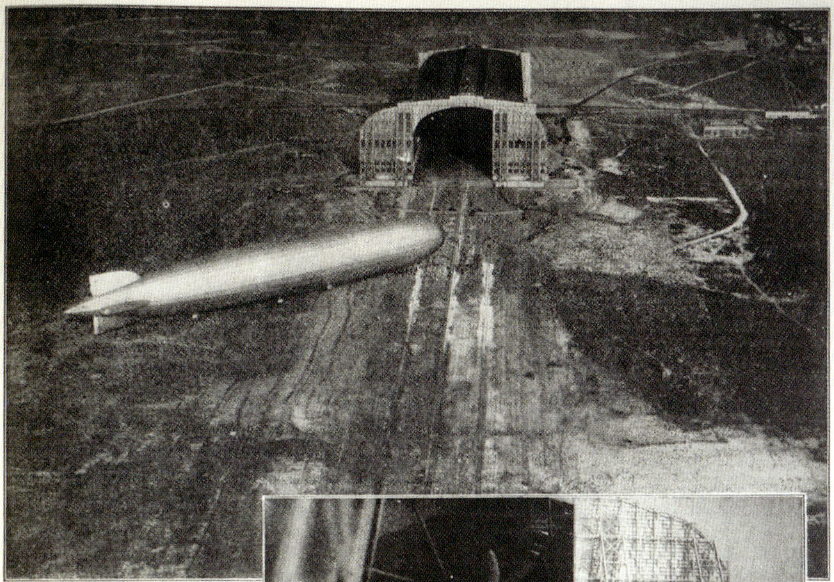

Ankunft in Lakehurst nach der Ueberquerung des nordamerikanischen Kontinents: „Graf Zeppelin" vor der Luftschiffhalle. Fot. P. & A.

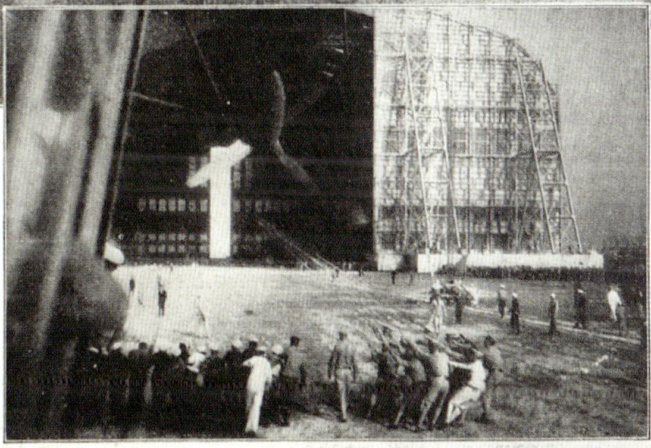

Die Landung in Lakehurst: Einbringung des Luftschiffes durch amerikanische Marinesoldaten. Fot. v. Perckhammer.

sançon diagonal durch Frankreich nach seinem Heimatshafen Friedrichshafen zurück, wo am 4. September, Mittwoch vormittag gegen halb 10 Uhr, die Landungsseile wieder auf deutschen Boden fielen. Unter den Passagieren dieser Weltfahrt durch den Aether waren außer Deutschland die Vereinigten Staaten, Frankreich, auch noch Australien, Japan, die Schweiz und Spanien vertreten. Ein gutes Omen für die Internationalität der Luftschiffahrt der Zukunft.

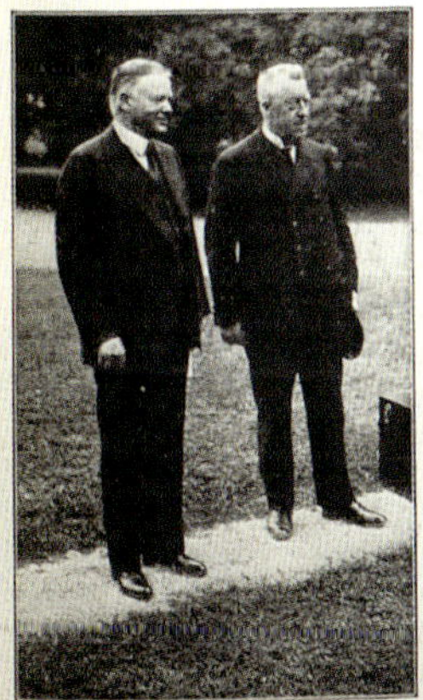

Dr. Eckener beim amerikanischen Präsidenten Hoover in Washington. Fot. P. & A.

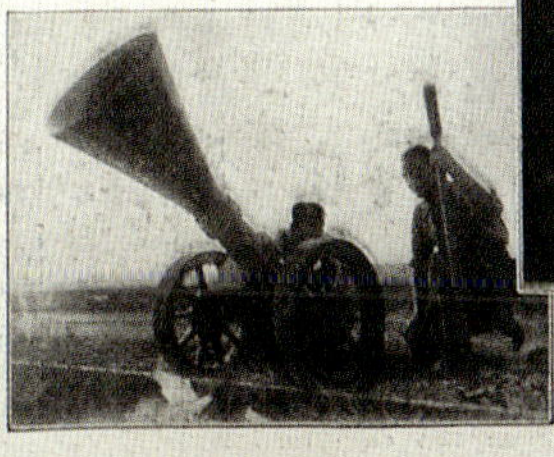

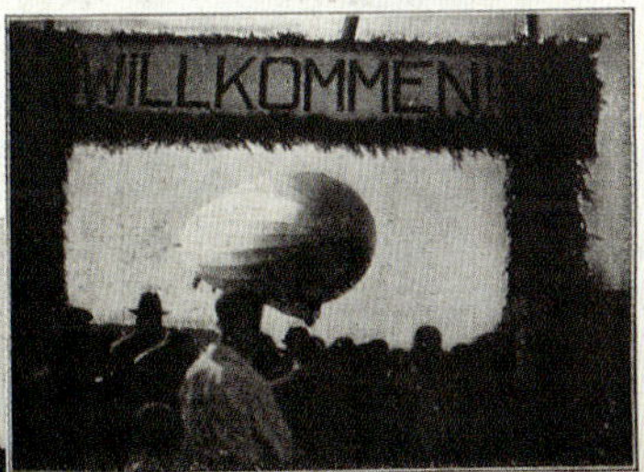

„Luftschiff in Sicht!" Böllerschüsse verkündeten in Friedrichshafen die Annäherung des Luftschiffes nach Beendigung der Weltfahrt. Fot. Seanecke.

Die Heimkehr nach Friedrichshafen.

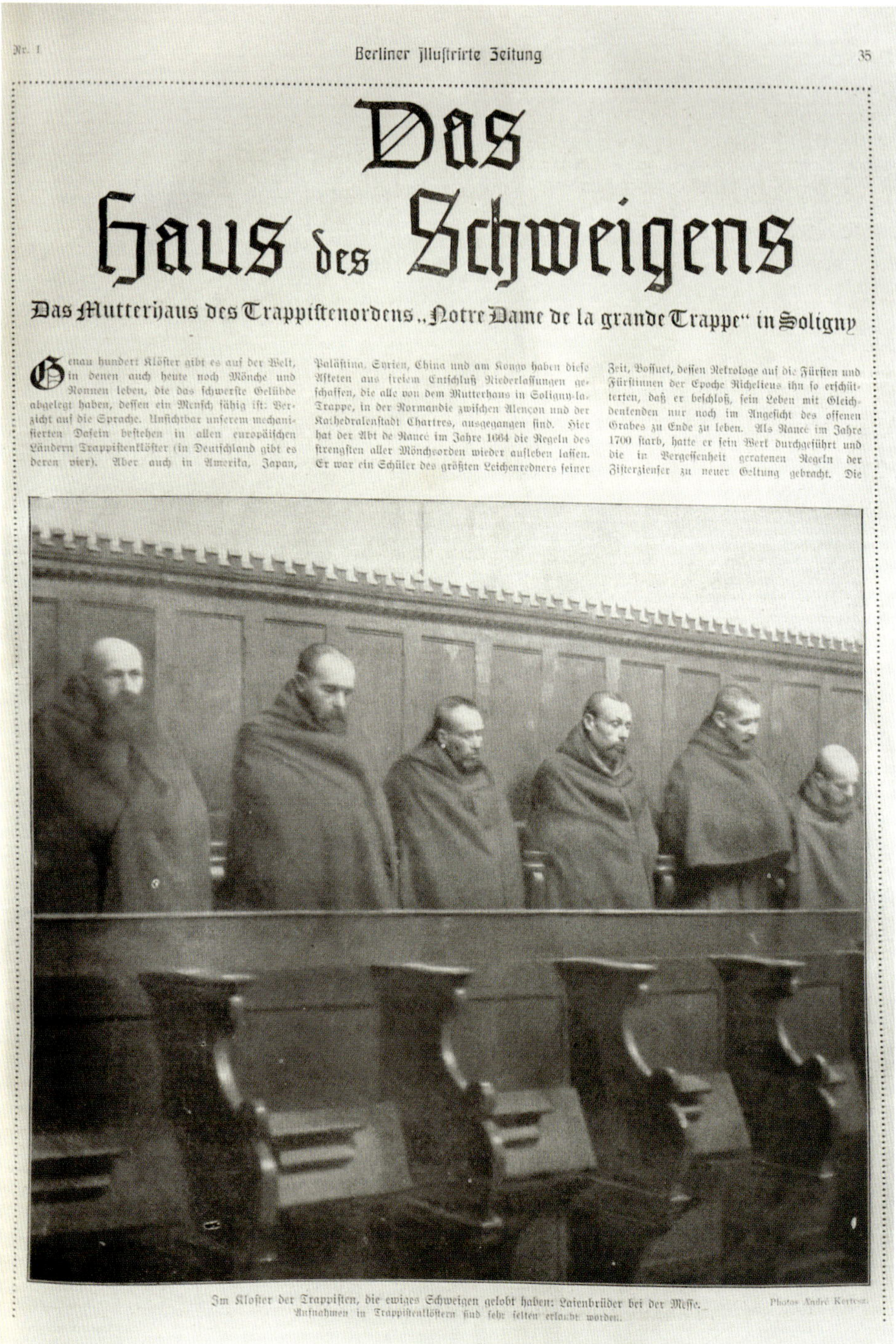

Nr. 1 Berliner Illustrirte Zeitung 35

Das Haus des Schweigens

Das Mutterhaus des Trappistenordens „Notre Dame de la grande Trappe" in Soligny

Genau hundert Klöster gibt es auf der Welt, in denen auch heute noch Mönche und Nonnen leben, die das schwerste Gelübde abgelegt haben, dessen ein Mensch fähig ist: Verzicht auf die Sprache. Unsichtbar unserem mechanisierten Dasein bestehen in allen europäischen Ländern Trappistenklöster (in Deutschland gibt es deren vier). Aber auch in Amerika, Japan, Palästina, Syrien, China und am Kongo haben diese Asketen aus freiem Entschluß Niederlassungen geschaffen, die alle von dem Mutterhaus in Soligny-la-Trappe, in der Normandie zwischen Alençon und der Kathedralenstadt Chartres, ausgegangen sind. Hier hat der Abt de Rancé im Jahre 1664 die Regeln des strengsten aller Mönchsorden wieder aufleben lassen. Er war ein Schüler des größten Leichenredners seiner Zeit, Bossuet, dessen Nekrologe auf die Fürsten und Fürstinnen der Epoche Richelieus ihn so erschütterten, daß er beschloß, sein Leben mit Gleichdenkenden nur noch im Angesicht des offenen Grabes zu Ende zu leben. Als Rancé im Jahre 1700 starb, hatte er sein Werk durchgeführt und die in Vergessenheit geratenen Regeln der Zisterzienser zu neuer Geltung gebracht. Die

Im Kloster der Trappisten, die ewiges Schweigen gelobt haben: Laienbrüder bei der Messe. Aufnahmen in Trappistenklöstern sind sehr selten erlaubt worden. Photos André Kertész

Figure 2.7 *Berliner Illustrirte Zeitung*, January 6, 1929, p. 35. Photograph by André Kertész.

Propagandist visual strategies

In November 1924, when the first *UHU* had just appeared and the first *Münchner Illustrierte Presse* was going to press, Willi Münzenberg, the German Communist Party's director of publications, added the magazine *Arbeiter Illustrierte Zeitung* (*AIZ*) to the German scene. In charge of propaganda for the Communist International—the Comintern—Münzenberg was building a veritable media empire, publishing and distributing newspapers, magazines, books (Kurt Tucholsky, John Heartfield), and films (Sergei Eisenstein). While very much part of the expanding magazine context in Germany at the time, *AIZ* stood out for its propagandist aims and its level of success: by 1931 it had a circulation of 450,000, putting it in third place nationally after *Berliner Illustrirte Zeitung* and *Münchner Illustrierte Presse*.[43] As an assertion both of the magazine's difference and its support for the Communist cause, Münzenberg and his editorial team made extensive use of photographs the cornerstone for remarkable visual strategies.

Taking a working class line counter to that of the middle class press that included *Berliner Illustrirte Zeitung* and *Münchner Illustrierte Presse*, *AIZ* established itself as the illustrated journal of the workers' movement. Initially a monthly, it went weekly in 1926. *AIZ* was the direct offspring of *Sowjet-Russland im Bild* (Soviet Russia in Pictures), launched in 1921 and the first Communist magazine to resort systematically to photography for propaganda purposes. Structured around its own photographs and photomontages of Russian Constructivist images, *Sowjet-Russland im Bild* morphed into *Sichel und Hammer* (Sickle and Hammer) in 1923, then *AIZ* the following year.[44] Since the magazine could not be sold on newsstands, Münzenberg fell back on an alternative network—as many as 46,000 people by 1931 for distribution in parks, at public meetings, in the workplace, and to the homes of activists.[45] Münzenberg also founded the Association of Worker Photographers, which supplied the illustrated press (including *AIZ*) with a politically committed vision of the working classes. A firm opponent of Nazism, *AIZ* was forced into exile in Prague after Hitler's election in 1933, and ceased publication in 1938.

Like its competitors—perhaps more so, given its mode of distribution—*AIZ* used its covers to catch potential readers' attention. In the publishing context of the time photography was seen as a potent instrument of communication; but where Kurt Korff demanded that a photograph embody "the most intense possible concentration,"[46] Münzenberg sought efficacy in the virtues of photomontage. As Communist artist John Heartfield, who had begun working for *AIZ* in 1930, put it in a lecture at the Moscow Polygraphic Institute in 1931, "The bourgeoisie is very much aware of the effectiveness [of photography] and has done its best to use it in its own interests. These attempts, though, have only had lackluster results: *Photomontage was and remains the weapon of revolutionary artists*."[47] *AIZ*, with its mix of text and images, became the vehicle of choice

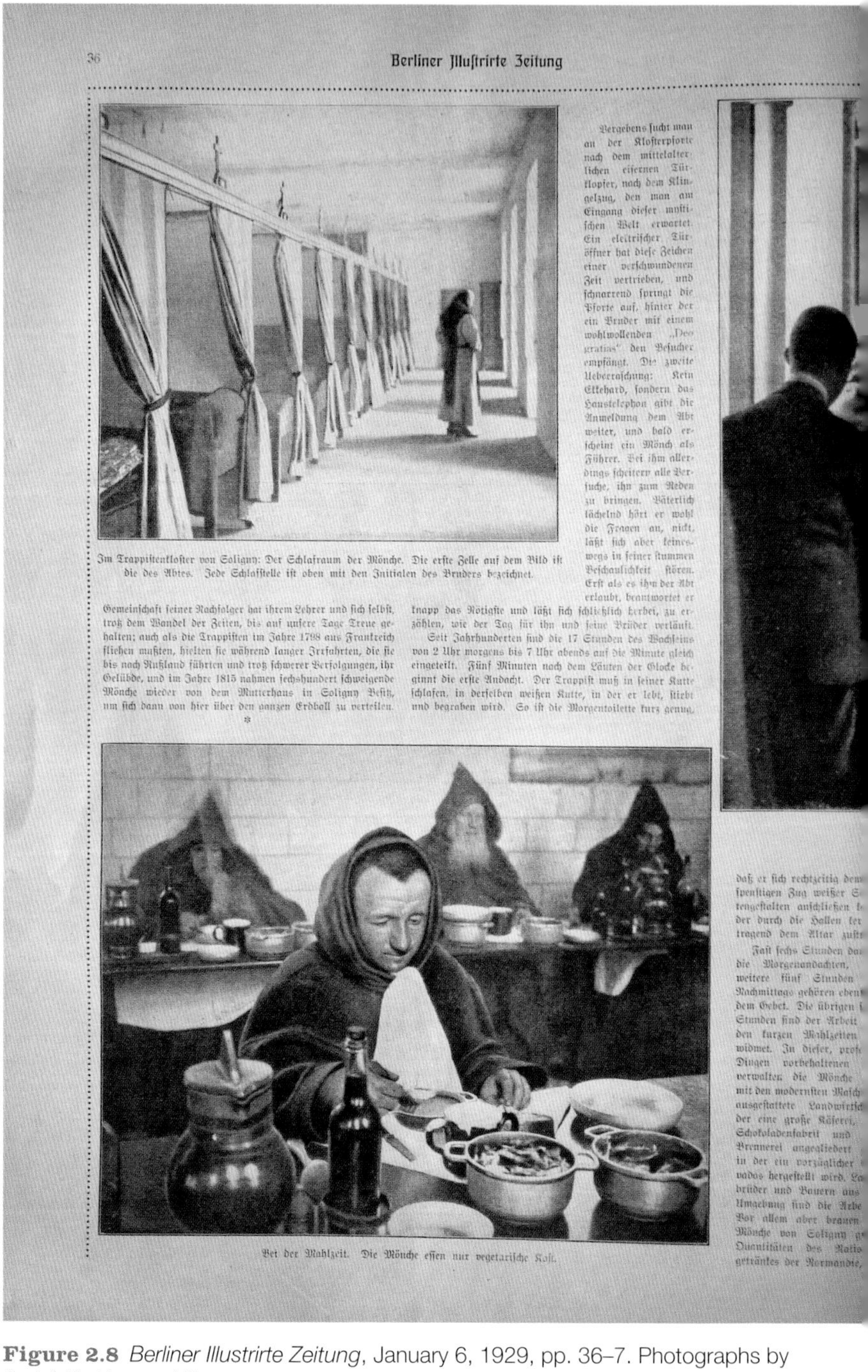

36 Berliner Illustrirte Zeitung

Im Trappistenkloster von Soligny: Der Schlafraum der Mönche. Die erste Zelle auf dem Bild ist die des Abtes. Jede Schlafstelle ist oben mit den Initialen des Bruders bezeichnet.

Vergebens sucht man an der Klosterpforte nach dem mittelalterlichen eisernen Türklopfer, nach dem Klingelzug, den man am Eingang dieser mystischen Welt erwartet. Ein elektrischer Türöffner hat diese Zeichen einer verschwundenen Zeit vertrieben, und schnarrend springt die Pforte auf, hinter der ein Bruder mit einem wohlwollenden „Deo gratias" den Besucher empfängt. Die zweite Ueberraschung: Kein Ekkehard, sondern das Haustelephon gibt die Anmeldung dem Abt weiter, und bald erscheint ein Mönch als Führer. Bei ihm allerdings scheitern alle Versuche, ihn zum Reden zu bringen. Väterlich lächelnd hört er wohl die Fragen an, nickt, läßt sich aber keineswegs in seiner stummen Beschaulichkeit stören. Erst als es ihm der Abt erlaubt, beantwortet er knapp das Nötigste und läßt sich schließlich herbei, zu erzählen, wie der Tag für ihn und seine Brüder verläuft.

Gemeinschaft seiner Nachfolger hat ihrem Lehrer und sich selbst, troß dem Wandel der Zeiten, bis auf unsere Tage Treue gehalten; auch als die Trappisten im Jahre 1798 aus Frankreich fliehen mußten, hielten sie während langer Irrfahrten, die sie bis nach Rußland führten und troß schwerer Verfolgungen, ihr Gelübde, und im Jahre 1815 nahmen sechshundert schweigende Mönche wieder von dem Mutterhaus in Soligny Besitz, um sich dann von hier über den ganzen Erdball zu verteilen.

*

Seit Jahrhunderten sind die 17 Stunden des Wachseins von 2 Uhr morgens bis 7 Uhr abends auf die Minute gleich eingeteilt. Fünf Minuten nach dem Läuten der Glocke beginnt die erste Andacht. Der Trappist muß in seiner Kutte schlafen, in derselben weißen Kutte, in der er lebt, stirbt und begraben wird. So ist die Morgentoilette kurz genug.

Bei der Mahlzeit. Die Mönche essen nur vegetarische Kost.

daß er sich rechtzeitig dem
spenstigen Zug weißer S
tengestalten anschließen k
der durch die Hallen ker
tragend dem Altar zust

Fast sechs Stunden da
die Morgenandachten,
weitere fünf Stunden
Nachmittags gehören eben
dem Gebet. Die übrigen
Stunden sind der Arbeit
den kurzen Mahlzeiten
widmet. In dieser, prof
Dingen vorbehaltenen
verwalten die Mönche
mit den modernsten Masch
ausgestattete Landwirtsch
der eine große Käserei,
Schokoladenfabrik und
Brennerei angegliedert
in der ein vorzüglicher
vados hergestellt wird. La
brüder und Bauern aus
Umgebung sind die Arbe
Vor allem aber brauen
Mönche von Soligny g
Quantitäten des Natio
getränkes der Normandie,

Figure 2.8 *Berliner Illustrirte Zeitung*, January 6, 1929, pp. 36–7. Photographs by André Kertész and Piermay.

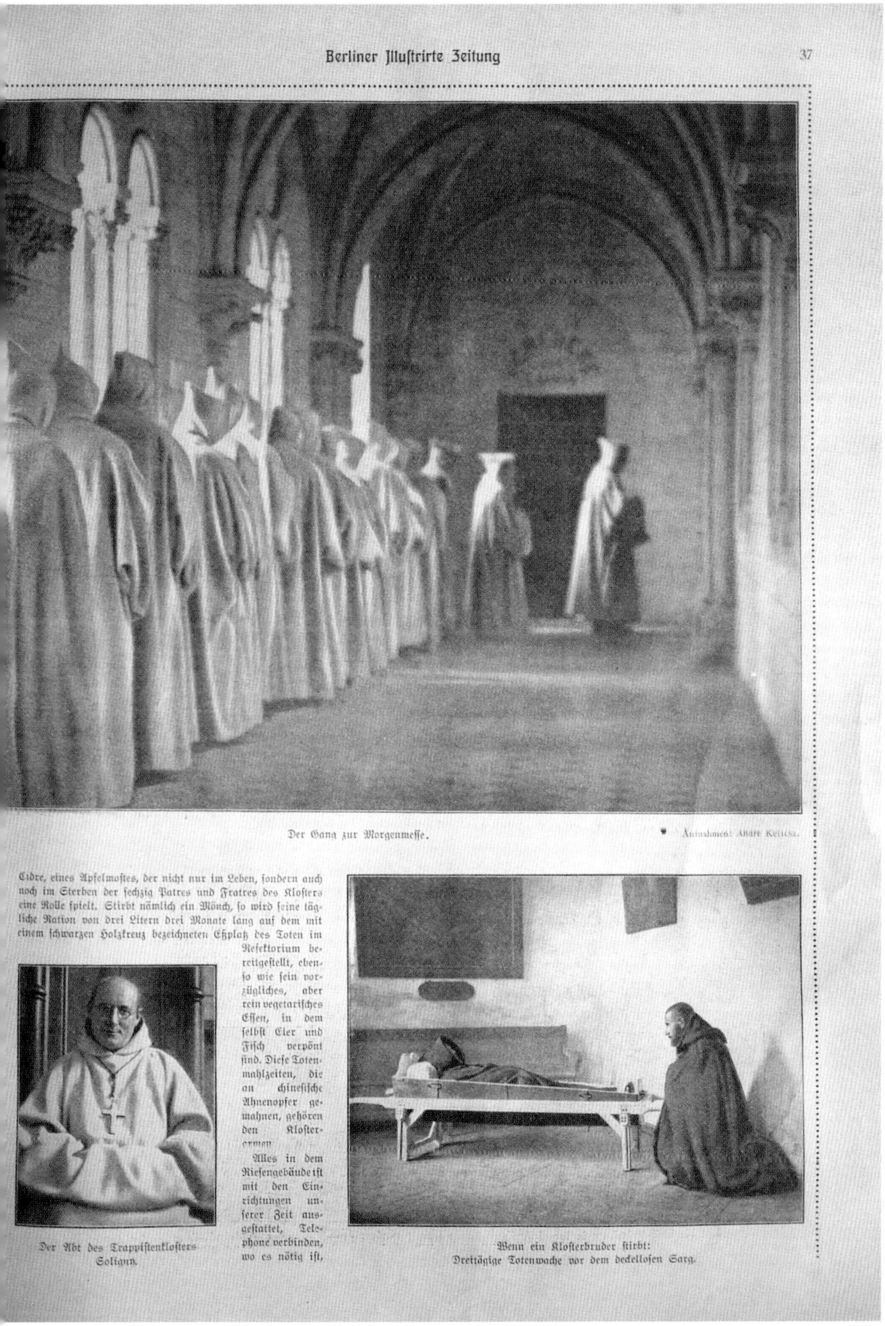

Berliner Illustrirte Zeitung 37

Der Gang zur Morgenmesse.

Aufnahmen: André Kertész.

Cidre, eines Apfelmostes, der nicht nur im Leben, sondern auch noch im Sterben der sechzig Patres und Fratres des Klosters eine Rolle spielt. Stirbt nämlich ein Mönch, so wird seine tägliche Ration von drei Litern drei Monate lang auf dem mit einem schwarzen Holzkreuz bezeichneten Eßplatz des Toten im Refektorium bereitgestellt, ebenso wie sein vorzügliches, aber rein vegetarisches Essen, in dem selbst Eier und Fisch verpönt sind. Diese Totenmahlzeiten, die an chinesische Ahnenopfer gemahnen, gehören den Klosterarmen.

Alles in dem Riesengebäude ist mit den Einrichtungen unserer Zeit ausgestattet, Telephone verbinden, wo es nötig ist,

Der Abt des Trappistenklosters Soligny.

Wenn ein Klosterbruder stirbt:
Dreitägige Totenwache vor dem deckellosen Sarg.

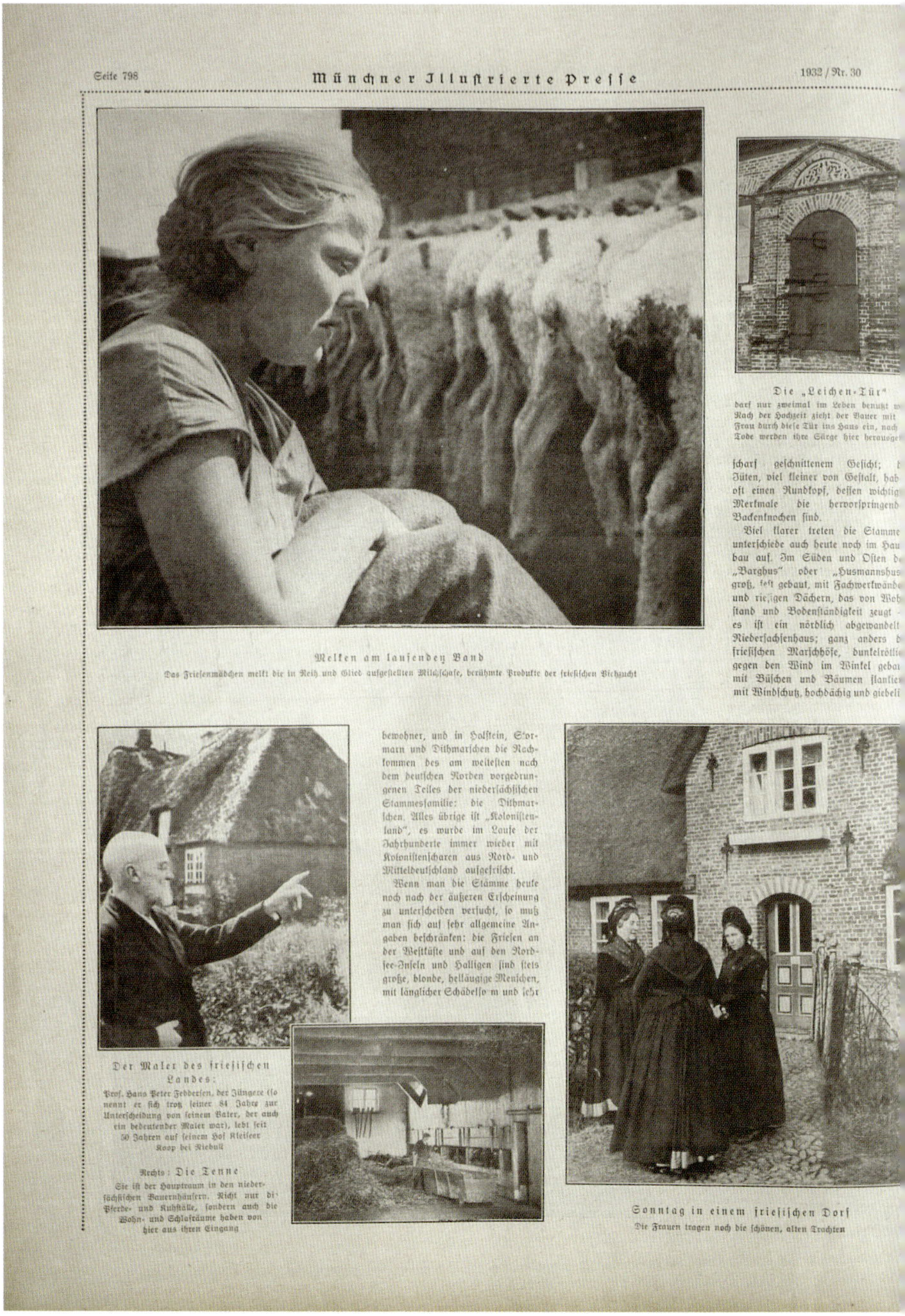

Seite 798 Münchner Illustrierte Presse 1932 / Nr. 30

Melken am laufenden Band
Das Friesenmädchen melkt die in Reih und Glied aufgestellten Milchschafe, berühmte Produkte der friesischen Viehzucht

Die „Leichen-Tür"
darf nur zweimal im Leben benutzt w
Nach der Hochzeit zieht der Bauer mit
Frau durch diese Tür ins Haus ein, nach
Tode werden ihre Särge hier herausge

bewohner, und in Holstein, Stormarn und Dithmarschen die Nachkommen des am weitesten nach dem deutschen Norden vorgedrungenen Teiles der niedersächsischen Stammesfamilie: die Dithmarschen. Alles übrige ist „Kolonistenland", es wurde im Laufe der Jahrhunderte immer wieder mit Kolonistenscharen aus Nord- und Mitteldeutschland aufgefrischt.

Wenn man die Stämme heute noch nach der äußeren Erscheinung zu unterscheiden versucht, so muß man sich auf sehr allgemeine Angaben beschränken: die Friesen an der Westküste und auf den Nordsee-Inseln und Halligen sind stets große, blonde, helläugige Menschen, mit länglicher Schädelform und sehr scharf geschnittenem Gesicht; d
Jüten, viel kleiner von Gestalt, hab
oft einen Rundkopf, dessen wichtig
Merkmale die hervorspringend
Backenknochen sind.

Viel klarer treten die Stamme
unterschiede auch heute noch im Hau
bau auf. Im Süden und Osten d
„Barghus" oder „Husmannshus
groß, fest gebaut, mit Fachwerkwänd
und riesigen Dächern, das von Woh
stand und Bodenständigkeit zeugt -
es ist ein nördlich abgewandelt
Niedersachsenhaus; ganz anders d
friesischen Marschhöfe, dunkelrötli
gegen den Wind im Winkel geba
mit Büschen und Bäumen flankie
mit Windschutz, hochdächig und giebeli

Der Maler des friesischen Landes:
Prof. Hans Peter Feddersen, der Jüngere (so nennt er sich trotz seiner 84 Jahre zur Unterscheidung von seinem Vater, der auch ein bedeutender Maler war), lebt seit 50 Jahren auf seinem Hof Kleiseer Koop bei Niebüll

Rechts: Die Tenne
Sie ist der Hauptraum in den niedersächsischen Bauernhäusern. Nicht nur di Pferde- und Kuhställe, sondern auch die Wohn- und Schlafräume haben von hier aus ihren Eingang

Sonntag in einem friesischen Dorf
Die Frauen tragen noch die schönen, alten Trachten

Figure 2.9 *Münchner Illustrierte Presse*, July 24, 1932, pp. 798–9. Photographs by Felix H. M
(Dephot).

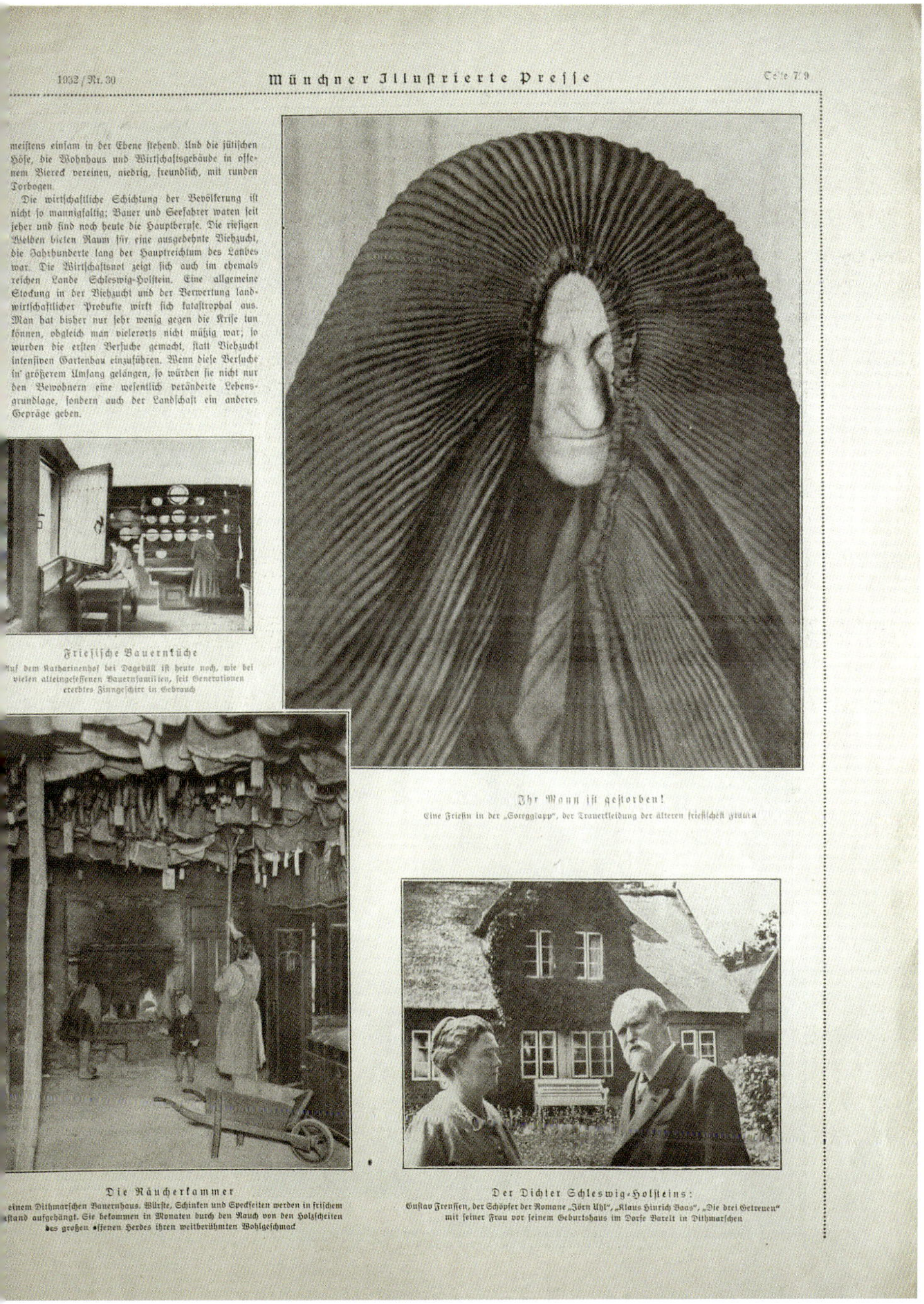

meistens einsam in der Ebene stehend. Und die jütischen Höfe, die Wohnhaus und Wirtschaftsgebäude in offenem Viereck vereinen, niedrig, freundlich, mit runden Torbogen.

Die wirtschaftliche Schichtung der Bevölkerung ist nicht so mannigfaltig; Bauer und Seefahrer waren seit jeher und sind noch heute die Hauptberufe. Die riesigen Welden bieten Raum für eine ausgedehnte Viehzucht, die Jahrhunderte lang der Hauptreichtum des Landes war. Die Wirtschaftsnot zeigt sich auch im ehemals reichen Lande Schleswig-Holstein. Eine allgemeine Stockung in der Viehzucht und der Verwertung landwirtschaftlicher Produkte wirkt sich katastrophal aus. Man hat bisher nur sehr wenig gegen die Krise tun können, obgleich man vielerorts nicht müßig war; so wurden die ersten Versuche gemacht, statt Viehzucht intensiven Gartenbau einzuführen. Wenn diese Versuche in größerem Umfang gelängen, so würden sie nicht nur den Bewohnern eine wesentlich veränderte Lebensgrundlage, sondern auch der Landschaft ein anderes Gepräge geben.

Friesische Bauernküche

Auf dem Katharinenhof bei Dagebüll ist heute noch, wie bei vielen alteingesessenen Bauernfamilien, seit Generationen ererbtes Zinngeschirr in Gebrauch

Ihr Mann ist gestorben!

Eine Friesin in der „Sorreglapp", der Trauerkleidung der älteren friesischeñ Frauen

Die Räucherkammer

einem Dithmarschen Bauernhaus. Würste, Schinken und Speckseiten werden in frischem stand aufgehängt. Sie bekommen in Monaten durch den Rauch von den Holzscheiten des großen offenen Herdes ihren weitberühmten Wohlgeschmack

Der Dichter Schleswig-Holsteins:

Gustav Frenssen, der Schöpfer der Romane „Jörn Uhl", „Klaus Hinrich Baas", „Die drei Getreuen" mit seiner Frau vor seinem Geburtshaus im Dorfe Barelt in Dithmarschen

for activist artists like Heartfield, for whom the photograph, far from being a mere recording of events, was a malleable raw material all of whose visual resources could be exploited in acting "powerfully on the masses."[48] Heartfield was producing his photomontages for *AIZ* at a time when numerous theoretical texts on photography were appearing: among others Siegfried Kracauer, Walter Benjamin and László Moholy-Nagy[49] were defining the camera as a political tool capable of challenging traditional modes of representation and creating a new vision for the working class. At *AIZ* editors, graphic designers and photographers were busily transgressing the conventions perpetuated by magazines like *Berliner Illustrirte Zeitung* and *Münchner Illustrierte Presse*, putting their faith in a visual freedom rooted in the dynamics and graphic approaches pioneered by the artistic avant-garde.

Set designer, book illustrator and creator of political posters, Heartfield collaborated with Berlin Dadaist George Grosz on photocollages using fragments of magazine pages to create a "deliberately provocative satirical form."[50] In *AIZ* he denounced the social-democrat Weimar Republic's political compromises and power plays, then went on to pillory National Socialism for its violations of freedom and personal integrity. Composed of different photographs rearranged to form a new image, his covers were graphically limpid and immediately comprehensible. The one for November 27, 1932, titled "Der Sinn von Genf" (The Meaning of Geneva), shows a dove of peace skewered on a bayonet as a symbol of the consequences of Germany's withdrawal from the Conference for the Reduction and Limitation of Armaments[51] (see Figure 2.10). Comprising at least three separate photographs (the dove, the bayonet, the building in the background) and retouched to highlight certain details (the Swiss flag, the feathers, the olive branch), the image nonetheless betrays few signs of montage on a strange, provocative cover that makes intriguing play with reality. In the course of the 1930s Heartfield published some 230 equally complex photomontages,[52] challenging social representations and recontextualizing events to provide them with an unequivocal message that fit the *AIZ* line.

Opening the magazine, the AIZ reader found graphic compositions associating typographic variations with pictures provided by photographic agencies, the Association of Worker Photographers and the Soviet press.[53] The page layouts used different photographic points of view to play up different subjects (high angle for political figures, low angle for the masses) and a variety of formats (half or quarter page, streamer, vignette) sequenced to recount the passing of a parade or—as in the issue of November 20, 1932—to stress the size of the turnout for the fifteenth anniversary of the Russian Revolution.[54] With an eye to instructing the reader, the layouts also featured graphs and statistics elucidating the overall message (see Figure 2.11).

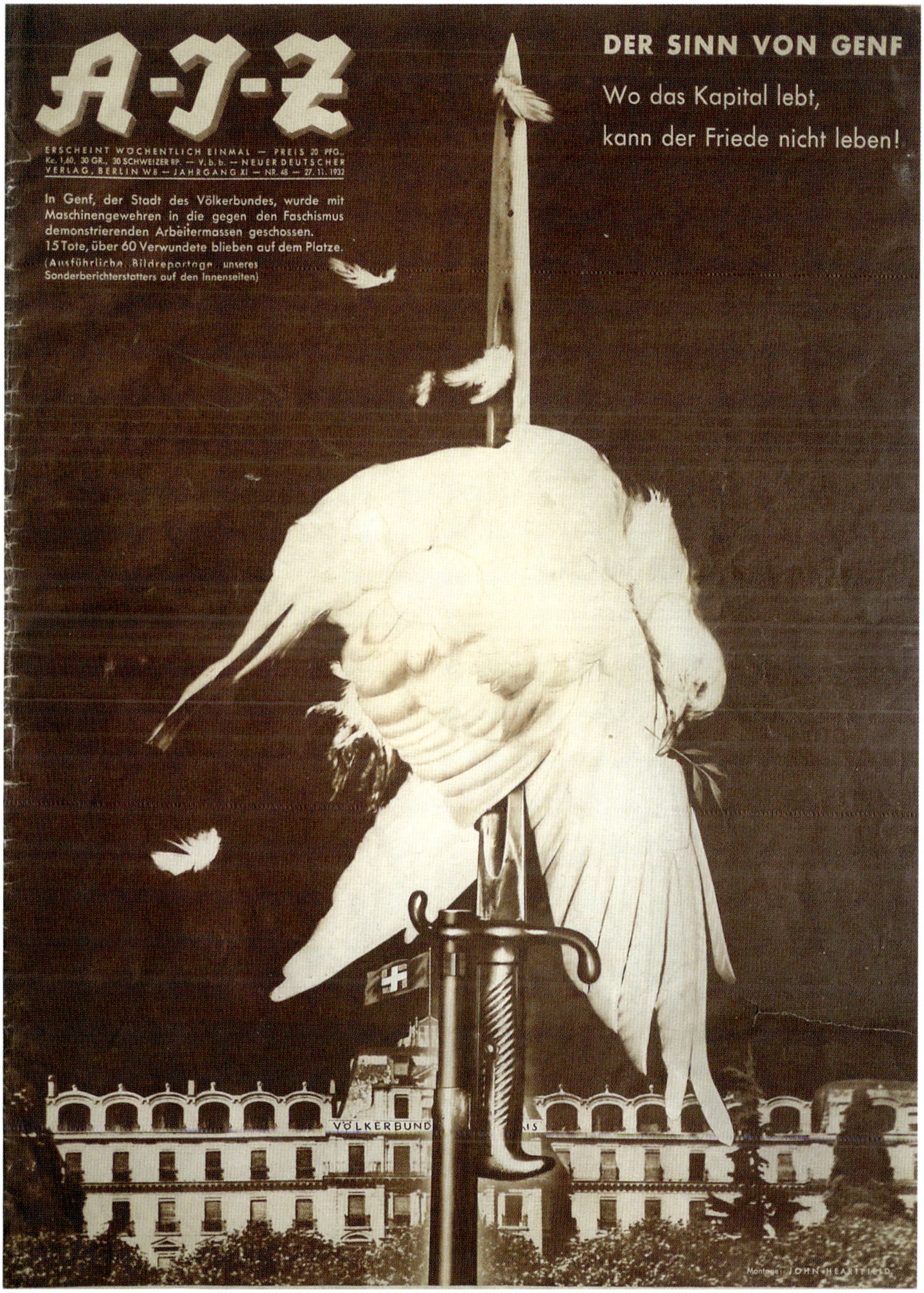

Figure 2.10 *AIZ*, November 20, 1932, cover. Photomontage by John Hearfield.

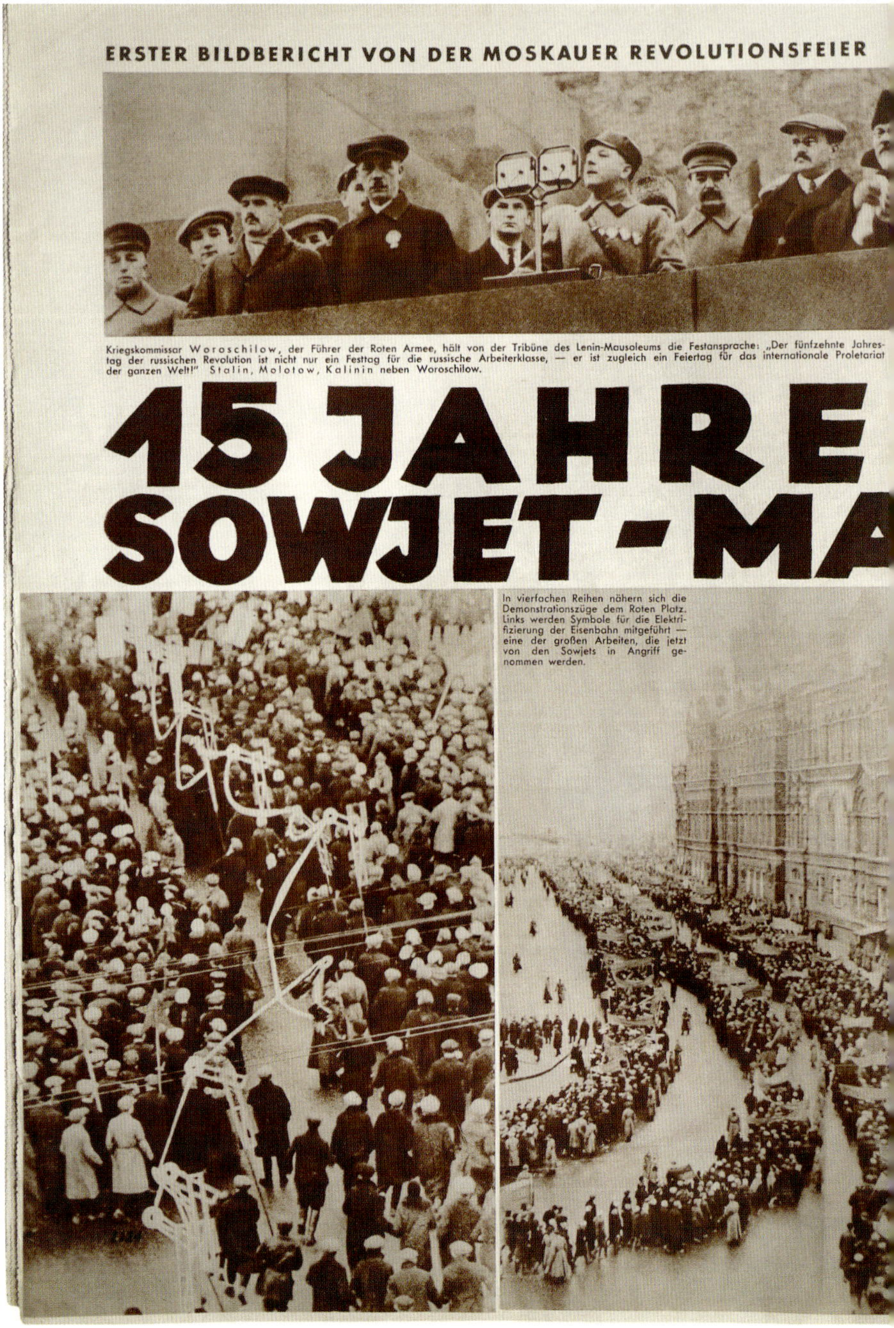

ERSTER BILDBERICHT VON DER MOSKAUER REVOLUTIONSFEIER

Kriegskommissar Woroschilow, der Führer der Roten Armee, hält von der Tribüne des Lenin-Mausoleums die Festansprache: „Der fünfzehnte Jahrestag der russischen Revolution ist nicht nur ein Festtag für die russische Arbeiterklasse, — er ist zugleich ein Feiertag für das internationale Proletariat der ganzen Welt!" Stalin, Molotow, Kalinin neben Woroschilow.

15 JAHRE
SOWJET-MA

In vierfachen Reihen nähern sich die Demonstrationszüge dem Roten Platz. Links werden Symbole für die Elektrifizierung der Eisenbahn mitgeführt — eine der großen Arbeiten, die jetzt von den Sowjets in Angriff genommen werden.

Figure 2.11 *AIZ*, November 20, 1932, pp. 1124–5.

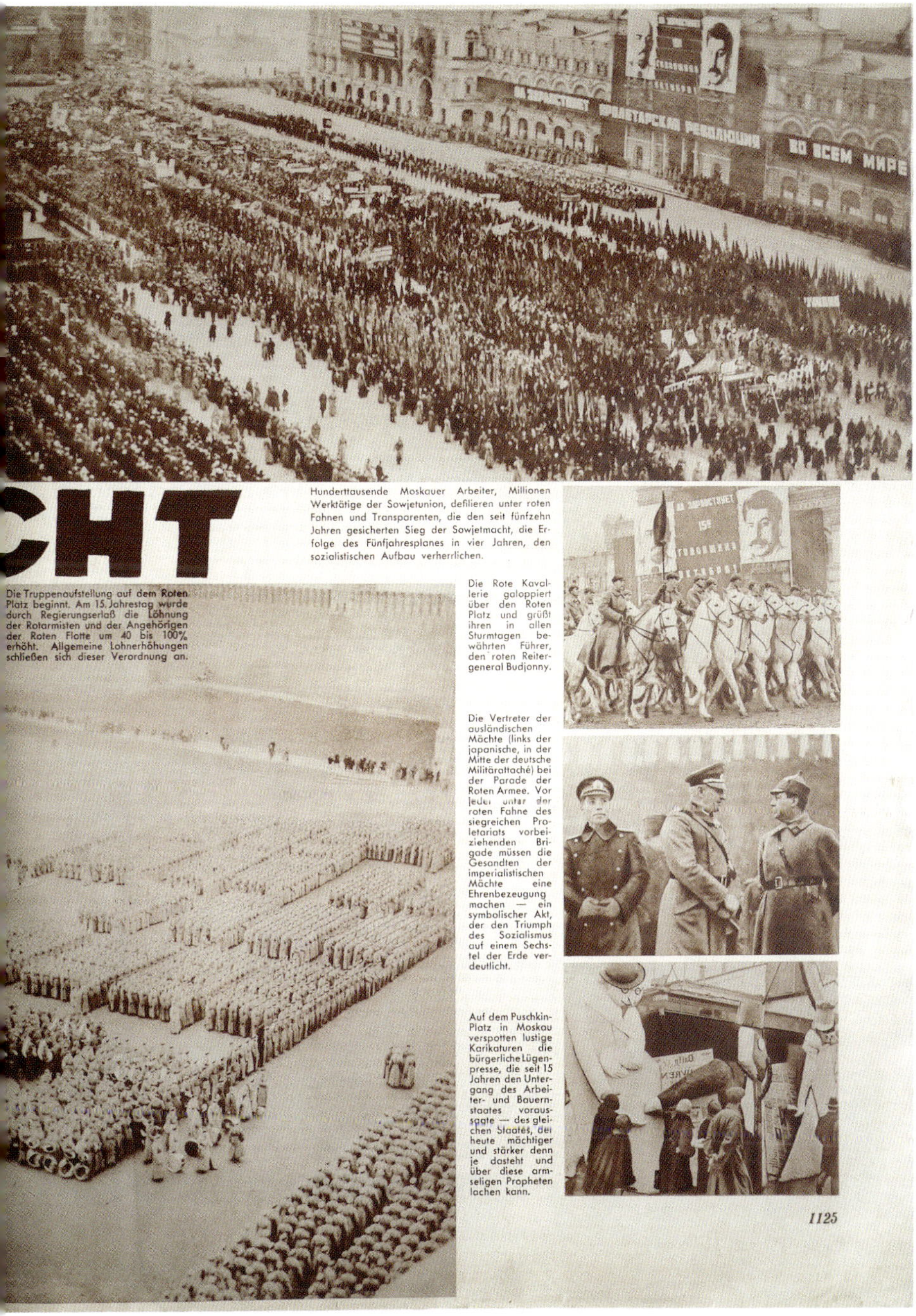

CHT

Hunderttausende Moskauer Arbeiter, Millionen Werktätige der Sowjetunion, defilieren unter roten Fahnen und Transparenten, die den seit fünfzehn Jahren gesicherten Sieg der Sowjetmacht, die Erfolge des Fünfjahresplanes in vier Jahren, den sozialistischen Aufbau verherrlichen.

Die Truppenaufstellung auf dem Roten Platz beginnt. Am 15. Jahrestag wurde durch Regierungserlaß die Löhnung der Rotarmisten und der Angehörigen der Roten Flotte um 40 bis 100% erhöht. Allgemeine Lohnerhöhungen schließen sich dieser Verordnung an.

Die Rote Kavallerie galoppiert über den Roten Platz und grüßt ihren in allen Sturmtagen bewährten Führer, den roten Reitergeneral Budjonny.

Die Vertreter der ausländischen Mächte (links der japanische, in der Mitte der deutsche Militärattaché) bei der Parade der Roten Armee. Vor jeder unter der roten Fahne des siegreichen Proletariats vorbeiziehenden Brigade müssen die Gesandten der imperialistischen Mächte eine Ehrenbezeugung machen — ein symbolischer Akt, der den Triumph des Sozialismus auf einem Sechstel der Erde verdeutlicht.

Auf dem Puschkin-Platz in Moskau verspotten lustige Karikaturen die bürgerliche Lügenpresse, die seit 15 Jahren den Untergang des Arbeiter- und Bauernstaates voraussagte — des gleichen Staates, der heute mächtiger und stärker denn je dasteht und über diese armseligen Propheten lachen kann.

1125

In 1932 the French Communist Party decided it needed its own press mouthpiece. This took the form of *Regards sur le monde du travail* (Looking at the World of Work), a title shortened to *Regards* in September 1933. The new magazine drew on the successful aspects of its German predecessor and put similar visual strategies to work in the interests of communication, education and the class struggle. Like *AIZ*, *Regards* saw itself as the crucial counterweight to a mendacious bourgeois press that was the enemy of the proletariat, and portrayed the working class world in photographs whose subjects and styles could be grasped immediately. Its covers personified worker resistance in photomontages and low angle shots that reversed contextual proportions: transformed into colossi looking down commandingly on buildings or landscapes, these proletarian figures overtly asserted their powerfulness (see Figure 2.12). The same graphic structures, the same personages—the Frenchman Henri Barbusse, the Russian Maxim Gorky—and in some cases the same images circulated from one magazine to another. A notable example is Heartfield's photomontage showing Nazi field marshal Hermann Göring setting the world alight with a flaming torch: after appearing on the cover of *AIZ* on February 28, 1935, it resurfaced two months later on the cover of *Regards*.[55]

Heartfield's photomontages also found their way into the Russian propaganda magazine *USSR in Construction*, which first appeared in 1929. Published in Moscow and distributed by the State Publishing House, it devoted each issue to a specific theme—collective farms, the Red Army, major state construction projects, the workers, and parades and processions—designed to show the world the country's successes under Stalin (see Figure 2.13). Here Heartfield's work was associated with that of the Soviet Constructivists El Lissitzky and Alexander Rodchenko.[56] Lissitzky produced photomontages and Rodchenko and Barbara Stepanova worked on layouts that ensured the visual effectiveness of numerous issues. Inventive maskings and associations generated arresting compositional effects, while the magazine made generous use of high and low angle shots to convince its readership of the modernity of the Soviet Union. *USSR in Construction* became a veritable image reservoir and some of its photographs found their way into *Regards* and *AIZ*. Thus the high and low angle shots, montages and photomontages, and perspective and flattening were put to work by the Communist propaganda press to get its message across convincingly (see Figure 2.14). These visual choices were also intended to target the gambits of the "bourgeois" general news outlets, as denounced in 1931 by Bertolt Brecht: "The immense amount of photo-material that the presses spew out on a daily basis and which does have the appearance of truth really only serves to obscure the facts. The camera can lie just like the typesetting machine."[57]

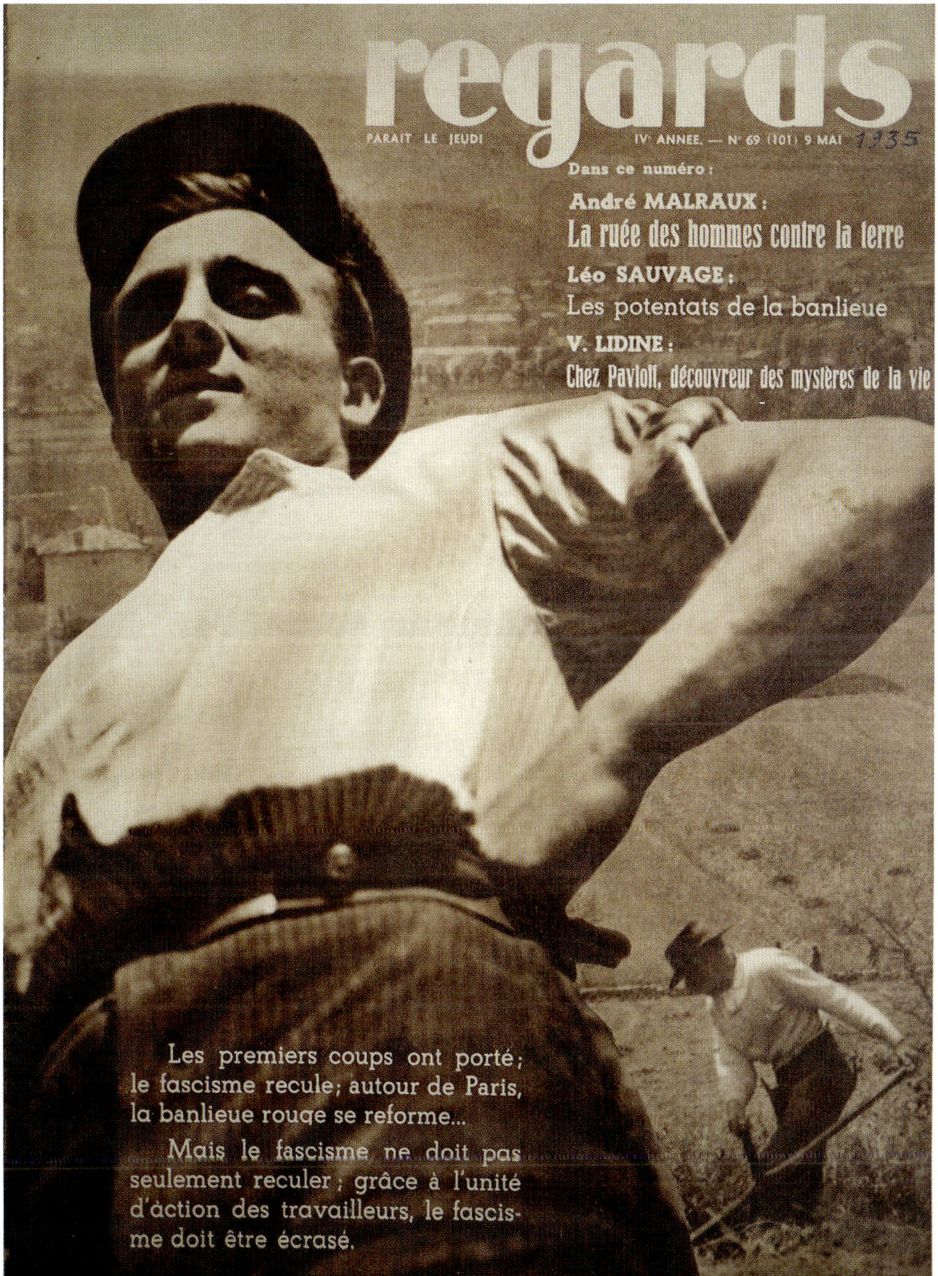

Figure 2.12 *Regards*, May 9, 1935, cover.

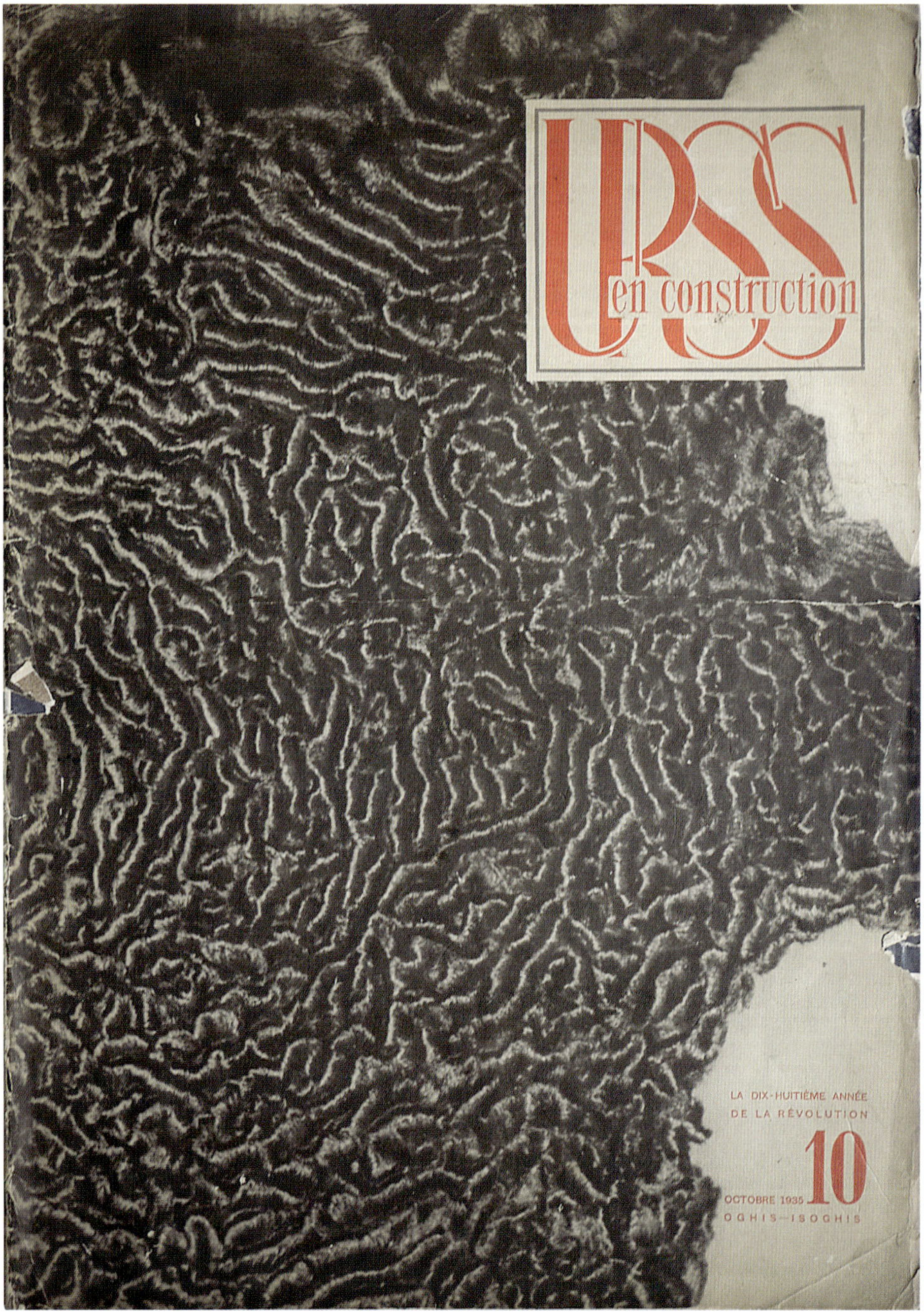

Figure 2.13 *URSS en construction*, October 1935, cover.

A style for news magazines

In the late 1920s the German illustrated press had all the available photography sources at its fingertips. It had contract photographers like Martin Munkácsi, who worked for the Ullstein group, could call on agencies like Wide World Photo, Associated Press and Dephot, and negotiated directly with freelancers. The demand for news photographs, the competition between the two main general news magazines, and the exactingness of editors worked to the advantage of the photographers, who enjoyed demonstrating their originality and stylistic distinctiveness. Their images circulated not only among the various periodicals belonging to the same publishing house, but also among rival weeklies, and found outlets in Germany, France, England and the United States.

The most readily identifiable style was probably that of Erich Salomon (1886–1944), whose photographs left their stamp on their era and are considered by Tim Gidal a milestone in the history of modern photojournalism.[58] Born into a banking family, Salomon was a Doctor of Law who had fallen on hard times during Germany's postwar crisis and ultimately found work in Ullstein's advertising department.[59] Just how this forty-something bourgeois began a career in photography remains unclear, but we know that the camera he used was an Ermanox, a brand that came onto the German market in 1924. Combining a huge lens with a small body that could take 4.5 × 6 cm sheet film, this weird-looking piece of equipment enabled indoor shots without a flash.[60] This allowed Salomon to work in courtrooms, where photography was forbidden, then at dinners and meetings where he secretly photographed the powerful of this world. Public figures had always been a major concern for the illustrated press: in its first issue *L'Illustration* declared, "We hope that not very long from now there will not bo a single personage in Europe . . . who has not paid our magazine the tribute of his portrait. As we all know, we understand the words and actions of a man better when we have seen his features."[61] Salomon's photographs met this requirement and provided portraits in context over which he had almost exclusive control. Taken in the casino at Monte Carlo, on the first-class decks of an ocean liner, at a dinner for the Berlin Secession artists, or at the Lausanne Conference,[62] his pictures are characterized by a recognizable personal aesthetic (see Figures 2.15 and 2.16). Hiding his camera in a bag or a top hat, he opted for unusual, often slightly low-angled points of view, rather than the habitual eye-height of a photographer looking through a viewfinder. His images are also often marked by dark, blurred areas caused by a person or a piece of furniture between himself and his subject; the effect was to direct the eye toward the sharp focus area, where the enhanced values help the viewer identify famous people at the gaming table or absorbed in discussion. In the list of his adventures Salomon, later followed by his commentators, unfailingly mentions the altercation that took place in 1929

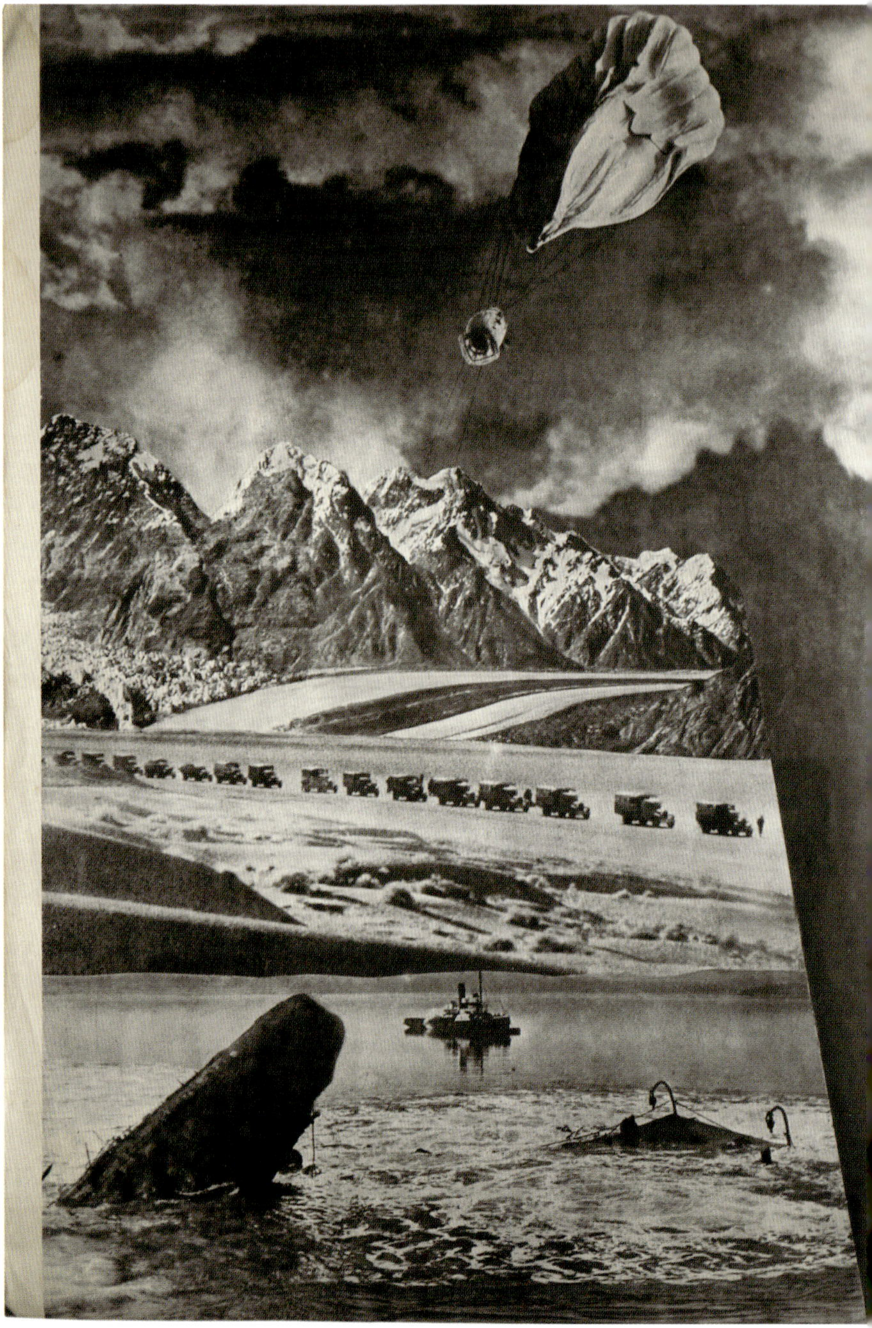

Figure 2.14 *URSS en construction,* February 1934, pp. 1–2.

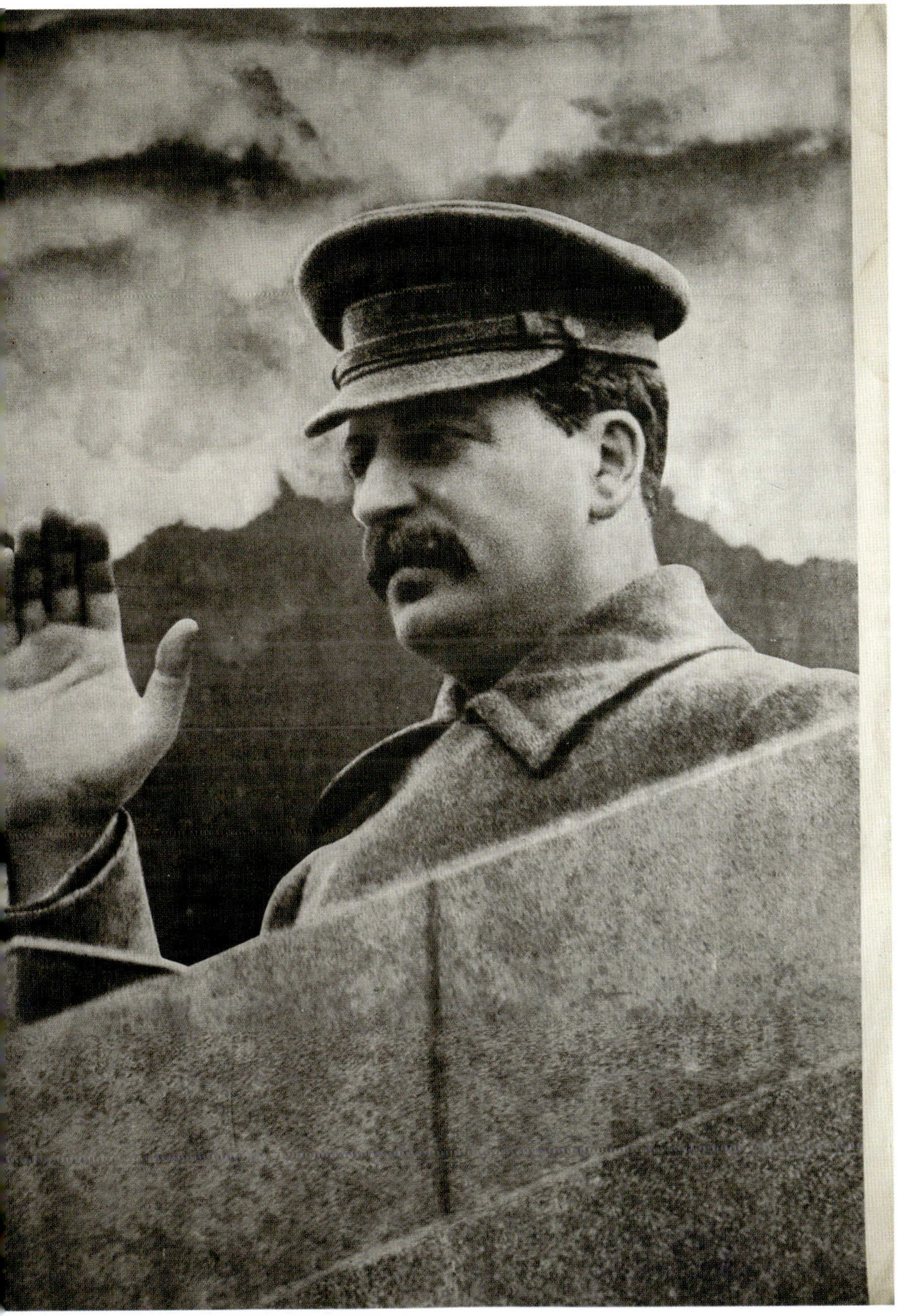

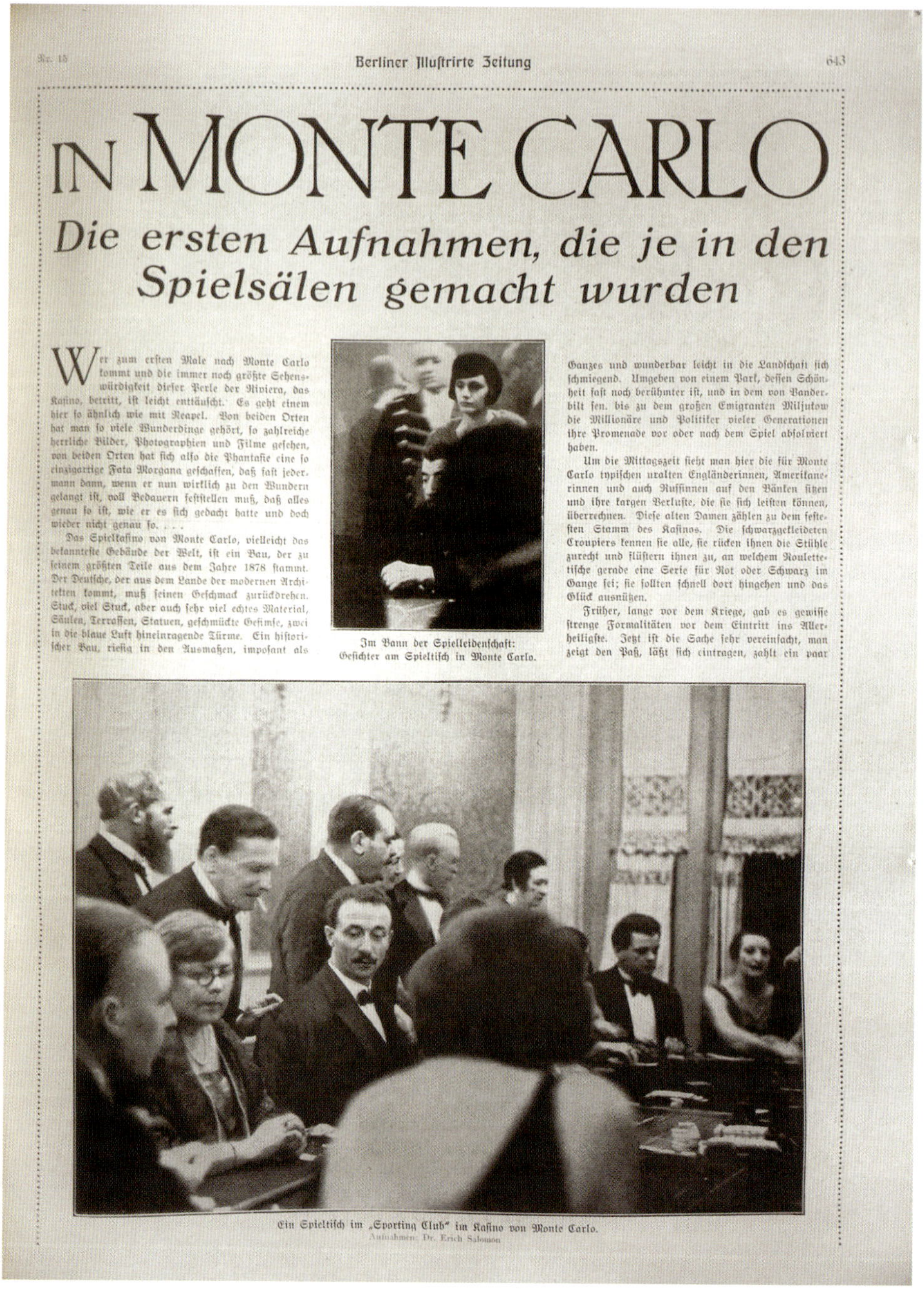

Nr. 15 Berliner Illustrirte Zeitung 643

IN MONTE CARLO

Die ersten Aufnahmen, die je in den Spielsälen gemacht wurden

Wer zum ersten Male nach Monte Carlo kommt und die immer noch größte Sehenswürdigkeit dieser Perle der Riviera, das Kasino, betritt, ist leicht enttäuscht. Es geht einem hier so ähnlich wie mit Neapel. Von beiden Orten hat man so viele Wunderdinge gehört, so zahlreiche herrliche Bilder, Photographien und Filme gesehen, von beiden Orten hat sich also die Phantasie eine so einzigartige Fata Morgana geschaffen, daß fast jedermann dann, wenn er nun wirklich zu den Wundern gelangt ist, voll Bedauern feststellen muß, daß alles genau so ist, wie er es sich gedacht hatte und doch wieder nicht genau so. . . .

Das Spielkasino von Monte Carlo, vielleicht das bekannteste Gebäude der Welt, ist ein Bau, der zu seinem größten Teile aus dem Jahre 1878 stammt. Der Deutsche, der aus dem Lande der modernen Architekten kommt, muß seinen Geschmack zurückdrehen. Stuck, viel Stuck, aber auch sehr viel echtes Material, Säulen, Terrassen, Statuen, geschmückte Gesimse, zwei in die blaue Luft hineinragende Türme. Ein historischer Bau, riesig in den Ausmaßen, imposant als Ganzes und wunderbar leicht in die Landschaft sich schmiegend. Umgeben von einem Park, dessen Schönheit fast noch berühmter ist, und in dem von Vanderbilt sen. bis zu dem großen Emigranten Miljukow die Millionäre und Politiker vieler Generationen ihre Promenade vor oder nach dem Spiel absolviert haben.

Um die Mittagszeit sieht man hier die für Monte Carlo typischen uralten Engländerinnen, Amerikanerinnen und auch Russinnen auf den Bänken sitzen und ihre kargen Verluste, die sie sich leisten können, überrechnen. Diese alten Damen zählen zu dem festesten Stamm des Kasinos. Die schwarzgekleideten Croupiers kennen sie alle, sie rücken ihnen die Stühle zurecht und flüstern ihnen zu, an welchem Roulettetische gerade eine Serie für Rot oder Schwarz im Gange sei; sie sollten schnell dort hingehen und das Glück ausnützen.

Früher, lange vor dem Kriege, gab es gewisse strenge Formalitäten vor dem Eintritt ins Allerheiligste. Jetzt ist die Sache sehr vereinfacht, man zeigt den Paß, läßt sich eintragen, zahlt ein paar

Im Bann der Spielleidenschaft: Gesichter am Spieltisch in Monte Carlo.

Ein Spieltisch im „Sporting Club" im Kasino von Monte Carlo.
Aufnahmen: Dr. Erich Salomon

Figure 2.15 *Berliner Illustrirte Zeitung*, April 14, 1929, p. 643. Photographs by Erich Salomon.

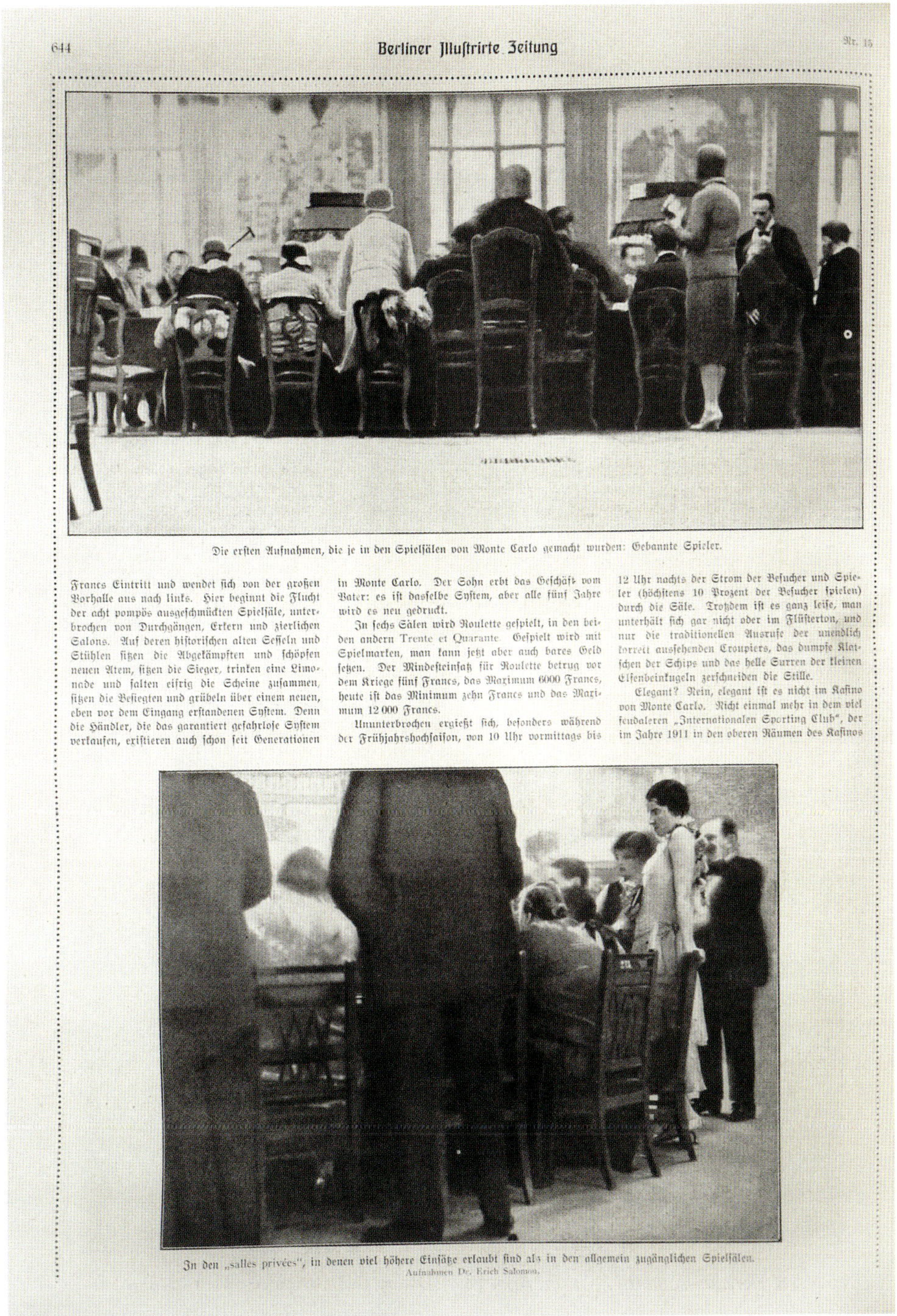

644 Berliner Illustrirte Zeitung Nr. 15

Die ersten Aufnahmen, die je in den Spielsälen von Monte Carlo gemacht wurden: Gebannte Spieler.

Francs Eintritt und wendet sich von der großen Vorhalle aus nach links. Hier beginnt die Flucht der acht pompös ausgeschmückten Spielsäle, unterbrochen von Durchgängen, Erkern und zierlichen Salons. Auf deren historischen alten Sesseln und Stühlen sitzen die Abgekämpften und schöpfen neuen Atem, sitzen die Sieger, trinken eine Limonade und falten eifrig die Scheine zusammen, sitzen die Besiegten und grübeln über einem neuen, eben vor dem Eingang erstandenen System. Denn die Händler, die das garantiert gefahrlose System verkaufen, existieren auch schon seit Generationen in Monte Carlo. Der Sohn erbt das Geschäft vom Vater: es ist dasselbe System, aber alle fünf Jahre wird es neu gedruckt.

In sechs Sälen wird Roulette gespielt, in den beiden andern Trente et Quarante. Gespielt wird mit Spielmarken, man kann jetzt aber auch bares Geld setzen. Der Mindesteinsatz für Roulette betrug vor dem Kriege fünf Francs, das Maximum 6000 Francs, heute ist das Minimum zehn Francs und das Maximum 12 000 Francs.

Ununterbrochen ergießt sich, besonders während der Frühjahrshochsaison, von 10 Uhr vormittags bis 12 Uhr nachts der Strom der Besucher und Spieler (höchstens 10 Prozent der Besucher spielen) durch die Säle. Trotzdem ist es ganz leise, man unterhält sich gar nicht oder im Flüsterton, und nur die traditionellen Ausrufe der unendlich korrekt aussehenden Croupiers, das dumpfe Klatschen der Schips und das helle Surren der kleinen Elfenbeinkugeln zerschneiden die Stille.

Elegant? Nein, elegant ist es nicht im Kasino von Monte Carlo. Nicht einmal mehr in dem viel feudaleren „Internationalen Sporting Club", der im Jahre 1911 in den oberen Räumen des Kasinos

In den „salles privées", in denen viel höhere Einsätze erlaubt sind als in den allgemein zugänglichen Spielsälen.
Aufnahmen Dr. Erich Salomon.

Figure 2.16 *Berliner Illustrirte Zeitung*, April 14, 1929, p. 644. Photographs by Erich Salomon.

when the Secretary of the Royal Academy in London remonstrated that his way of working was unheard of. To which he riposted, "That is just why I am doing it."[63]

A similar story is told of Léon Gimpel, come to photograph a bus that had fallen into the Seine in Paris in 1911. The police suggested he should join the other journalists, who had all taken up vantage points on the riverbank: "That's exactly why I don't want to go there,"[64] he told them, and proceeded to take a high-angle shot from the bridge. Like Salomon, Gimpel aimed to set himself apart, and in doing so established a news photography style of his own.[65] The sole difference between the two was that Salomon's style was unacceptable to the Belle Époque. In 1909 Gimpel succeeded in getting the only two shots of the ceremonial lunch given for the Russian sovereigns on their official visit to Cherbourg. The photographs were taken from a gun turret and although the view is largely blocked by the stock of a cannon, in both of them we can make out the main subjects—the Russian royals and France's President Fallières—busy with their food or gazing distractedly at their surroundings. These pictures, though, did not suit *L'Illustration*'s editors, who were bent on providing a serene image of Franco–Russian friendship; so they called in an illustrator to cut out and assemble the acceptable visual elements of each, and thus provide the classical official composition deemed necessary for the cover for August 7, 1909. While it was true that Gimpel's Spido Gaumont was less sensitive and more cumbersome that Salomon's Ermanox, it still allowed him to take all the interior pictures he wanted, even at night. For aspiration, and not just technique, was an issue here: the Salomon aesthetic was sought after as much by photographers as by the weeklies that published them, enabling the latter to attract attention in a competitive market by highlighting the investigative role of the photographer and the different vision of the news it opened up for readers. Salomon's style became his visual signature and the magazines began crediting him on their covers. The style, however, was not exclusively his, and other photographers like Felix H. Man and Alfred Eisenstaedt drew on it to help get their work published.[66] The cover of *L'Illustration* for June 1, 1929, featuring three photographs by Jean Clair-Guyot of the King and Queen of Spain at a dinner in Barcelona, shows even the French weekly adapting to this aesthetic.[67]

The other photographer whose style guaranteed him hundreds of appearances in the German and French press was Martin Munkácsi (1896–1963). His picture of three young Liberians running into the sea became famous after Henri Cartier-Bresson singled it out as the only image that had influenced him in the course of his entire career.[68] In June 1930 Munkácsi was sent by *Berliner Illustrirte Zeitung* to Liberia on the assignment announced on the cover for June 22 as "Four Weeks in a Modern Negro State: Martin Munkácsi visits Liberia for the *Berliner Illustrirte*."[69] As historian Enno Kaufhold has pointed out, *Berliner Illustrirte Zeitung* did not include the famous image, preferring to emphasize the modernity of the country with photographs of a lawyer defending his client and young women out shopping in the European manner.[70] The picture of the young Liberians finally came out (still within the Ullstein fold) in *Die Dame* in July 1931; a month later in the Hungarian magazine *Pesti Napló*; and then in *Arts et Métiers graphiques*, where Cartier-Bresson discovered it on his return from his own stay in West Africa: "There is such intensity in this image, such spontaneity, such *joie de vivre*, such miraculousness, that even today it still bowls me over."[71]

In the summer of 1928 Munkácsi left Hungary, where he had a studio and had been supplying the illustrated press with portraits and sports images. Arriving in Berlin, he immediately began working for Ullstein, while retaining the right to publish with the competition. Most of his work appeared in *Berliner Illustrirte Zeitung*, *Die Dame* and the dailies *Berliner Morgenpost* and *Tempo* (all owned by Ullstein), but he also published in *Die Woche* (owned by Hugenberg-Konzern). During his six years in Berlin he sometimes covered breaking news—Hitler in Potsdam in 1933, for example[72]—and photographed various personalities, among them the Turkish president Mustafa Kemal Pasha leading the first dance at his daughter's wedding in 1929;[73] but he was most often called on for cultural events, voyages of discovery, and everyday life (see Figure 2.17) Whatever the actual working context, Munkácsi had no time for the new 35 mm cameras, preferring a 9 × 12 cm body or even a 24 × 30 cm view camera. He sometimes staged his photographs, or used distorting lenses to produce compositions whose balance was unfailingly flawless.[74] Above all he made use of every possible viewpoint: working the entire range from high to low angle, he sabotaged classical perspective in favor of emphasizing the lines and forms of his subjects. Skiers and dancers, soldiers and children, workers and summer holidaymakers: photographed from ground level or from the sky, they entirely fill images from which the horizon line has vanished; indeed, in July 1932 *Berliner Illustrirte Zeitung* had to rotate a picture and modify its page layout to restore a group of soldiers in Rio to the vertical.[75]

As already mentioned, Munkácsi subscribed neither to The New Vision nor The New Objectivity, but with Albert Renger-Patzsch he did write an article on amateur photography for *UHU*, which had published photograms by László Moholy-Nagy.[76] By the late 1920s the German illustrated press had become a nerve center where the ambitions of avant-garde artists coincided with those of press photographers and editors. In particular, Munkácsi's concern with composition and his mastery of the snapshot gave his photographs the elegance and spontaneity that so impressed Cartier-Bresson. The sports pictures he had taken in Budapest indicated not only his interest in snapshot forms, but also the sheer dexterity he brought to this kind of image. On his way to Liberia in 1930 he photographed dancers in the street in Seville, in a high shot that enabled an overall treatment of his subject. The camera angle highlights the swirl of dresses transformed by the snapshot into corollas, while in the foreground Munkácsi has captured the transit of a

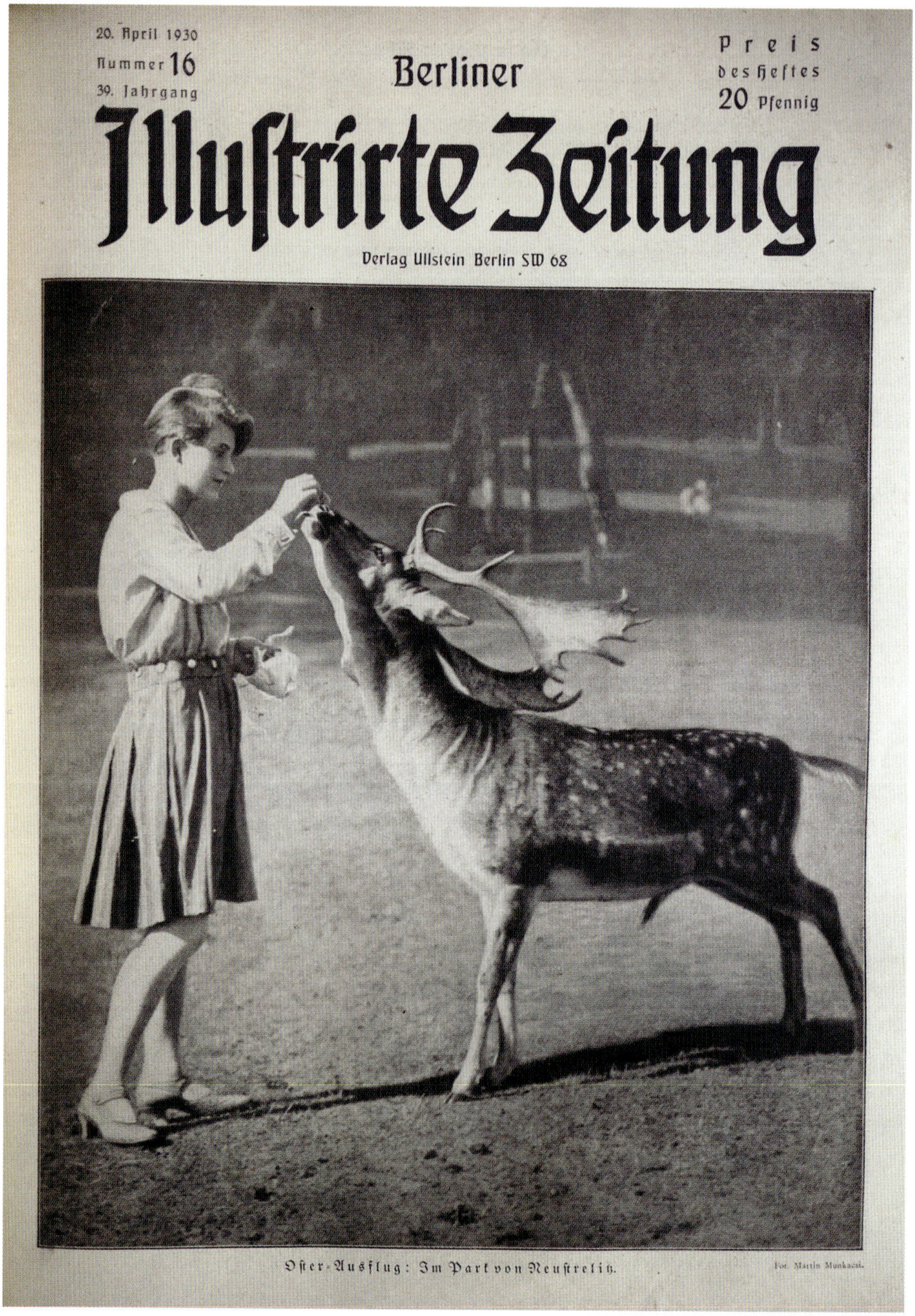
20. April 1930
Nummer 16
39. Jahrgang

Berliner
Illustrirte Zeitung

Preis
des Heftes
20 Pfennig

Verlag Ullstein Berlin SW 68

Oster-Ausflug: Im Park von Neustrelitz.

Fot. Martin Munkácsi.

Figure 2.17 *Berliner Illustrirte Zeitung*, April 20, 1930, cover. Photograph by Martin Munkácsi.

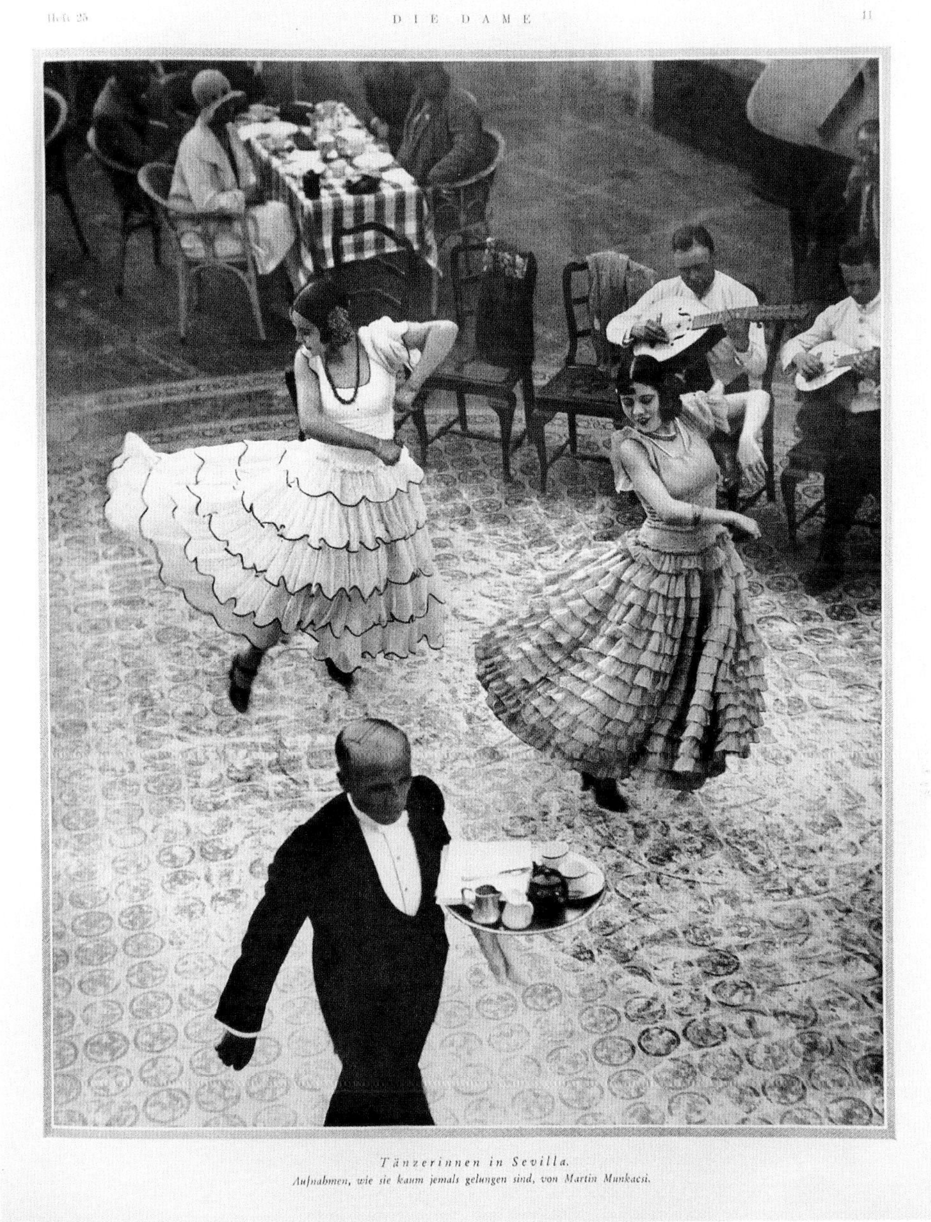

Figure 2.18 *Die Dame*, September 1, 1930, p. 11. Photograph by Martin Munkácsi.

café waiter whose arm and leg movements, despite their cropping by the framing of the image, mimic and underscore those of the dancers. This photograph appeared as a full page in *Die Dame* for September 1, 1930, accompanied by four others, giving the magazine the chance to publish an article on Spanish dance[77] (see Figure 2.18).

Two years later, in a reportage on the recently opened Victor-Gsovsky school of classical dance in Berlin, Munkácsi adopted a low-angle approach, highlighting the lightness and elegance of movement caught at its pinnacle as he suspended the dancers in the air. As André Gunthert has emphasized, catching movement and making it visible had become the crux of a snapshot aesthetic developed by amateur photographers in the late nineteenth century.[78] Photographers had realized that the shutter had to be released at the culmination of the leap—the "pause"[79]—when the movement has slowed. By 1932 the tenseness of the great nineteenth-century leapers had given way to the grace of the Gsovsky school, whose formal distinctiveness Munkácsi beautifully captures in his sober compositions. The series was published in *Die Dame* in Germany and some years later in France, in *Le Miroir du Monde*, *VU* and *Art et Médecine*.[80] Munkácsi's technical virtuosity and his interest in balanced composition did not go unnoticed by the editors at *Berliner Illustrirte Zeitung* who, as a kind of authorial added value, mentioned him by name on his many covers and even in the headings for his reportages: "Martin Munkácsi visits Liberia for the *Berliner Illustrirte*"[81] and "Martin Munkácsi's contribution to the 'Berlin–Rio de Janeiro'."[82] Working in very different genres, Erich Salomon and Martin Munkácsi both gained professional recognition as journalists capable of carrying out investigations and giving eloquent expression to their findings.

An aesthetics of transparency

In his history of modern photojournalism, a field in which he himself was a major actor, Tim Gidal lists many photographers working directly for publishers or an agency, or both. Felix H. Man (1893–1985) and Alfred Eisenstaedt (1898–1995) were both born into the German bourgeoisie, both fought in the First World War (from which Man brought back some photographs), and both experienced the postwar crisis before becoming press photographers.[83] Man abandoned his career as an illustrator—along with his aspirations as a painter—in order to sell his photographs to the daily press (Ullstein), and in 1929 joined the Dephot agency, founded by Simon Guttmann the year before. Eisenstaedt gave up his job as a sales representative in favor of photography and his pictures began to be distributed by Associated Press in 1929. Both started out with Kodaks before moving on to 35 mm Leicas, but they also used plate cameras like the Nettel Man worked with in 1933. Their long careers began in Germany, but Man left for England in 1933 and

Eisenstaedt for the United States in 1935; respectively they played a part in the founding of *Picture Post* (1938) and *Life* (1936). They shared the same ambitions in terms of their practice and the kind of image they wanted: each sought not to impose a personal presence, but rather to remain invisible while letting the situation reveal itself naturally. In 1931, when Man was given permission to photograph Mussolini, he put his Ermanox on a tripod in the Palazzo Venezia office—the camera was highly sensitive, but its use indoors still demanded considerable expertise—and took his pictures when his subjects had forgotten he was there. One result was the famous photograph of the Duce—behind his desk, lost amid the gargantuan splendor of the setting—whose appearance in both *Münchner Illustrierte Presse* and *Berliner Illustrirte Zeitung* had a negative effect on Man's relationship with Stefan Lorant[84] (see Figure 2.19). Eisenstaedt's approach was identical when in the summer of 1930 he photographed Gerhart Hauptmann, winner of the 1912 Nobel Prize for Literature, comfortably installed in the garden of his new home on the island of Hiddensee.[85] Whatever the theme or the personality to be covered, Man and Eisenstaedt rejected both staging and sittings. The upshot was a colossal corpus of aesthetically elusive images that led Henry Luce to remark of Eisenstaedt, "I do not see a man with a camera; I simply see a man looking, a man unobtrusively, quietly, but intently looking."[86] Nonetheless both refused to be considered as mere machines: they claimed a sense of the ephemeral whose simplicity distinguished it from mere candid photography, and even spoke of a style, one dictated by each situation rather than by rules of composition. Man invoked a "new conception"[87] of photojournalism definable by its transparency: transparency of a method whose prime mover deliberately effaces himself, and transparency of an aesthetic that automatically ensures inner consistency of photographic output (see Figure 2.20).

This concern with transparency was a major argument in the rhetoric of photojournalistic self-legitimation, with images being described as "mirrors" reflecting current events or, to quote Nadar, windows that allow the reader to become the "spectator, as if he were actually present."[88] The difference now was that this conception of things was contributing to the definition of the nascent profession of photojournalist. In his analysis of the "books written by professionals for photojournalists" that appeared in the 1930s and in considerably greater numbers after the Second World War, Vincent Lavoie highlights the emphasis on content at the expense of aesthetics; formal mediocrity was even seen as an asset in informational terms.[89] In this context of professionalization the interest of images depended above all on a narrative power to be served by form and layout. And while Pierre Lafitte in 1909 and Kurt Korff in 1927 had both made reference to the moving image in justifying the use of photographic illustrations in their magazines, in the intervening period, as film historian André Gaudreault makes clear, the cinema had abandoned the fondness for experimentation of its early years, and moved into the era of the narrative.[90]

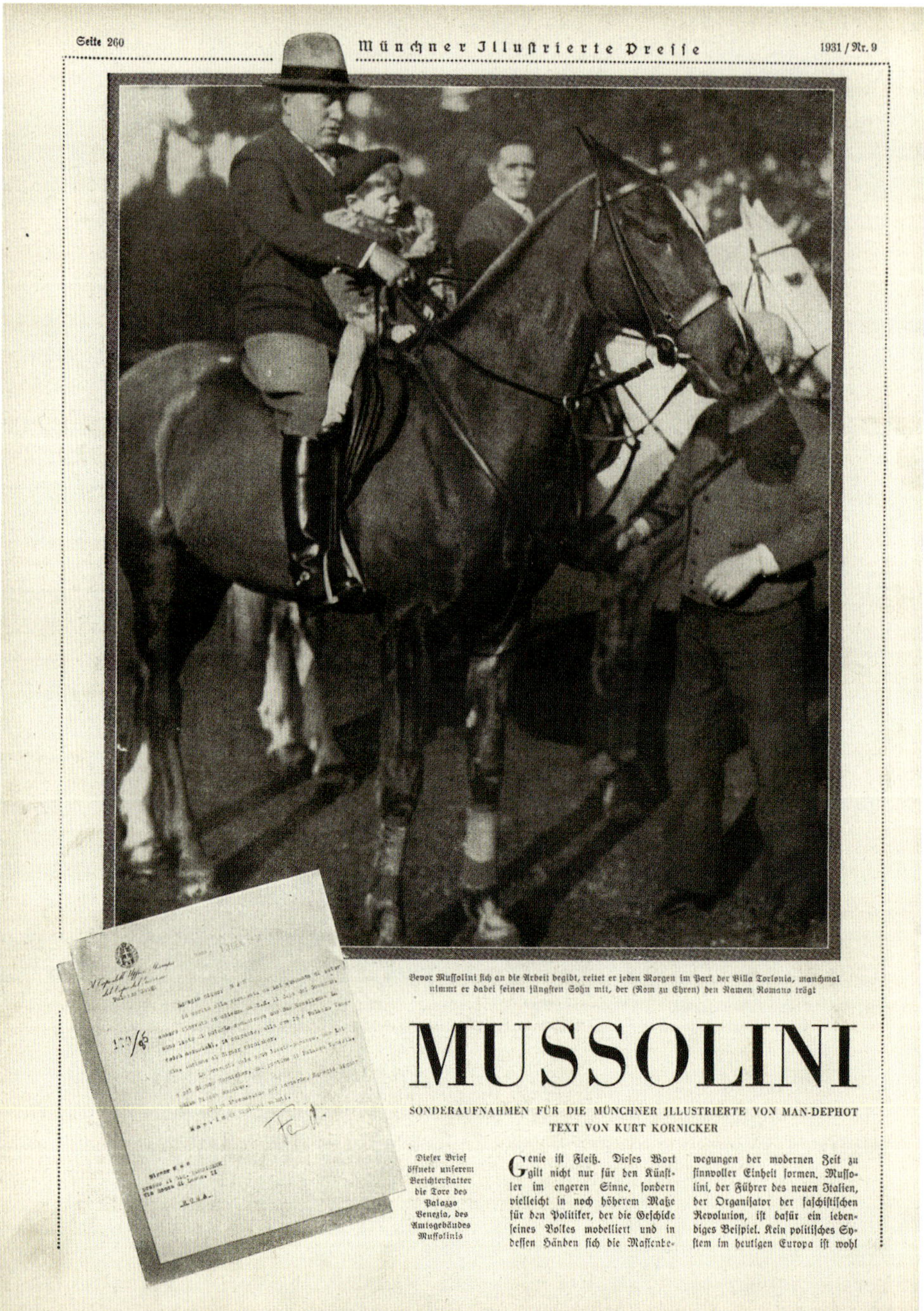

Seite 260 Münchner Illustrierte Presse 1931 / Nr. 9

Bevor Mussolini sich an die Arbeit begibt, reitet er jeden Morgen im Park der Villa Torlonia, manchmal nimmt er dabei seinen jüngsten Sohn mit, der (Rom zu Ehren) den Namen Romano trägt

MUSSOLINI

SONDERAUFNAHMEN FÜR DIE MÜNCHNER JLLUSTRIERTE VON MAN-DEPHOT
TEXT VON KURT KORNICKER

Dieser Brief öffnete unserem Berichterstatter die Tore des Palazzo Venezia, des Amtsgebäudes Mussolinis

Genie ist Fleiß. Dieses Wort gilt nicht nur für den Künstler im engeren Sinne, sondern vielleicht in noch höherem Maße für den Politiker, der die Geschicke seines Volkes modelliert und in dessen Händen sich die Massenbewegungen der modernen Zeit zu sinnvoller Einheit formen. Mussolini, der Führer des neuen Italien, der Organisator der faschistischen Revolution, ist dafür ein lebendiges Beispiel. Kein politisches System im heutigen Europa ist wohl

Figure 2.19a *Münchner Illustrierte Presse*, March 1, 1931, pp. 260–1. Photographs by Felix H. Man (Dephot).

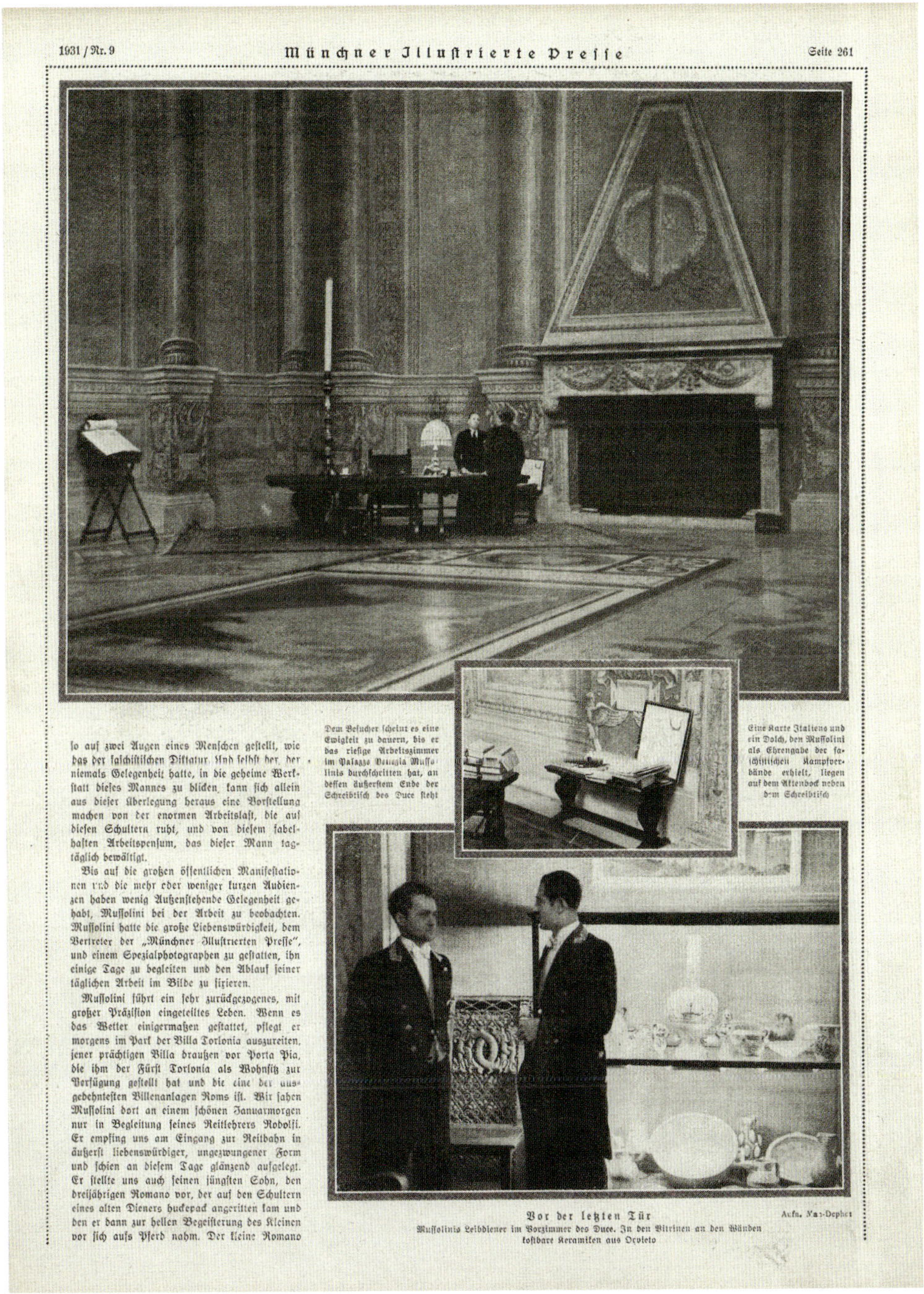

1931 / Nr. 9 **Münchner Illustrierte Presse** Seite 261

so auf zwei Augen eines Menschen gestellt, wie das der faschistischen Diktatur. Und selbst der, der niemals Gelegenheit hatte, in die geheime Werkstatt dieses Mannes zu blicken, kann sich allein aus dieser Überlegung heraus eine Vorstellung machen von der enormen Arbeitslast, die auf diesen Schultern ruht, und von diesem fabelhaften Arbeitspensum, das dieser Mann tagtäglich bewältigt.

Bis auf die großen öffentlichen Manifestationen und die mehr oder weniger kurzen Audienzen haben wenig Außenstehende Gelegenheit gehabt, Mussolini bei der Arbeit zu beobachten. Mussolini hatte die große Liebenswürdigkeit, dem Vertreter der „Münchner Illustrierten Presse", und einem Spezialphotographen zu gestatten, ihn einige Tage zu begleiten und den Ablauf seiner täglichen Arbeit im Bilde zu fixieren.

Mussolini führt ein sehr zurückgezogenes, mit großer Präzision eingeteiltes Leben. Wenn es das Wetter einigermaßen gestattet, pflegt er morgens im Park der Villa Torlonia auszureiten, jener prächtigen Villa draußen vor Porta Pia, die ihm der Fürst Torlonia als Wohnsitz zur Verfügung gestellt hat und die eine der ausgedehntesten Villenanlagen Roms ist. Wir sahen Mussolini dort an einem schönen Januarmorgen nur in Begleitung seines Reitlehrers Rodolfi. Er empfing uns am Eingang zur Reitbahn in äußerst liebenswürdiger, ungezwungener Form und schien an diesem Tage glänzend aufgelegt. Er stellte uns auch seinen jüngsten Sohn, den dreijährigen Romano vor, der auf den Schultern eines alten Dieners huckepack angeritten kam und den er dann zur hellen Begeisterung des Kleinen vor sich aufs Pferd nahm. Der kleine Romano

Dem Besucher scheint es eine Ewigkeit zu dauern, bis er das riesige Arbeitszimmer im Palazzo Venezia Mussolinis durchschritten hat, an dessen äußerstem Ende der Schreibtisch des Duce steht

Eine Karte Italiens und ein Dolch, den Mussolini als Ehrengabe der faschistischen Kampfverbände erhielt, liegen auf dem Aktenbock neben dem Schreibtisch

Vor der letzten Tür

Mussolinis Leibdiener im Vorzimmer des Duce. In den Vitrinen an den Wänden kostbare Keramiken aus Orvieto

Aufn. Max-Dephot

Figure 2.19b

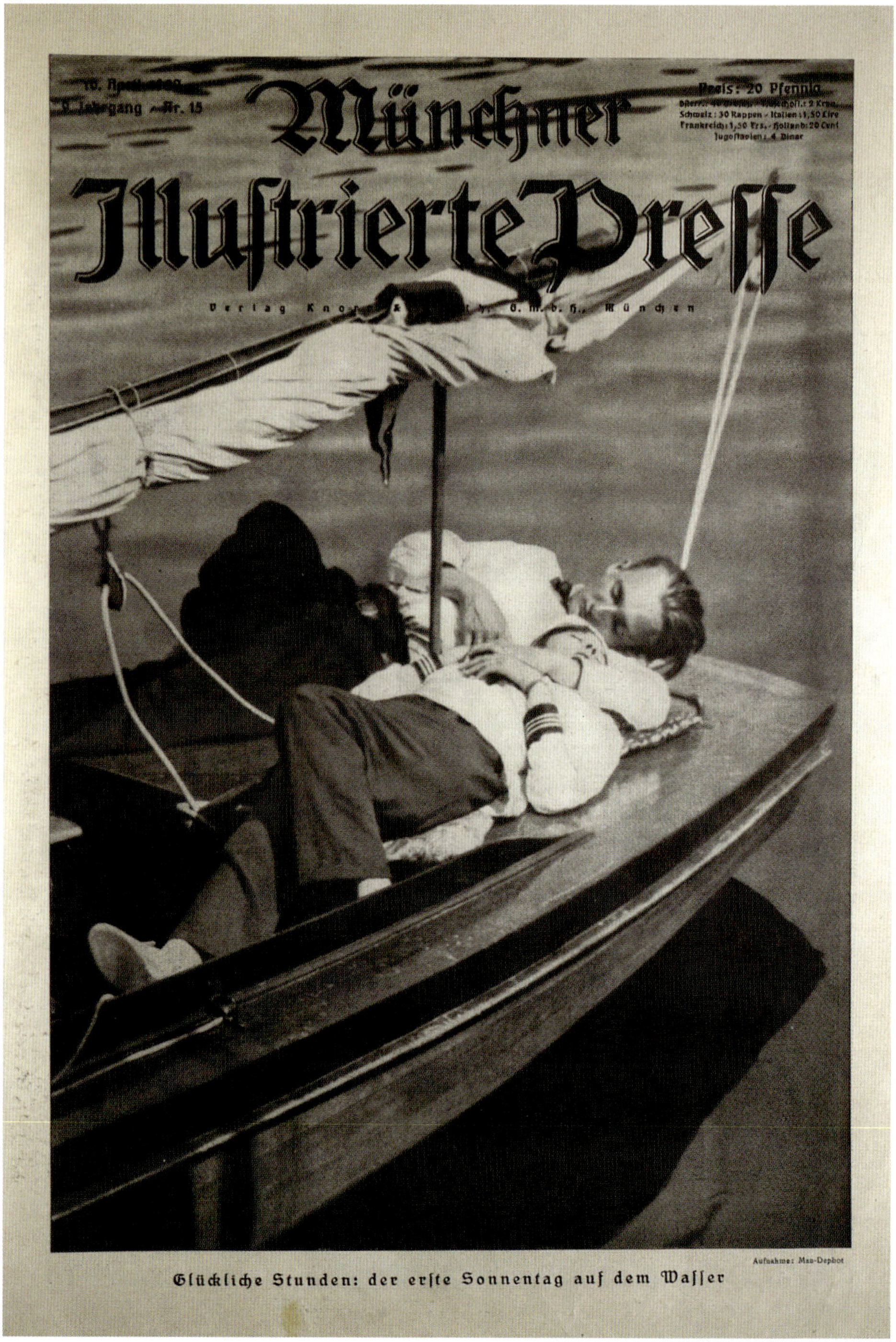

Figure 2.20 *Münchner Illustrierte Presse*, April 10, 1932, cover. Photograph by Felix H. Man (Dephot).

By the beginning of the 1930s, in the press as in the cinema, mass production was defining the terms and conditions of visual representation.

VU: a photographic workshop

In his introductory to the first issue of *VU: illustré de la semaine*, dated March 21, 1928, Lucien Vogel (1886–1954) also made reference to the cinema: "Lively as a wonderful film, *VU* will be eagerly awaited every week by all its readers."[91] And even before the launch of the weekly, the Pathé film *Un grand journal illustré moderne* (A Great, Modern Illustrated Magazine) was made by Edmond Gréville and screened with the newsreels.[92] *VU* was not named as the film's subject but the logo designed by the celebrated graphic artist Cassandre and the image of Lucien Vogel at his work table were readily identifiable. After the title came a panel: "The hectic life of today prevents us from reading . . ."; this was followed by two tilted cityscapes and a further panel declaring, "Seeing is what counts; we are in the century of the image."[93] Reminiscent of Kurt Korff's 1927 announcements of the aims of *Berliner Illustrirte Zeitung*[94]—and those of Moholy-Nagy—these declarations are the linchpins of the article laying down the new magazine's program: in order to give expression to "the frantic rhythm of present-day life . . . *VU* is offering a new formula: the illustrated reporting of world news."[95] In addition to the sense of shared urgency only photography can communicate, Korff and Vogel brought an attentiveness to the new generation of photographers and the artistic role of the medium. Their aims, however, were radically different: *VU*'s rotogravure images were dispersed over the whole of an issue varying from twenty to thirty-two pages, the result being a more uncluttered exercise in quality printing.

Like the Germans illustrateds, *VU* published an episode from a serialized novel each week; but by according it only two pages (including a photograph) it avoided the characteristic grey area of the German periodicals. *VU* means "seen" in French, and sections titled "VU this week," "VU in the world," and sometimes "VU in France" or "VU in Europe" brought together different kinds of images, mostly from agencies. From its inception *VU* had recourse to French agencies founded before the War, like Rol, Trampus and Henri Manuel, but the editors also enjoyed special relationships with the international agencies that had just opened in Paris: fresh from its successes in London and Berlin, Keystone set up at 25 Rue Royale in 1927, and Wide World, a subsidiary of the *New York Times*, moved into offices on Rue de la Paix the same year.[96] The "VU in . . ." sections took the form of independent—but not standardized—pages at the beginning and end of the issue and provided a weekly visual version of the news with images interrelated via superposition and detailed captions as the only text. The last page

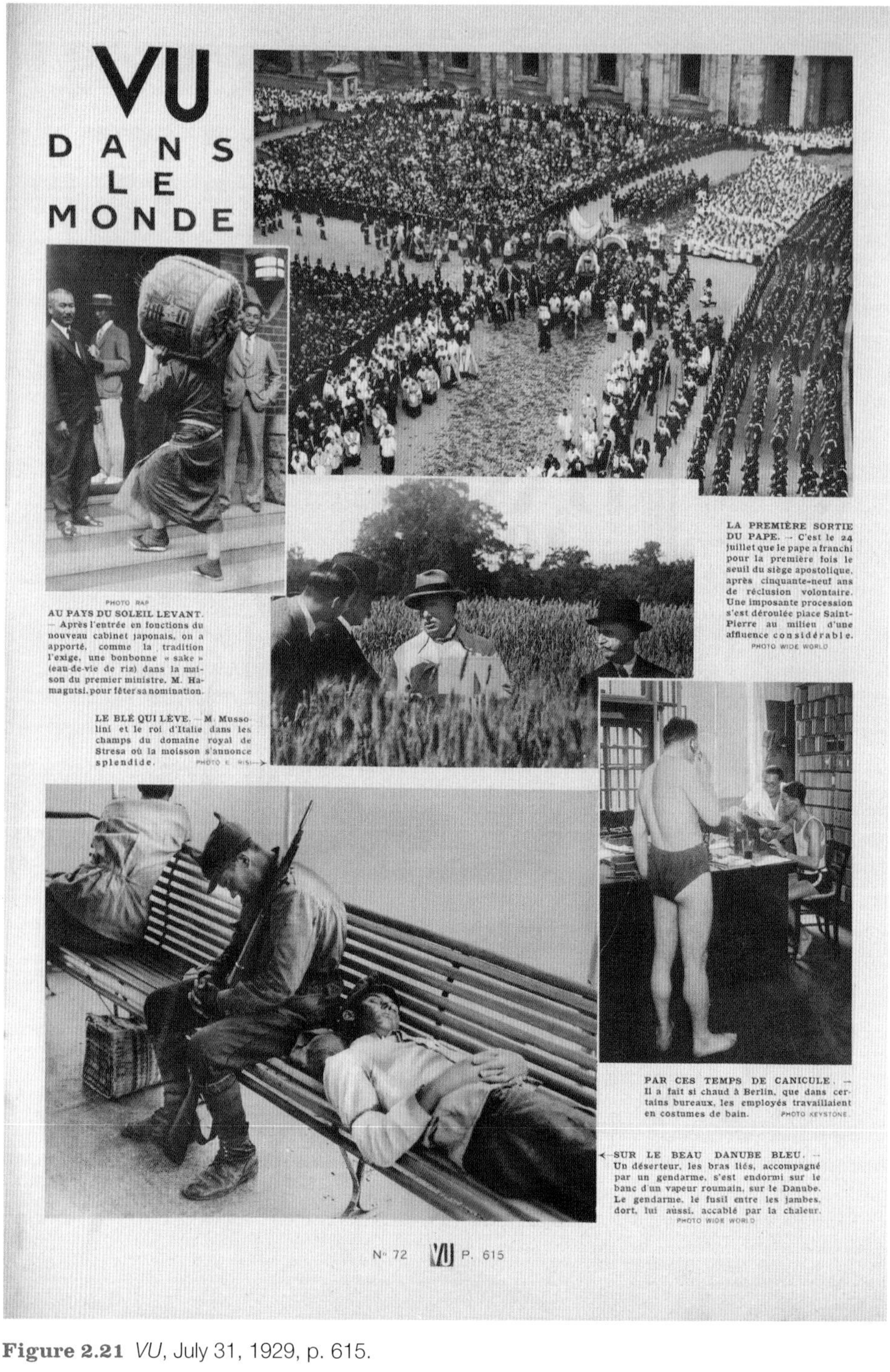

VU DANS LE MONDE

PHOTO RAP

AU PAYS DU SOLEIL LEVANT. — Après l'entrée en fonctions du nouveau cabinet japonais, on a apporté, comme la tradition l'exige, une bonbonne « sake » (eau-de-vie de riz) dans la maison du premier ministre, M. Hamagutsi, pour fêter sa nomination.

LE BLÉ QUI LÈVE. — M. Mussolini et le roi d'Italie dans les champs du domaine royal de Stresa où la moisson s'annonce splendide. PHOTO E. RISI →

LA PREMIÈRE SORTIE DU PAPE. — C'est le 24 juillet que le pape a franchi pour la première fois le seuil du siège apostolique, après cinquante-neuf ans de réclusion volontaire. Une imposante procession s'est déroulée place Saint-Pierre au milieu d'une affluence considérable. PHOTO WIDE WORLD

PAR CES TEMPS DE CANICULE. — Il a fait si chaud à Berlin, que dans certains bureaux, les employés travaillaient en costumes de bain. PHOTO KEYSTONE.

← **SUR LE BEAU DANUBE BLEU.** — Un déserteur, les bras liés, accompagné par un gendarme, s'est endormi sur le banc d'un vapeur roumain, sur le Danube. Le gendarme, le fusil entre les jambes, dort, lui aussi, accablé par la chaleur. PHOTO WIDE WORLD

N° 72 VU P. 615

Figure 2.21 *VU*, July 31, 1929, p. 615.

of the issue of July 31, 1929, for instance, used five photographs credited Wide World (2), Keystone (1), Rap (1) and E. Risi (1)[97] to cover the investiture of the Japanese prime minister, Mussolini's meeting with the King of Italy, Pope Pius XI's first appearance on Saint Peter's Square, and the heatwave in Germany and Romania (see Figure 2.21). The eclecticism of the subjects is underscored by a highly anecdotal choice of images including the delivery of a demijohn of saké to the prime minister's office and German office staff working in swimsuits.

Recently carried out by the Musée Nicéphore Niépce, the colossal task of indexing all the photographs published in *VU* gives an insight into the role of the agencies in supplying material for the magazine.[98] Of the French agencies, Manuel was the major contributor, with over 620 photographs illustrating 371 different articles. The figures for Associated Press were 720 photographs for 488 articles, but it is the statistics for Keystone and Wide World that confirm the superior performance of the American agencies, already pointed out by the historian Françoise Denoyelle in her study of the uses of photograph in the interwar years:[99] Keystone contributed some 2,190 images to 1,308 articles, while the figures for Wide World were over 2,850 pictures for 1,435 articles. As Carlo Rim, who became *VU*'s editor in chief in March–April 1930, explained two years later, "Every day, from morning to night, people come to the office . . . lugging briefcases stuffed with more or less successful photographs . . . They're bringing us our raw material. Our editorial and photolab staff know how to get the most out of their stories and pictures."[100] Together with the dispatches that came in, this material enabled the editors to come up with the content of an issue meeting the criteria listed by journalist Jacques Berr in his 1929 article "Comment on fait *VU*" (How *VU* Is Made): "timeliness, significance of the subject, novelty, picturesqueness, originality." "Then" Berr continues, "the search for material begins. Either photojournalists take new pictures or, on the contrary, you just consult the specialist agencies and their mass of stuff from all over the world."[101] According to the statistics collected by historian Danielle Leenaerts, the agencies and anonymous photographers supplied from 58 percent to 93 percent of the images published in individual issues of *VU* between 1928 and 1940.[102] The rest came from a list of freelancers that includes Berenice Abbott (6 photos), Cecil Beaton (1), Margaret Bourke-White (4), Robert Capa (35), Henri Cartier-Bresson (10), Florence Henri (1), Man Ray (45), Martin Munkácsi (13), Roger Parry (7), Albert Renger-Patzsch (12), Edward Steichen (2)—to name but a few—and speaks volumes about international connections and editorial interest in young artistic photographers. There was also an inner circle of photographers who published regularly and in quantity, among them Brassaï (94 photos), Eli Lotar (132), Germaine Krull (283), André Kertész (442), Roger Schall (620), and—by far the largest individual contribution of all—Gaston Paris (1,290). Nor should we forget the magazine's director, Lucien Vogel, who personally provided over 700 pictures.

VU's editors called on these photographers to improve their documentation or for specific assignments such as Kertész's portrait of the Cistercian monks of Soligny Abbey: four pages including additional photography by Eli Lotar and Piermay.[103] Michel Frizot and Annie-Laure Wanaverbecq have identified thirty-six "photographic essays" by Kertész in *VU*, as well as numerous "illustrations."[104] According to the index compiled by the Musée Nicéphore Niépce, Kertész contributed in all to 147 articles, of which only a quarter included five or more photographs. Such famous series as those on the cost of living (1932) and Paris's Latin Quarter (1933)[105] were rounded out by the editors with illustrations and agency photographs,[106] while Kertész's eighteen artistically less distinguished photographs for the article "La Journée des enfants" (Children's Day) were published unaccompanied by other images and represent his largest single series for *VU*.[107]

The situation was similar for the magazine's other photographers, who supplied illustrative material as well as series. Twenty-six photographs by Germaine Krull appeared in four issues as illustrations for Emmanuel Berl's long article "Les Ouvrières de Paris" (Working Women of Paris, see Figures 2.22 and 2.23). The first part comprises exclusively images by Krull; other photographers were then called in and ultimately supplied almost all of the pictures for the following segments.[108] Thus these illustrated articles sometimes drew on a reportage by a specific photographer, but the final choice of images always fell to the *VU* editors, who decided on the layout and added to the visual narrative when necessary.

These photographic series were given two, three, or four pages, but rarely more. Florent Fels's "Les Mystères de la foire aux puces" (Mysteries of the Flea Market) was published in the issue of June 6, 1928 with seven photographs by Germaine Krull: snapshots of sellers and buyers amid the mishmash of objects that make the Porte de Clignancourt market such a delight.[109] With their varied formats set edge to edge and sometimes overlapping, the images form a sequence, but do not so much tell a story as communicate an atmosphere. Jean Gallotti's article on glassblowers is spread over three pages, with six photographs by Kertész.[110] The text begins on a double page, with four photographs taken in the workshop capturing the sureness and precision of the workers whose traditional métier is described by the writer. Although he had bought a Leica in 1925, Kertész liked working with a 9 x 12 cm plate camera, whose sensitivity he could control better and which offered the clarity of detail he wanted.[111] The tonal variety and exactness of framing of the pictures of the glassblowers bespeak an attention to image quality that was further highlighted by large-format reproduction and sobriety of layout.

For its conveying of Mussolini's busy schedule *VU* went to the Trampus and Keystone agencies, which came up with six photographs of the Duce and his daughter. The text and the images were laid out symmetrically, stressing—not without a touch of irony—"the method and orderliness" the dictator boasted of in his handling of the six ministries he had

Les Ouvrières de Paris

par Emmanuel Berl

I

REPORTAGE
PHOTOGRAPHIQUE
GERMAINE KRULL

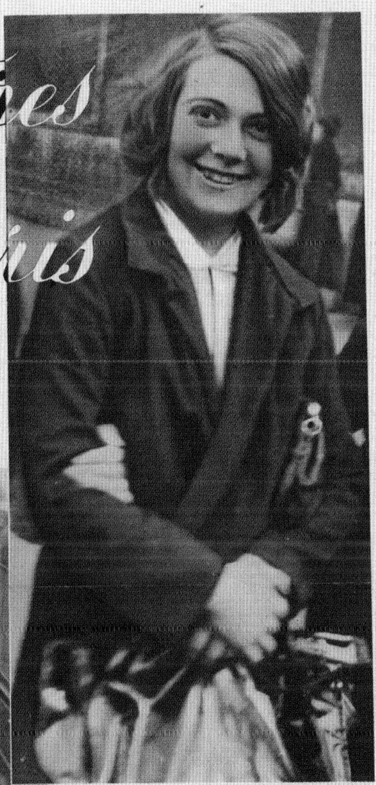

Celle-là aime l'usine.

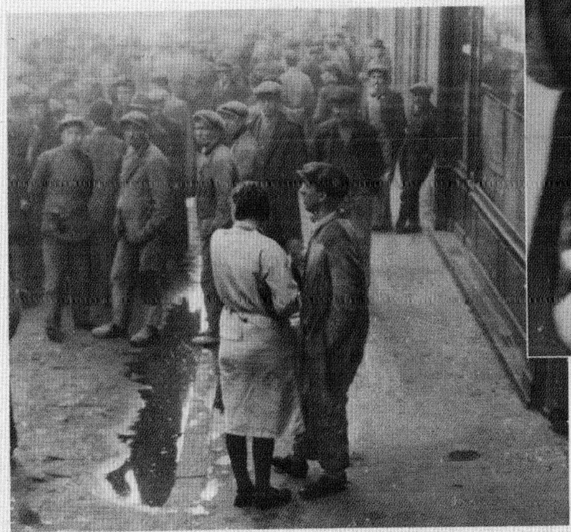

La rue est soumise au rythme des heures.

PHOTO BRODSKY

Il faut voir à la ceinture de Paris, dans ces quartiers neufs tellement anonymes qu'ils se situent plutôt dans le temps que dans l'espace, ces milliers de femmes sans âge, presque sans sexe, dont les corps n'expriment plus rien que le travail accumulé. Certaines avenues de Grenelle, de Javel pourraient aussi bien être dans la banlieue de Lyon ou de Liége qu'auprès de la Tour Eiffel dont la pointe apparaît soudain au bout d'une rue pour vous avertir que vous êtes à Paris, quand même. Qu'ont à faire avec lui ces faites bas qui arrêtent l'élan toujours repris des murs de brique ? Quartiers abstraits. Les mouvements démographiques, les variations des tarifs et des changes modifient jusqu'à la couleur des peaux des hommes, des femmes qui se promènent là comme des passagers sur le pont d'un navire. Comme les ponts des navires, ces rues sont soumises rigoureusement au rythme des heures. De huit heures à midi, elles sont vides. A treize heures, elles sont pleines de châles tricotés. A treize heures trente, elles sont de nouveau vides. A dix-huit heures, elles grouillent de nouveau, joie de la journée finie. Suprématie du temps sur le lieu, caractère principal du monde moderne où le mot : contemporain fait sonner la fraternité la plus effective. Les jeunes sont là, indifférentiées dans leur solitude, en attendant la solitude de la chaine.

Une ouvrière avec son homme. Il la mène gentiment jusqu'au bout de la ruelle. Ils restent un moment à côté l'un de l'autre. Ils ne parlent pas. Puis un baiser assez long. L'homme s'en va. Il doit travailler plus loin, entrer par une autre porte dans un autre atelier. Autour d'eux, je perçois le silence de cette foule. Je ne l'avais pas remarqué.

Maintenant, les ouvrières montent les marches. Le soleil disparaît derrière le mur de droite. Il n'éclaire la rue qu'une heure par jour. Ce mur est celui d'une petite fabrique. Il a des fenêtres. Aux fenêtres, des ouvrières qui sourient. L'ombre gagne. La lourde porte de fer, en haut de l'escalier, qui était ouverte, se referme. Une sirène sonne. Les ouvrières quittent les fenêtres. Il n'y a plus rien.

⁂

L'usine d'isolants. Les femmes travaillent huit heures de suite à couler dans des moules une matière brûlante. Il faut faire bien attention : à chaque moule cassé, une semaine de mise à pied ; à chaque éclaboussure, une plaie douloureuse et mauvaise. Quelques centaines de femms, leur canette de bière à côté d'elles. Quand elles ont trop chaud, elles boivent une gorgée de cette bière tiédie, puis reprennent la coulée dangereuse. Sept sur dix ont le bras abimé. Je les interroge. Elles ne répondent guère. Fermées sur leurs existences dures et pareilles : les heures de travail, le déjeuner à la cantine, le dîner qu'on n'a pas le courage de cuire, auquel on substitue chaque soir, par lassitude, le Kub, le Viandox délayé, la charcuterie qu'on achète en passant. L'enfant qu'on met en garde quand on part pour l'usine, qu'on lave, qu'on endort, le ménage, la lessive qu'il faut faire, l'homme aussi

N° 247 VU P. 1925

Figure 2.22 *VU*, December 7, 1932, p. 1925. Photographs by Germaine Krull.

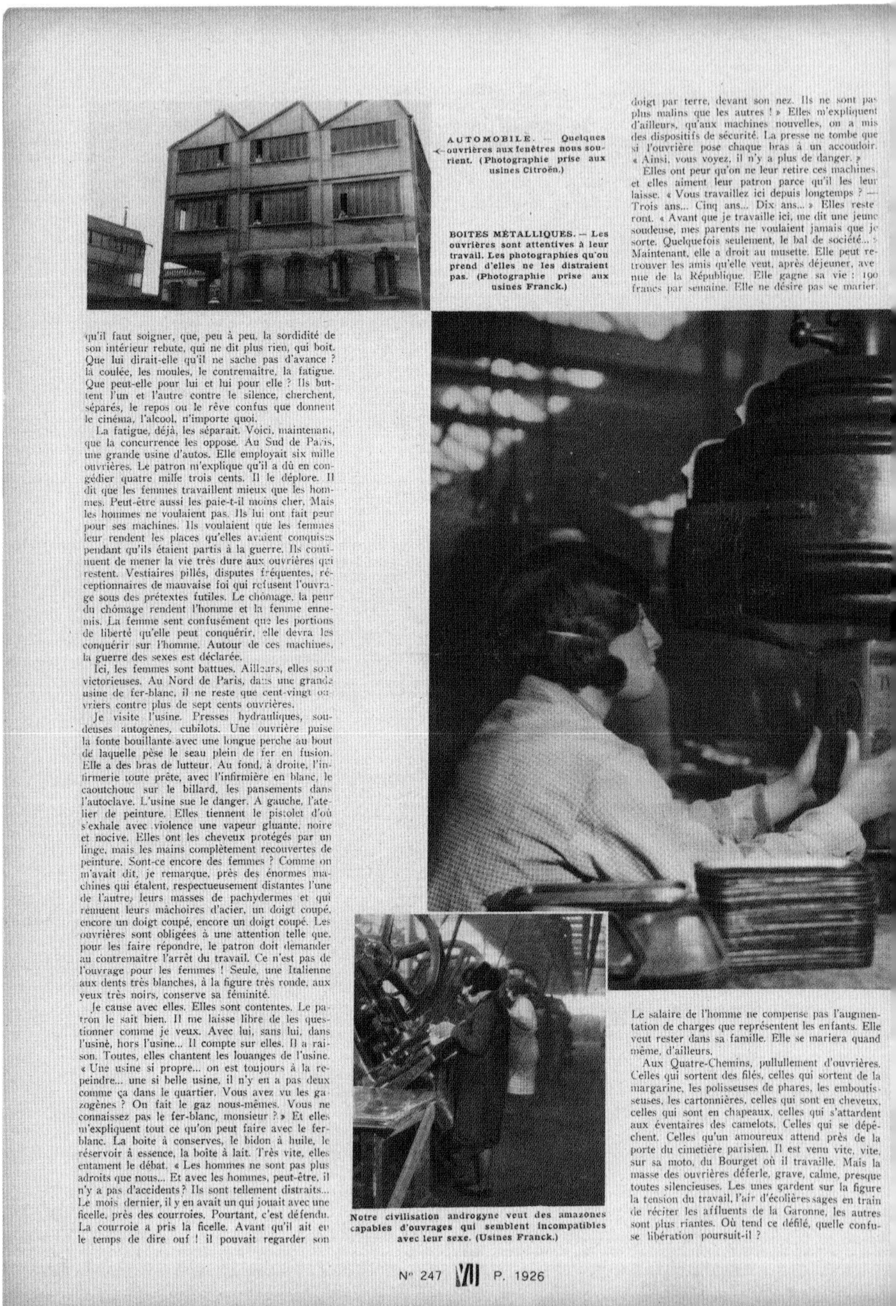

AUTOMOBILE. — Quelques ouvrières aux fenêtres nous sourient. (Photographie prise aux usines Citroën.)

BOITES MÉTALLIQUES. — Les ouvrières sont attentives à leur travail. Les photographies qu'on prend d'elles ne les distraient pas. (Photographie prise aux usines Franck.)

qu'il faut soigner, que, peu à peu, la sordidité de son intérieur rebute, qui ne dit plus rien, qui boit. Que lui dirait-elle qu'il ne sache pas d'avance ? la coulée, les moules, le contremaître, la fatigue. Que peut-elle pour lui et lui pour elle ? Ils buttent l'un et l'autre contre le silence, cherchent, séparés, le repos ou le rêve confus que donnent le cinéma, l'alcool, n'importe quoi.

La fatigue, déjà, les séparait. Voici, maintenant, que la concurrence les oppose. Au Sud de Paris, une grande usine d'autos. Elle employait six mille ouvrières. Le patron m'explique qu'il a dû en congédier quatre mille trois cents. Il le déplore. Il dit que les femmes travaillent mieux que les hommes. Peut-être aussi les paie-t-il moins cher. Mais les hommes ne voulaient pas. Ils lui ont fait peur pour ses machines. Ils voulaient que les femmes leur rendent les places qu'elles avaient conquises pendant qu'ils étaient partis à la guerre. Ils continuent de mener la vie très dure aux ouvrières qui restent. Vestiaires pillés, disputes fréquentes, réceptionnaires de mauvaise foi qui refusent l'ouvrage sous des prétextes futiles. Le chômage, la peur du chômage rendent l'homme et la femme ennemis. La femme sent confusément que les portions de liberté qu'elle peut conquérir, elle devra les conquérir sur l'homme. Autour de ces machines, la guerre des sexes est déclarée.

Ici, les femmes sont battues. Ailleurs, elles sont victorieuses. Au Nord de Paris, dans une grande usine de fer-blanc, il ne reste que cent-vingt ouvriers contre plus de sept cents ouvrières.

Je visite l'usine. Presses hydrauliques, soudeuses autogènes, cubilots. Une ouvrière puise la fonte bouillante avec une longue perche au bout de laquelle pèse le seau plein de fer en fusion. Elle a des bras de lutteur. Au fond, à droite, l'infirmerie toute prête, avec l'infirmière en blanc, le caoutchouc sur le billard, les pansements dans l'autoclave. L'usine sue le danger. A gauche, l'atelier de peinture. Elles tiennent le pistolet d'où s'exhale avec violence une vapeur gluante, noire et nocive. Elles ont les cheveux protégés par un linge, mais les mains complètement recouvertes de peinture. Sont-ce encore des femmes ? Comme on m'avait dit, je remarque, près des énormes machines qui étalent, respectueusement distantes l'une de l'autre, leurs masses de pachydermes et qui remuent leurs mâchoires d'acier, un doigt coupé, encore un doigt coupé, encore un doigt coupé. Les ouvrières sont obligées à une attention telle que, pour les faire répondre, le patron doit demander au contremaître l'arrêt du travail. Ce n'est pas de l'ouvrage pour les femmes ! Seule, une Italienne aux dents très blanches, à la figure très ronde, aux yeux très noirs, conserve sa féminité.

Je cause avec elles. Elles sont contentes. Le patron le sait bien. Il me laisse libre de les questionner comme je veux. Avec lui, sans lui, dans l'usine, hors l'usine... Il compte sur elles. Il a raison. Toutes, elles chantent les louanges de l'usine. « Une usine si propre... on est toujours à la repeindre... une si belle usine, il n'y en a pas deux comme ça dans le quartier. Vous avez vu les gazogènes ? On fait le gaz nous-mêmes. Vous ne connaissez pas le fer-blanc, monsieur ? » Et elles m'expliquent tout ce qu'on peut faire avec le fer-blanc. La boite à conserves, le bidon à huile, le réservoir à essence, la boîte à lait. Très vite, elles entament le débat. « Les hommes ne sont pas plus adroits que nous... Et avec les hommes, peut-être, il n'y a pas d'accidents ? Ils sont tellement distraits... Le mois dernier, il y en avait un qui jouait avec une ficelle, près des courroies. Pourtant, c'est défendu. La courroie a pris la ficelle. Avant qu'il ait eu le temps de dire ouf ! il pouvait regarder son doigt par terre, devant son nez. Ils ne sont pas plus malins que les autres ! » Elles m'expliquent d'ailleurs, qu'aux machines nouvelles, on a mis des dispositifs de sécurité. La presse ne tombe que si l'ouvrière pose chaque bras à un accoudoir. « Ainsi, vous voyez, il n'y a plus de danger. »

Elles ont peur qu'on ne leur retire ces machines, et elles aiment leur patron parce qu'il les leur laisse. « Vous travaillez ici depuis longtemps ? — Trois ans... Cinq ans... Dix ans... » Elles resteront. « Avant que je travaille ici, me dit une jeune soudeuse, mes parents ne voulaient jamais que je sorte. Quelquefois seulement, le bal de société... » Maintenant, elle a droit au musette. Elle peut retrouver les amis qu'elle veut, après déjeuner, avenue de la République. Elle gagne sa vie : 190 francs par semaine. Elle ne désire pas se marier. Le salaire de l'homme ne compense pas l'augmentation de charges que représentent les enfants. Elle veut rester dans sa famille. Elle se mariera quand même, d'ailleurs.

Aux Quatre-Chemins, pullulement d'ouvrières. Celles qui sortent des filés, celles qui sortent de la margarine, les polisseuses de phares, les emboutisseuses, les cartonnières, celles qui sont en cheveux, celles qui sont en chapeaux, celles qui s'attardent aux éventaires des camelots. Celles qui se dépêchent. Celles qu'un amoureux attend près de la porte du cimetière parisien. Il est venu vite, vite, sur sa moto, du Bourget où il travaille. Mais la masse des ouvrières déferle, grave, calme, presque toutes silencieuses. Les unes gardent sur la figure la tension du travail, l'air d'écolières sages en train de réciter les affluents de la Garonne, les autres sont plus riantes. Où tend ce défilé, quelle confuse libération poursuit-il ?

Notre civilisation androgyne veut des amazones capables d'ouvrages qui semblent incompatibles avec leur sexe. (Usines Franck.)

N° 247 VU P. 1926

Figure 2.23 *VU*, December 7, 1932, pp. 1926–7. Photographs by Germaine Krull.

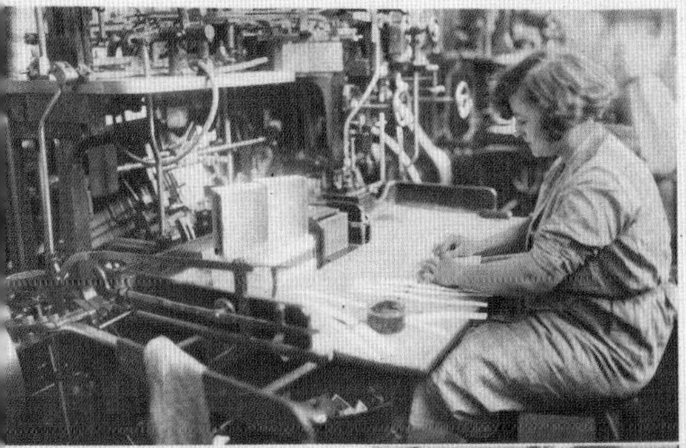

ELOPPES ET PAPIER A LETTRES. — Il y a de grandes nes toutes neuves qui prennent le papier, le plient, nment, le doublent. D'autres, semblables à d'anciennes nes à coudre, fonctionnent grâce à un mouvement édales. (Photographies prises aux usines Blancan.)

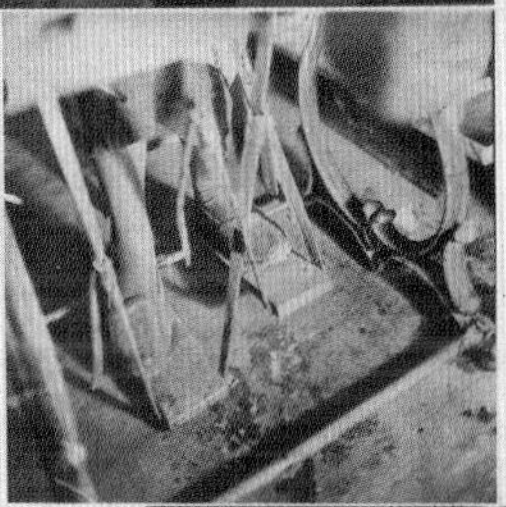

MANUFACTURES

La manufacture d'enveloppes est plus attardée, plus rassurante aussi. Brocheuses et plieuses n'ont pas beaucoup changé depuis Huysmans. L'extrême diversité des modèles s'oppose aux progrès de la rationalisation. Sans doute, je vois de belles machines neuves, qui plient le papier, le gomment, doublent l'enveloppe, la débitent par paquets de cinq cents devant l'ouvrière qui n'a plus qu'à les recueillir. Mais d'autres machines demeurent tout à fait rudimentaires, actionnées par un simple mouvement de pédales. Cela suffit pour les petites commandes.

Même le pliage à la main subsiste. En haut de la salle, sur une espèce de balcon. On y est bien tranquille. On aperçoit l'immense développement de l'usine, la forêt des courroies et soi-même on reste caché. Les ouvrières ne sont pas mieux payées que dans l'industrie lourde. Pourtant, elles sont beaucoup plus élégantes. L'usine exale un parfum de féminité. Avec ses monceaux de papier multicolore, ses tas d'enveloppes bleu clair, rose clair, beige clair, gris clair, ses femmes en blouses blanches, ses bancs propres, derrière lesquels je vois, collées, les photos des vedettes que les plieuses préfèrent : Henri Garat, Douglas junior. C'est du travail pour les femmes, parce que les femmes aiment le papier, les lettres, la poste restante. Elles sont entrées ici pour ne pas enlaidir et gardent leur coquetterie même à l'intérieur de l'usine. Presque toutes ont les cheveux bien arrangés, les lèvres fardées, les visages poudrés. Les dernières modes de Paris sont immédiatement suivies au pliage à la main. « Quand même, il y a ici de belles femmes ! » me dit avec orgueil un contremaître qui m'accompagne. C'est vrai. J'en remarque une qui ressemble à Annabella. Un souffle d'aventure circule. Le pliage à la main, d'ailleurs, a ses légendes : une plieuse est devenue danseuse acrobatique, elle est au Chili ; une autre est devenue actrice, elle joue dans un théâtre près de la rue de la Paix ; une autre a un ami très riche, une belle auto. Elle vient parfois le soir à la porte de l'usine montrer ses bijoux neufs à ses anciennes camarades. La contremaitresse est ici depuis quarante deux ans. Elle connaît la vie. Elle sait les jours où l'atelier bourdonne d'une nouvelle importante : des fiançailles, une grossesse, un accouchement ; où il faut laisser passer le vent ; et, au contraire, ceux où on peut rétablir, avec un peu d'autorité, la discipline : « Dépêchez-vous. Il y a une grosse commande du B. M. » Elle a vu naitre beaucoup de ses ouvrières. Elle a connu leurs mères, assisté à leurs mariages. Mais elle a de la discrétion.

Mais cette sorte d'usines, cette sorte d'ouvrières tendent à être supprimées par le progrès mécanique. Le nombre des machines neuves augmente et celui des plieuses diminue. Jadis, à côté d'elles, dans l'usine de parfumerie, les ouvrières étaient jolies et coquettes, elles aussi. On me les avait beaucoup vantées. J'aurais voulu voir leur usine. Je trouve les portes closes : les administrateurs craignent, parait-il, pour les secrets de fabrication. Je doute que ces secrets soient tellement secrets. Peut-être ne désirent-ils pas qu'on prenne une mesure exacte de la crise qui les frappe. Il me reste, en tout cas, le droit de guetter les sorties. Je suis très déçu. Le concierge m'explique pourquoi : on a réduit le personnel, débauché les plus jeunes : celles qui restent le sont moins. D'autre part, la facilité croissante des transports a métamorphosé en dactylos, en vendeuses, les parfumeuses du temps jadis. Il n'y aura bientôt plus que des ouvrières et des artisanes. La manufacturière aura disparu.

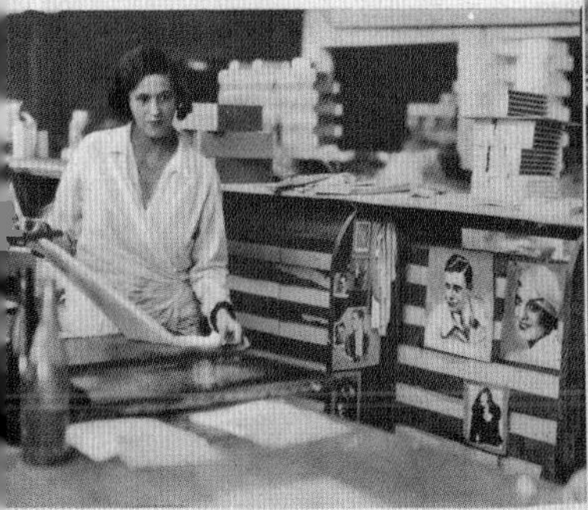

ère leurs bancs, les cartonnières ont collé les photos de leurs acteurs préférés : Ramon Novarro, Henry Garat... (Usines Blancan.)

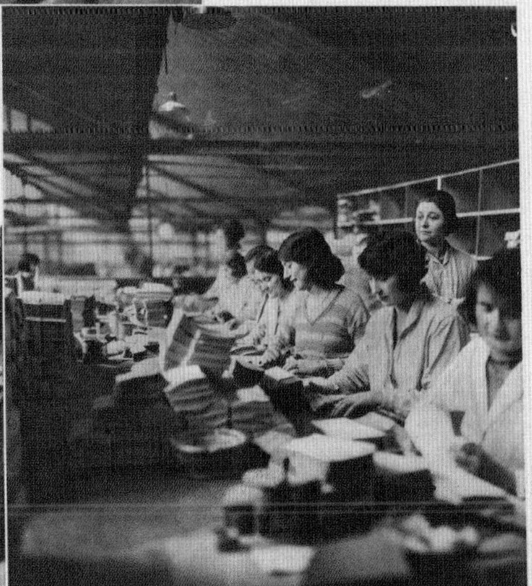

Dans la manufacture d'enveloppes, le pliage à main subsiste. (Usine Blancan.)

N° 247 VU P. 1927

allotted himself.[112] These illustrated articles were freestanding entities, sometimes punctuated by pages of advertising, but above all orchestrated around the double page spread. In the *VU* of the 1920s and 1930s this central space remained a showcase for the creative talents of the art director. This post was held by Irène Lidova, who had Alexander Liberman as one of her assistants from 1933 onwards.[113]

As Michel Frizot and Cédric de Veigy point out, page composition was technically facilitated by the use of rotogravure.[114] Not only did rotogravure give images a tonal richness and satin finish that were beyond the reach of halftone—witness the drabness of Germany's *Berliner Illustrirte Zeitung* and *Münchner Illustrierte Presse* at the same period—it also hinged on the use of transparent films comprising text and images, which the art director assembled on a lighted layout table. Easier to work with than in the lead type/copper plates combination, photographs reproduced on film could be easily masked, associated, and mixed in with typeset or handwritten text. In the article of March 1929 mentioned above, Jacques Berr's enthusiastic description of the main steps in the process was not uninfluenced by the fact that he was plugging the services of the Desfossés-Néogravure printing works, whose owner was one of *VU*'s principal shareholders.[115]

As was also the case at *La Vie au grand air*, the double pages at the center of *VU* were given over to complex graphic compositions. One example was the series of photographs by Brassaï titled "Un homme tombe dans la rue" (A Man Falls in the Street):[116] eight identical format high angle snapshots taken from a window, presented in two groups of four and numbered to relate the brief, tragic story of a man collapsing in the street in Paris. The article, images, typography, and layout all put the accent on the event's ephemerality as underscored by the sequencing of the photographs, and on its character as a parable of city life. Irène Lidova sometimes harnessed the visual impact of a single photograph: a view of La Scala in Milan, for example, with the rising succession of balconies filling the two pages;[117] but her principal aim was to play on photographic styles and varied, unexpected typographical effects in compositions marrying form and content. Photographs of parachutists, tennis players, skaters and numerous other sportspeople were silhouetted and subtly associated in layouts accompanied by brief texts. Apart from the compositional flexibility exemplified by these layouts, her typographical effects marked a real difference between the double page spreads in *VU* and those of Lucien Faure in *La Vie au grand air* during the Belle Époque. Sometimes the headings were handwritten, the better to follow the line of a masking; sometimes they cut free of the horizontal to accentuate the oblique movement of skiers on a slope or to align themselves with the sights of a hunter's gun.[118] These pages are also notable for their use of full-bleed reproduction, as in Schall's photographs from the shipyards at Saint Nazaire during the building of the liner *Normandy*. (see Figure 2.23).[119] In three cases the edge of the page forms the edge of the photograph, underscoring the marriage of "elegance and strength" in the constructing of a ship too huge to be contained within the page.

Most *VU* covers feature a striking image overlaid with the title at the top and, at the bottom, a brown streamer bearing the basic information about the issue and the caption for the image.[120] The magazine also published numerous montages, some of them the work of Alexander Liberman, who went on to become a mainstay at Condé Nast in the United States. Liberman took full advantage of the flexible montage allowed by rotogravure and delighted in introducing an element of strangeness into his compositions. The strategy behind the structuring of the covers of the issue of February 21, 1934, devoted to "La Voix de la province" (A Word from the Provinces), and the special number dated March 3, 1934, devoted to colonialism, is identical. a color for the background, an evocative title that enables the decoding of the montage, and most importantly, contrasts of scale. On the first cover two weather-beaten peasants in working clothes are leaning on a table whose surface is an aerial view of the French capital (see Figure 2.25); while the second shows a barechested colored man carrying on his head a dish out of which are rising skyscrapers and factory chimneys.[121]

Narrating the news

In 1928 the press wing of the French publishing house Gallimard launched the magazine *Détective*, following up with *Voilà* in 1931 and *Marianne* in 1932. *Voilà* was described as "the illustrated news reporting weekly" whose "contributors . . . famous names in journalism and literature, will cover the local scene as well as world events and thus open up hitherto unexplored reporting territory . . . All the reports in *Voilà* will be accompanied by photographs, visual material offering the image in all its variety and dynamism. No text without image, no image without text."[122] *Voilà* used a larger format than *VU*, but it too was printed in rotogravure and each page had its photographs. The first issues were overseen by Joseph Kessel, until then in charge of *Détective*,[123] with layout by Pierre Laguarrigue.[124] During the magazine's first year the photographs went uncredited; often small, they were adapted to the column width of the "Voici" and "Reportages indiscrets" segments, and were sometimes assembled as photomontages. The use of photographs on the cover—in one instance an image of Hitler giving the Nazi salute overlaid on an aerial view of Paris—occasionally resembled that of the Communist magazine *Regards*, but mostly settled for a selection of masked, eye-catchingly arranged pictures signaling the content. Sometimes the effect was overtly seductive—rare indeed were the issues without an article illustrated with unclad female bodies.[125]

While an article like Léo Larguier's "La Cour des miracles"—a portrait of a rundown part of central Paris—provides credits for Alfred Eisenstaedt's street photographs in a layout reflecting the author's "stroll" through the area,[126] most of the images are part of

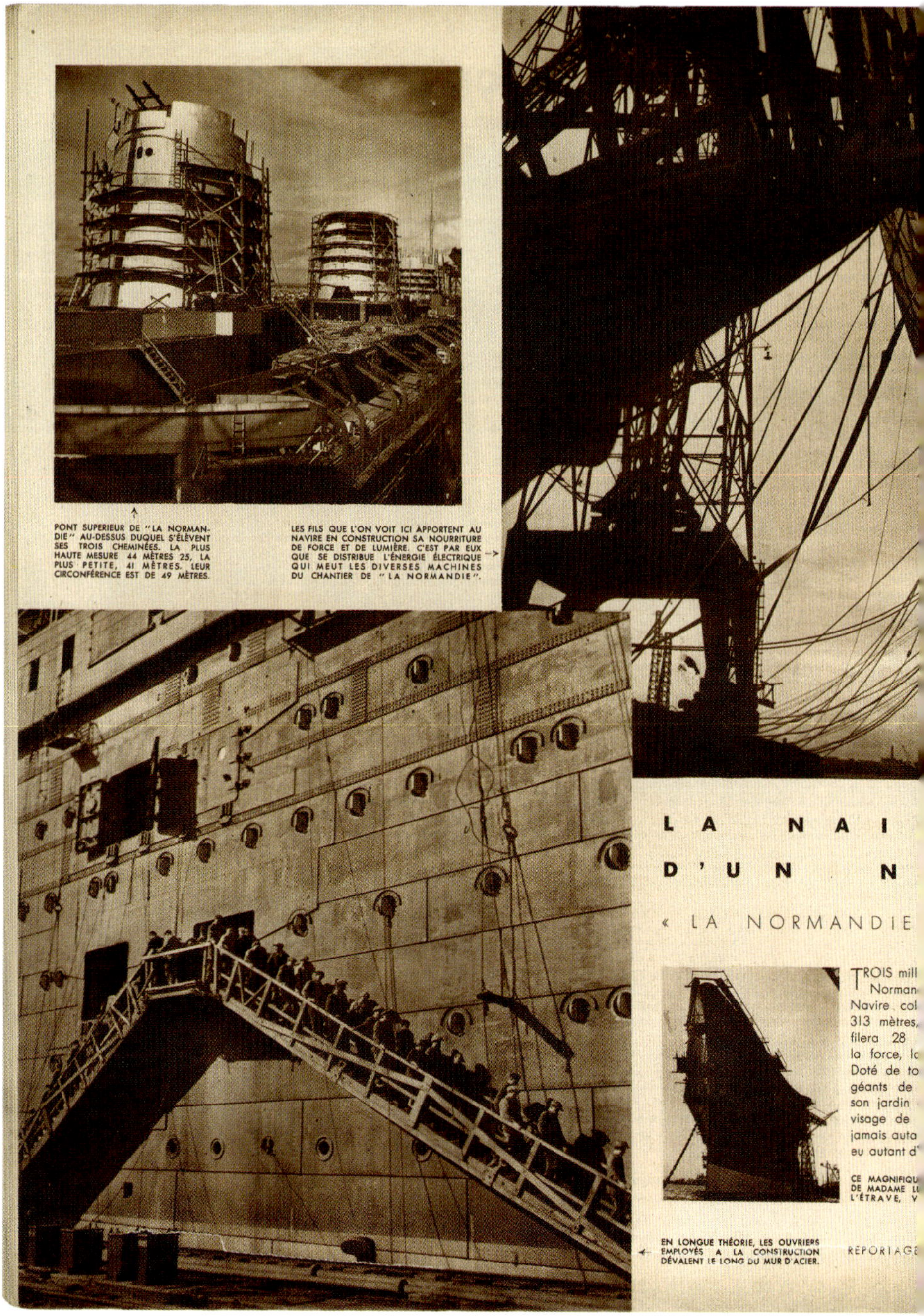
PONT SUPERIEUR DE "LA NORMANDIE" AU-DESSUS DUQUEL S'ÉLÈVENT SES TROIS CHEMINÉES. LA PLUS HAUTE MESURE 44 MÈTRES 25, LA PLUS PETITE, 41 MÈTRES. LEUR CIRCONFÉRENCE EST DE 49 MÈTRES.

LES FILS QUE L'ON VOIT ICI APPORTENT AU NAVIRE EN CONSTRUCTION SA NOURRITURE DE FORCE ET DE LUMIÈRE. C'EST PAR EUX QUE SE DISTRIBUE L'ÉNERGIE ÉLECTRIQUE QUI MEUT LES DIVERSES MACHINES DU CHANTIER DE "LA NORMANDIE". →

LA NAI
D'UN N
« LA NORMANDIE

TROIS mill
Norman
Navire col
313 mètres,
filera 28
la force, lo
Doté de to
géants de
son jardin
visage de
jamais auta
eu autant d'

CE MAGNIFIQU
DE MADAME LI
L'ÉTRAVE, V

← EN LONGUE THÉORIE, LES OUVRIERS EMPLOYÉS A LA CONSTRUCTION DÉVALENT LE LONG DU MUR D'ACIER.

REPORTAGE

Figure 2.24 *VU*, October 10, 1934, pp. 1268–9. Photographs by Roger Schall.

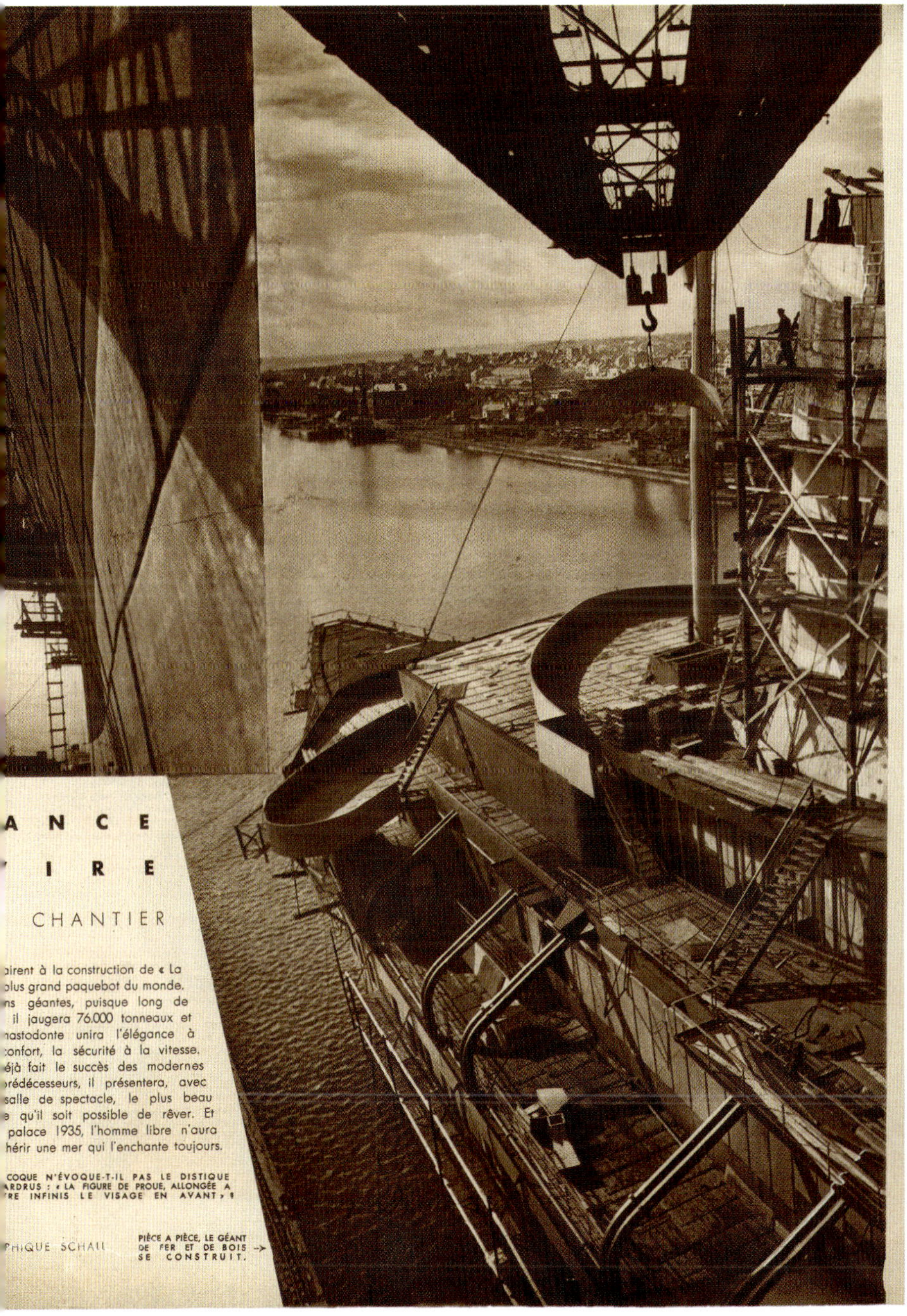

ANCE
IRE
CHANTIER

airent à la construction de « La
plus grand paquebot du monde.
ns géantes, puisque long de
il jaugera 76.000 tonneaux et
nastodonte unira l'élégance à
confort, la sécurité à la vitesse.
éjà fait le succès des modernes
prédécesseurs, il présentera, avec
salle de spectacle, le plus beau
e qu'il soit possible de rêver. Et
palace 1935, l'homme libre n'aura
hérir une mer qui l'enchante toujours.

COQUE N'ÉVOQUE-T-IL PAS LE DISTIQUE
ARDRUS : « LA FIGURE DE PROUE, ALLONGÉE A
RE INFINIS LE VISAGE EN AVANT » ?

PHIQUE SCHALL

PIÈCE A PIÈCE, LE GÉANT
DE FER ET DE BOIS →
SE CONSTRUIT.

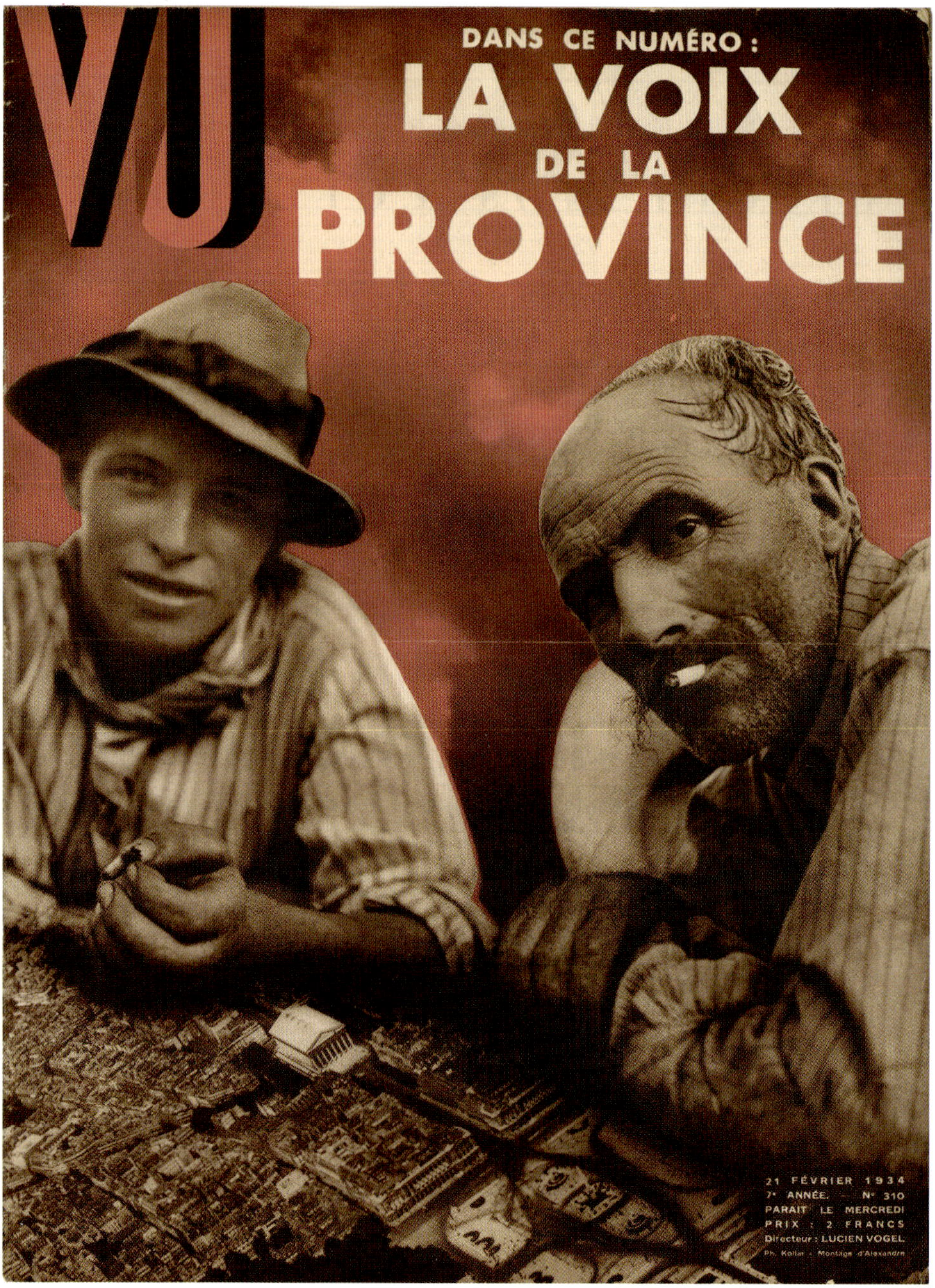

Figure 2.25 *VU*, February 21, 1934, cover.

photomontages (see Figure 2.24). The photographs are associated to form a single image over which the eye roves, from one page to the other. For Antoine Zischka's article "Un nouvel empire du fer" (A New Empire of Iron) a photomontage of factories, workers taking care of machines, a tractor park, and high-angle faces, frames the three columns of text (see Figure 2.27).[127] The "Europe 33" piece in the issue of April 29, 1933 sets its five columns of text in the upper part of the center page spread and a ten-image photomontage in the lower part. Here the use of films for the composition has enabled the transparent overlaying of the title of the article in an arc spanning the five columns. This was the seventh and last article in "the major survey by [our] special correspondent": Georges Simenon. From March 18 to April 29, 1933 the famous novelist described his travels through Europe in an account backed up by a few of his own photographs and many others from agencies, with layouts that varied from one issue to another.[128] ZED, the company that published *Détective*, *Voilà*, and *Marianne*, regularly called on well-known Gallimard authors to fuel its weeklies,[129] but in addition to these celebrity presences what emerges in *Voilà* is the treatment of news as a serial to be followed from issue to issue. In the course of 1934 we accompany Titaÿna on her voyage of discovery in the Indian Ocean;[130] follow May Reeves's nine-part portrayal of the private life of Charlie Chaplin;[131] and continue with Pierre Scize's "objective account" of a summer climbing accident in the Alps.[132]

In all these cases the editors put together a mixed bag of images including intimate snapshots and formal poses from such different sources as the article's author and various photographic agencies. These were cut out, juxtaposed and associated not only with the text, but also with graphic elements like geometrical signs evoking the Toraja people of Indonesia and the film rebate and sprocket holes of Hollywood movies. In this context the photographs back up the text, which in turn justifies the association and publication of the images as a contribution to the news narrative. Just as the covers of *Berliner Illustrirte Zeitung* mentioned the titles of the Vicki Baum novels to be found inside, *Voilà* announced the contributions of the reporters who had taken the news and turned it into stories.

Structurally and formally, then, *VU* and *Voilà* differ only minimally from the turn-of-the-century *La Vie au grand air*. Each period saw art directors composing pages, double page spreads and covers, using groups of photographs and fitting text into the remaining space. These pages offered subjects that could be read independently of the rest of the magazine and thus left the reader free to leaf through at will. However, the editorial boards at *VU* and *Voilà*, many of whose members worked for both, had new tools at their disposal which facilitated the business of layout, encouraged graphic creativity, and provided a remarkable finish for the images. They also had access to photographic agencies with more diverse and better organized resources, as well as to a network of freelance

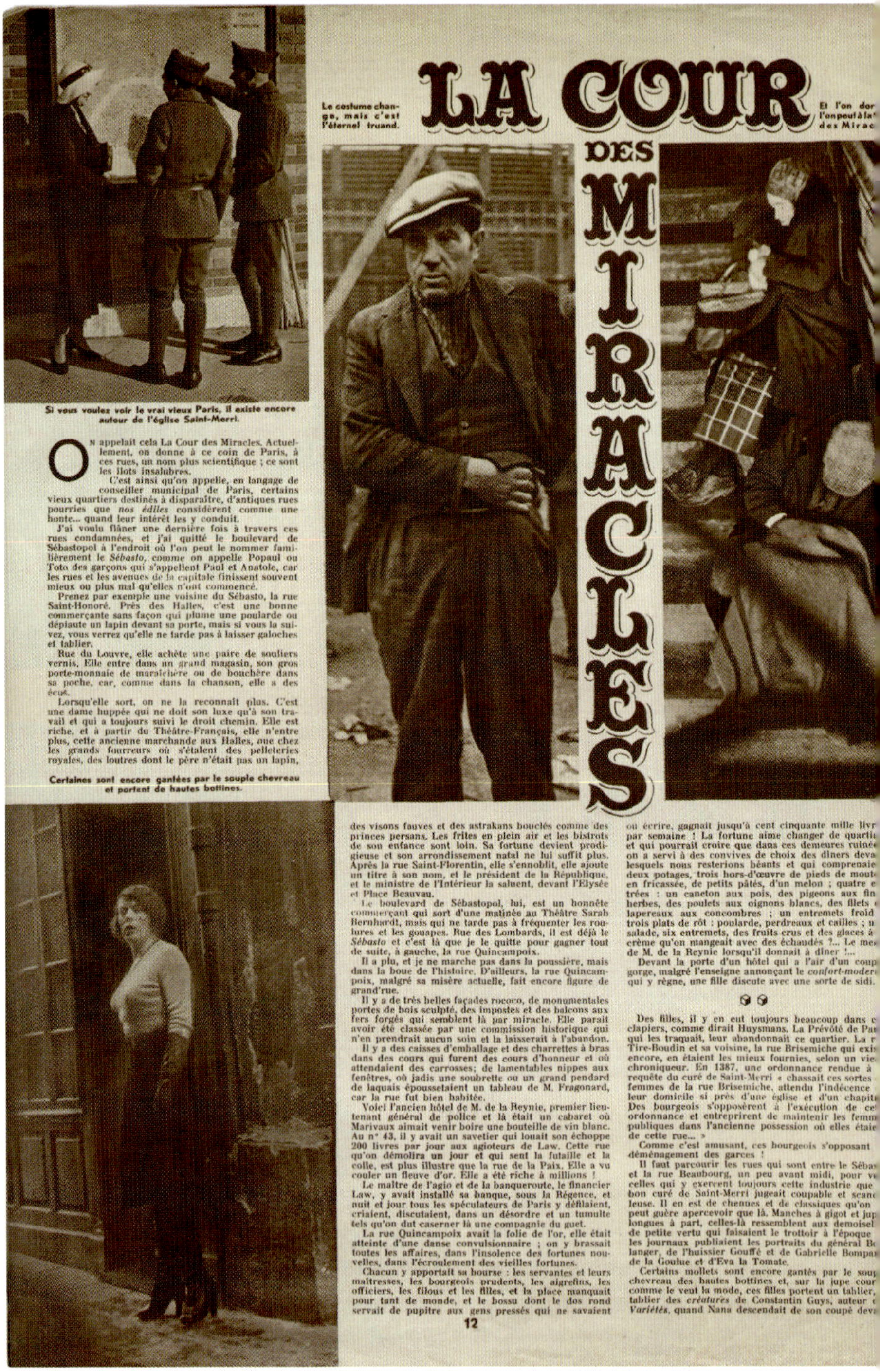

LA COUR DES MIRACLES

Le costume change, mais c'est l'éternel truand.

Et l'on dor l'onpeut à la des Mirac

Si vous voulez voir le vrai vieux Paris, il existe encore autour de l'église Saint-Merri.

On appelait cela La Cour des Miracles. Actuellement, on donne à ce coin de Paris, à ces rues, un nom plus scientifique ; ce sont les îlots insalubres.

C'est ainsi qu'on appelle, en langage de conseiller municipal de Paris, certains vieux quartiers destinés à disparaître, d'antiques rues pourries que *nos édiles* considèrent comme une honte… quand leur intérêt les y conduit.

J'ai voulu flâner une dernière fois à travers ces rues condamnées, et j'ai quitté le boulevard de Sébastopol à l'endroit où l'on peut le nommer familièrement le *Sébasto*, comme on appelle Popaul ou Toto des garçons qui s'appellent Paul et Anatole, car les rues et les avenues de la capitale finissent souvent mieux ou plus mal qu'elles n'ont commencé.

Prenez par exemple une voisine du Sébasto, la rue Saint-Honoré. Près des Halles, c'est une bonne commerçante sans façon qui plume une poularde ou dépiaute un lapin devant sa porte, mais si vous la suivez, vous verrez qu'elle ne tarde pas à laisser galoches et tablier.

Rue du Louvre, elle achète une paire de souliers vernis. Elle entre dans un grand magasin, son gros porte-monnaie de maraîchère ou de bouchère dans sa poche, car, comme dans la chanson, elle a des écus.

Lorsqu'elle sort, on ne la reconnaît plus. C'est une dame huppée qui ne doit son luxe qu'à son travail et qui a toujours suivi le droit chemin. Elle est riche, et à partir du Théâtre-Français, elle n'entre plus, cette ancienne marchande aux Halles, que chez les grands fourreurs où s'étalent des pelleteries royales, des loutres dont le père n'était pas un lapin,

Certaines sont encore gantées par le souple chevreau et portent de hautes bottines.

des visons fauves et des astrakans bouclés comme des princes persans. Les frites en plein air et les bistrots de son enfance sont loin. Sa fortune devient prodigieuse et son arrondissement natal ne lui suffit plus. Après la rue Saint-Florentin, elle s'ennoblit, elle ajoute un titre à son nom, et le président de la République, et le ministre de l'Intérieur la saluent, devant l'Elysée et Place Beauvau.

Le boulevard de Sébastopol, lui, est un honnête commerçant qui sort d'une matinée au Théâtre Sarah Bernhardt, mais qui ne tarde pas à fréquenter les roulures et les gouapes. Rue des Lombards, il est déjà le *Sébasto* et c'est là que je le quitte pour gagner tout de suite, à gauche, la rue Quincampoix.

Il a plu, et je ne marche pas dans la poussière, mais dans la boue de l'histoire. D'ailleurs, la rue Quincampoix, malgré sa misère actuelle, fait encore figure de grand'rue.

Il y a de très belles façades rococo, de monumentales portes de bois sculpté, des impostes et des balcons aux fers forgés qui semblent là par miracle. Elle paraît avoir été classée par une commission historique qui n'en prendrait aucun soin et la laisserait à l'abandon.

Il y a des caisses d'emballage et des charrettes à bras dans des cours qui furent des cours d'honneur et où attendaient des carrosses; de lamentables nippes aux fenêtres, où jadis une soubrette ou un grand pendard de laquais époussetaient un tableau de M. Fragonard, car la rue fut bien habitée.

Voici l'ancien hôtel de M. de la Reynie, premier lieutenant général de police et là était un cabaret où Marivaux aimait venir boire une bouteille de vin blanc. Au n° 43, il y avait un savetier qui louait son échoppe 200 livres par jour aux agioteurs de Law. Cette rue qu'on démolira un jour et qui sent la futaille et la colle, est plus illustre que la rue de la Paix. Elle a vu couler un fleuve d'or. Elle a été riche à millions !

Le maître de l'agio et de la banqueroute, le financier Law, y avait installé sa banque, sous la Régence, et nuit et jour tous les spéculateurs de Paris y défilaient, criaient, discutaient, dans un désordre et un tumulte tels qu'on dut caserner là une compagnie du guet.

La rue Quincampoix avait la folie de l'or, elle était atteinte d'une danse convulsionnaire ; on y brassait toutes les affaires, dans l'insolence des fortunes nouvelles, dans l'écroulement des vieilles fortunes.

Chacun y apportait sa bourse : les servantes et leurs maîtresses, les bourgeois prudents, les aigrefins, les officiers, les filous et les filles, et la place manquait pour tant de monde, et le bossu dont le dos rond servait de pupitre aux gens pressés qui ne savaient

12

ou écrire, gagnait jusqu'à cent cinquante mille livr par semaine ! La fortune aime changer de quarti et qui pourrait croire que dans ces demeures ruiné on a servi à des convives de choix des dîners deva lesquels nous resterions béants et qui comprenaie deux potages, trois hors-d'œuvre de pieds de mout en fricassée, de petits pâtés, d'un melon ; quatre e trées : un caneton aux pois, des pigeons aux fin herbes, des poulets aux oignons blancs, des filets lapereaux aux concombres ; un entremets froid trois plats de rôt : poularde, perdreaux et cailles ; u salade, six entremets, des fruits crus et des glaces à crème qu'on mangeait avec des échaudés ?… Le me de M. de la Reynie lorsqu'il donnait à dîner !…

Devant la porte d'un hôtel qui a l'air d'un coup gorge, malgré l'enseigne annonçant le *confort-moder* qui y règne, une fille discute avec une sorte de sidi.

Des filles, il y en eut toujours beaucoup dans c clapiers, comme dirait Huysmans. La Prévôté de Pa qui les traquait, leur abandonnait ce quartier. La r Tire-Boudin et sa voisine, la rue Brisemiche qui exi encore, en étaient les mieux fournies, selon un vie chroniqueur. En 1387, une ordonnance rendue à requête du curé de Saint-Merri « chassait ces sortes femmes de la rue Brisemiche, attendu l'indécence leur domicile si près d'une église et d'un chapit Des bourgeois s'opposèrent à l'exécution de ce ordonnance et entreprirent de maintenir les femm publiques dans l'ancienne possession où elles étaie de cette rue… »

Comme c'est amusant, ces bourgeois s'opposant démènagement des garces !

Il faut parcourir les rues qui sont entre le Séba et la rue Beaubourg, un peu avant midi, pour v celles qui y exercent toujours cette industrie que bon curé de Saint-Merri jugeait coupable et scan leuse. Il en est de chenues et de classiques qu'on peut guère apercevoir que là. Manches à gigot et ju longues à part, celles-là ressemblent aux demoisel de petite vertu qui faisaient le trottoir à l'époque les journaux publiaient les portraits du général B langer, de l'huissier Gouffé et de Gabrielle Bompa de la Goulue et d'Eva la Tomate.

Certains mollets sont encore gantés par le sou chevreau des hautes bottines et, sur la jupe cour comme le veut la mode, ces filles portent un tablier, tablier des *créatures* de Constantin Guys, auteur *Variétés*, quand Nana descendait de son coupé dev

Figure 2.26 *Voilà*, March 11, 1933, pp. 12–13. Photographs by Alfred Eisenstaedt.

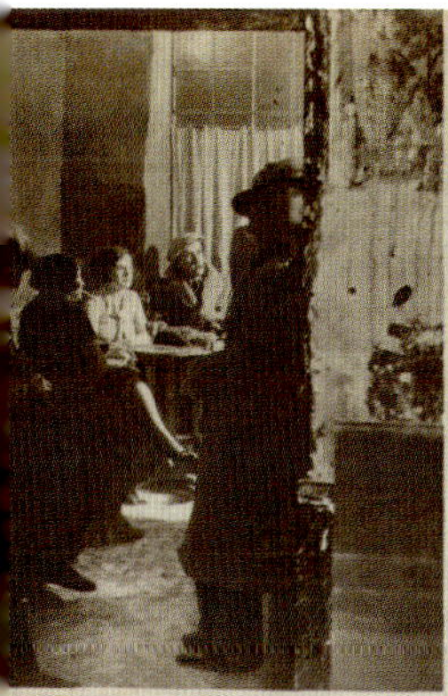

Il y a pourtant quelques bistrots, quelques authentiques assommoirs.

éâtre, et que les sergents de ville avaient la grosse stache et l'impériale de Badinguet.

ne doit pas être difficile rue des Etuves, rue des -Consuls, rue du Cloître Saint-Merri, rue Brise-e, rue Pierre-au-Lard, et le recrutement est triste. u de margoulettes enfarinées, d'yeux agrandis par rayon et de lèvres artificiellement rafraîchies. La art ressemblent à des souillons en savates, à des vaises ménagères délaissant leur cambuse pour le ot, et, en cette saison, sous le manteau minable qui du *décrochez-moi-ça* et de la confection, on voit ainages pauvres, un cache-nez et un chandail.

s brunes, minces et plus vives, ont l'air de teignes nplies, de cigarières en grève ; les grosses sont illes à de molles pochardes ; les plus chevronnées un teint de clochard et cette viande que font les s ratatouilles, les apéritifs et les alcools falsifiés, upidité des jours vides et les sommeils dans des is qui puent.

s plus reluisantes sont sans doute les sirènes de la e noce pour les garçons qui ont escorté jusqu'aux s des charretées de légumes et qui, leur cargaison e, sont *pleins de sous.*

apportent avec eux les honnêtes parfums de la -et-Oise, des banlieues maraîchères et comme une fée de poésie rustique aux filles qui font toutes, leurs meublés lugubres, un rêve que les plus chan-es ne réaliseront jamais et qui songent à une petite on à volets verts, sous de grands arbres, avec des es et des lapins, un jardin plein de salades, de , de capucines, et, à deux pas, le bois, les blés d'or s de coquelicots, tout un décor de romance senti-ale sous l'azur d'un beau dimanche campagnard et cent.

Les brunes ont l'air de teignes accomplies, de cigarières en grève.

C'est un peu avant midi que tout cela grouille et qu'il y a, dans ces misérables sentines, un air de fête. L'heure sent l'apéritif et la friture. Le tramway Montrouge-Gare de l'Est s'arrête là-bas, à chaque instant, parce que le Sébasto est embouteillé par les charrettes qui viennent des Halles ou qui y vont. On marche sur des feuilles de choux et des fanes de carottes. Un artichaut qui a roulé d'une corbeille a l'air d'une grenade non éclatée. Il y a des odeurs d'équarrissoir et de jardin après la pluie, des parfums d'oranges et des relents de triperie ; un camion est plein de moutons décapités, et un vieux bonhomme pousse une carriole sur laquelle s'entassent des chrysanthèmes pour les morts et des roses fraîches pour les belles vivantes.

Le pernod et quelques autres sirops font voir la vie en beau. Sous les tricots de laine et les blouses, les portefeuilles sont bourrés de billets et voici le

DAIS'Y-HOTEL
Chauffage central
Confort moderne

avec ses chambres *à la semaine, à la journée* et même à l'heure !...

Rue de la Reynie et rue des Etuves,
Des Juges-Consuls, de la Verrerie ;
Rue Simon-le-Franc et rue de Venise,
Rue Pierre-au-Lard, rue Aubry-le-Boucher,
Rue Quincampoix et rue du Cloître Saint-
[Merri,
Rue Saint-Bon et rue Brisemiche...

Les noms seuls de ces ruelles décriées imprimés de la sorte et réglés par une cadence intérieure, ressemblent à de vieux vers français, mais continuons cette promenade

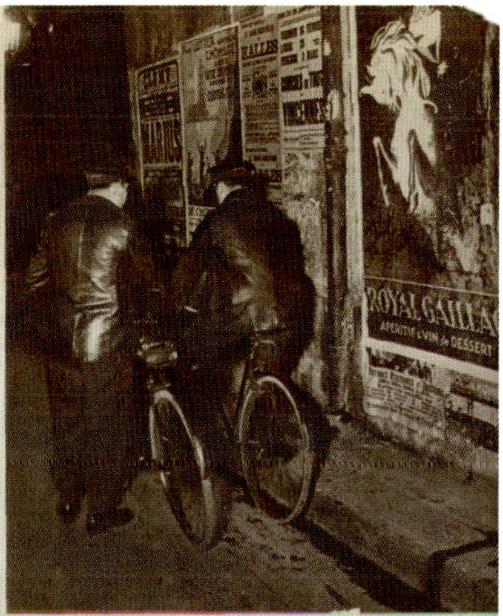

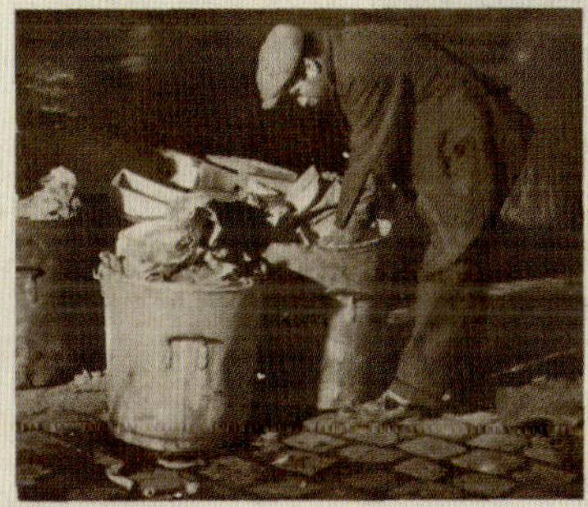

Voici la rue Brisemiche, la plus sinistre de toutes assurément.

Un client entre dans une boutique dont l'enseigne porte en lettres maladroites ces deux mots :

COIFFEUR POPULAIRE

Mais ce n'est pas un homme du Tiers-Etat qui va se faire accommoder là. Il appartient à une quatrième classe, il a du sidi et du clochard, et sans doute mieux vaudrait ne pas se servir du peigne qui va carder sa tignasse.

A côté du barbier, un gros tuyau de fonte qui vient peut-être de quelque lavoir et qui est crevé en deux endroits, laisse échapper des jets de vapeur fade, collé contre le mur noir comme une plaque de cuirassé ou un blindage de machine. Sur un seuil, sanguinolentes et roses, des tripes, de la fressure qu'un chien regarde et n'attaque pas.

Ailleurs, derrière les Gobelins, par exemple, les trop vieilles bicoques étalent tout de même un certain pittoresque. Les badigeons qui ont coulé sous les pluies sont encore clairs ; les murs ont des maladies de peau, des eczémas, des dartres que saupoudre une farine de plâtre, et un arbre rabougri se penche fraternellement vers une croisée dont les vitres cassées ont été remplacées par du carton, mais, ici, tout est tragique, et les pierres des maisons solides qui datent du XIVe, du XVe et du XVIe siècle, souffrent d'une maladie noire et semblent mortes du choléra et de la peste.

Cela tient de la cave et du souterrain, du mur de lazaret et de cachot, du quai gras qui borde un égout, du puisard où l'on jetait au moyen âge les ordures des maladreries.

Un tapis qu'on a mis à sécher sur l'appui d'une croisée est pareil à ces loques abandonnées devant les remparts d'une ville d'Asie, décimée par une effroyable épidémie, et presque tous les rez-de-chaussée sont inhabitables.

Il y a pourtant quelques bistrots, quelques authentiques *assommoirs*, comme disaient les romanciers naturalistes.

Au bruit de mon pas qui sonne sur l'antique pavé comme devait sonner celui d'un sergent du guet en 1360, des clients qui cassent la croûte lèvent le nez et regardent.

Que peuvent-ils manger à ces tables de soupes populaires et d'asiles de nuit ? Quels arlequins et quelle fressure ?

Dans une *resserre* où clignote une lampe-pigeon, un vieux essuye contre la manche de sa veste des pommes qu'il jette ensuite sur une charrette à bras, et je souris en imaginant les doux nigauds, les bons végétariens qui croient aux vitamines et qui y mordront demain à belles dents, sans les éplucher.

C'est un truqueur et un commerçant avisé : il astique et il ravive le vernis de *la Canada !*

Je sors de la rue Brisemiche comme on sortait d'un boyau pendant la guerre, comme on pouvait sortir de la Bastille par un souterrain. Elle s'élargit un peu en allant vers la rue Saint-Merri, elle tombe sur une école maternelle, sur une solide et récente bâtisse de la ville, qui abrite une bibliothèque municipale où les livres sont prêtés gratuitement, et comme si je revenais du fond du XIVe siècle, j'ai envie d'entrer, de prier le préposé aux bouquins de me laisser feuilleter ce volume où Octave Mirbeau, las d'une ville hantée par un passé redoutable, murmurait un cantique familier à la louange de notre époque : « *Avec quelle joie purifiante, avec quelle dévotion consolatrice, je me plais à évoquer vos vertueux hauts-de-forme et vos honnêtes habits noirs... bons radicaux et radicaux-socialistes de notre temps...* »

Léo LARGUIER.

(Reportage photographique Eisenstaedt).

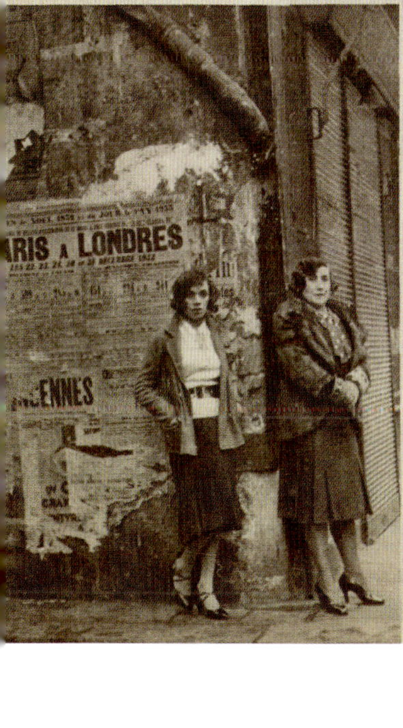

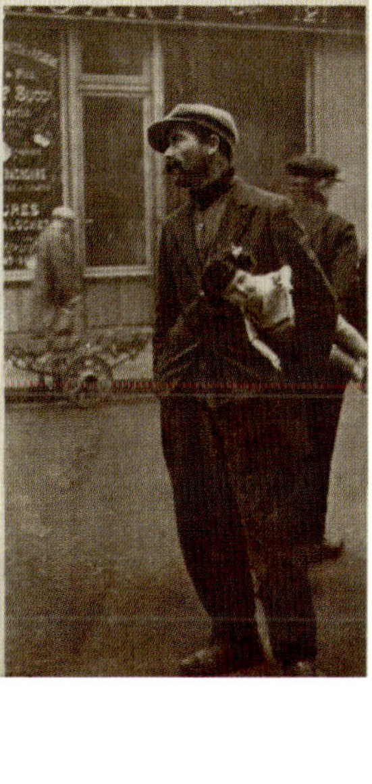

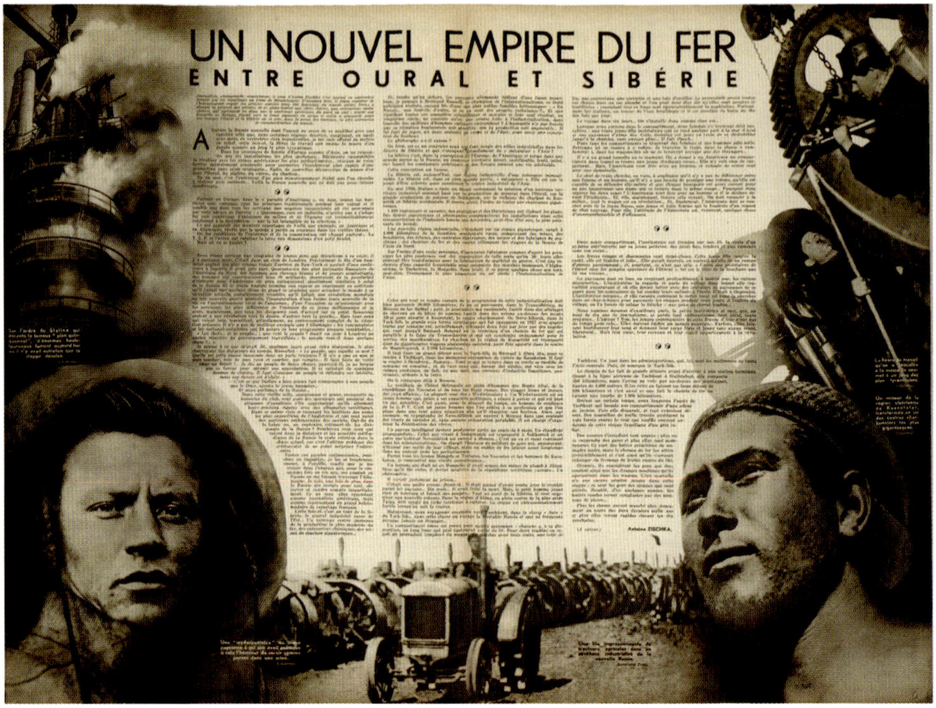

Figure 2.27 *Voilà*, May 14, 1932, pp. 8–9.

photographers whose artistic aspirations they applied to news coverage. The big difference in relation to *La Vie au grand air*, though, had to do with content: *VU* dealt with "all aspects of contemporary life"[133] and *Voilà* with "today's world news."[134] The graphic and photographic presentation that suited only sports news during the Belle Époque made a successful adaptation to general news in the interwar years.

This approach to general, and more precisely political news really came into its own in *VU* during the Spanish Civil War. While less politically committed than at *Regards*, the *VU* editorial team took an anti-Franco stand and regularly published photographs taken on the Republican side of the lines. Indeed, it was in the issue of September 23, 1936 that Robert Capa's photograph of a Republican soldier struck down by a bullet was published for the first time.[135] Set to the left in the double page spread headed "The Civil War in Spain," this photograph was accompanied by another, taken from the same vantage point, of a second soldier falling backwards as he met the same fate. Both images were vivid illustrations of "how they fell," but only one of them achieved iconic status as a representation not only of the war in Spain, but also of the photographer's method, role and dedication. Their publication came in the wake of the special issue of *VU*, "En Espagne: la défense de la République" (In Spain: the Defense of the Republic), in which Lucien Vogel mounted an unequivocal denunciation of "the conservative French bourgeoisie"[136] and its support for the fascist movements then wreaking havoc on Europe's political landscape. This overt stance triggered a loss of advertising and angered the magazine's wealthy owners, who called for Vogel's resignation.[137] His name disappeared from the cover and he was replaced as director by Alfred Mallet, who played down the magazine's politics. Gradually the layout lost its stylishness, entire pages of text were reintroduced, and in a symbolic change, with the issue of May 12, 1937, the title became *VU et LU* (Seen and Read).

In time with the rising importance of photography in the general news press over the interwar period, and the magazines' foregrounding of the role of reporters and photographers, the work of journalists was undergoing a process of institutionalization that culminated in the creation of a profession as such.[138] As Arnaud Mercier has explained, this process began in 1918 with the founding of the Syndicat National des Journalistes (National Union of Journalists), a body which, in the course of the 1920s–1930s would consolidate and organize journalists and legitimize their work by laying down aims and methods. Now set apart from amateurs and his predecessors, "the true journalist allied the work of investigation with a respect for higher moral demands. Journalism was becoming a calling, the epitome of dedication and probity."[139] The movement spread its wings with the founding of the International Federation of Journalists in 1926, and the legal status of journalists as professionals was enshrined in the law of March 29, 1935 in France. The status of photographers, by contrast, wavered between that of technician and of journalist, and only those working full-time for the press were accorded journalist status in 1937.[140] Then came their own striving for institutional legitimation and the drawing up of a code of professional ethics.[141] The handbooks for photojournalists that appeared between the wars and, later, bodies like the National Press Photographers Association (1946) and World Press Photo (1955), would lay down the necessary parameters and establish a framework for the profession of photojournalist.

Thus the interwar years saw the uses of photography in the general news press loom larger as they incorporated formal and layout approaches previously restricted to the sports and leisure press. There was an increasing emphasis on channeling and legitimizing their use, and the principal actors came together to assert their rights in a visual information economy that had become financially attractive. It was hardly surprising, then, that Marxist thinkers like Siegfried Kracauer and Walter Benjamin began looking into the workings of this process. In his article "Photography," published in 1927, Kracauer said of the illustrated press:

> Never before has an age been so informed about itself, if being informed means having an image of objects that resembles them in a photographic sense . . . In the illustrated magazines people see the very world that the illustrated magazines prevent them from perceiving. The spatial continuum from the camera's perspective predominates the spatial appearance of the perceived object; the likeness that the image bears to it effaces the contours of the object's 'history'. Never before has a period known so little about itself.[142]

Four years later, in his "Small History of Photography" Benjamin took a fresh look at the famous remark by László Moholy-Nagy, "But shouldn't the photographer who cannot read his own images count as no less an illiterate? Is the caption not destined to become the essential component of the shot?"[143] Benjamin is suggesting here the ambiguity of photographic representation and its uses. Both commentators underscore the quantitative and qualitative importance of photographs in the news press, as well as their cultural significance and political role, and stress the need for an understanding of their historical circumstances.

Chapter 3

The *Life* Model and the Standardization Of News Magazines (1936–1976)

The period after the Second World War is regarded as a high point in the history of press photography. In their *Kiosk: eine Geschichte der Fotoreportage* (Kiosk: A History of Photojournalism, 2001) Bodo von Dewitz and Robert Lebeck speak of an "apogee", and close their account with the last issue of *Life*, published in 1972.[1] In *Things As They Are: Photojournalism in Context since 1955*, Mary Panzer and Christian Caujolle challenged the legitimacy of this "golden age", but nonetheless opted for beginning their study with "the era of W. Eugene Smith's legendary stories for *Life* magazine."[2] These authors analyze both the production and circulation of photographs, but single out the photographic essay as the most fully realized form of photojournalism. What exactly, though, is a photographic essay? And what exactly is the difference between Jimmy Hare's sequences in *L'Illustration*[3] and Eugene Smith's in *Life*?

The term "photographic essay" has come to cover any series or group of images centered on the same subject and appearing on one or more pages of a magazine. But before being subsumed under this vague concept, the genre had been defined within a specific historical context: the creation of *Life* magazine. After the success of *Time Magazine* (founded in 1923) and *Fortune* (founded in 1930), Henry R. Luce (1898–1967) consolidated the Time Inc. empire with the launch of *Life* on November 23, 1936.[4] The following spring saw the photographic essay defined in the article "The Camera as Essayist", which prescribed and justified the use of photographs in the new magazine.[5] This definition chimed with the journalistic approach Luce had practiced since the first issue of *Time*: the overt plugging of personal standpoints at the expense of objectivity.[6]

Whereas photography had always been justified in the general press as a necessarily impartial tool,[7] it was presented in *Life* as a means of expression capable of possessing a style. This stance set *Life* apart from other magazines like *Picture Post* in England and *Paris Match* in France, which had no misgivings about using images to convey their opinions on the news, but never actually acknowledged the fact. Founded late in the summer of 1937, the "Photographic Essay" embodied *Life*'s concept and became a significant element in the magazine's table of contents.

Success for *Life* was immediate and its print run was on the rise continuously until 1966, when it passed the 7.7 million mark, international sales included.[8] Publication in *Life* rapidly became a grail for photographers, bringing with it an unprecedented level of recognition and generous pay checks into the bargain.[9] The magazine's structure and format would also become a yardstick and a model for many of the general and specialist periodicals launched in the years that followed.

Even so, the photographic essay represented few pages of any given issue of *Life*—around 10 percent of the total. The celebrities on the cover and inside, together with contents varied enough to attract a wide readership, accounted for a substantial part of the weekly's success. *Life*, moreover, made groundbreaking use of the magazine form: because its articles were unrelated to each other, they could be interspersed with advertisements that took up as much as 50 percent of the available space. At the same time the role attributed to photography in the essays helped shape the myth of the photojournalist and of the magazine itself, which still exists today. A study of the launching of *Life* offers an insight into the European influences in its conception, its international aura during the decades to come, its specific characteristics in terms of the treatment of images and, above all, the discrepancies between its statements of intent regarding photography and its actual uses of the medium. The photographic essay concept offered photographers unheard-of recognition and prestige, but at the practical level it imposed clear restrictions on their role, generated a great deal of frustration, and underscored the limitations of the system.

From idea to actuality: the beginnings of *Life*

In the America of the early 1930s the idea of starting a magazine that could compete with such long-established institutions as *Collier's* and *Saturday Evening Post* was beginning to take root among various press publishers. In a memo to Condé Nast dated May 9, 1931, Clare Boothe Brokaw, then working at *Vanity Fair*, suggested:

> [I]f the Condé Nast publications were to consider buying *Life* [a declining humorous monthly] I can suggest a new editorial formula which . . . I dare to believe would make the magazine a success. I should like to pattern an American magazine—and one bearing the title *Life* is admirably adapted to its contents—after the Parisian *VU*. It would be a weekly and would contain some of the editorial elements of *Time*, *Fortune* and even *Vanity Fair*, plus its own special angle, which would be reporting, not all the news nor, necessarily, the most important news, but the most interesting and exciting news, in photographs, and interpreting it editorially through articles by capable writers and journalists.[10]

The suggestion was not taken up, just as William Randolph Hearst rejected the idea for a magazine based on a dummy designed by Berliner Kurt Safranski in the autumn of 1934. That same year Henry Luce set up an experimental department within Time Inc. whose purpose was to collect and evaluate publishing projects that included a picture magazine. The department, though, failed to come up with the hoped-for results and was shut down six months later. Plenty of ideas went the rounds, but none of them were considered worth investing in.[11]

Time Inc., of course, already owned an illustrated magazine, the luxury monthly *Fortune*, launched in 1930 "to reflect Industrial Life in ink and paper and work and picture as the finest skyscraper reflects it in skill and architecture."[12] Launched during the Depression, *Fortune* was a publishing and financial gamble aimed at celebrating the power of American capitalism. Its articles spoke of the world's great industrial families, science, technological progress, political and cultural life, and finance. Expensive and available only on subscription, it targeted wealthy businessmen and stood out for the quality of its photography and its overall aesthetic. Its sparse, meticulously designed layout underscored its emphasis on typography and big pictures (the magazine measured 35.5 x 27.9 cm) partially printed in photogravure. In the images black and white alternated with color in a layout whose sobriety and balance highlighted them perfectly. In its numerous photographic commissions on industry the magazine appropriated the graphic principles of Surrealism, the New Vision and the New Objectivity and applied them to a glamorization of the world of work. Margaret Bourke-White's February 1930 series on a pig slaughterhouse—Luce had invited her onto the *Fortune* team in July 1929[13]—illustrates the emphasis on form in the images.[14] On elegantly laid-out pages the photographs offer dramatic play on light and shade, low angle shots of the suspended animals and an insistence on the repetitive nature of the slaughtering process. There is, too, an overall stress on the strangeness of this out-of-the-way place and on the industrialization of the American economy (see Figure 3.1). Thus by the late 1920s Henry Luce was wagering on the impact of photography and Time Inc. had the team required by *Fortune*'s needs in the

Across the narrow alley are Swift's by-product plants. Heaped outside the bone house are the heads of cattle, in awful pile; inside are grinders which belch forth clouds of dust. The odor is not pleasant. Swift supplies the workmen here with filter masks. Some use them and some do not. It is wiser to use them.

Thus the Packingtown in which the farmer's finished product finds itself.

The hog is disassembled

The major adjustment which the hog makes as it moves to the last quarter of its year is of course the change from life to death. This is the only adjustment which can conceivably be of concern to the hog, and it is a curious thing that it should be of such little concern to Swift & Company. If killing is the chief function of a butcher, then the Swifts are not butchers. Exactly 25 minutes elapse between the time the live hog reaches the killing floor and the time the dressed carcass goes to the cooler. By the left hind foot he is hoisted athwart a giant wheel, then delivered to a conveyor from which he hangs, squealing, head downward. A mammoth being with a spear-like knife makes a quick, deft thrust at the hog's throat. The adjustment is made.[2]

Beautifully certain are the ministrations of the killing room to the rows of carcasses which were hogs. An incredibly intricate nest of blunt knives scrapes every hair from the hog's skin; nearby stand government inspectors, slicing the neck-glands, to search for tiny white spots which are tuberculosis. Off comes the head; it is put to one side. One deft ripping motion and the inside of the carcass is as clean as the outside. A twist of giant tweezers and the toenail clatters to the floor. Now the procession moves through a bath of fire to singe off the last of the hair, a bath of water to cool. The rhythmic rise and fall of a cleaver rends the backbone. On and on come the carcasses, perhaps 20,000 of them, a fat pink parade curling through blades of steel.

From the killing floor the carcass moves to the cooler for twenty-four hours, then to the floors where men and machines carve it into dollars and cents. Here is a mechanical saw which grinds through the shoulder; there is a draw knife like a curved adz which scoops out the loin. Hundreds of white-sleeved arms swing back and forth. Hundreds of funnels gulp the morsels the knives flip aside. Some gulp lean trimmings; these will make sausage. Some gulp fats; these will make lard. Down one chute go the hams, trimmed to within ⅛-inch of standardization; down another pour shoulders. To the waiting refrigerator cars is rushed the fresh meat, ready to travel to a branch house in Seattle or Atlanta. But the hams and the bacon must go to the curing cellars, there to remain from 30 to 90 days—and the toenails, the hair, the fats, the lips, still have long weeks to wait before their processing is complete, before the hog has been perfectly destroyed.

In this gradual dissolution there is no accident, no happenstance. When the live 250-lb. hog begins his run across the viaduct to the killing-floor, he is already divided and subdivided as exactly as a suburban real estate development. Swift knows that when the knives are through with him, there will remain:

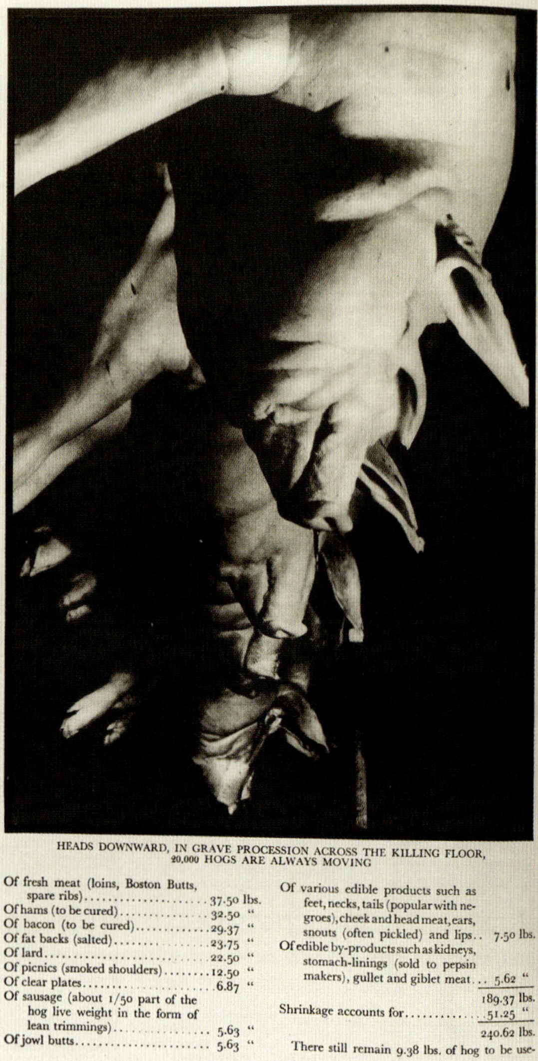

HEADS DOWNWARD, IN GRAVE PROCESSION ACROSS THE KILLING FLOOR, 20,000 HOGS ARE ALWAYS MOVING

Of fresh meat (loins, Boston Butts, spare ribs)	37.50 lbs.
Of hams (to be cured)	32.50 "
Of bacon (to be cured)	29.37 "
Of fat backs (salted)	23.75 "
Of lard	22.50 "
Of picnics (smoked shoulders)	12.50 "
Of clear plates	6.87 "
Of sausage (about 1/50 part of the hog live weight in the form of lean trimmings)	5.63 "
Of jowl butts	5.63 "
Of various edible products such as feet, necks, tails (popular with negroes), cheek and head meat, ears, snouts (often pickled) and lips	7.50 lbs.
Of edible by-products such as kidneys, stomach-linings (sold to pepsin makers), gullet and giblet meat	5.62 "
	189.37 lbs.
Shrinkage accounts for	51.25 "
	240.62 lbs.

There still remain 9.38 lbs. of hog to be use-

· 58 ·

Figure 3.1 *Fortune*, February 1930, p. 58. Photograph by Margaret Bourke-White.

image field. However, their network of photographers, way of working, and image publishing skills seemed of uncertain value in terms of creating a general news weekly.

The political changes that left their mark on Europe in the 1930s had a direct impact on those working in the illustrated press. In March 1933, only weeks after Hitler's appointment as Chancellor of the Reich, Stefan Lorant, editor of the *Münchner Illustrierte Presse*, was arrested; he would spend six months in prison before making his way to London in 1934.[15] Ullstein, the publishing house responsible for the illustrated periodicals *Berliner Illustrirte Zeitung*, *UHU* and *Die Dame*, gradually lost control of its publications, and its main staffers—among them Kurt Korff, Kurt Safranski, Martin Munkácsi, Felix H. Man, and Alfred Eisenstaedt—left Germany between 1933 and 1935. With the exception of Man, who went to London and worked there with Lorant, the others pursued their careers in the illustrated press in New York. In the years that followed André Kertész, Man Ray and Alexander Liberman left France for North America. The transatlantic inspiration for press publishers in New York was no longer a matter of mere statements intended to set oneself apart from one's colleagues, but a concrete situation based on a transfer of skills from Europe.[16]

When Luce and Daniel Longwell met with Kurt Korff and Kurt Safranski in the Time Inc. offices on December 11, 1934, the aim was a sharing of their experiences as publishers. On the agenda was a plan for a general news magazine and how to get it running, together with an examination of a mock-up originally proposed by Safranski to Hearst. Luce would later acknowledge that this meeting, and the mock-up in particular, gave substance to ideas that had already been under discussion for several years.[17] From there on the two German émigrés went their separate but complementary ways: Korff worked as a consultant for Time Inc., joining the secretly revived experimental department now gravitating around Longwell, who was *Time Magazine's* picture coordinator.[18] From January 1935 to July 1936, Korff met regularly with members of the team, had lengthy discussions with Longwell, turned out numerous memoranda and wrote a document titled "Essential Outline for a New Illustrated Magazine".[19] In the latter he suggested covering cultural news, never using the same subject twice in the same issue and, of course, paying close attention to the choice of images: "Sometimes it is sufficient to have *one* very good, thrilling, artistic picture or illustrated article in *one* issue."[20] The strategies underlying the success and the reputation of the *Berliner Illustrirte Zeitung*—among them negotiation of exclusive rights and good rates for photographers—were also brought on board, guaranteeing the quality of the images. Thus Korff shared his experience with pictures, insisting on the best ways of obtaining and selecting them and on enhancing them editorially. During this period of gestation Korff remained in the background; he realized that he was not going to be offered the job of editor-in-chief, and resigned from Time Inc. in June 1936.[21]

Four photographers were hired to ensure the supply of images for the upcoming magazine: Margaret Bourke-White, who had been with Time Inc. since the late 1920s; Alfred Eisenstaedt, recommended by Korff and a New York resident since 1935; Thomas D. McAvoy; and Peter Stackpole. Apart from Bourke-White, a devotee of medium and large view cameras, the others all used portables of the Leica and Rolleiflex type in the interests of working discreetly. Longwell also set up connections with European press publishers and Time Inc. ensured the cooperation of the main images sources, such as Associated Press, Wide World and Keystone, while also cultivating a close relationship with the newly created Black Star agency.

It was in December 1935, after more than a year working in the American press, that Kurt Safranski, realizing what was needed in the way of images and what his own skills were worth, got together with Ernest Mayer and Kurt Kornfeld to set up Black Star.[22] Mayer had founded the Mauritius agency in Germany in 1929 and drew on this established network to meet Longwell in 1936 and offer him Black Star's services. The upshot of the meeting was that for a fee of 5,000 dollars Time Inc. was given a year's special access to all images taken by Black Star's photographers and all those the agency acquired overseas. Time Inc. was thus acquiring the services of picture editors experienced in innovative journalistic practice. Black Star, in effect, was offering the magazine both a supply of images and proposals for projects the agency would carry out. This editorial aspect was enhanced by the care the agency brought to the treatment of its subjects, with the snapshot overriding the use of posed material. Mayer also recalls having convinced the American publishers of the interest of the photographic series that were more profitable for Black Star than individual illustrations.[23]

In October 1936 Luce—who had married Clare Booth Brokaw in November 1935—finally bought the title *Life* from the nineteenth-century magazine in question for $92,000.[24] He put the editorial team together with himself as editor, assisted by John Shaw Billings. Daniel Longwell was made picture editor and Howard Richmond art director. In the spring of 1937 Wilson Hicks left Associated Press, joined the team and took over the selection and organization of photographs for the magazine.[25] The first issue went out on November 23, 1936, priced 10 cents: it comprised 100 pages, sixteen of them in color, with over 250 photographs and thirty-five pages of advertising (see Figure 3.2). The articles varied in length from half a page to nine pages. The sections "*Life* on the American News front" and "The Camera Overseas" grouped together photographs from different parts of the world; and "Speaking of Pictures", which began in the second issue, featured and discussed photographs provided by readers.[26] The subjects—local and exotic, socio-political and cultural—included series or groups of images in various, and sometimes crowded, layouts characterized by tight silhouetting, symmetrical composition, jokey associations, and numbered sequences on a white or black ground.

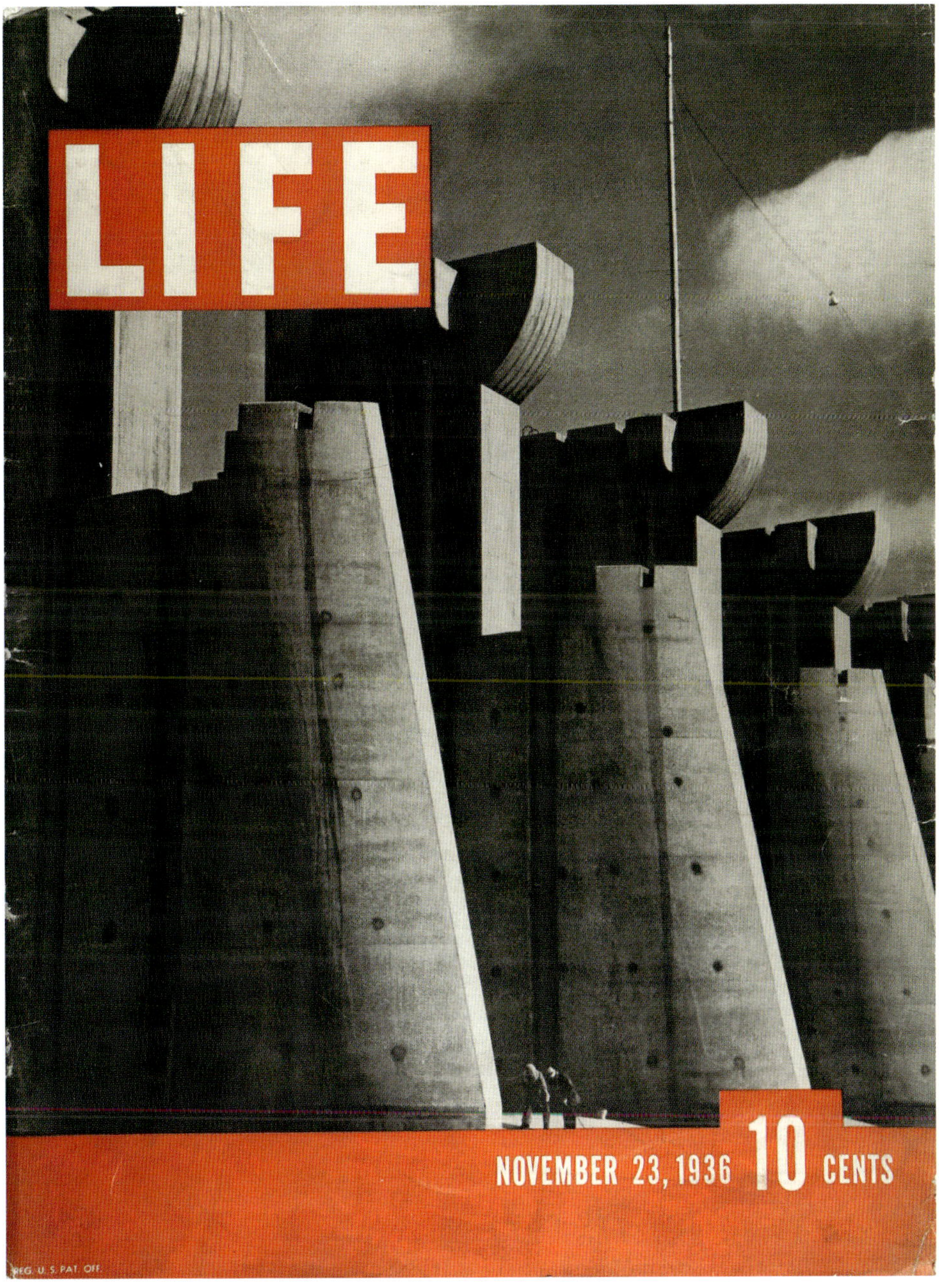

Figure 3.2 *Life*, November 23, 1936, cover. Photograph by Margaret Bourke-White.

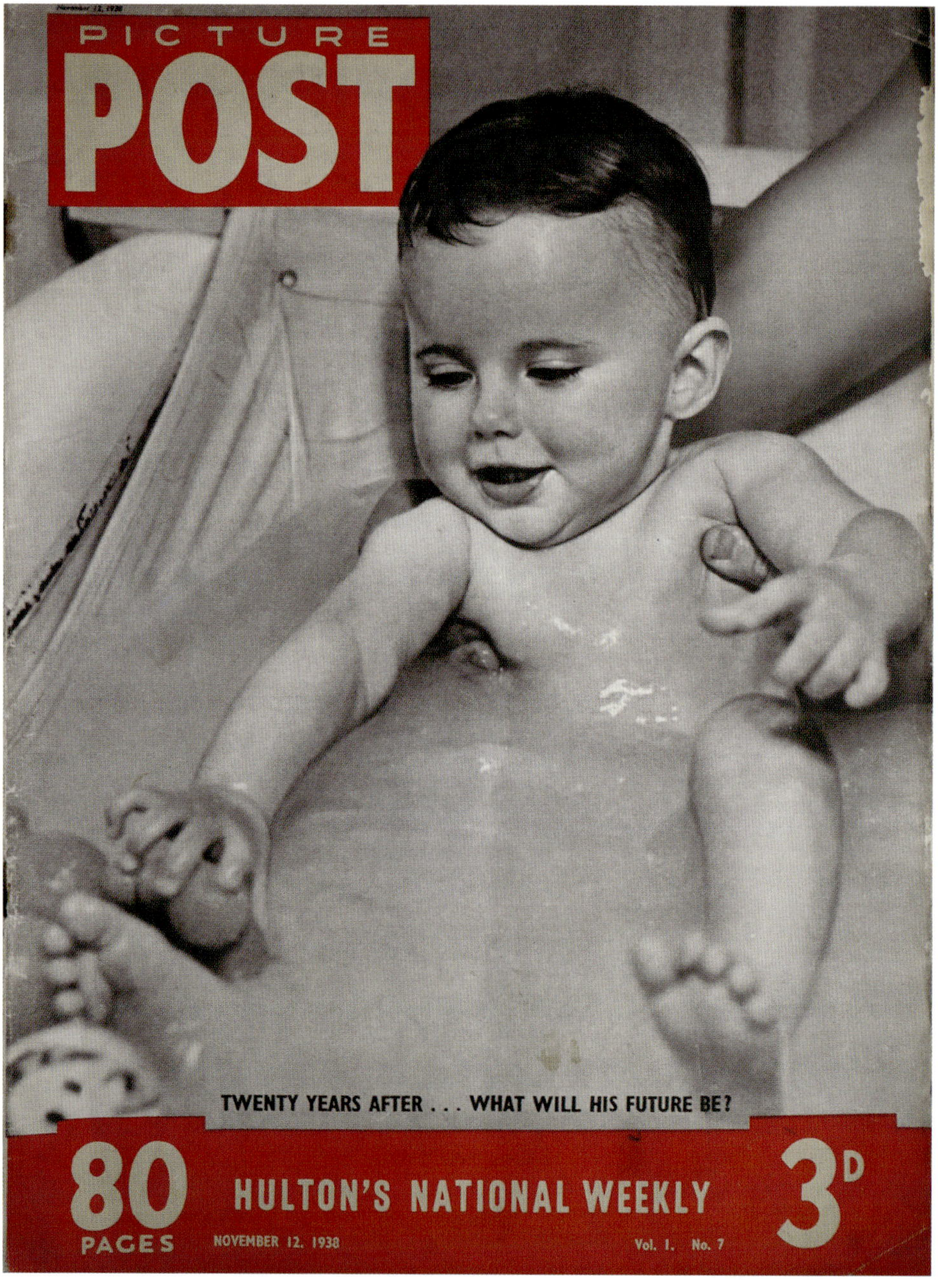

Figure 3.3 *Picture Post*, November 12, 1938, cover.

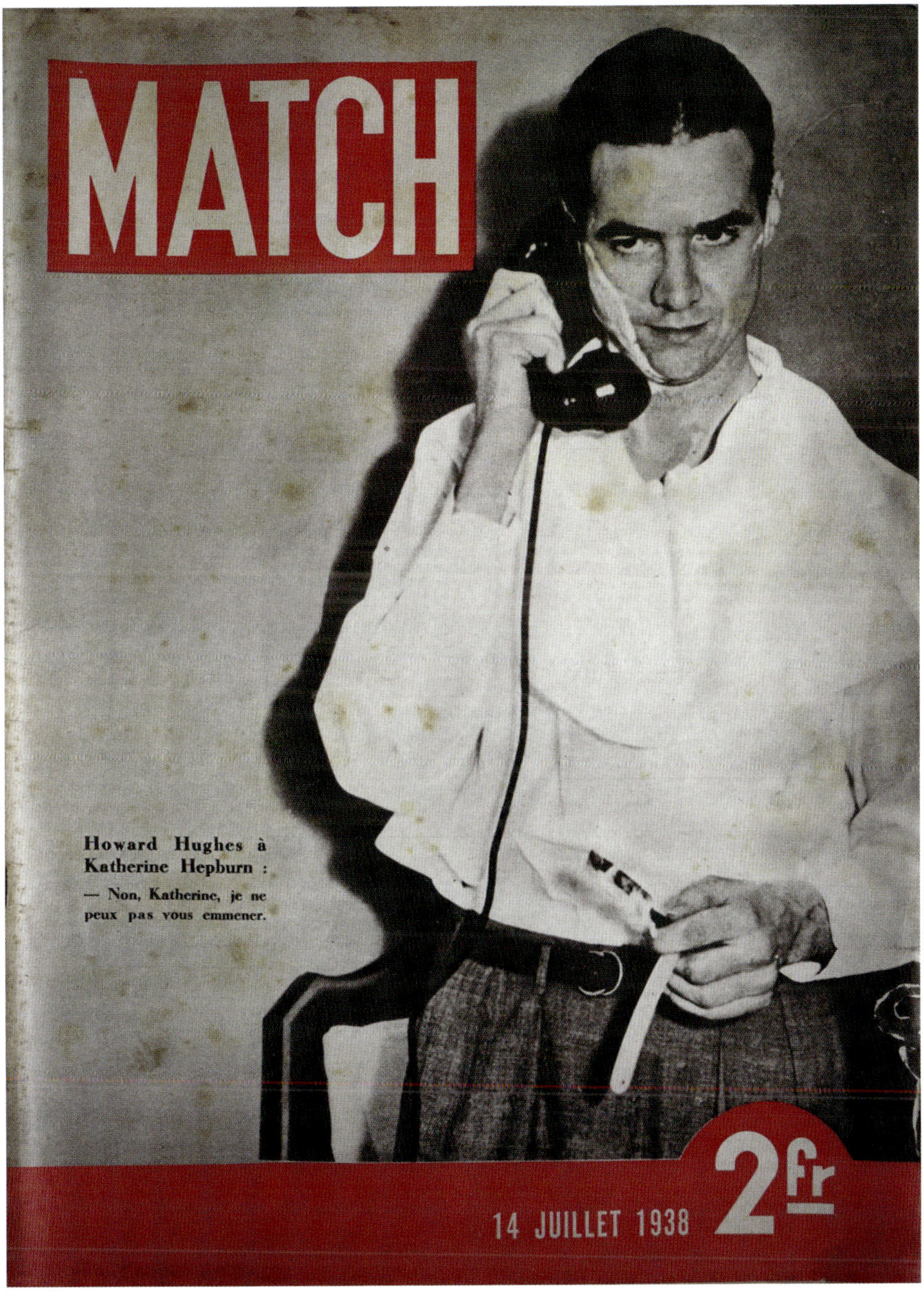

Figure 3.4 *Match*, July 14, 1938, cover.

Advertising, to which *VU*'s Lucien Vogel had wanted to accord "the place it occupied in modern life",[27] took on unprecedented importance. Advertisements filled 20 percent of the space in *Life* in 1938, 35 percent in 1940 and 45–50 percent from 1942 onwards.[28] The independence of the pages and of the double page spreads that distinguished the magazine from the illustrated weekly allowed the reader to flip back and forth according to his or her interests. This editorial feature also meant that advertising material could be inserted to fit with the content of the articles: thus the magazine became a "marketing vehicle" whose efficacy tied in with the rationalization of work implemented by Henry Ford in his assembly-line plants after the First World War.[29] *Life* identified with this emphasis on large-scale capitalist production via a product addressed to a wide readership which, nonetheless, still largely belonged to the affluent classes. *Life*'s success was immediate: on January 4, 1937 it published the print runs for its first six issues, declaring that it had progressed from 380,000 to 600,000 copies in a few weeks.[30]

Of layout as initially practiced at the magazine Wilson Hicks remarks, "The early issues of *Life* contained many pages of physically abused photographs which now have a unique value as horrible examples."[31] These issues included many photographs—around 200 each[32]—in a compact layout that the designers tried to brighten up with some heavy-handed ornamentation. As the years passed the pictures became fewer and bigger, and the layout gained in elegance. Hicks points out that the task was "to develop art editors and layout men who could make pictures tell a story coherent in form."[33] Thus it took the editorial team several months to find its feet and come up with a visual identity for the magazine; nonetheless the *Life* formula, revolving around groups of photographs (and advertisements) emphasizing a snapshot aesthetic, had repercussions as far afield as Europe: like *Life*, the first covers of *Picture Post* in London and *Match* in Paris (see Figures 3.3 and 3.4) adopted a white title on a red ground, with a banner for the price, date and issue number.[34]

Dramatizing the news

In England the first number of the weekly *Picture Post* appeared on October 1, 1938, published by Edward Hulton with Stefan Lorant as editor in chief. Its success was on the same scale as *Life*'s: after an initial print run of 700,000, it had a circulation of 1.7 million by the spring of 1939.[35] The graphics of its first covers were directly inspired by *Life*, but the layout and the role of photography were an extension of editorial practices Lorant had been working on for a decade.

Not long after his arrival in London in 1934, Lorant had picked up where he had left off as a pressman and began working on the new formula for the magazine *Clarion*, published by Odhams Press. He gave it a news focus, changed its name to *Weekly Illustrated* (1934–1939) and published the work of photographers he had met in Germany, among them Brassaï, Alfred Eisenstaedt and Fritz Goro.[36] In July 1937, as a personal venture, he launched the magazine *Lilliput* (1937–1960), a small format (19 x 13 cm) monthly of a hundred or so pages whose cover, interest in photography and general style were reminiscent of those of *UHU*, published by Ullstein in Berlin. *Lilliput* included articles, short stories, illustrations and photographs published as a section apart, independently of the texts and, as a general rule, with one per page. The photographers on its credits list had been working in photojournalism since the 1920s: Felix H. Man, Alfred Eisenstaedt, Erich Salomon and Tim Gidal, whom Lorant knew from the *Münchner Illustrierte Presse*; the Parisians Erwin Blumenfeld, Brassaï, André Kertész, Philippe Halsman, Germaine Krull, Robert Capa, Emmanuel Sougez and Pierre Verger; and the Englishmen Bill Brandt and Cecil Beaton. The magazine's photographic sections were enlivened by visual associations created by Lorant, and there were double-page pairs of images that triggered meaningful thematic and formal comparisons. Humor was a key aspect of the image associations: in 1937 Lorant set a photograph of a woman at the hairdresser's with her hair hooked into a network of electric curlers, captioned "Almost ready", alongside one of a spiky-crested bird, captioned "Ready".[37] Satire also provided an outlet for Lorant's political opinions, with plenty of double pages deriding fascism in Europe and German Nazism in particular: one portrait of a bellowing Hitler brandishing his fists was titled "The German Head of State" and paired with an image of a chimp in similar pose and the caption "The Terror of the Zoo"[38] (see Figure 3.5). This kind of juxtaposition was eloquent in itself, but was always backed up by a caption. At *Lilliput* Lorant made use of the network of photographers he had built up in the preceding years, and his association of aesthetic and political concerns was proof of real savoir-faire in the image field. By the spring of 1938 the magazine had a circulation of 75,000 and a balanced budget.[39] Lorant was then approached by Hulton Press, with an offer to buy *Lilliput* and launch an illustrated magazine: the contract was signed in May and Lorant began thinking out the form and content of what would be *Picture Post*.

For Lorant, "The photograph should not be posed, rather the camera should be as the notebook of a trained reporter, recording contemporary events as they happen, without trying to stop them to make a picture; people should be photographed as they really are and not as they would like to appear."[40] In November 1938, barely two months after its launching, *Picture Post* published "With the Candid Camera in the Café of Artists," on a café in Regent Street in London[41] (see Figure 3.6). The article's five pages gave a brief résumé of the seventy years of existence of a café whose customers went there "to see and be seen." The text was accompanied by sixteen photographs, fifteen of them showing the animated life of the café as seen from one table and borrowing the artistic codes

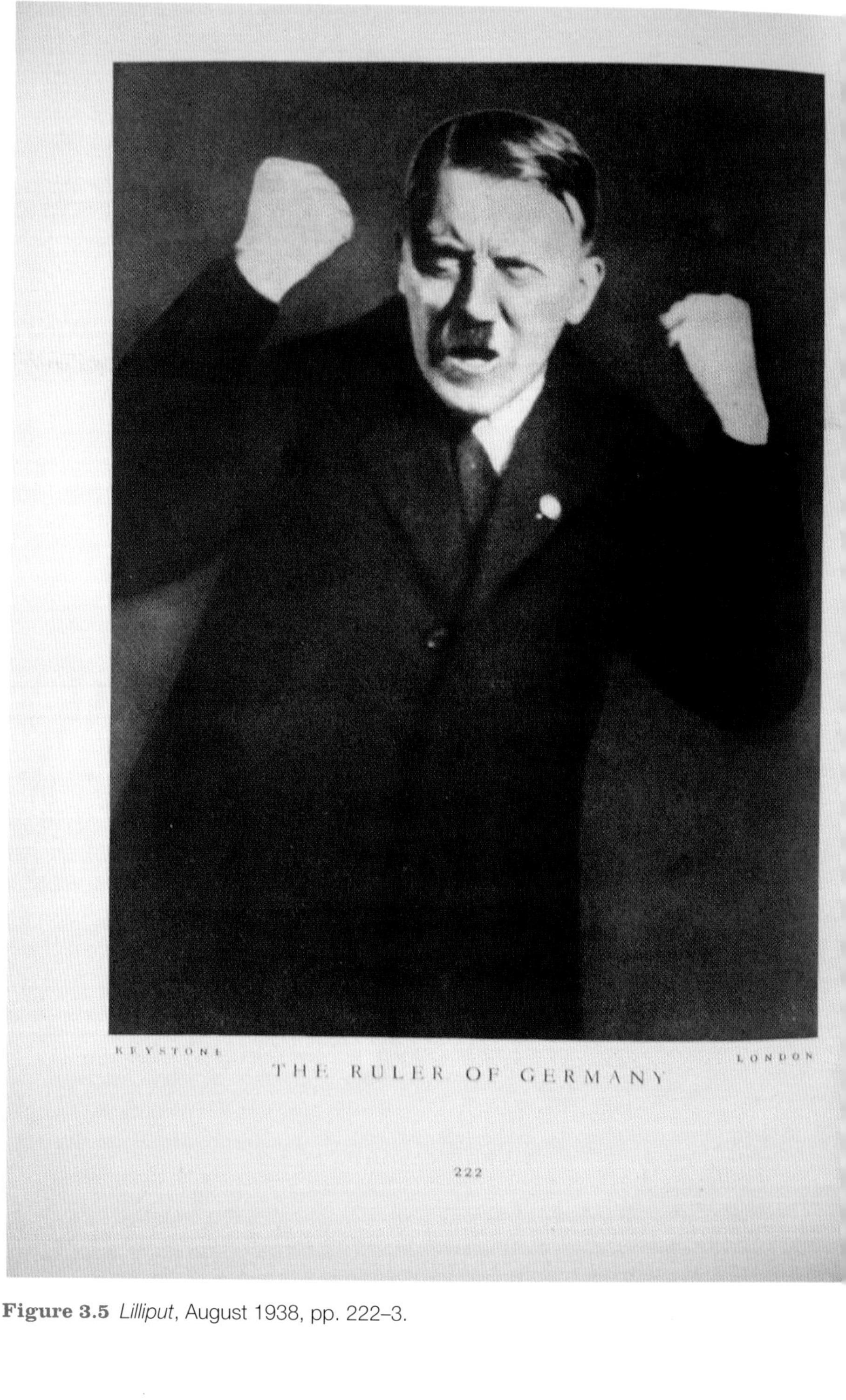

Figure 3.5 *Lilliput*, August 1938, pp. 222–3.

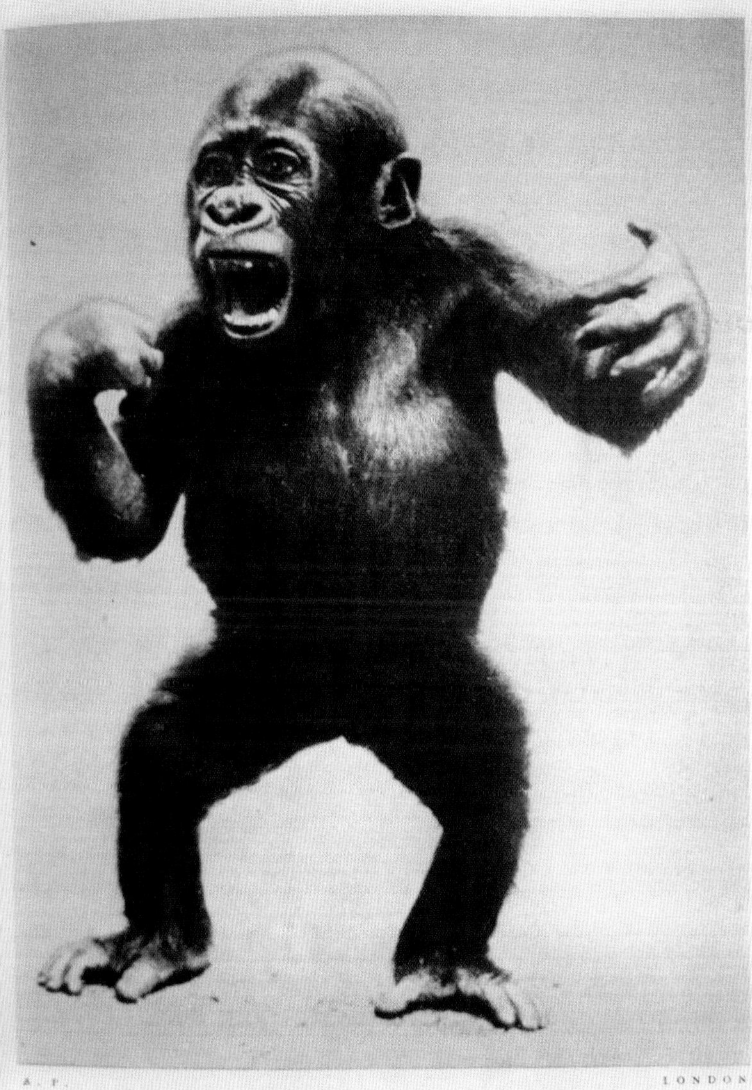

A. P. LONDON

THE TERROR OF THE ZOO

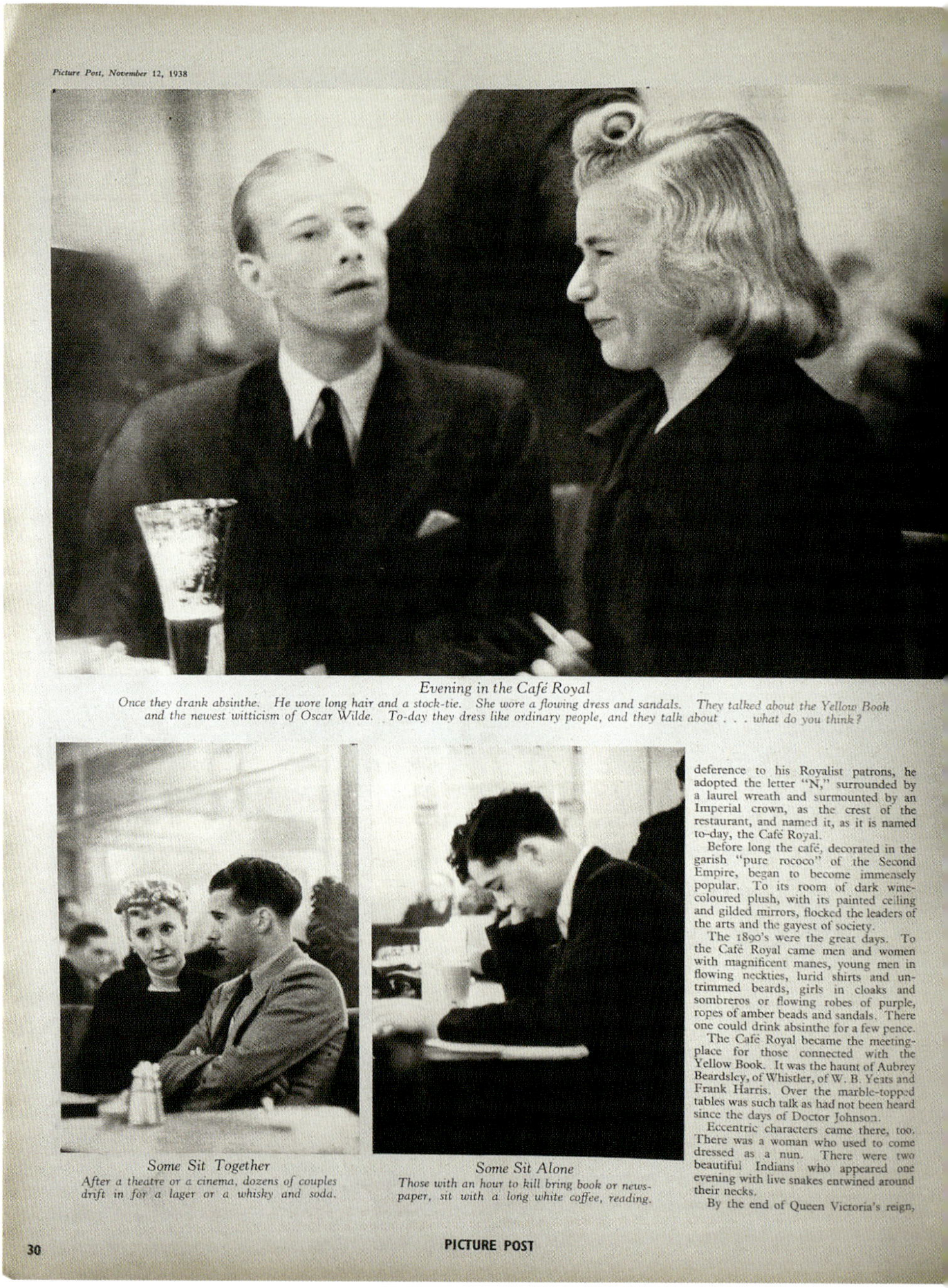
Picture Post, November 12, 1938

Evening in the Café Royal

Once they drank absinthe. He wore long hair and a stock-tie. She wore a flowing dress and sandals. They talked about the Yellow Book and the newest witticism of Oscar Wilde. To-day they dress like ordinary people, and they talk about . . . what do you think?

Some Sit Together

After a theatre or a cinema, dozens of couples drift in for a lager or a whisky and soda.

Some Sit Alone

Those with an hour to kill bring book or newspaper, sit with a long white coffee, reading.

deference to his Royalist patrons, he adopted the letter "N," surrounded by a laurel wreath and surmounted by an Imperial crown, as the crest of the restaurant, and named it, as it is named to-day, the Café Royal.

Before long the café, decorated in the garish "pure rococo" of the Second Empire, began to become immensely popular. To its room of dark wine-coloured plush, with its painted ceiling and gilded mirrors, flocked the leaders of the arts and the gayest of society.

The 1890's were the great days. To the Café Royal came men and women with magnificent manes, young men in flowing neckties, lurid shirts and untrimmed beards, girls in cloaks and sombreros or flowing robes of purple, ropes of amber beads and sandals. There one could drink absinthe for a few pence.

The Café Royal became the meeting-place for those connected with the Yellow Book. It was the haunt of Aubrey Beardsley, of Whistler, of W. B. Yeats and Frank Harris. Over the marble-topped tables was such talk as had not been heard since the days of Doctor Johnson.

Eccentric characters came there, too. There was a woman who used to come dressed as a nun. There were two beautiful Indians who appeared one evening with live snakes entwined around their necks.

By the end of Queen Victoria's reign,

30 PICTURE POST

Figure 3.6 *Picture Post*, November 12, 1938, pp. 30–1.

Picture Post, November 12, 1938

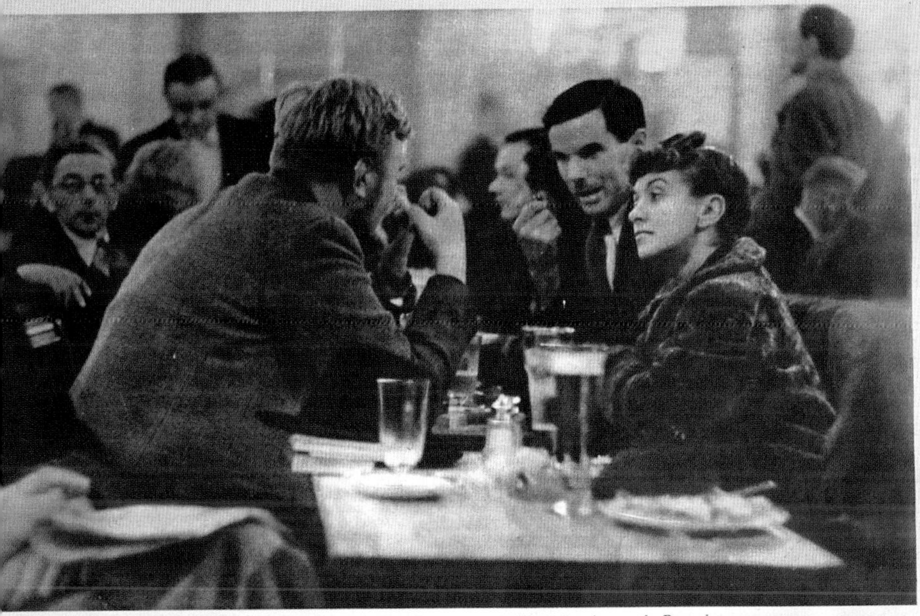

Discussion Among the Beer-glasses

One of the few public places in London where you still hear vehement discussion on literature or art, is the Café Royal. Bearded film-producer Arthur Elton (left) argues with a couple of friends.

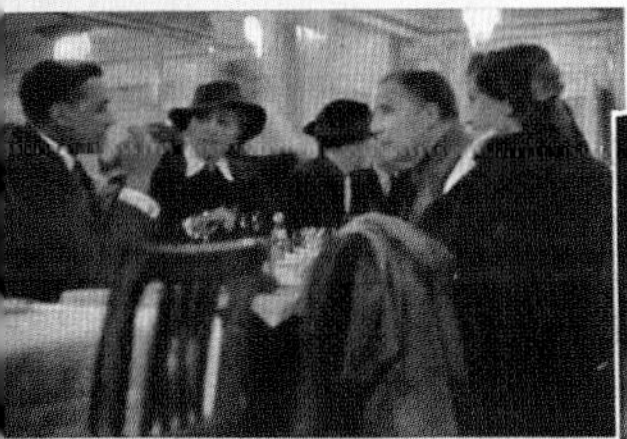

Mrs. "Feather" Looks In

Jeanne de Casalis ("Mrs. Feather" of the radio) and her husband Douglas Stephenson (left) chat to artist-actor Elliot Seabrooke and his dress-designer wife.

even Polite Society had begun to frequent the Café Royal. It was filled with fashionable actresses, sporting peers and wealthy financiers. King Edward VII was a patron. It was at the Café Royal that there occurred that deplorable incident when Lily Langtry, the "Jersey Lily," the beauty of the age, so far forgot herself as to put an ice-cream down His Majesty's back.

The second great period of the Café Royal was between 1910-1914—the days of the Post-Impressionists, the Futurists, the Vorticists, the Cubists. To the Café Royal now came Walter Sickert, Orpen, C. R. W. Nevinson and Augustus John, bearded, brawny, and dressed in rough

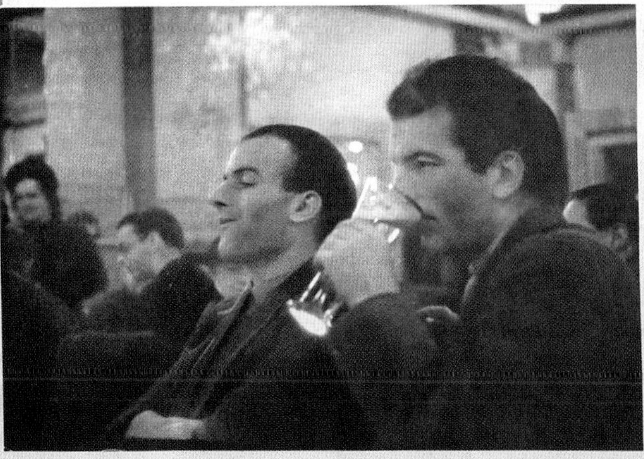

In the Haunt of Wilde and Whistler

The Café Royal, in its various forms, has probably heard more brilliant conversation in seventy years than any other London restaurant. It hears some of other kinds as well.

PICTURE POST 31

popularized by Erich Salomon in the German press ten years earlier. The subjects were a mix of well-known and anonymous figures, alone or in company, and sitting with a coffee or a beer; they are shot from a slightly low angle, the framing is sometimes erratic, and there are the shadow and blur elements specific to the "stolen" photograph. The final image, which takes up half a page, gives the photographer's game away: the camera is a briefcase equipped with a lens, placed on the table and camouflaged by a newspaper the photographer is holding. Snapshots masking the photographer's presence would be the basic material for Lorant's creation of a news narrative in pictures.

Lorant was assisted by Tom Hopkinson, whom he had met at *The Weekly Illustrated*, and two emigrant German photographers Felix H. Man and Kurt Hutton.[42] In a format similar to *Life*'s, a typical 1939 issue of *Picture Post* comprised sixty pages, included over eighty photographs, and in structural terms reflected Lorant's editorial experience.[43] The table of contents was down-to-earth and contained only three sections: "Pictorial Features," "Special Features" and "Articles." The first two of these were devoted exclusively to photographic subjects, while "Articles" summarized the editorial material and the advertising, which were evenly distributed through the opening and closing pages of each issue, without ever interrupting the sequence of the photographic series. Lorant took charge of the selection and placement of the images, leaving Hopkinson to write the captions and texts comprising only a few paragraphs. While the "Articles" varied in length and could sometimes run to ten pages, the layout itself changed little and drew extensively on the graphic possibilities of the double page. As he had done at the *Münchner Illustrierte Presse*, Lorant arranged headings, text, captions and images symmetrically, with the binding as the vertical axis. In this constant search for equilibrium he used a range of formats to highlight the photographs he saw as making his point most effectively.

The first numbers of *Picture Post* covered the last maneuvers of the Spanish Civil War, notably with long series by Robert Capa. In the issue dated December 3, 1938 Lorant devoted eleven pages and a sequence of twenty-six photographs to the Republican attack on Franco's positions along the Rio Segre. At a time when German and Italian military aid to Franco was intensifying, when international support for the Republicans was drying up, and when part of the International Brigades had been repatriated, the victory on the Rio Segre was a flicker of hope in the struggle against fascism.[44] This reportage was first published in the French Communist magazine *Regards*, for which Capa had been working since the beginning of the conflict, then in *Picture Post* (see Figure 3.7), *Life*, and finally *Match* in December.[45] Capa's snapshots—of discussions of strategy, troop movements, shells bursting, soldiers cut down by bullets, stretcher-bearers aiding the fallen, care for the wounded behind the lines—were all numbered and captioned in sequence on the pages of *Picture Post*, whose layout stuck closely to the rules of symmetry so dear to Lorant. Moreover the images and captions were printed on a black background that made their ordering visually coherent. Tight shots of specific movements and concentrated faces, out-of-focus obstacles, camera shake caused by sudden movement or the impact of an explosion—all these factors, in the course of the series, guaranteed the presence and proximity of the photographer and, by extension, his journalistic credibility. In the title paragraph the editors are at pains to make it clear that the photographs "are not presented as propaganda for or against either side. They are simply a record of modern war seen from the inside."[46] Nonetheless, this does not detract from the heroic story of men barely equipped to face the artillery and planes provided by a Germany trying out explosives which, as the article suggests, might one day be used to bomb London. One of the photographs is printed as a double page panorama, showing a group of Republican soldiers sheltering under a rock as a shell explodes on the hill behind them. Captioned "At the heart of the battle: the most remarkable war photograph ever taken," this image is in fact a montage of two photographs designed to produce an impactful double-page spread. Thus Lorant, while using the snapshot aesthetic to shore up the journalistic aspect of his account, was indulging in an editorial practice that failed to respect the integrity of his material.

This long sequence is introduced by a page presenting Robert Capa, accompanied by a portrait in profile showing him looking into his viewfinder. The caption declares him "the greatest war-photographer in the world" and "a passionate democrat [who] lives to take photographs."[47] The subject, the serial approach, the international circulation of the pictures and the sealing of Capa's reputation recall the press strategies used in the early twentieth century to plug Jimmy Hare as "the greatest of war photographers."[48] Hare's photographs of the Russo–Japanese war in 1904 had been run in *L'Illustration* as a portrayal of "A day in battle . . . photographed hour by hour."[49] The concept of action in the process of unfolding was elaborated on by *Picture Post*'s use of Capa's photographs. The French magazine *Match* took up the idea of the black background and the numbering of the images, made a selection that included some previously unpublished material, and wrote its own captions (see Figure 3.8).[50] *Match* also offered a panoramic montage, with the group of images spread over eight pages and illustrating "an hour on the attack" or "the film of one hour, of sixty minutes more densely packed, more eventful, more terrible than an entire lifetime."[51]

For both Hare and Capa the serial presentation of their images was the most appropriate publishing gambit, but the magazines of the late 1930s went further in terms of formal acceptance and enhancement. Whereas the sequencing the editors adopted for Hare's work in *L'Illustration* was an experimental approach to the aesthetic problems posed by the photographs,[52] that of Capa's pictures in *Picture Post* and *Match* had now become the desired and accepted form. Producing visual stories became the goal of magazines and photographers alike. Another consideration was that risk-taking by photographers, which had served to justify Hare's "slightly less than perfect"[53] pictures for readers of

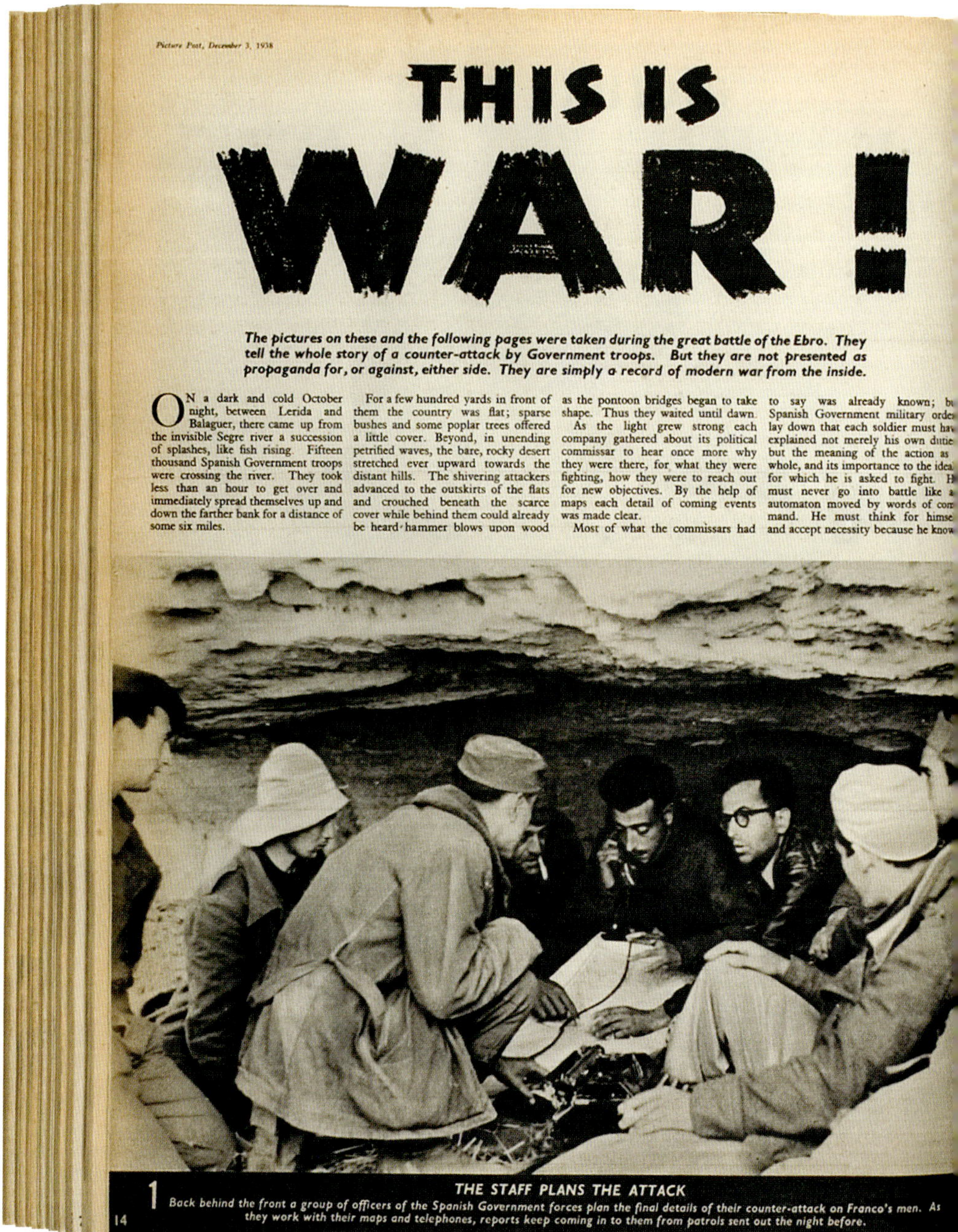

Picture Post, December 3, 1938

THIS IS WAR!

The pictures on these and the following pages were taken during the great battle of the Ebro. They tell the whole story of a counter-attack by Government troops. But they are not presented as propaganda for, or against, either side. They are simply a record of modern war from the inside.

ON a dark and cold October night, between Lerida and Balaguer, there came up from the invisible Segre river a succession of splashes, like fish rising. Fifteen thousand Spanish Government troops were crossing the river. They took less than an hour to get over and immediately spread themselves up and down the farther bank for a distance of some six miles.

For a few hundred yards in front of them the country was flat; sparse bushes and some poplar trees offered a little cover. Beyond, in unending petrified waves, the bare, rocky desert stretched ever upward towards the distant hills. The shivering attackers advanced to the outskirts of the flats and crouched beneath the scarce cover while behind them could already be heard hammer blows upon wood as the pontoon bridges began to take shape. Thus they waited until dawn.

As the light grew strong each company gathered about its political commissar to hear once more why they were there, for what they were fighting, how they were to reach out for new objectives. By the help of maps each detail of coming events was made clear.

Most of what the commissars had to say was already known; bu Spanish Government military orde lay down that each soldier must hav explained not merely his own dutie but the meaning of the action as whole, and its importance to the idea for which he is asked to fight. H must never go into battle like a automaton moved by words of com mand. He must think for himse and accept necessity because he know

1 THE STAFF PLANS THE ATTACK

Back behind the front a group of officers of the Spanish Government forces plan the final details of their counter-attack on Franco's men. As they work with their maps and telephones, reports keep coming in to them from patrols sent out the night before.

14

Figure 3.7 *Picture Post*, December 3, 1938, pp. 14–15. Photographs by Robert Capa. © Robert Capa, courtesy of International Center of Photography.

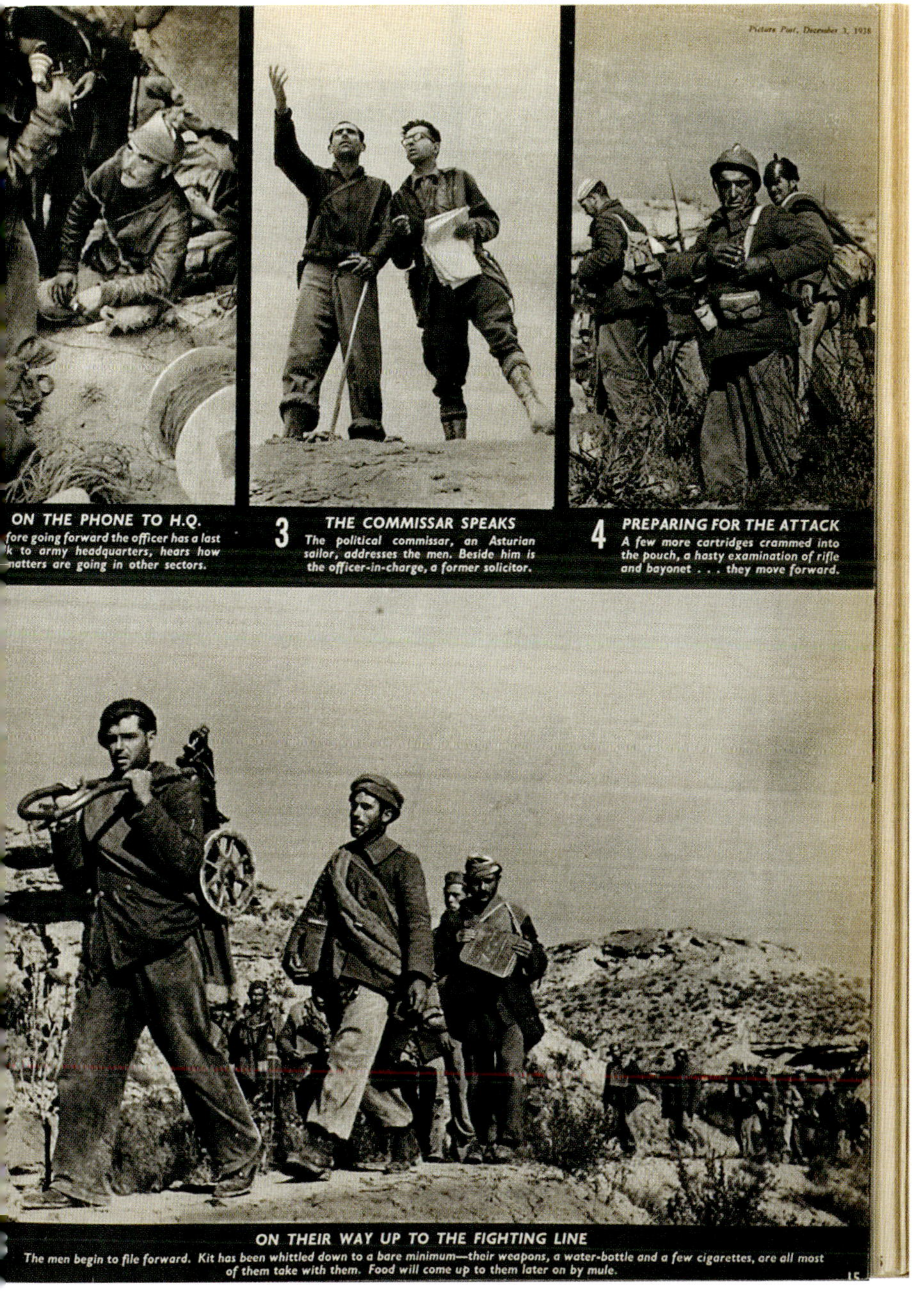

Picture Post, December 3, 1938

ON THE PHONE TO H.Q.
fore going forward the officer has a last
k to army headquarters, hears how
natters are going in other sectors.

3 THE COMMISSAR SPEAKS
The political commissar, an Asturian sailor, addresses the men. Beside him is the officer-in-charge, a former solicitor.

4 PREPARING FOR THE ATTACK
A few more cartridges crammed into the pouch, a hasty examination of rifle and bayonet . . . they move forward.

ON THEIR WAY UP TO THE FIGHTING LINE
The men begin to file forward. Kit has been whittled down to a bare minimum—their weapons, a water-bottle and a few cigarettes, are all most of them take with them. Food will come up to them later on by mule.

15

L'Illustration, had become a dramatic driving force for the narrative processes being applied to the reportages—"one hour . . . more terrible than an entire lifetime"—which was further boosted by the commitment of that "passionate democrat", the photographer. In this context Capa's blurred shots were played up as much as those he had taken on the fly. They too were chosen for a double page feature in *Life* of December 12, 1938 titled "Life's Camera Gets Closer to Spanish War Than Any Camera Has Ever Got Before."[54]

Picture Post presented these images as "simply a record", *Match* as "capturing those terrible seconds in which man becomes inhuman", and *Life* as the product of a camera working as a free agent for the magazine. This rhetoric reminds us of the standard line taken since photographs first made their appearance in the press in the nineteenth century, with the same emphasis on the veracity ensured by the medium's mechanical character. All these magazines, then, laid claim to a form of photographic objectivity whose aura and credibility they exploited to get their own message across. The *Life* team, however, stood out in according the camera the power to express a point of view.

From the photographic essay to the pictorial essay

In discussions about the profession of journalist, Henry Luce's position was clear-cut: any notion of objectivity was illusory.[55] He summoned his editorial teams to take sides and vent a point of view. The task was no longer to reflect reality, but to make it the stuff of an editorial line that stood up for a capitalist vision of the world economy and American power. *Life* shared this perspective and used photography as a media tool.[56] In the short article "The Camera as Essayist," published in the issue dated April 26, 1937, the editors, with five months' experience to their credit, outlined their view of the medium:

> When people think of the camera in journalism they think of it as a reporter—the best of reporters; the most accurate of reporters; the most convincing of reporters. Actually, as *Life* has learned in its first few months, the camera is not merely a reporter. It can also be a commentator. It can interpret as it presents. It can picture the world as a seventeenth century essayist or a twentieth century columnist would picture it.[57]

So where the standard discourse on the legitimacy of photography in the news media usually centered on the medium's mechanical character, *Life* took a contrary stance in presenting the camera not as an incontrovertible recording tool, but as just another means of recounting reality via the media. The typewriter and the camera were thus equivalent in that they enabled expression of ideas. Words and images were two forms of communication used by journalists to convey a point of view on current affairs. The article continued, "A photographer has his style as an essayist has his. He will select his subjects with equal individuality. He will present them with equal manner. The sum total of what he has to say will be equally his own."[58]

In this brief statement *Life*'s editors rejected the authority of the purely mechanical and took for granted the photographer's adoption of a style for his account of a given event. The photograph was no longer put forward as a window on the world, but as a representation, intimately connected with its referent but the result of a formal act on the part of the photographer. Thus did *Life* redefine the role of the photographer and the medium in the general press; and in August 1937 it put its theory into practice by adding the "Photographic Essay" to its list of contents.

The first photographic essay appeared in the issue of August 30, 1937. Of the 1,292 such essays published between that year and 1962, 769 made up the feature in its entirety and 418 of them were the work of a single photographer.[59] Yet even if the editors had promoted the photographer to the role of essayist, the weekly still kept a firm hand on things, including the style and make-up of the essays. That initial essay of August 30, 1937 comprised thirty photographs spread over eight pages under the title "The Japanese: the World's Most Conventional People."[60] For this ambiguously titled essay the editors drew on nine different sources, among them freelance photographers (Masao Horino) and the Associated Press, Wide World, Keystone, Pix and Black Star agencies. At the time Black Star represented Fritz Henle and, most notably, Yonosuke Natori, thirteen of whose photographs were included. Natori's images made up the main body of the essay, with descriptions of the daily life of the Japanese—urban scenes, public baths, farming, education—in which a snapshot approach was balanced out by formal composition, although without defining a distinctive style. The essay's images were in different formats, sometimes printed right to the edge of the page and in all cases accompanied by short, descriptive legends stressing criticism at the expense of information for the curious. The portrait of a young woman bears a reminder that only 5 percent of Japan's population receive an education comparable to that available in the West; and the photograph of a peasant woman in a rice paddy is coupled with an ironic remark about how patriotic the Japanese are, despite their appalling working conditions. In this essay—split in half by two pages of color advertisements for cigarettes and whisky—the editors responsible for the miscellany of images and the captions are imposing their own ideological vision. The aesthetic discretion of the photographs thus becomes an asset, enabling a kind of malleability in terms of the meaning the editors can assign to the images. Natori's picture of the peasant woman in the rice field has been slightly cropped to highlight its subject (see Figure 3.9).[61] The backs of the Natori prints held by the Ryerson Image Centre in

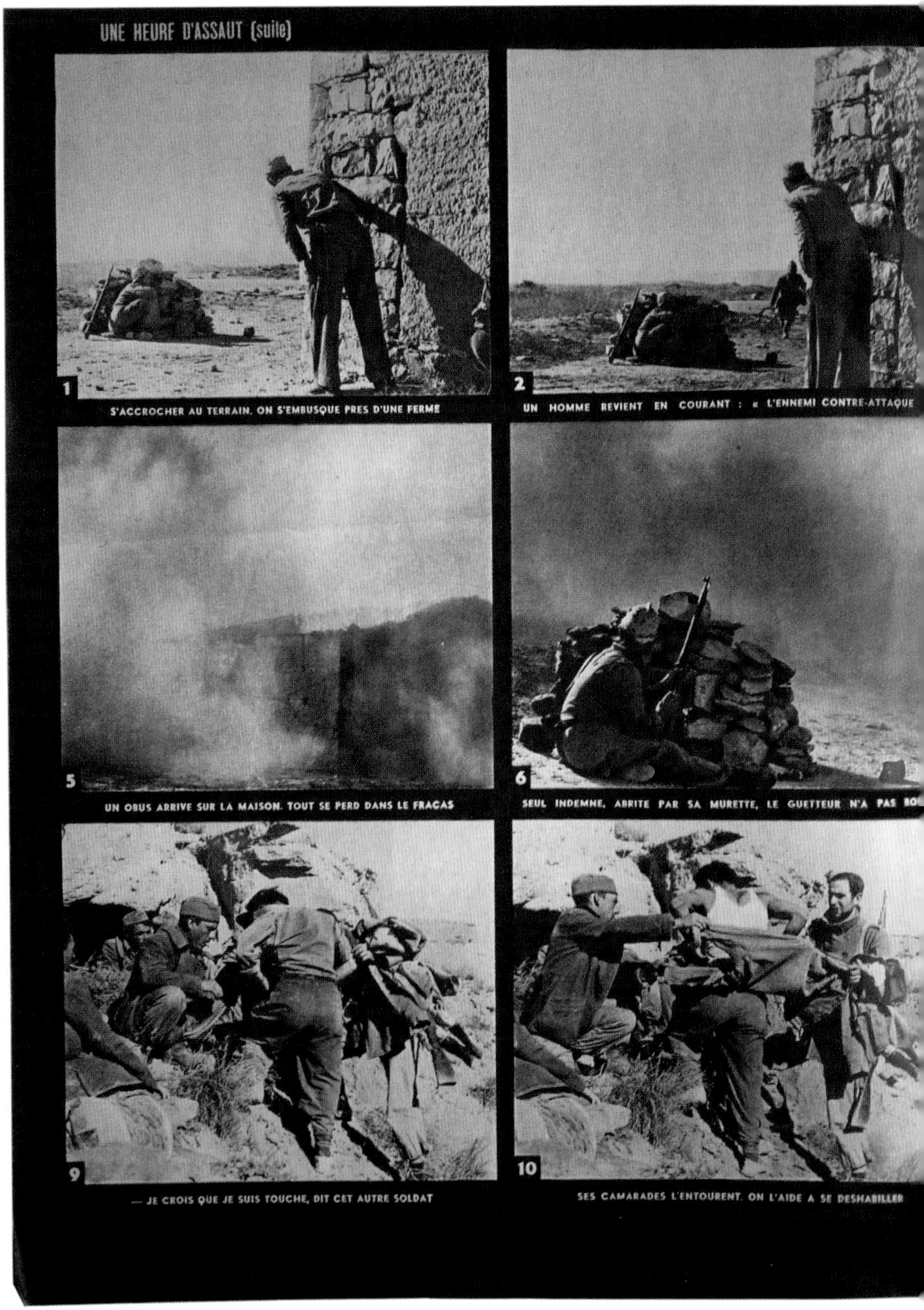

Figure 3.8 *Match*, December 22, 1938, pp. 24–5. Photographs by Robert Capa.

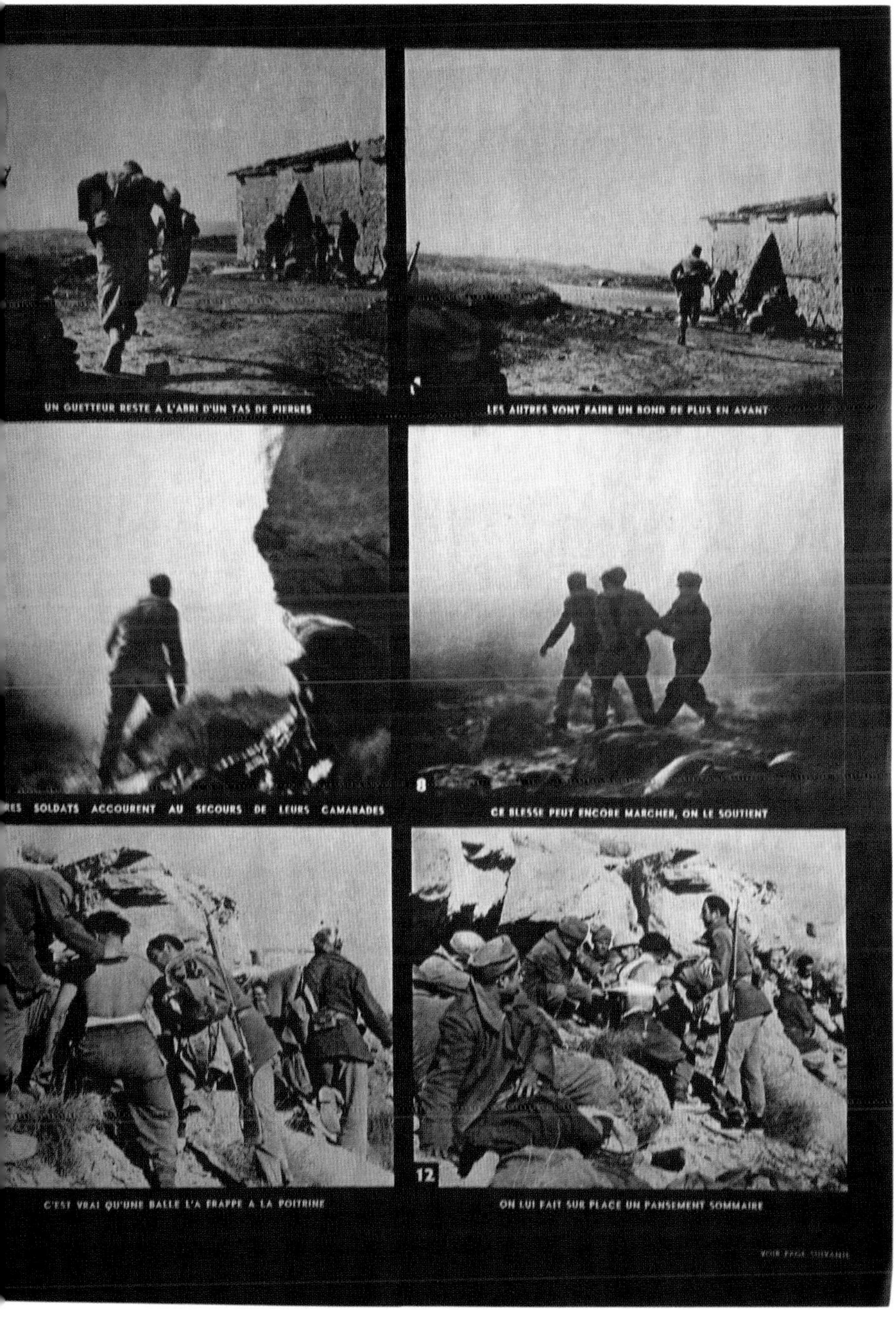
UN GUETTEUR RESTE A L'ABRI D'UN TAS DE PIERRES
LES AUTRES VONT FAIRE UN BOND DE PLUS EN AVANT
RES SOLDATS ACCOURENT AU SECOURS DE LEURS CAMARADES
8
CE BLESSE PEUT ENCORE MARCHER, ON LE SOUTIENT
C'EST VRAI QU'UNE BALLE L'A FRAPPE A LA POITRINE
12
ON LUI FAIT SUR PLACE UN PANSEMENT SOMMAIRE

CONTINUED

Page 44

The World's Most Conventional People

The world's most amazing mass human effort is the Japanese farmer's attempt to feed 70,000,000 Japanese from the arable fringes of Japan's rocky backbone. Growing little else but rice (which yields ten more bushels to the acre than any other grain), he still cannot supply Japan's demand for rice. Normally this would mean that the price of rice would long since have gone up but the Government has kept it down and kept the Japanese farmer husk-poor.

His family makes their own clothes, mats, baskets and charcoal, and the whole village helps him build his house. He uses chiefly rice for money. To save land, he is buried squatting. He keeps no dog, hen or cow. He flattens the winter snowdrifts to hasten their melting. He learned about soil improvement hundreds of years ago. He has a richly satisfying village life, goes on group trips to look at famed cherry trees or chrysanthemums, enjoys weddings, funerals, house-buildings and gets drunk twice a week on *shochu* (rice liquor).

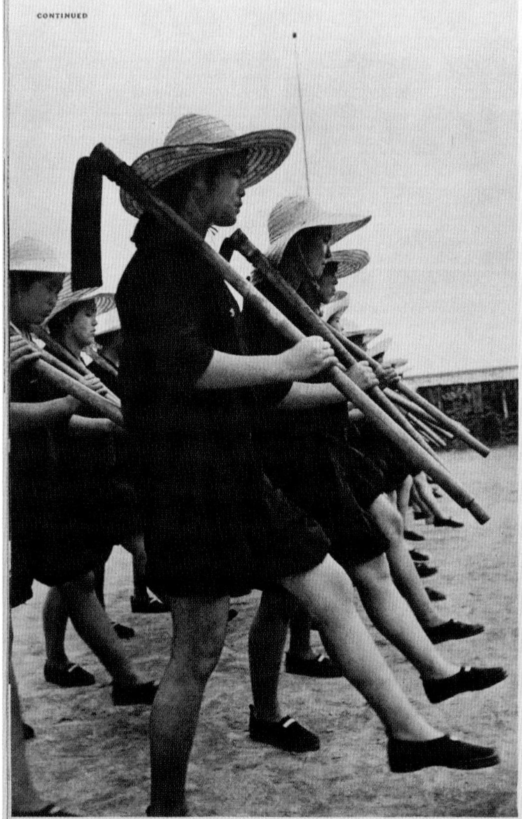

The farmer's daughter in Japan has practically no legal rights in herself. At 13, she may be sold to factory or brothel. Those above are getting a fortunate year at a Government school to learn wifehood. Their long-bladed hoes they will hold onto for the greater part of their waking lives.

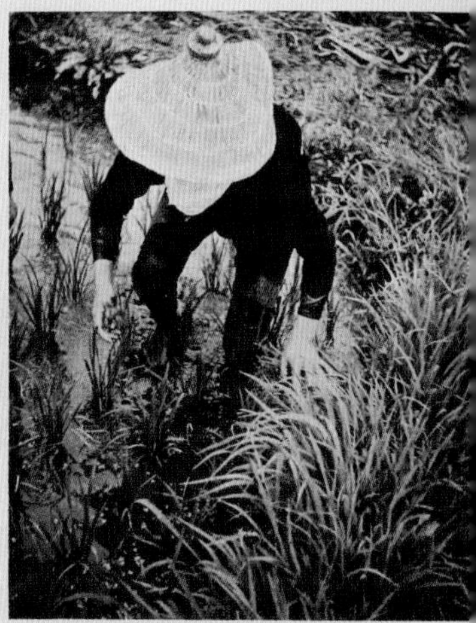

This is rice in June. The farmer in grass hat, cotton shirt, drawers and leggings is at the interminable wet work of cultivation. For all the terrible grinding labor, Japanese like no other climate and no other place than Japan

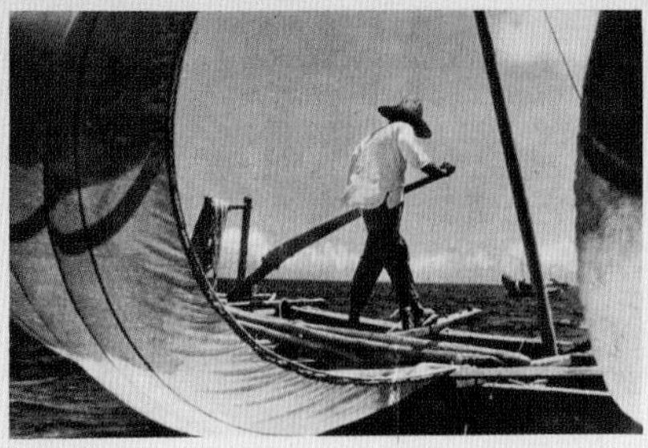

This fishing sampan is out for *tai* (sea bream), best-liked of Japan's 300 varieties of fish. This is a one-sail sampan. Another's sail bulges at the right. Some 1,500,000 Japanese fishermen and 360,000 boats supply the mite of cold, cooked fish to go with rice.

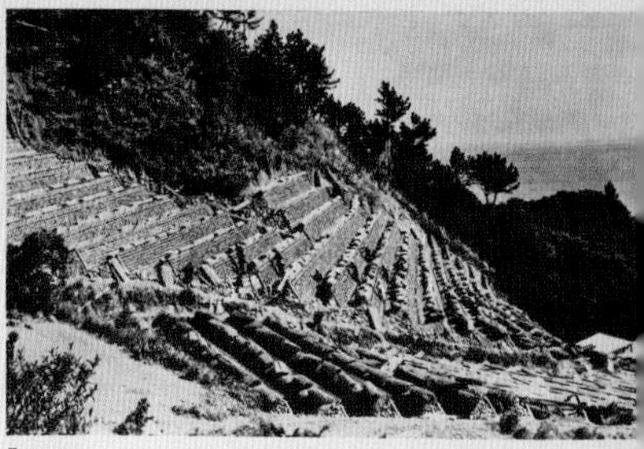

Terraces turn the last possible inch of Japanese earth up to the sun. Only one sevent of Japan is cultivable. The walled-up hillside (*above*), too barren for rice, is set to straw berries, shown covered with cold-weather matting. The berries grow big as onions

CONTINUED ON PAGE 4

Figure 3.9 *Life*, August 30, 1937, pp. 44–5. Photographs by Yonosuke Natori.

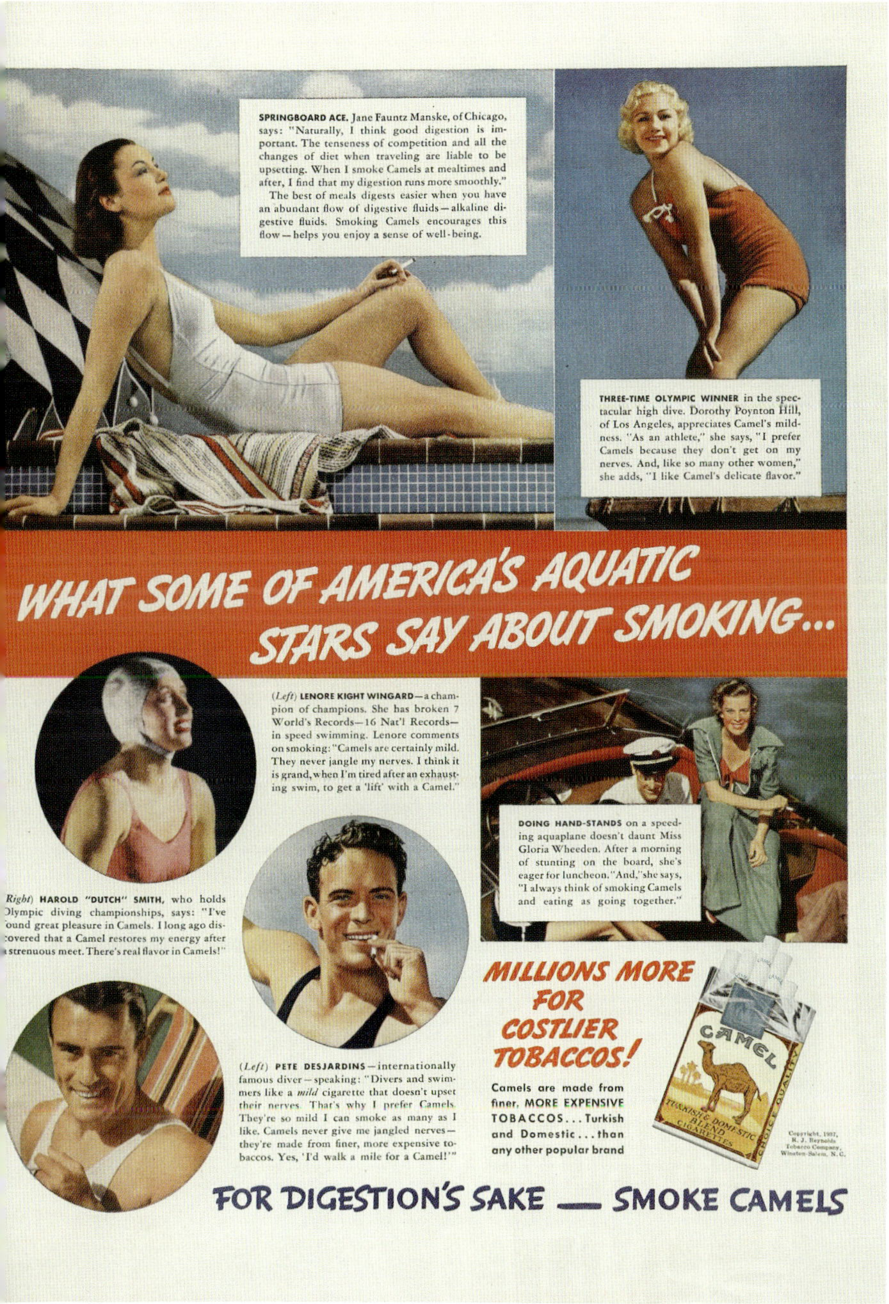
SPRINGBOARD ACE. Jane Fauntz Manske, of Chicago, says: "Naturally, I think good digestion is important. The tenseness of competition and all the changes of diet when traveling are liable to be upsetting. When I smoke Camels at mealtimes and after, I find that my digestion runs more smoothly."
The best of meals digests easier when you have an abundant flow of digestive fluids—alkaline digestive fluids. Smoking Camels encourages this flow—helps you enjoy a sense of well-being.
THREE-TIME OLYMPIC WINNER in the spectacular high dive. Dorothy Poynton Hill, of Los Angeles, appreciates Camel's mildness. "As an athlete," she says, "I prefer Camels because they don't get on my nerves. And, like so many other women," she adds, "I like Camel's delicate flavor."
WHAT SOME OF AMERICA'S AQUATIC STARS SAY ABOUT SMOKING...
(Left) LENORE KIGHT WINGARD—a champion of champions. She has broken 7 World's Records—16 Nat'l Records—in speed swimming. Lenore comments on smoking: "Camels are certainly mild. They never jangle my nerves. I think it is grand, when I'm tired after an exhausting swim, to get a 'lift' with a Camel."
DOING HAND-STANDS on a speeding aquaplane doesn't daunt Miss Gloria Wheeden. After a morning of stunting on the board, she's eager for luncheon. "And," she says, "I always think of smoking Camels and eating as going together."
Right) HAROLD "DUTCH" SMITH, who holds lympic diving championships, says: "I've ound great pleasure in Camels. I long ago discovered that a Camel restores my energy after strenuous meet. There's real flavor in Camels!"
(Left) PETE DESJARDINS—internationally famous diver—speaking: "Divers and swimmers like a mild cigarette that doesn't upset their nerves. That's why I prefer Camels. They're so mild I can smoke as many as I like. Camels never give me jangled nerves—they're made from finer, more expensive tobaccos. Yes, 'I'd walk a mile for a Camel!'"
MILLIONS MORE FOR COSTLIER TOBACCOS!
Camels are made from finer, MORE EXPENSIVE TOBACCOS... Turkish and Domestic... than any other popular brand
CAMEL
TURKISH & DOMESTIC BLEND CIGARETTES
CHOICE QUALITY
Copyright, 1937, R. J. Reynolds Tobacco Company, Winston-Salem, N. C.
FOR DIGESTION'S SAKE — SMOKE CAMELS

Toronto have been stamped "Natori-Photographs should not be used for anti-Japanese purposes."[62] And so *Life*'s first photographic essay expresses a point of view going frankly counter to that of the photographer.

Between 1937 and 1962 102 different photographers contributed to these long essays.[63] The most prolific of them was Alfred Eisenstaedt (twenty-eight essays), followed by Margaret Bourke-White (twenty), Nina Leen (twenty), Eliot Elisofon (nineteen), Andreas Feininger (seventeen) and Dmitri Kessel (seventeen). Among the many other famous photographers who published in this section in the course of their careers were Werner Bischof, Henri Cartier-Bresson, Bruce Davidson, David Douglas Duncan, Philippe Halsman, Yousuf Karsh, Dorothea Lange, Martin Munkácsi, Gordon Parks, George Rodger, William Eugene Smith, Edward Steichen and William Vandivert. According to the period, the styles vary from one photographer to another. Eisenstaedt's success depended partly on his considerable adaptability, but also on his use of a specific aesthetics: the style he had developed in Germany sought to mask the photographer's presence the better to underscore the spontaneity—authentic or simulated—of the people and situations portrayed.[64] This formula could be readily accommodated to editorial intentions and a wide range of subjects: Eisenstaedt was equally at ease photographing the life of the Ainu—the aboriginal people of Japan—on the island of Hokkaido (1946), the strangeness of a Massachusetts beach resort in winter (1963, see Figure 3.10), and Sophia Loren at the peak of her Hollywood career, in the Naples suburb where she had grown up (1961).[65] The Eisenstaedt style was not that of Henri Cartier-Bresson, whose images are characterized by an identifiable compositional balance,[66] or of Gordon Parks and the somber, saturated black and white pictures he took in Harlem[67] (see Figure 3.11) and the favelas of Rio de Janeiro.[68] While sometimes diverging from the photographers' artistic or political stances, the *Life* essays brought access to a wide audience, together with recognition and status. For Gordon Parks, "*Life* was *the* magazine as far as photographers were concerned . . . [and] a prestigious base for me to work from."[69]

Photographers' styles and personal motivation came together in a way that sometimes clashed with the editorial team's objectives. In 1963, for instance, George P. Hunt, *Life*'s managing editor, published a short article titled "To Gene Smith, Welcome Back":

> In this issue we welcome back to our pages a name that has become a legend in photography—W. Eugene Smith . . . It was only natural that the intensity and passion that Smith put into his photography would carry over into the delicate job of selecting which pictures to print and how to arrange them. Often disagreements flared between Smith and the editors. Eight years ago one such disagreement led Smith to resign from our staff.[70]

Hunt was referring to *Life*'s publication of the celebrated essay "A Man of Mercy" on November 15, 1954.[71] Charles Tudor's layout for the twelve pages of Smith's reportage on Dr Albert Schweitzer in his hospital in Lambaréné, Gabon, annoyed Smith, who felt that his perspective on the 1952 Nobel Peace Prize winner had not been respected.[72] The exchange of letters between Smith and managing editor Edward Thompson lasted several months, focusing on the photographer's role in the publication of photoreportages, with Thompson stressing the importance of editorial objectivity in doing justice to photographs and Smith striving for total control over publication of his images.

Smith had joined the *Life* photography team on April 23, 1945.[73] Two weeks earlier a first long reportage, "The Battlefield of Iwo," had appeared as the magazine's "Photographic Essay": nine pages of meticulously framed photographs that shared the news segment with "The Week's Events"—Robert Capa's snapshots of Allied troops being parachuted into Germany.[74]

Smith gradually gained his independence at *Life* and played an increasing part in the editorial work.[75] Initially he sent his negatives to the magazine's laboratory, where they were printed and the results sent on for editing. This was still the procedure in September 1948, when his essay "Country Doctor"[76] was published (see Figure 3.12). The essay's eleven pages comprised numerous snapshots—using various points of view, but always tight angle—of the many-faceted business of being a rural doctor. Smith, though, was dissatisfied, feeling that the prints produced in-house were lacking in tonal depth. He then presented his personal print of the opening picture, showing the doctor walking alone beneath a dark, cloudy sky, with a marked emphasis on chiaroscuro. From there on Smith was in charge of making his own prints, choosing the framing and the tonal intensity and picking out those that were to go to the editors. The difference is patent in his next photographic essay, an account of long and arduous auditions in theatres on Broadway. All the pictures of the actors were taken indoors and are marked by deep blacks and gleaming whites (see Figure 3.13). These tonal contrasts combine very effectively with the grain of the film and a range of framings whose somber, out-of-focus areas bring dramatic depth to the situations portrayed.[77] This work on the prints rounded off the journalistic approach of a photographer who took the time to observe his subjects and gain their confidence. Smith spent twenty-three days with the country doctor and three months in South Carolina for his essay on Maude Callen, published as "Nurse Midwife" in *Life* on November 5, 1951.[78]

In May–June 1950 he was in Spain for two months gathering the material for "Spanish Village," published in *Life* on April 9, 1951.[79] The 2,500 negatives he brought back yielded a selection of fifty-seven prints, seventeen of which were ultimately chosen by the editors for a ten-page essay laid out by Bernard Quint. As deputy editor Maitland Edey emphasized, this economical use of images—"Country Doctor" had comprised twenty-eight and "Nurse

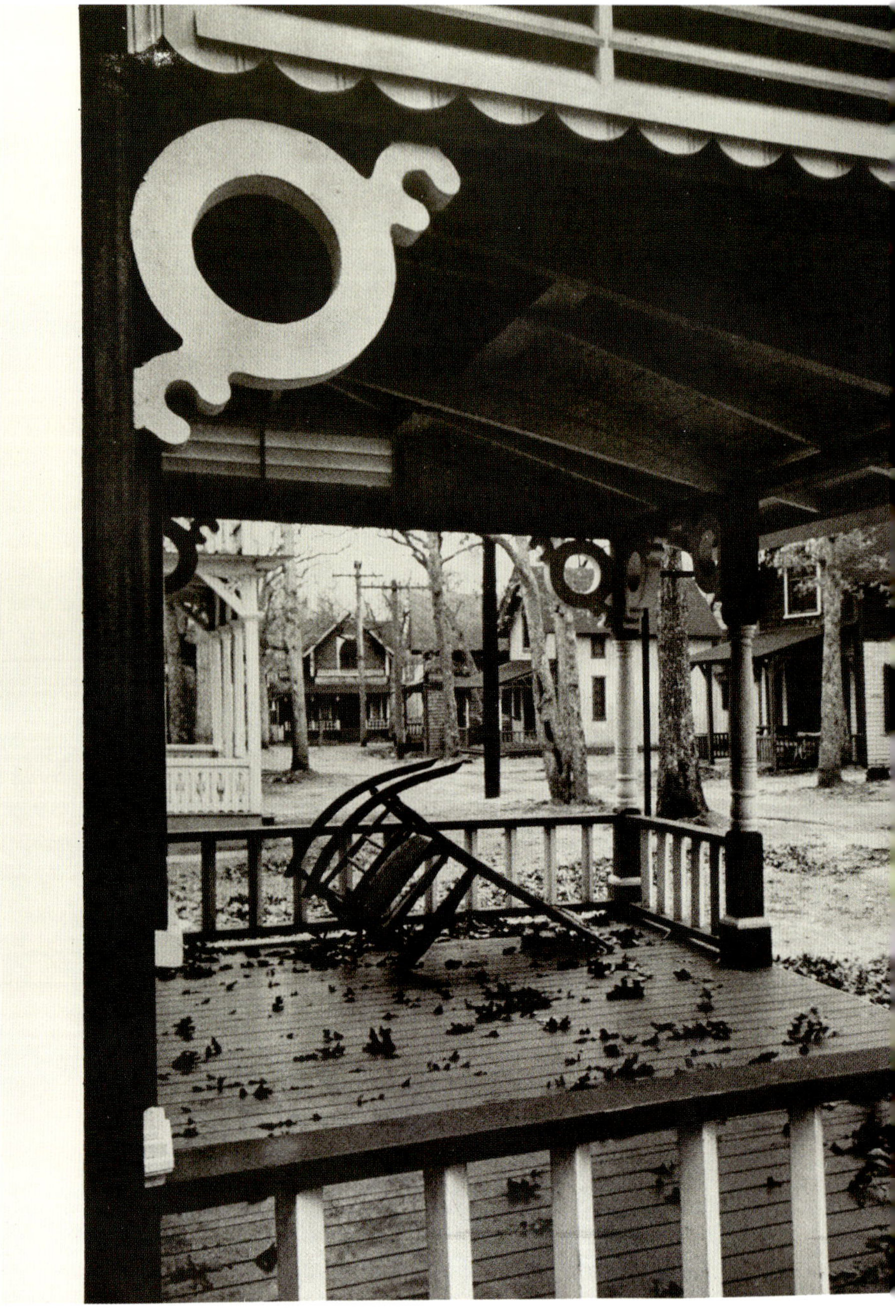

Figure 3.10 *Life*, January 26, 1953, pp. 94–5. Photographs by Alfred Eisenstaedt.

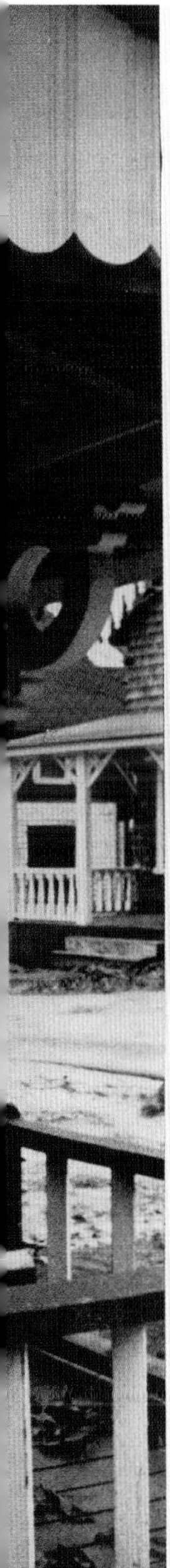

EMPTY HOUSES (*left*) in the gingerbread town of Oak Bluffs stand shuttered against wind and rain. Oak Bluffs houses nearly 15,000 people in summer, only 1,500 in winter.

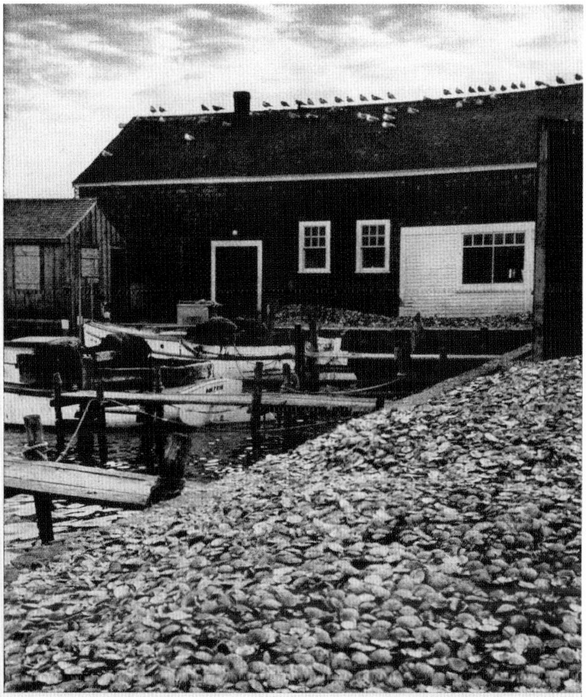

SCALLOP SEASON, in winter brings gulls to docks to wait for returning boats. Gulls eat scallop remains while shells (*foreground*) are used to surface parking lots, private roads.

A Summer Resort in Winter

Emptied Martha's Vineyard takes on a bleak beauty

PHOTOGRAPHED FOR LIFE BY ALFRED EISENSTAEDT

To millions of American vacationers a summer resort is a place that does not really exist except between the Fourth of July and Labor Day. Even when a vacationer keeps going back to the same place summer after summer until he knows every road and every house, he tends to think of it always as a land of warm sun and bathing suits, of afternoon sailboat races and Saturday night dances. But sooner or later every summer visitor gets around to asking a question of some year-round resident. "What's it like here in the winter?"

The pictures on these pages answer the question by showing what happens to Martha's Vineyard after the last vacation visitor has gone. This 100-square-mile island off the coast of Massachusetts undergoes its great annual emptying-out in early September when the population suddenly drops from more than 40,000 to less than 6,000. Those who stay behind slowly recuperate from the bustle of summer, prepare (*pp. 96, 97*) for the next year's tourist invasion and find time at last for all the social life they have been too busy to enjoy. Most of the island's stores, restaurants and hotels are closed. There is no longer a parking problem on the town streets nor a traffic jam every time the steamer arrives from the mainland. Town meetings, church socials and lodge parties take the place of beach picnics and yacht club dinners. Winters are mild with few heavy snowfalls, and permanent residents feel that in spite of the emptiness the Vineyard is a friendlier place, for now everyone knows everyone else. They inherit an island that is restfully quiet and beautiful in the bleakness of its boarded-up houses and its snow-swept beaches.

CONTINUED ON NEXT PAGE 95

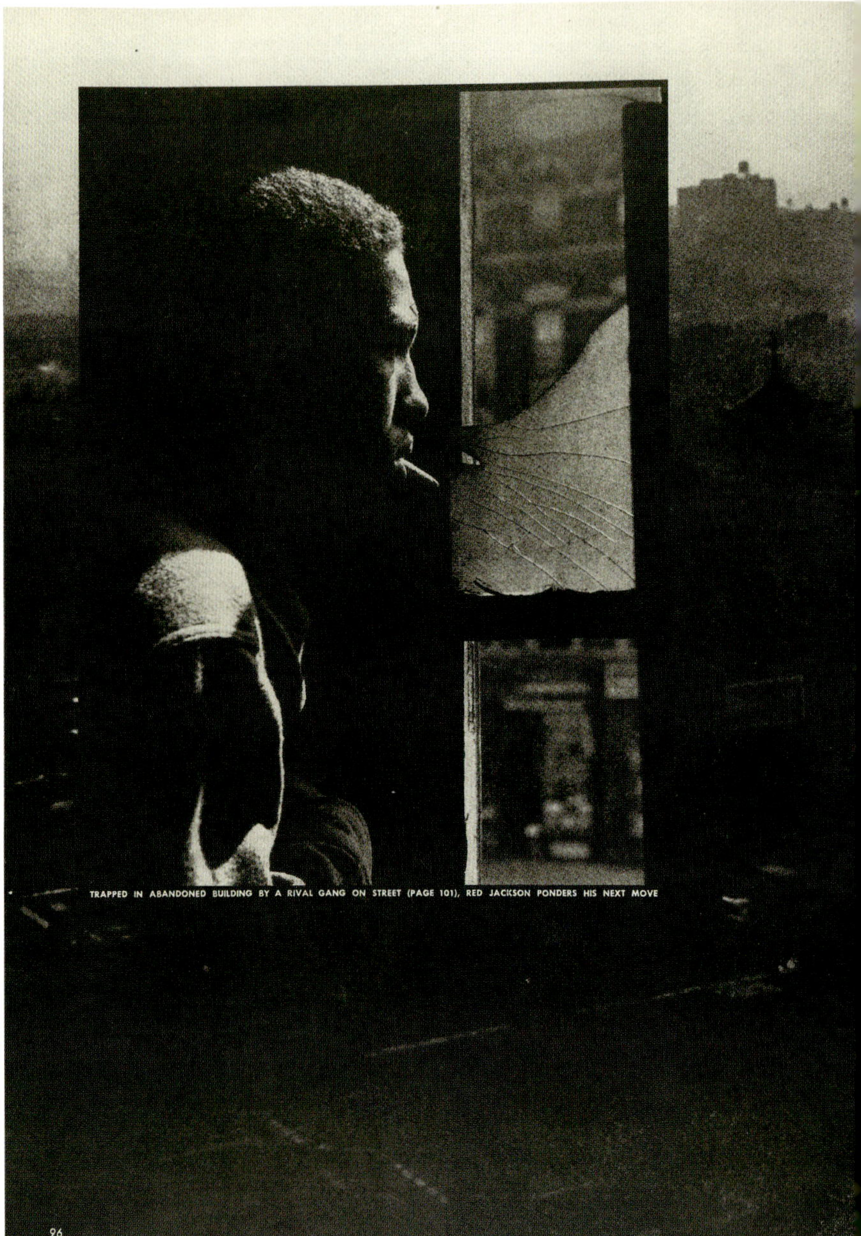

Figure 3.11 *Life*, November 1, 1948, pp. 96–7. Photographs by Gordon Parks.

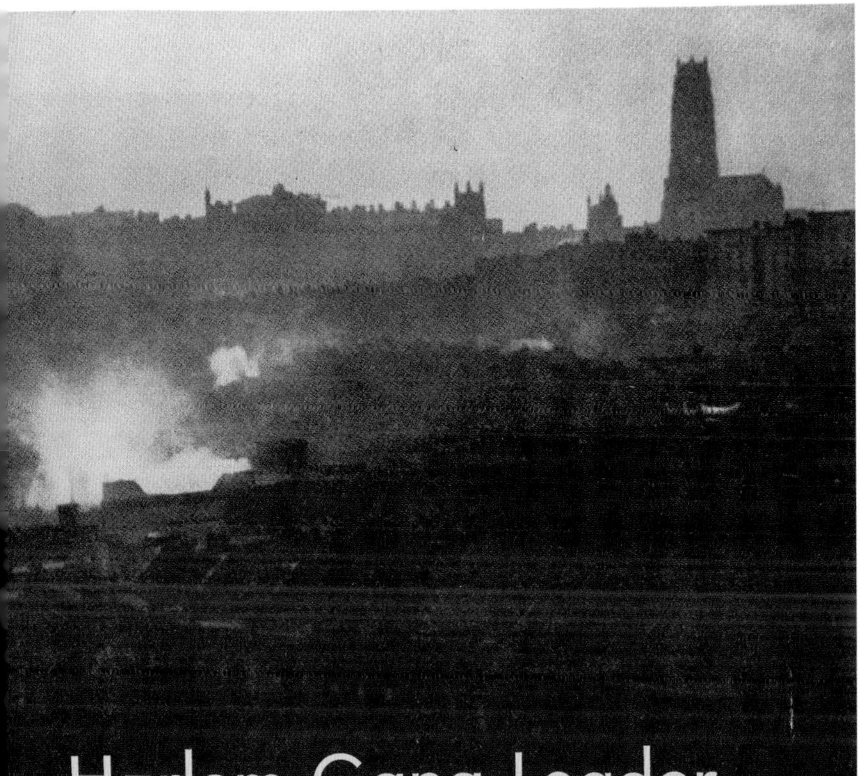

Harlem Gang Leader

Red Jackson's life is one of fear, frustration and violence

Photographs for LIFE by Gordon Parks

The tower in the upper right-hand corner of this page belongs to New York City's famous Riverside Church. Stretching off to the left of it are the classic buildings of Columbia University and the elegant apartments of some of the city's leading citizens. Nestled just below these, under the smoke and haze, are the crowded tenements and the cluttered, dreary streets of Harlem, the U.S.'s biggest Negro community. Here 500,000 people live, crammed into a ghettolike section built originally to hold less than half that number. Schools, like housing, are crowded and run-down, and at the close of each day overworked teachers are glad to turn their restless pupils back into the streets. With little to do but roam around, the children often band together into street gangs—at their best, organized athletic teams, at their worst, roving bands of hoodlums held together by a common spirit of rebellion and a need for security. Leonard ("Red") Jackson, 17, is the tough and successful leader of such a gang.

When he was about 12, Red got tired of getting beaten up by older boys in the block and of paying "protection" in order to get to school. And when he was hungry, which was often, he needed a little help in stealing apples from the sidewalk stands. So he joined a gang for self-protection and for a chance to express his own personal defiance.

Red's gang fights other Harlem gangs like itself. Their acts of violence are no worse than those of white gangs in Brooklyn and other sections of the city, but with more to be frustrated about, and to fear, they have helped to give Harlem one of the highest delinquency rates in the nation. The photographs on these and the following pages are by Gordon Parks, a young Negro photographer who won Red Jackson's confidence and then stuck with him for four hectic weeks to make a chronicle of Red's unhappy life.

CONTINUED ON NEXT PAGE 97

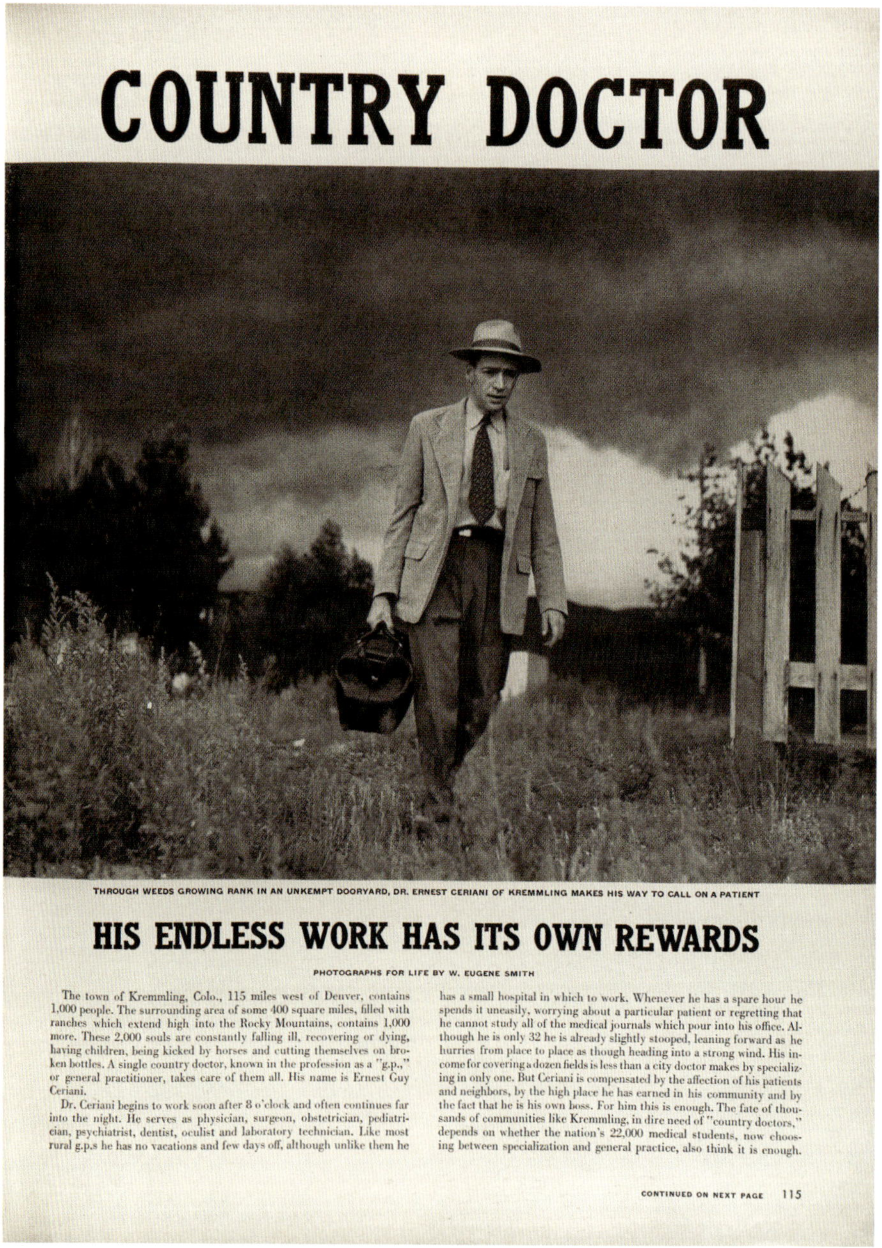

COUNTRY DOCTOR

THROUGH WEEDS GROWING RANK IN AN UNKEMPT DOORYARD, DR. ERNEST CERIANI OF KREMMLING MAKES HIS WAY TO CALL ON A PATIENT

HIS ENDLESS WORK HAS ITS OWN REWARDS

PHOTOGRAPHS FOR LIFE BY W. EUGENE SMITH

The town of Kremmling, Colo., 115 miles west of Denver, contains 1,000 people. The surrounding area of some 400 square miles, filled with ranches which extend high into the Rocky Mountains, contains 1,000 more. These 2,000 souls are constantly falling ill, recovering or dying, having children, being kicked by horses and cutting themselves on broken bottles. A single country doctor, known in the profession as a "g.p.," or general practitioner, takes care of them all. His name is Ernest Guy Ceriani.

Dr. Ceriani begins to work soon after 8 o'clock and often continues far into the night. He serves as physician, surgeon, obstetrician, pediatrician, psychiatrist, dentist, oculist and laboratory technician. Like most rural g.p.s he has no vacations and few days off, although unlike them he has a small hospital in which to work. Whenever he has a spare hour he spends it uneasily, worrying about a particular patient or regretting that he cannot study all of the medical journals which pour into his office. Although he is only 32 he is already slightly stooped, leaning forward as he hurries from place to place as though heading into a strong wind. His income for covering a dozen fields is less than a city doctor makes by specializing in only one. But Ceriani is compensated by the affection of his patients and neighbors, by the high place he has earned in his community and by the fact that he is his own boss. For him this is enough. The fate of thousands of communities like Kremmling, in dire need of "country doctors," depends on whether the nation's 22,000 medical students, now choosing between specialization and general practice, also think it is enough.

CONTINUED ON NEXT PAGE 115

Figure 3.12 *Life*, September 20, 1948, p. 115. Photograph by W. Eugene Smith.

Midwife" thirty—helped to make the most of the white page and enhance the singularity of each photograph.[80]

Sometimes printed to the edge of the page, the pictures were of different sizes and were arranged across double pages without regard for the gutter or the usual text column layout. The published images showed everyday secular and religious activities—plowing the fields, taking communion—in the hamlet of Deleitosa, and stressed the precariousness of the villagers' existence. They were different from the contact sheets, having been modified by Smith in his laboratory: the original image of the three Civil Guards was cropped to provide a tight focus portrait which cuts through the hat of the figure in the foreground; and the saturation and contrast of the picture of a group of women watching over an old man's deathbed were obtained during the printing. Amid this picture's intense chiaroscuro, Smith highlights the faces of the dead man and the grieving women against a sooty background; the effect is to endow this photograph, the last in the series and printed borderless on a double page, with the power to conjure up the Biblical scene of the Lamentation of Christ (see Figure 3.14). Because of this shaping process, applied equally to the images making up "the most famous of all *Life*'s photographic essays"[81] and to the layout, the piece was presented under the heading "Pictorial Essay." The need to replace "photographic" with "pictorial" in the description of Smith's essay arose from the visibility of the photographer's style, the non-topical character of the subject matter and an authorial affirmation which the editors referred to as "artistic sensibility."[82]

The "Pictorial Essay" section was launched in the issue dated March 3, 1947 as a home for articles on "the history and development of Western culture" exemplified by "the work of men who both create and record the culture of their times: the artists."[83] This new section brought together numerous articles of the nineteenth-century "useful knowledge" kind,[84] eclectically illustrated with paintings, stained glass, drawings, engravings and photographs. Between 1947 and 1961, 181 issues out of a total of 1,335 included this section, with articles as on subjects as varied as *Les Très Riches Heures du duc de Berry*, fishing for Chinook salmon and the geography of the universe.[85] As for the photographic essays, the editors chose the illustrative material, whose suppliers and media were very diverse. This section was marked by meticulous attention to the reproduction of images that were often in color: Swiss painter Walter Linsenmaier's animal illustrations and Howard Sochurek's helicopter safari photographs were particularly notable in this respect.[86] Color functioned here as a formally appealing added extra whose use underscored an entertaining and/or artistic intention. The publication of Smith's essay from Spain in this setting demonstrated the change of status accorded to both the reportage and the photographer himself. The editors' attentiveness to Smith's stylistic approach led Edward Thompson to describe him as a "creative journalist."[87] But while Smith enjoyed special recognition and status in photojournalistic circles, he never

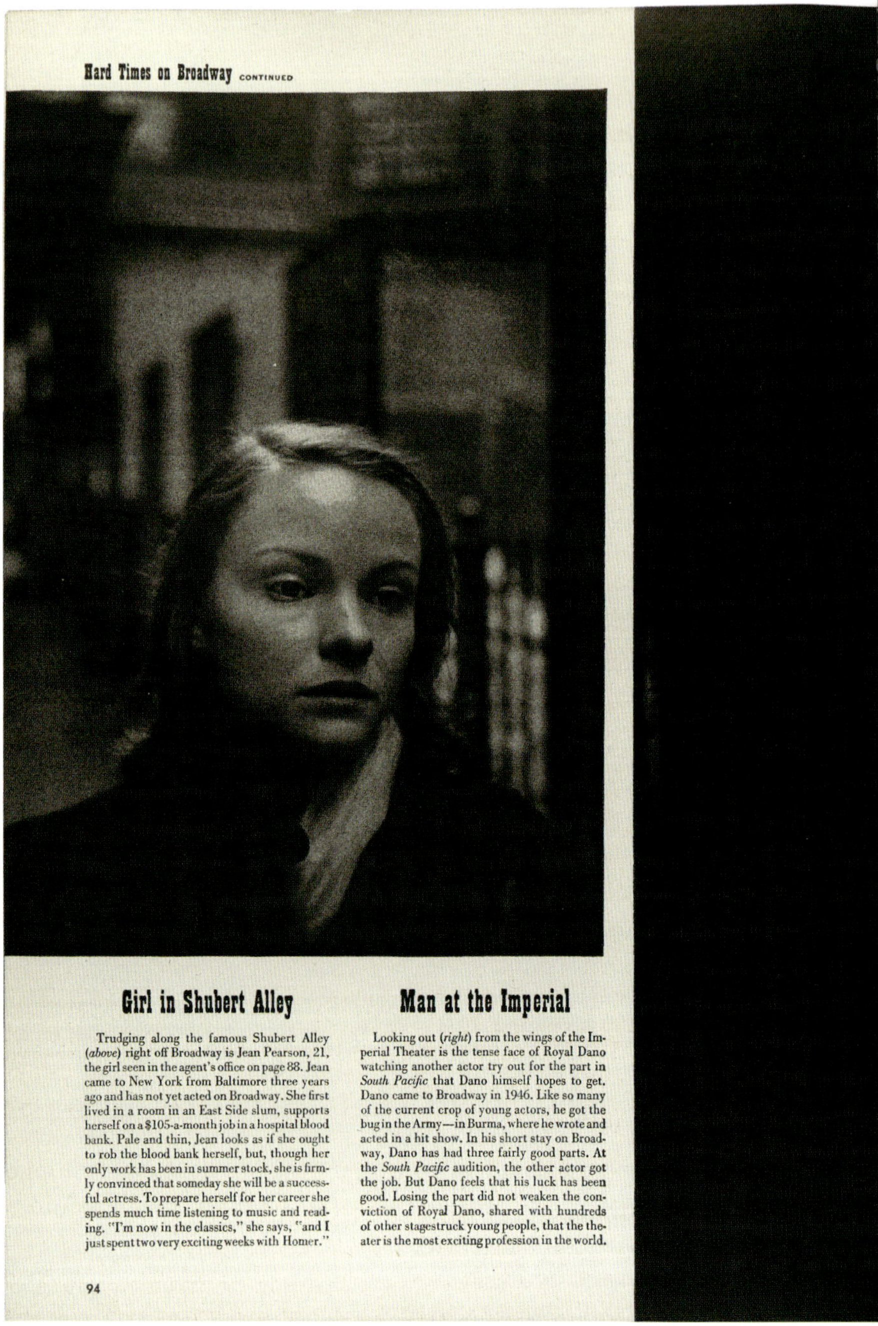
Hard Times on Broadway CONTINUED

Girl in Shubert Alley

Trudging along the famous Shubert Alley (*above*) right off Broadway is Jean Pearson, 21, the girl seen in the agent's office on page 88. Jean came to New York from Baltimore three years ago and has not yet acted on Broadway. She first lived in a room in an East Side slum, supports herself on a $105-a-month job in a hospital blood bank. Pale and thin, Jean looks as if she ought to rob the blood bank herself, but, though her only work has been in summer stock, she is firmly convinced that someday she will be a successful actress. To prepare herself for her career she spends much time listening to music and reading. "I'm now in the classics," she says, "and I just spent two very exciting weeks with Homer."

Man at the Imperial

Looking out (*right*) from the wings of the Imperial Theater is the tense face of Royal Dano watching another actor try out for the part in *South Pacific* that Dano himself hopes to get. Dano came to Broadway in 1946. Like so many of the current crop of young actors, he got the bug in the Army—in Burma, where he wrote and acted in a hit show. In his short stay on Broadway, Dano has had three fairly good parts. At the *South Pacific* audition, the other actor got the job. But Dano feels that his luck has been good. Losing the part did not weaken the conviction of Royal Dano, shared with hundreds of other stagestruck young people, that the theater is the most exciting profession in the world.

94

Figure 3.13 *Life*, February 14, 1949, p. 94–5. Photographs by W. Eugene Smith.

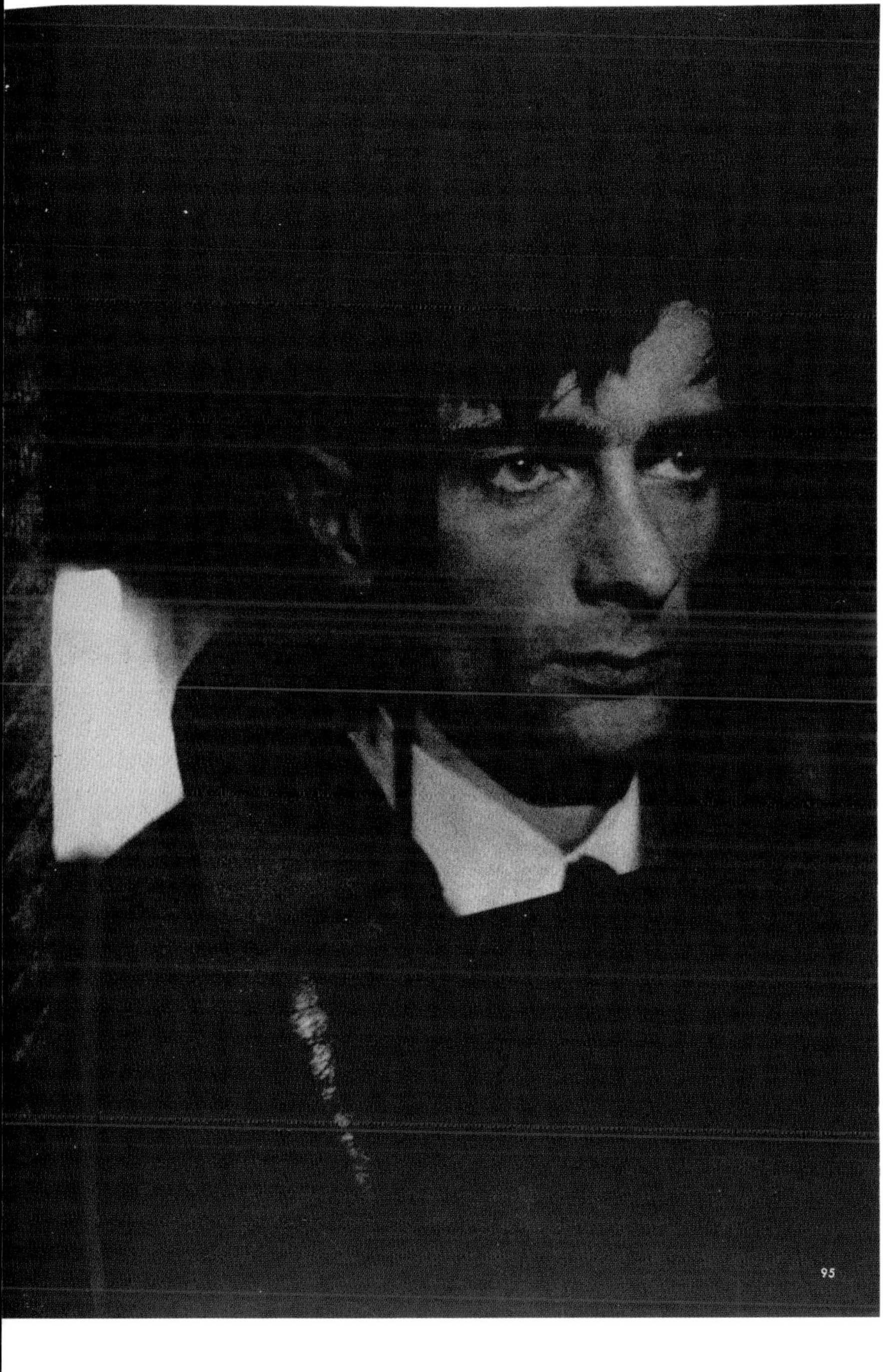
95

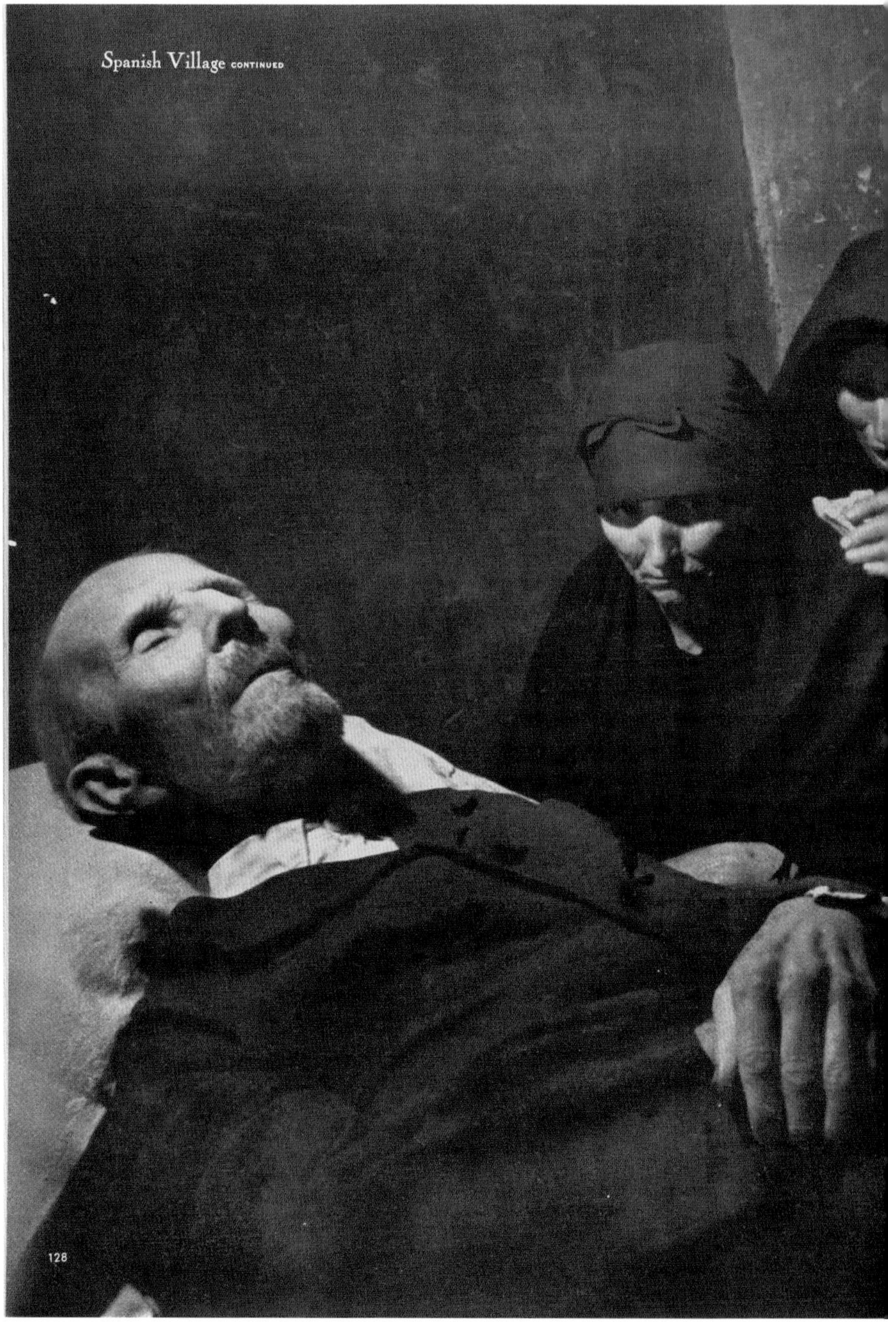

Figure 3.14 *Life*, April 9, 1951, pp. 128–9. Photograph by W. Eugene Smith.

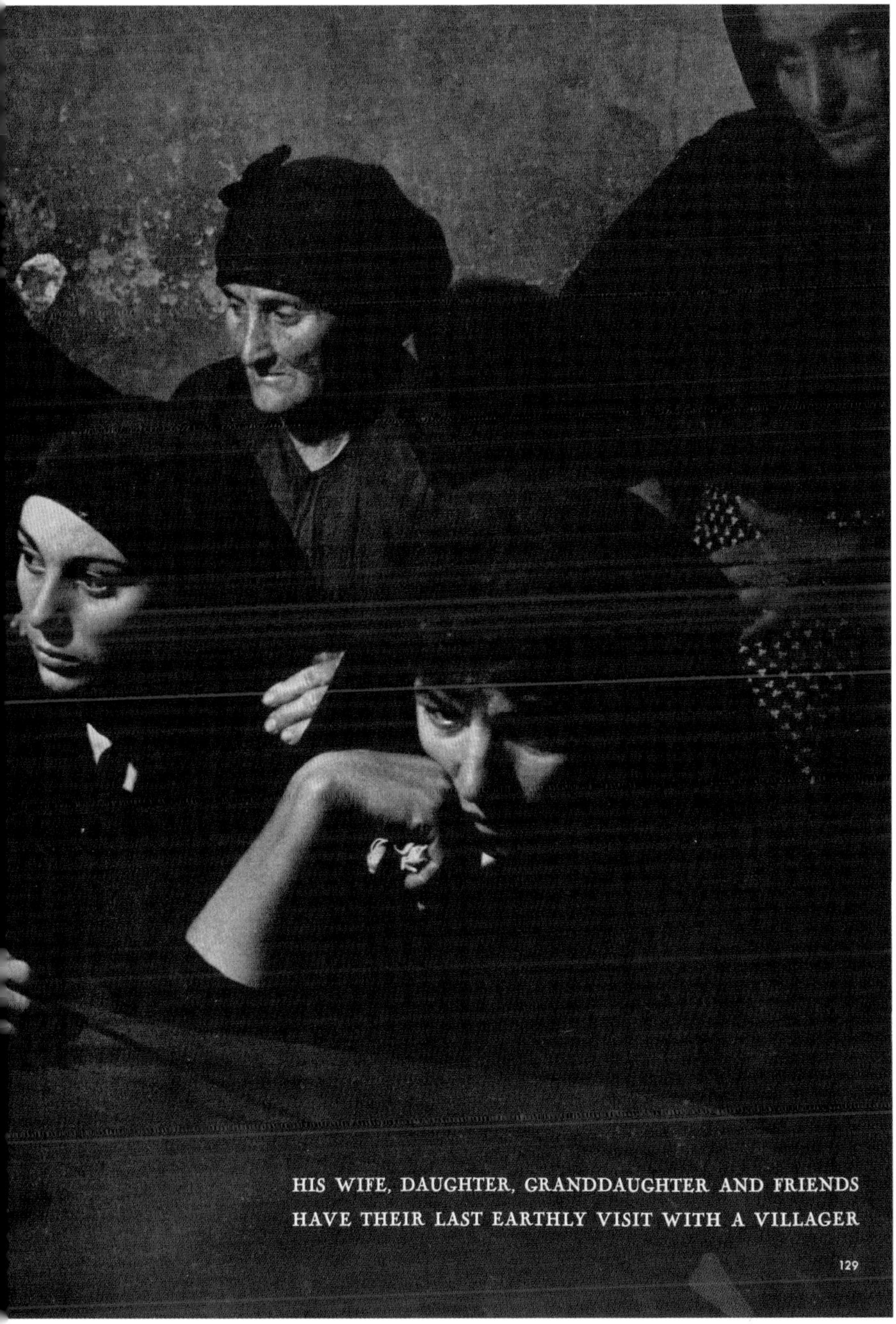
HIS WIFE, DAUGHTER, GRANDDAUGHTER AND FRIENDS
HAVE THEIR LAST EARTHLY VISIT WITH A VILLAGER

129

achieved total control of his work in the pages of *Life*. When he left *Life* for the Magnum agency early in 1955 the pragmatics of the photographic essay was in the hands of the magazine. Publication of an essay in *Life* was lucrative and prestigious, but henceforth the final decisions were taken by the editors, with or without the photographer's consent.

As the 1950s wore on, segmentation of the contents gradually lost its relevance, and long photographic series began to find their way into other sections: in 1955 the first part of Henri Cartier-Bresson's report on Russia appeared under "The Week's Events" heading, while the second part was published two weeks later as a "Pictorial Essay".[88] In 1961 "The Week's Events" became "Story of the Week" and a new section "The Color Spectacle" shared the image resources that had formerly been the exclusive property of the "Photographic Essay".[89] In 1963 these sections disappeared and the photographic essay evolved into a general concept embracing all the magazine's photographic series. Cartier-Bresson's report from Cuba (1963), the twenty-three photographs taken by Larry Burrows aboard the helicopter *Yankee Papa 13* during the war in Vietnam (1965), David Douglas Duncan's series on Khe Sanh (1968, see Figure 3.15) and Smith's Minimata images were presented in the same way as all the other illustrated articles.[90] For Wendy Kozol the weekly's use of the transparency of the images was part of a visual strategy of drawing on photographic "realism" to convey its political viewpoints to its readers.[91] These editorial choices would seem to explain the success of Eisenstaedt's photographs, which captured the spontaneity of his subjects while, most importantly, masking his own presence. However, the juxtaposition of images, the role of captions and texts, and the complexity of the layouts had the effect of toning down the realism of the photographs.[92] Moreover, alongside Eisenstaedt's transparent approach, *Life* explored numerous other visual gambits via the services of more overt stylists like Smith and Parks, whose meticulously wrought images generated dramatic tensions not only in informational but also in emotional terms.

Challenges to authority

In New York in 1947 Robert Capa, Henri Cartier-Bresson, David "Chim" Seymour, William Vandivert and George Rodger founded the agency Magnum Photos, Inc., their aim being to gain control of the editorial use of their photographs and "cut out the middle man" at distribution level.[93] The agency took the form of a cooperative, with its five founders as vice-presidents. The New York office was run by Rita Vandivert and the Paris office by Maria Eisner, who had set up the Alliance Photos agency before the war and distributed the work of Seymour, Capa and Cartier-Bresson.[94] Cartier-Bresson's work was being shown by Beaumont Newhall at the Museum of Modern Art (MoMA) the same year, and the Magnum photographers were able to take advantage of this artistic and institutional recognition to enforce their rights as authors in terms of the use of their images. Magnum Photos members retained ownership of their negatives, stipulated that their images not be cropped and stamped the back of each with a warning that "This photograph can be reproduced only with the accompanying caption or with text strictly in the spirit of its caption."[95] All of them were experienced photographers and free to take on outside commissions, but within the agency each had his personal interests and his own specific work zone: Cartier-Bresson chose Asia, Chim covered Europe, Rodger opted for Africa and the Middle East, Vandivert concentrated on the United States, and Capa remained available for current events. Their reportages were principally intended for the press, but at the same time they were seeking other outlets that would allow them greater freedom. This variety of use tied in with their insistence on absolute respect for their images, and highlighted the limitations facing photographers in their relationships with magazine editors. A turn toward book publishing brought increased control over their output.

In 1947 Capa and writer John Steinbeck went to the USSR for a project on family life that fitted with the series "People Are People the World Over" which *Ladies' Home Journal* photography editor John Morris was preparing. Capa's reportage sold to the *Ladies' Home Journal* for $20,000 in February 1948.[96] It was also published in February in the French monthly *Réalités*, and on May 1, the English magazine *Illustrated* used sixty of Capa's images, in color and black and white, for its cover and a sixteen-page feature (see Figures 3.16 and 3.17).[97] The income accruing from these articles was gratifying, but that same year Steinbeck and Capa joined forces to produce *A Russian Journal*, which was "contrary to a large part of modern journalism, but for that very reason . . . might be a relief."[98] In *Death in the Making* (1938) and *Slightly Out of Focus* (1947) Capa had given an account of his own experience as a war photographer,[99] but for *A Russian Journal* he entrusted the narrative to a famous literary figure. The photographs appeared in the body of the text, without captions. Two years later he repeated the venture, this time with photographs taken after Palestine had been divided into two states. His pictures appeared first in *Illustrated* in August 1949 and then in *Look* in November of the same year (see Figure 3.18). In 1950 the photographs were brought together in the book *Report on Israel* with a text by writer Irwin Shaw.[100] Here the pictures were presented in free-standing thematic groups, arranged as double pages and printed in photogravure. Shaw pointed out in his introduction that this was "not a definitive study. It is a series of glimpses of a puzzling phenomenon."[101] The number of images, their arrangement and the point of view they advocated provided a broader vision of an historic moment which the book form set in a time frame freed from the hectic pace of the topical.

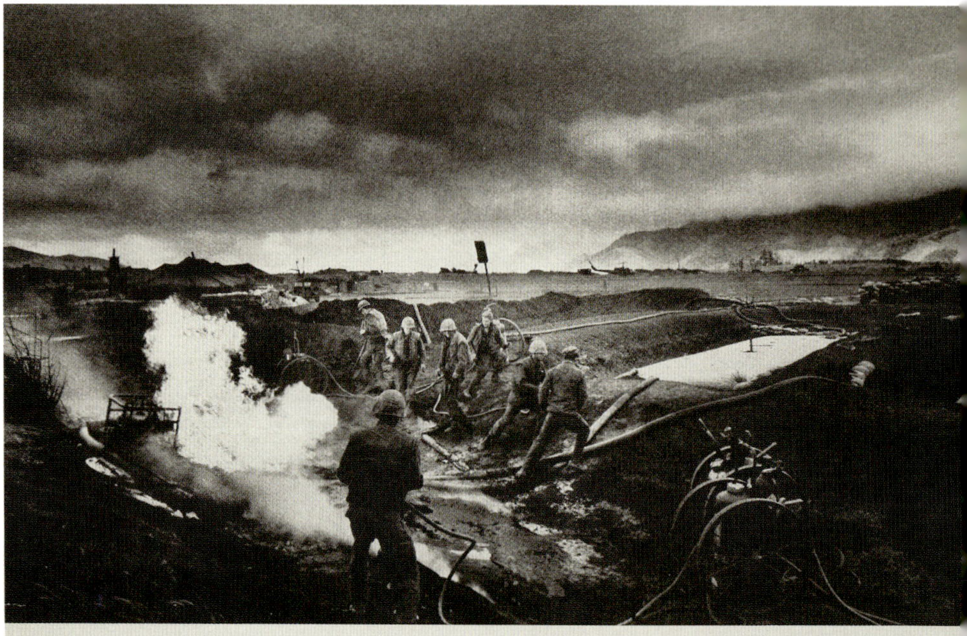

The only words that matter after a while are "Incoming!" and "Outgoing!" One day an incoming rocket ignited the aviation fuel hoses, turning them into sputtering fuses (*above*) leading straight to the main gasoline dump. A single wild spark might have sent the whole tank farm sky-high, but a handful of men doused the flames. Farther around the perimeter other Marines (*above right*) passed scorched but unexploded artillery shells—a deadly debris from direct hits on the main ammo dump—with tender precision into a hole for burial. By comparison "Outgoing!" is almost festive. There is the throaty whine of an artillery round and the reedy whistle of a mortar and, most spectacular of all, a close airstrike. Marines in Phantom jets strafe, hurl canisters of napalm and drop finned bombs (*right*) on enemy positions sometimes only yards beyond the front trenches (*far right*).

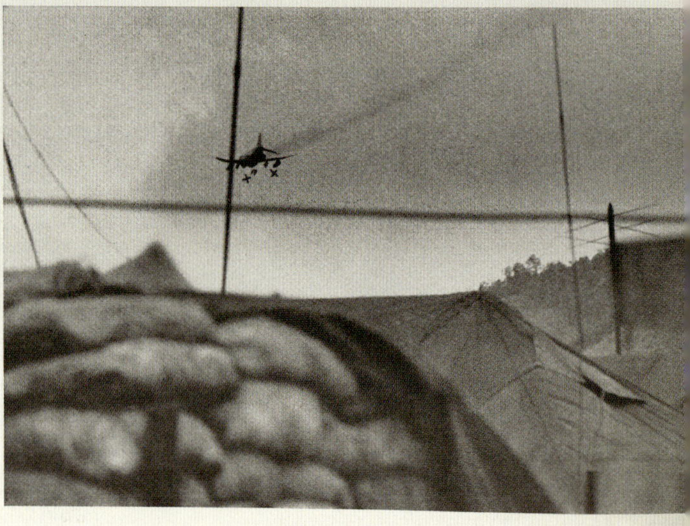

Tender precision, bombs slammed in close to the trenches

28

Figure 3.15 *Life*, February 23, 1968, pp. 28–9. Photographs by David Douglas Duncan.

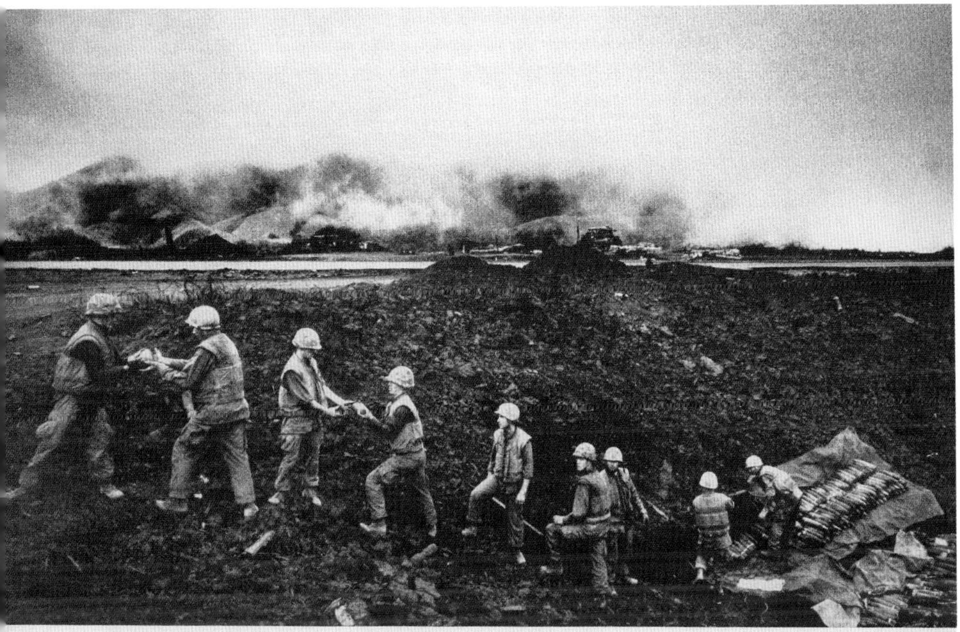

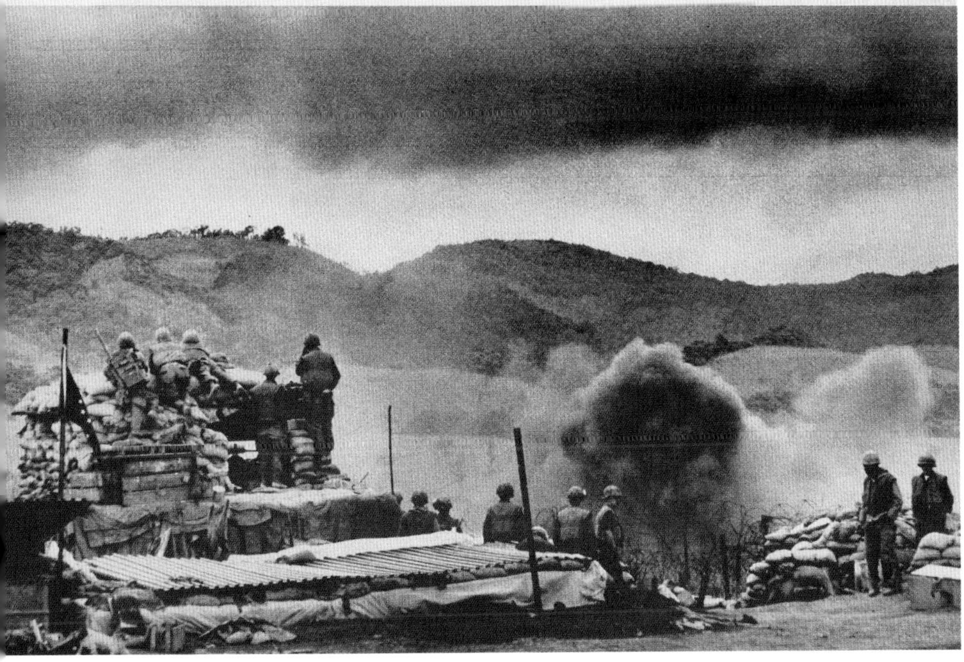

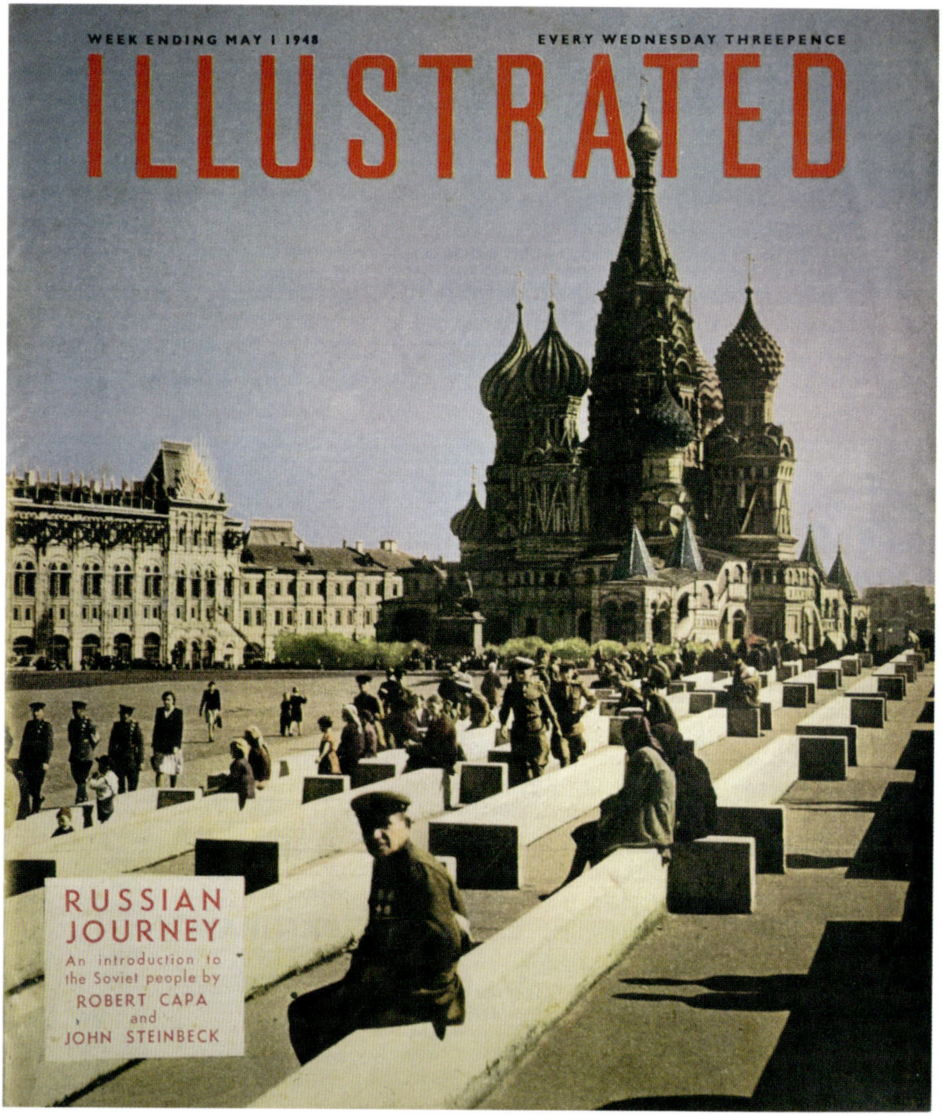

Figure 3.16 *Illustrated*, May 1, 1948, cover. Photograph by Robert Capa (Magnum).

Henri Cartier-Bresson displayed similar authorial ambitions.[102] After the war, and despite his MoMA exhibition, he abandoned art photography for photojournalism and threw himself wholeheartedly into the great Magnum adventure.[103] His output became more varied: he went off on press assignments to India (1948), China (1948–1949) and the USSR (1954), and undertook marketing and advertising work for IBM and Mercedes. His artistic reputation, his reportages from Communist countries (Cuba, 1963) and the efficiency of Magnum's distribution system gave his images a high profile and a wide audience. John Morris, who had begun working for Magnum in 1953, sold the Russian reportage to *Life* for $40,000 before heading for Europe and offering it to *Stern*, *Epoca*, *Picture Post* and *Paris Match*.[104] *Match* also published two Cartier-Bresson series titled "The Russian People," the first focused on Moscow and the second on other cities and regions.[105] *Life* and *Paris Match* contributed to shaping Cartier-Bresson's reputation by using similar strategies: in January 1955 both declared him "one of the world's greatest photographers,"[106] and stressed his intention of showing the everyday life of the Russian people after Stalin's death.

In the humanistic vein of the postwar period, Cartier-Bresson's snapshots had little to do with the traditional, caricatural images then fueling the Cold War—which did not prevent their being given entirely different emphases in the two weeklies. While *Match* adhered to the descriptive and well-researched captions furnished by Cartier-Bresson himself, *Life* adopted a tone that was less nuanced and—unsurprisingly—more critical of the Communist regime. A good illustration of this divergence is the double page devoted to childhood and education, for which both magazines used the same image of children in class, both arms raised vertically (see Figure 3.19 an 3.20).[107] In the French magazine the double page combines two borderless images, one vertical and the other horizontal, with a brief text that complements the photographs. *Life* uses only one of these, but fills the vacant space thus created with three others. Both titles mention the compulsory uniform, but *Life* adds in the glorification of the founding fathers. Image interpretation differs too: *Paris Match* uses Cartier-Bresson's explanation that the children are raising their arms to "imitate the shape of a cloud." *Life*, by contrast, sees this as an exercise in indoctrination. It also uses a photograph of two children in a holiday camp, surrounded by posters of party leaders, while *Match* opts for a more neutral image of a schoolboy walking down the street. From the outset, both weeklies are at pains to stress the apolitical nature of Cartier-Bresson's reportage, but the difference in their attitudes to the USSR is made clear throughout.

This issue of ideological exploitation of images found its way into theoretical discourse on photography in the 1960s. In his 1961 essay "The Photographic Message" Roland Barthes observes, "A photograph can change its meaning as it passes from the very conservative *L'Aurore* to the communist *L'Humanité*;"[108] he then goes on to

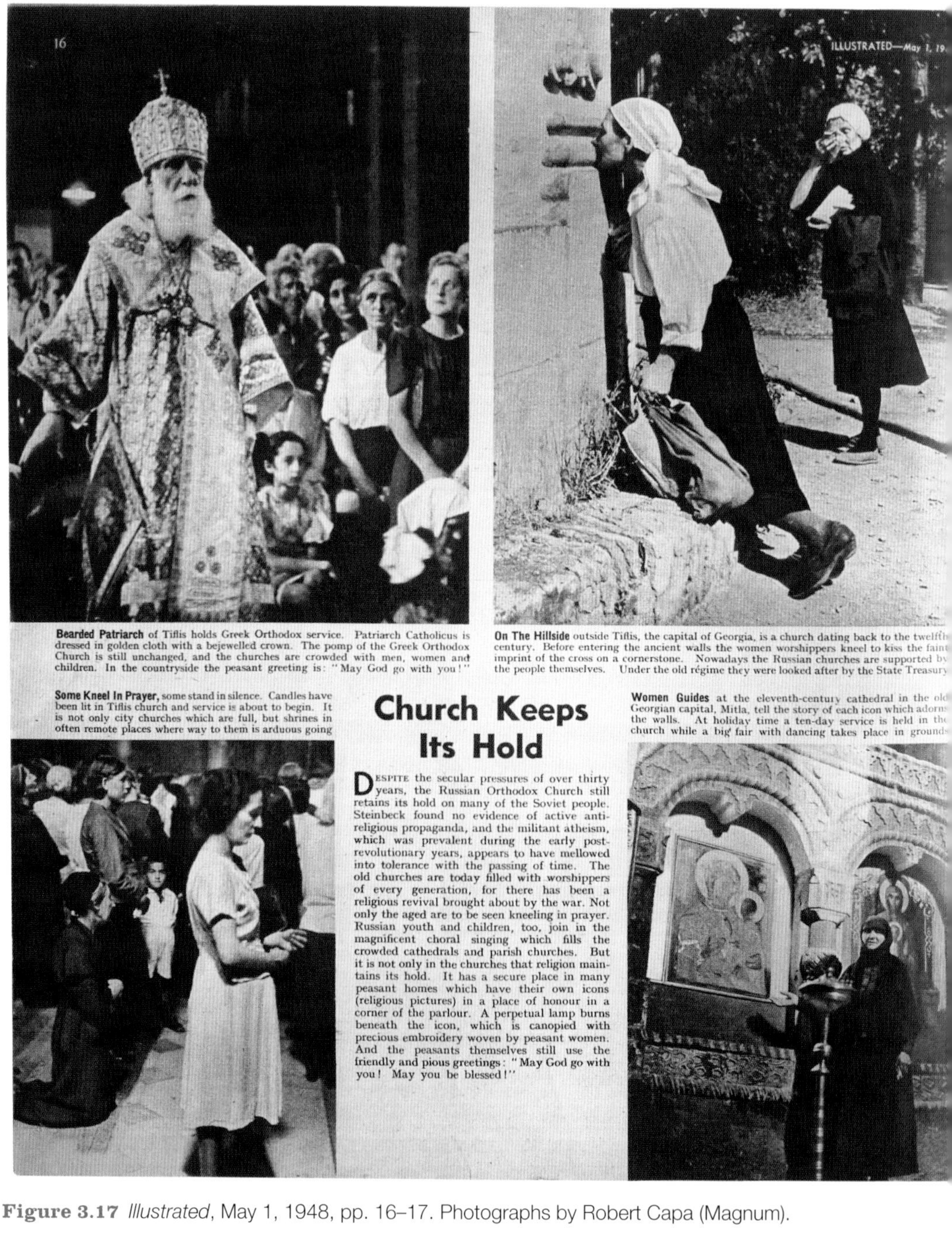
16

ILLUSTRATED—May 1, 19

Bearded Patriarch of Tiflis holds Greek Orthodox service. Patriarch Catholicus is dressed in golden cloth with a bejewelled crown. The pomp of the Greek Orthodox Church is still unchanged, and the churches are crowded with men, women and children. In the countryside the peasant greeting is: "May God go with you!"

On The Hillside outside Tiflis, the capital of Georgia, is a church dating back to the twelfth century. Before entering the ancient walls the women worshippers kneel to kiss the faint imprint of the cross on a cornerstone. Nowadays the Russian churches are supported by the people themselves. Under the old régime they were looked after by the State Treasury

Some Kneel In Prayer, some stand in silence. Candles have been lit in Tiflis church and service is about to begin. It is not only city churches which are full, but shrines in often remote places where way to them is arduous going

Church Keeps Its Hold

Despite the secular pressures of over thirty years, the Russian Orthodox Church still retains its hold on many of the Soviet people. Steinbeck found no evidence of active anti-religious propaganda, and the militant atheism, which was prevalent during the early post-revolutionary years, appears to have mellowed into tolerance with the passing of time. The old churches are today filled with worshippers of every generation, for there has been a religious revival brought about by the war. Not only the aged are to be seen kneeling in prayer. Russian youth and children, too, join in the magnificent choral singing which fills the crowded cathedrals and parish churches. But it is not only in the churches that religion maintains its hold. It has a secure place in many peasant homes which have their own icons (religious pictures) in a place of honour in a corner of the parlour. A perpetual lamp burns beneath the icon, which is canopied with precious embroidery woven by peasant women. And the peasants themselves still use the friendly and pious greetings: "May God go with you! May you be blessed!"

Women Guides at the eleventh-century cathedral in the old Georgian capital, Mitla, tell the story of each icon which adorns the walls. At holiday time a ten-day service is held in the church while a big fair with dancing takes place in grounds

Figure 3.17 *Illustrated*, May 1, 1948, pp. 16–17. Photographs by Robert Capa (Magnum).

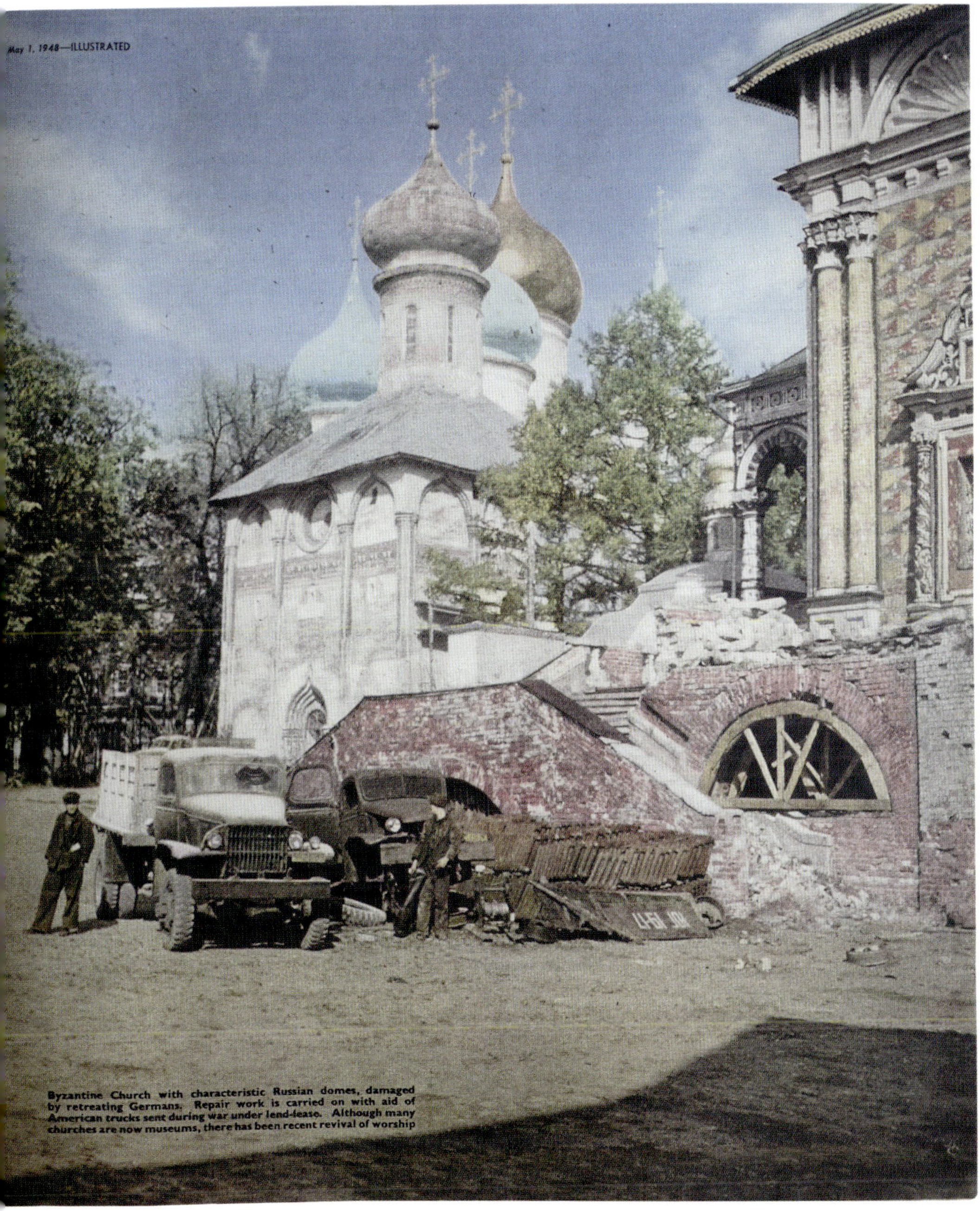
May 1, 1948—ILLUSTRATED

Byzantine Church with characteristic Russian domes, damaged by retreating Germans. Repair work is carried on with aid of American trucks sent during war under lend-lease. Although many churches are now museums, there has been recent revival of worship

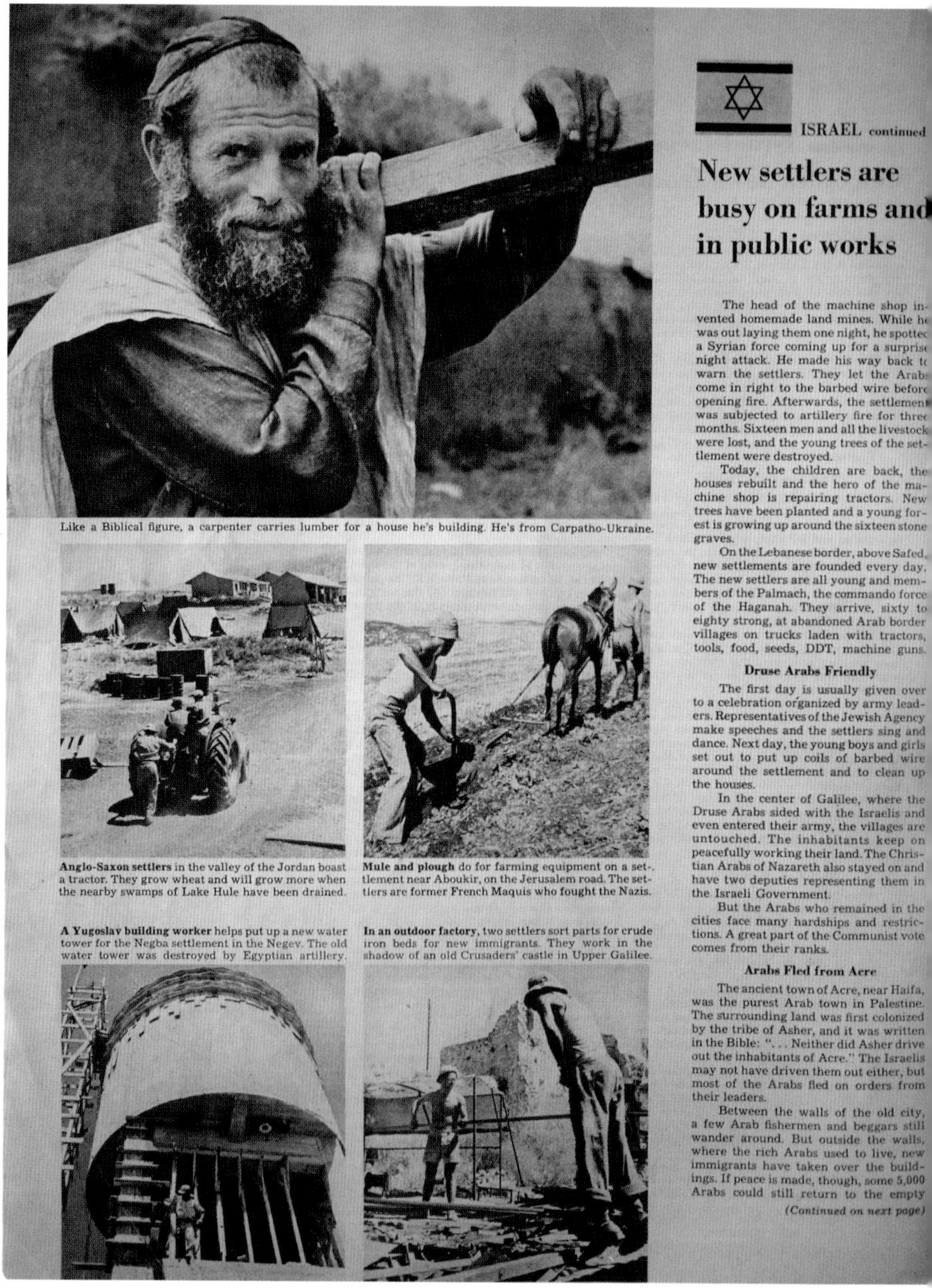

ISRAEL continued

New settlers are busy on farms and in public works

Like a Biblical figure, a carpenter carries lumber for a house he's building. He's from Carpatho-Ukraine.

Anglo-Saxon settlers in the valley of the Jordan boast a tractor. They grow wheat and will grow more when the nearby swamps of Lake Hule have been drained.

Mule and plough do for farming equipment on a settlement near Aboukir, on the Jerusalem road. The settlers are former French Maquis who fought the Nazis.

A Yugoslav building worker helps put up a new water tower for the Negba settlement in the Negev. The old water tower was destroyed by Egyptian artillery.

In an outdoor factory, two settlers sort parts for crude iron beds for new immigrants. They work in the shadow of an old Crusaders' castle in Upper Galilee.

The head of the machine shop invented homemade land mines. While h was out laying them one night, he spotte a Syrian force coming up for a surpris night attack. He made his way back t warn the settlers. They let the Arab come in right to the barbed wire befor opening fire. Afterwards, the settlemen was subjected to artillery fire for thre months. Sixteen men and all the livestock were lost, and the young trees of the settlement were destroyed.

Today, the children are back, the houses rebuilt and the hero of the machine shop is repairing tractors. New trees have been planted and a young forest is growing up around the sixteen stone graves.

On the Lebanese border, above Safed, new settlements are founded every day. The new settlers are all young and members of the Palmach, the commando force of the Haganah. They arrive, sixty to eighty strong, at abandoned Arab border villages on trucks laden with tractors, tools, food, seeds, DDT, machine guns.

Druse Arabs Friendly

The first day is usually given over to a celebration organized by army leaders. Representatives of the Jewish Agency make speeches and the settlers sing and dance. Next day, the young boys and girls set out to put up coils of barbed wire around the settlement and to clean up the houses.

In the center of Galilee, where the Druse Arabs sided with the Israelis and even entered their army, the villages are untouched. The inhabitants keep on peacefully working their land. The Christian Arabs of Nazareth also stayed on and have two deputies representing them in the Israeli Government.

But the Arabs who remained in the cities face many hardships and restrictions. A great part of the Communist vote comes from their ranks.

Arabs Fled from Acre

The ancient town of Acre, near Haifa, was the purest Arab town in Palestine. The surrounding land was first colonized by the tribe of Asher, and it was written in the Bible: "... Neither did Asher drive out the inhabitants of Acre." The Israelis may not have driven them out either, but most of the Arabs fled on orders from their leaders.

Between the walls of the old city, a few Arab fishermen and beggars still wander around. But outside the walls, where the rich Arabs used to live, new immigrants have taken over the buildings. If peace is made, though, some 5,000 Arabs could still return to the empty

(Continued on next page)

Figure 3.18 *Look*, November 8, 1949, pp. 28–9. Photographs by Robert Capa (Magnum).

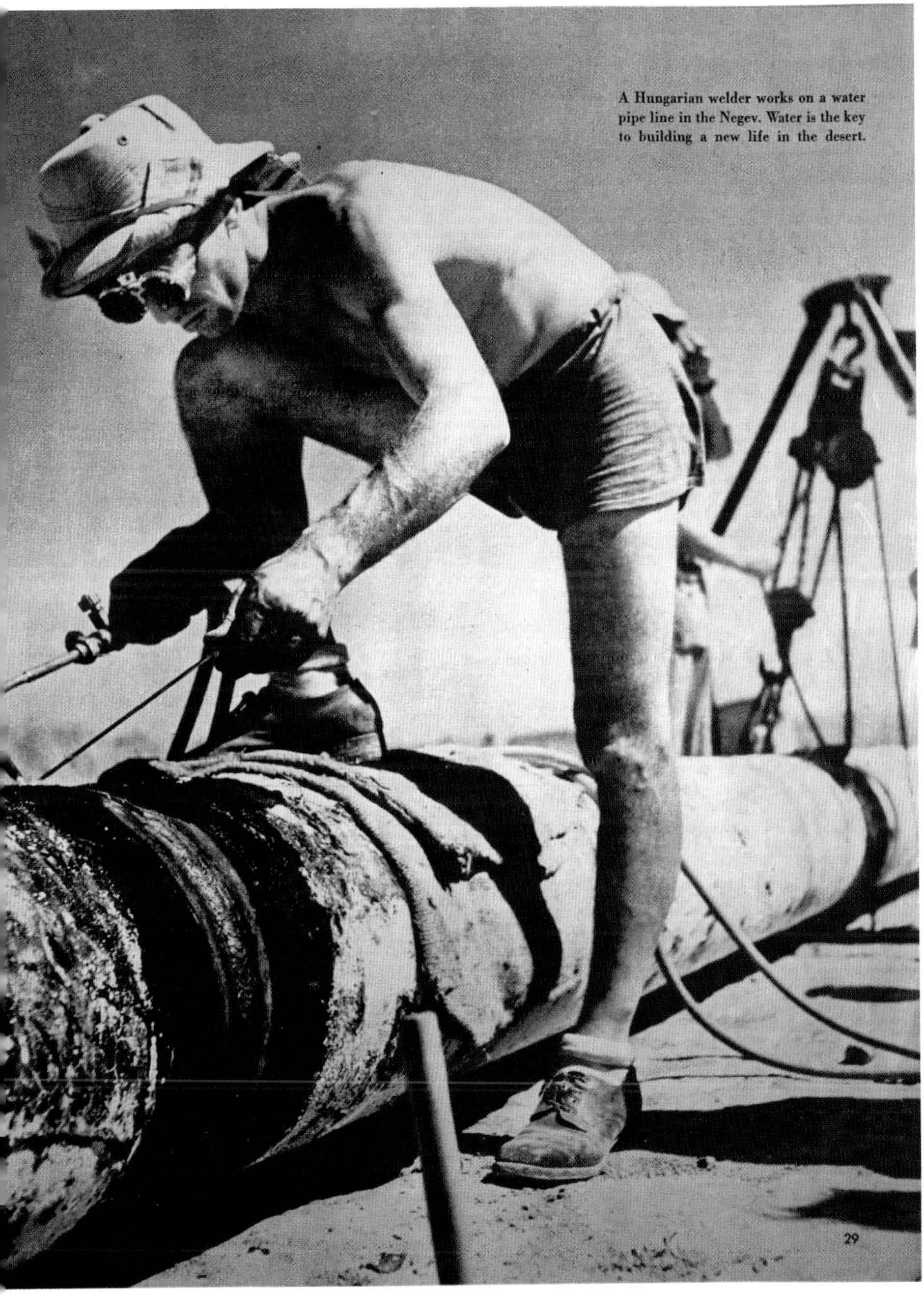

A Hungarian welder works on a water pipe line in the Negev. Water is the key to building a new life in the desert.

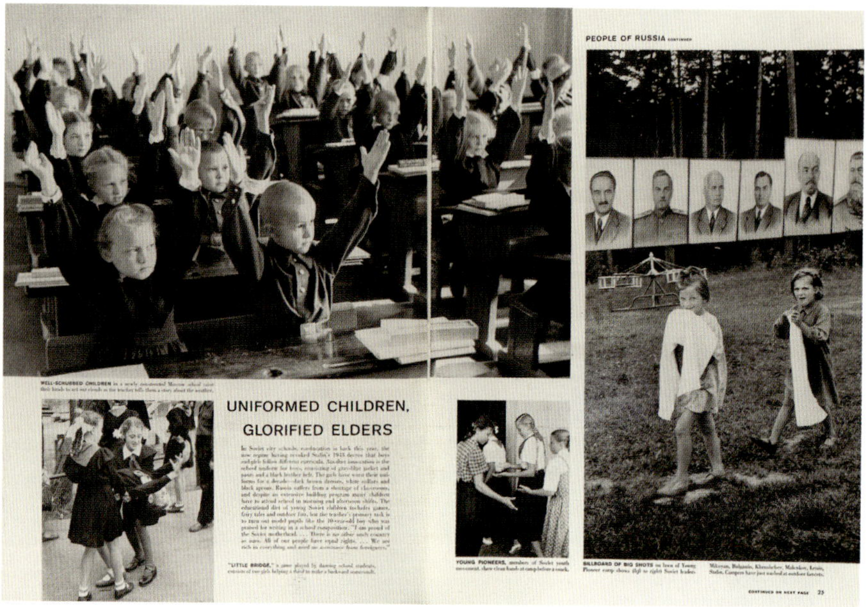

Figure 3.19 *Life*, January 17, 1955, pp. 24–5. Photographs by Henri Cartier-Bresson (Magnum).

analyze the different connotative modes of the photographic message, ranging from the actual taking of the photograph to the association of images and the writing of captions. While ever-attentive to the photographer's authority within the press economy, Magnum Photos was still unable to prevent *Match* from radically cropping the image of workers dancing during their break inside the Ukraine Hotel they were building in Moscow; nor from reversing the photograph of a summer vacationer on a chaise longue on the Black Sea coast, smiling at his lady friend opposite him as she protects her back from the sun with an umbrella.[109] In both cases the editorial approach offers a better visual fit with the layout: the cropping of the photograph of the dancers allows a focus on two couples and the matching of their size to that of the people in the other picture; while the reversal avoids the cropping of the vacationer's bodies by the gutter of the spread (see Figure 3.21). Thus these modifications of the images, effected in spite of the agency's instructions, enhance the aesthetics of the page with a view to increasing the reader's visual enjoyment.[110]

For the original 1955 French edition of *The People of Moscow*, Cartier-Bresson shared control of his images with the publisher, Robert Delpire. The pictures are harmoniously

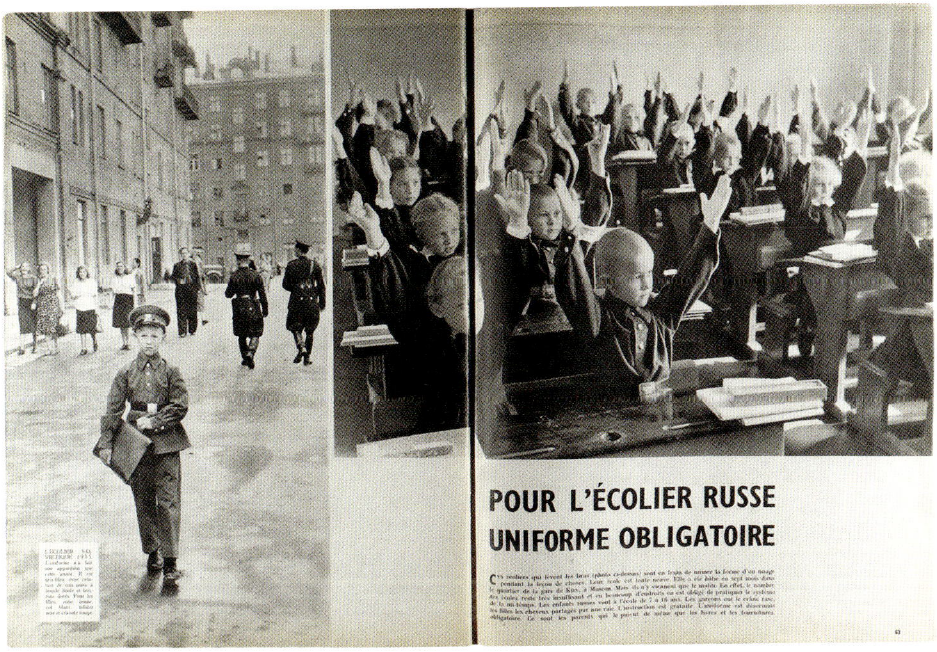

Figure 3.20 *Paris Match*, January 29, 1955, pp. 62–3. Photographs by Henri Cartier-Bresson (Magnum) © Paris Match / Scoop.

grouped by themes and the photographer himself wrote the captions and the brief introduction: "to those who ask me 'What did you see?', I reply: 'Let my eye speak for me'. These pictures are meant for them."[111] This reference to "my eye" allows the photographer to align himself with "all the writers who had previously taken the trip to the USSR . . . [and had] claimed to be 'eyes'."[112] While Cartier-Bresson had opted for reportage after the War, he was not about to be a mere photojournalist, and adopted an authorial strategy of his own, using the same images for different purposes. In that same year of 1955 a selection of his photographs from Russia was shown at the Musée des Arts Décoratifs in Paris as part of his first French retrospective.[113]

Other photographers, too, would circulate their images from the press to books and museums. David Douglas Duncan's photographs of an American base besieged by North Vietnamese forces first appeared in *Life* in 1968,[114] and soon afterwards were brought together in the book *I Protest!*, a denunciation of the American intervention in Vietnam.[115] Published in 1971, *Vietnam Inc.* by Philip Jones Griffiths grouped its photographs by such themes as "The Vietnamese Village" and "The Battle for the Cities," and condemned "the folly of the original view that deemed it possible for a society like

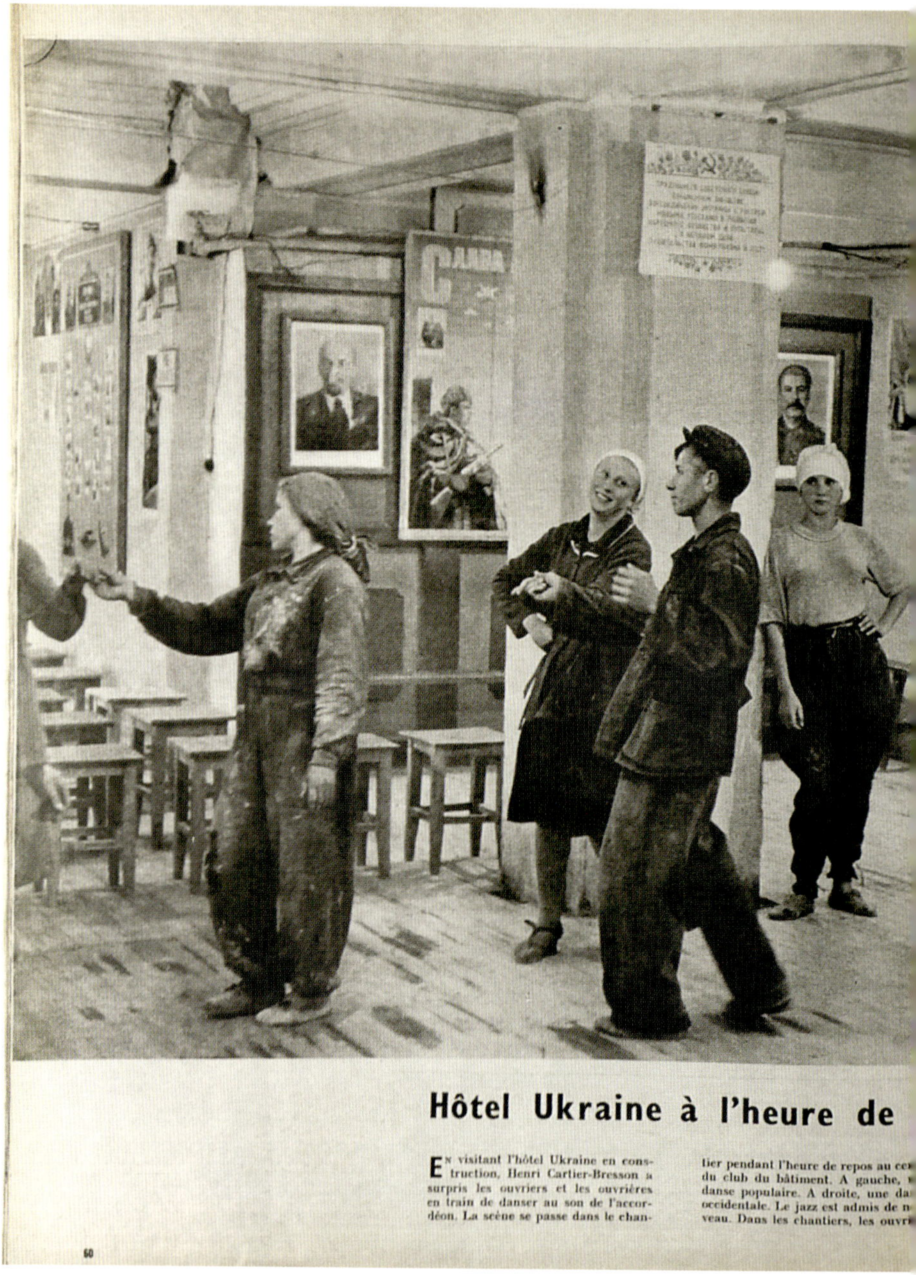

Hôtel Ukraine à l'heure de

En visitant l'hôtel Ukraine en construction, Henri Cartier-Bresson a surpris les ouvriers et les ouvrières en train de danser au son de l'accordéon. La scène se passe dans le chantier pendant l'heure de repos au ce
du club du bâtiment. A gauche,
danse populaire. A droite, une da
occidentale. Le jazz est admis de n
veau. Dans les chantiers, les ouvr

60

Figure 3.21 *Paris Match*, January 29, 1955, pp. 60–1. Photographs by Henri Cartier-Bresson (Magnum) © Paris Match / Scoop.

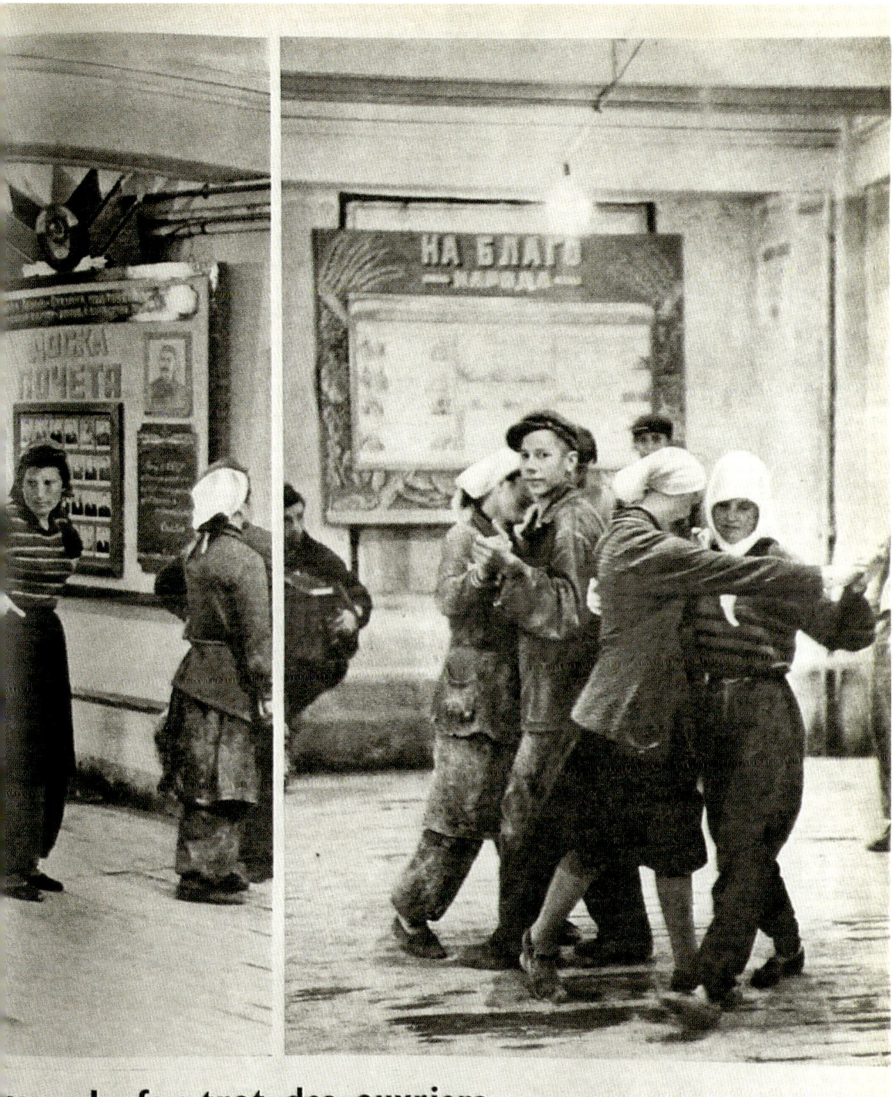

ıse : le fox-trot des ouvriers

vaillent en équipes de jour et de t. Il est cependant difficile pour construction de suivre la cadence l'augmentation de la population scovite. Toutes les maisons ancien-

nes ne sont pas détruites. Celles qui ont un intérêt artistique sont conservées. Si elles se trouvent dans la zone à reconstruire, on les déplace en les emmenant sur des rouleaux.

61

America's to impose itself on that of the Vietnamese."[116] Bent on controlling the use and circulation of his pictures, Griffiths joined Magnum in 1971. These explorations of alternatives reflect photographers' frustrations with regard to the press: in addition to challenging their own lack of editorial control, they were calling into question the role and the effectiveness of their work and of their political denunciations in the pages of the magazines.

Toward diversification

Nonetheless, photographers continued to practice their profession in local and global terms and in black and white and color, and to offer their work to magazines. Working in the tradition of Robert Capa, the Frenchman Gilles Caron used short focal length lenses to get as close as he could to his subjects. He played his part in the founding of the Gamma agency in Paris in 1967[117] by buying out photographer Léonard De Raemy, one of the instigators together with Hubert Henrotte, Hugues Vassal and Raymond Depardon. Gamma protected its members' copyright—unlike other agencies, which put their photographers on salary—while circulating their work to outlets and sharing expenses and income with them. The Sipa agency was born in 1969, followed by Sygma in 1973—in the wake of an internal dispute at Gamma—and Contact Press in 1976. All Paris-based, these agencies made the French capital the world's photojournalism nerve center.[118] In early June 1967 Caron went to Israel to cover the Six Day War between Israel and Egypt, Jordan and Syria. His reportage was sold a few days later to *Paris Match*, which devoted forty-four pages to the conflict in its issue of June 17.[119] Caron's pictures were associated with those of a dozen other photographers to form a multifaceted visual narrative that included the conquest of the Suez Canal, control of Gaza and Sinai, the taking of Jerusalem and access to the Wailing Wall. A handful of aerial photographs aside, the consistency of this mass of images testified to an aesthetic shared by the various photographers concerned. A mix of color and black and white, the *Paris Match* photographs highlighted the proximity and involvement of the photographers with tight framing of faces and situations, and points of view cluttered with the obstacles that provided the photographers with protection. The images were printed to the edge of the page and were so tightly packed that they left barely enough narrow white spaces for captions tersely specifying their content and the connections between them. The result was not conducive to contemplation; instead it underscored the urgent need to recount what the *Match* cover described as a "lightning war." Caron knew the relevant magazine codes and adapted his photographs accordingly. An Israeli soldier pressed passionately head to toe against the Wailing Wall signified the taking of Jerusalem, but at the same time symbolized the reconquest of the Holy City by the Jewish people (see Figure 3.22). In Biafra in 1968 Caron took the pictures needed to ensure publication: "If you come back from Biafra with photographs of some doleful African soldier, nobody gives a damn. What you need is the African soldier with his guts hanging out. It has to be bloody or it's not going to find any takers."[120] So the photographers homed in on the worst horrors: Caron and English photographer Don McCullin, whose paths crossed during the war in Biafra, both brought back images of those child victims of the conflict, their bodies branded with the unbearable marks of starvation.

The two had the journalistic vocation in common, but their aesthetic leanings were not the same. McCullin was a lover of somberly cloudy skies, of black smoke pouring out over industrial towns, of streets wrapped in impenetrable fog. Whether working on war in Vietnam, clashes in Derry City, conflict in Cambodia, London's homeless or civil strife in Beirut, McCullin turned out dense, graphic images, tightly focused and characterized by saturated blacks. His color and black and white reportages for the *Sunday Times Magazine*—he was a contributor from 1966 to 1984—were each accompanied by an article by a journalist (see Figures 3.23, 3.24 and 3.25). But while Caron and McCullin both worked for the press, they were uneasy about their legitimacy and their status as witnesses. Jimmy Hare's 1904 account in *L'Illustration* of a day of combat between Japanese and Russian troops closed with an image of the photographer himself administering first aid to the wounded, and raised questions and doubts about the reporter's role: should he be a photographer or a caregiver?[121] And so photographing yourself treating the wounded seemed one way of salving the conscience of photojournalist and publisher alike. In the 1930s the image of the committed reporter—like Capa, the "passionate democrat"—camouflaged these misgivings and legitimized the role of the photographer as a provider of visual information in the name of democratic values. However, the visual overkill triggered by the conflicts in Vietnam and Biafra, and the exploitation of the sensational side of their work gradually eroded the image of the photographer as hero. The information value of published images was called into question and by the late 1960s the "photographer's queasy conscience"[122] had unsettled the profession as a whole. Not only did photographers have to supply affecting but essentially ephemeral pictures, they also had to keep tabs on current news while indulging in the trivial local and international socializing that generated the profits their existence depended on. The list of Caron's assignments in the course of his brief career—he died in 1970—reveals that most of his time was devoted to celebrities. In May–June 1967, for example, he covered the Six Day War, but also pop star Sylvie Vartan, future French president Georges Pompidou, Jean-Paul Sartre, Queen Elizabeth II's visit to Normandy and singer Enrico Macias on tour in Israel.[123]

The quantity of major news stories published in magazines needs to be measured against the coverage given to celebrities in *Paris Match*. Alain Chenu, in his quantitative/

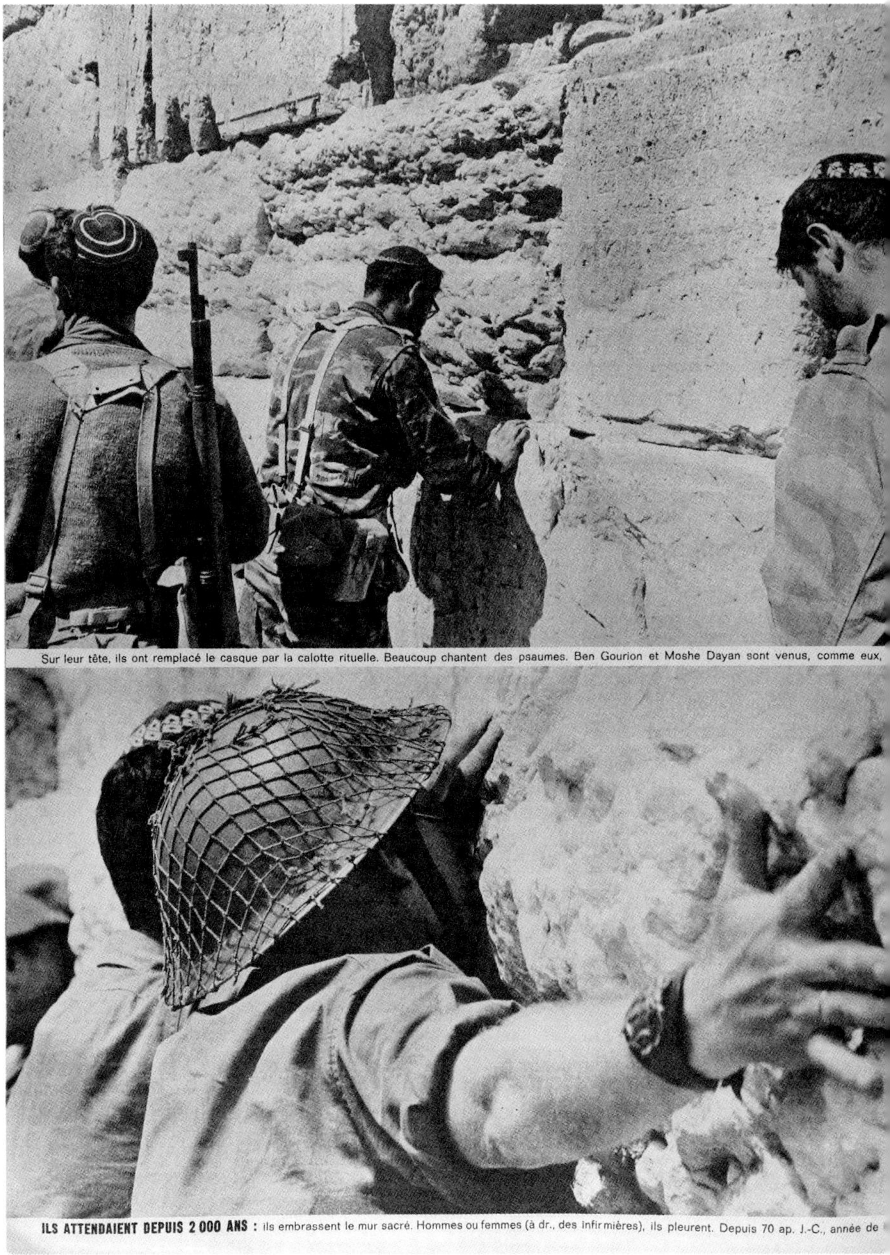

Figure 3.22 *Paris Match*, June 17, 1967, pp. 82–3. Photographs by Gilles Caron (Gamma) © Paris Match / Scoop.

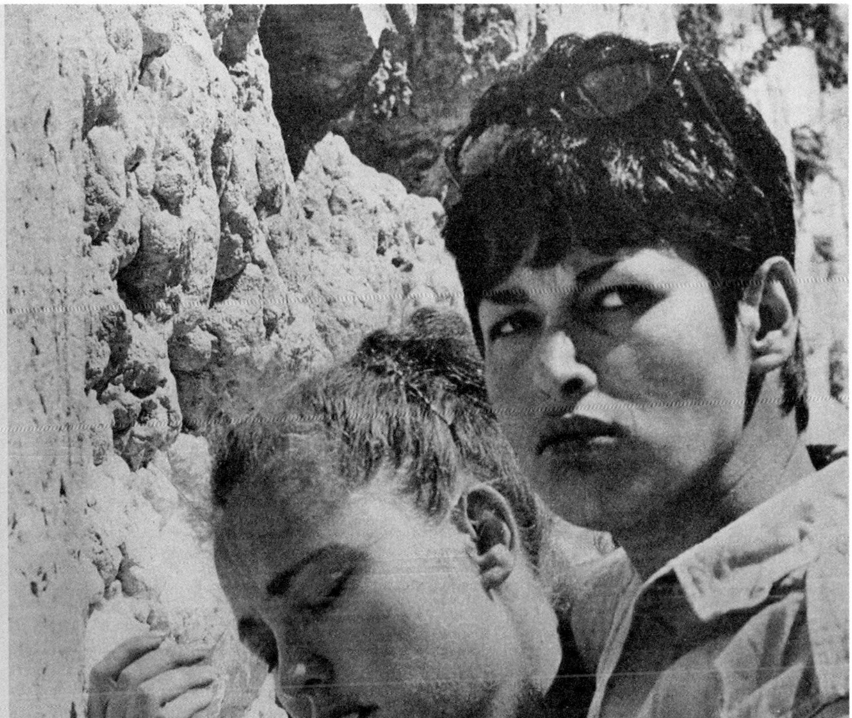

nple et de la dispersion du peuple juif, ce mur est le symbole de la patrie perdue. Ils disent : « Nous l'avons repris aux Arabes. Jamais nous ne le rendrons. »

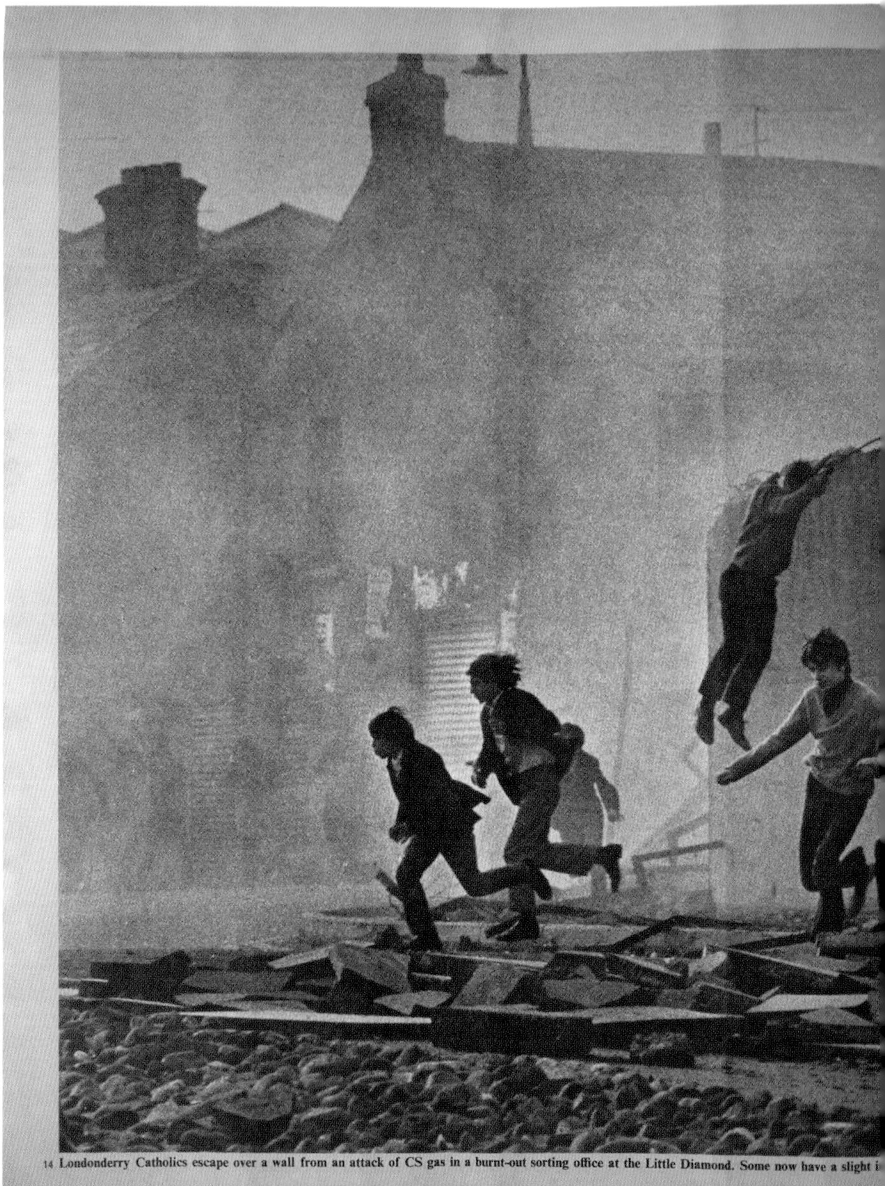

Figure 3.23 *The Sunday Times Magazine*, December 19, 1971, pp. 14–15. Photograph by Don McCullin.

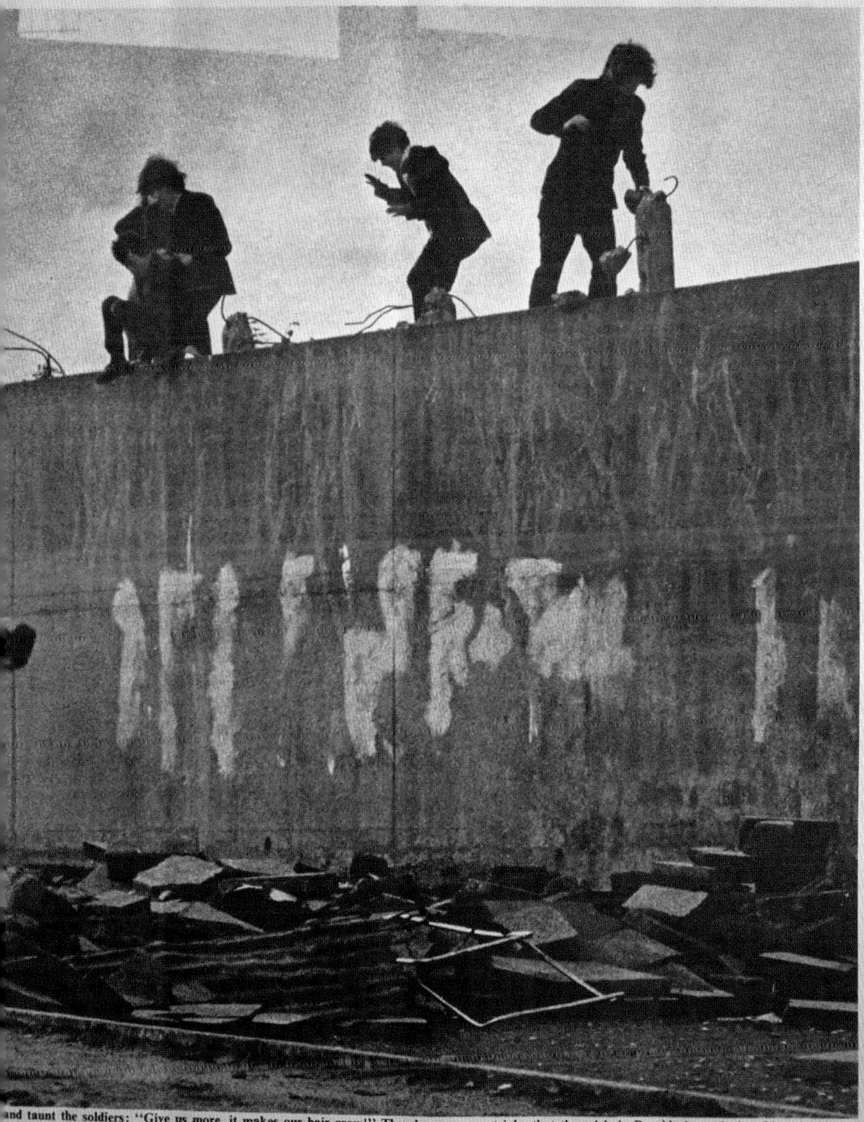

and taunt the soldiers: "Give us more, it makes our hair grow!" They have a current joke that the crisis in Bogside is producing Olympic athletes 15

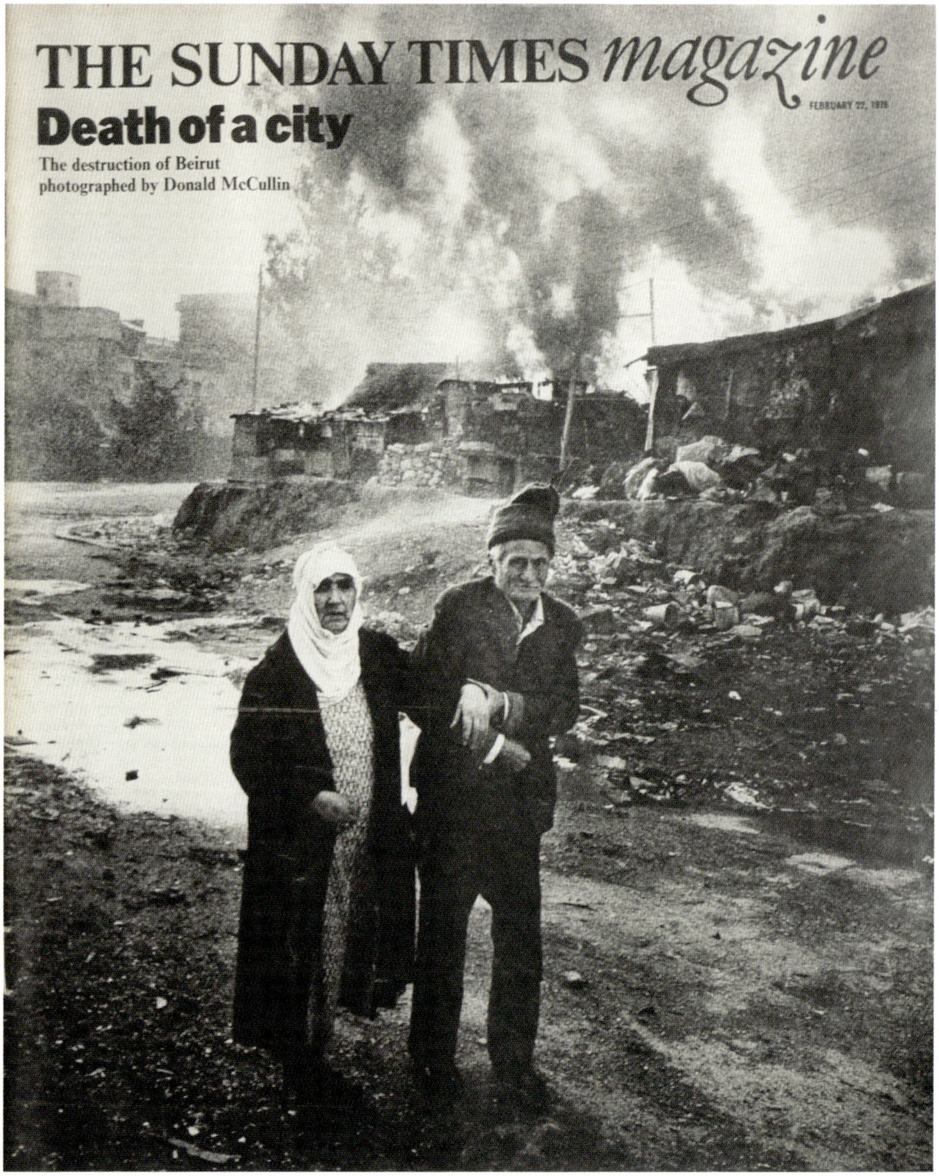

Figure 3.24 *The Sunday Times Magazine*, February 22, 1976, cover. Photograph by Don McCullin.

qualitative study of *Paris Match* covers from 1949 to 2005, shows that 85 percent of them use the faces of personalities from the aristocracy, the entertainment world and political and social life.[124] The crowning of the Queen of England, Prince Rainier of Monaco's marriage to Grace Kelly and the lives of the aristocracy in general were regularly followed up, accounting for one cover in every six.[125] The photoreportages inside the magazine were collections of snapshots agreed on with their subjects, showing them relaxing in private: a good example is the series by Howell Conant illustrating the article "Monaco intime" (Inside Monaco), published in 1959.[126] Color and black and white photographs of Grace and her children in the palace, the garden and the pool are presented as illustrations of life on "The Rock" taken from "the princess's private album" (see Figure 3.26). In Germany *Stern* showed the same interest in celebrities, and for its article on the Kennedy family in May 1963, drew on a similar repertoire of family snaps taken on the beach and in the Oval Office (see Figure 3.27).[127] Also in the spring of that year, both magazines' covers used the same portrait of Italian actress Monica Vitti, then shooting *Castle in Sweden* with director Roger Vadim.[128] The color photograph highlights her luxuriant blonde hair, her parted, pink-glossed lips, and the hazel eyes looking directly at the camera: a cover whose emphasis on the charm and seductiveness of her face is intended to catch the potential reader's eye (see Figure 3.28).

Stern had the same idea in mind when it ventured toward men's magazine soft porn with cover photographs of unclothed young women. Against an aqua-blue background the cover of May 26, 1976 revealed the bronzed, voluptuous torso of a woman shading her eyes against the sun so as to see the photographer better.[129] Of the titles on the cover, only the one mentioning the coming of summer has anything to do with an image that has quite blatantly been chosen for its sexual allure (see Figure 3.29).

The general news magazine went through a crisis in the late 1960s–early 1970s, a period that saw the last issues of *Saturday Evening Post* (1969), *Look* (1971) and *Life* (1972). Television, which was eating into readers' free time, winning more and more advertisers, and offering a flood of moving images in color, was largely responsible for this shift and forced publishers to aim their magazines elsewhere.[130] Daniel Filipacchi's acquisition of *Paris Match* in 1976 is an eloquent example. After beginning as a photographer at *Paris Match*, where he met Roger Thérond, Filipacchi bought *Cahiers du cinéma*, then launched a series of niche publications including *Salut les copains* (Hi, Gang!) in 1962, *Lui* (Man) in 1963, *Mademoiselle Âge Tendre* (Young Mademoiselle) in 1964, *Photo* and *Ski* in 1967, *Cuisine magazine* (Cuisine Magazine) in 1968, and *Son magazine* (Sound Magazine) in 1969. The number of publications and the sheer variety of their subject matter signaled a publishing trend away from general news and toward a wider magazine-buying range. When the Prouvost group decided to get rid of *Paris Match*, whose circulation had dropped from 1.8 million in 1958 to 200,000 in 1975, Filipacchi bought it and put his longtime friend

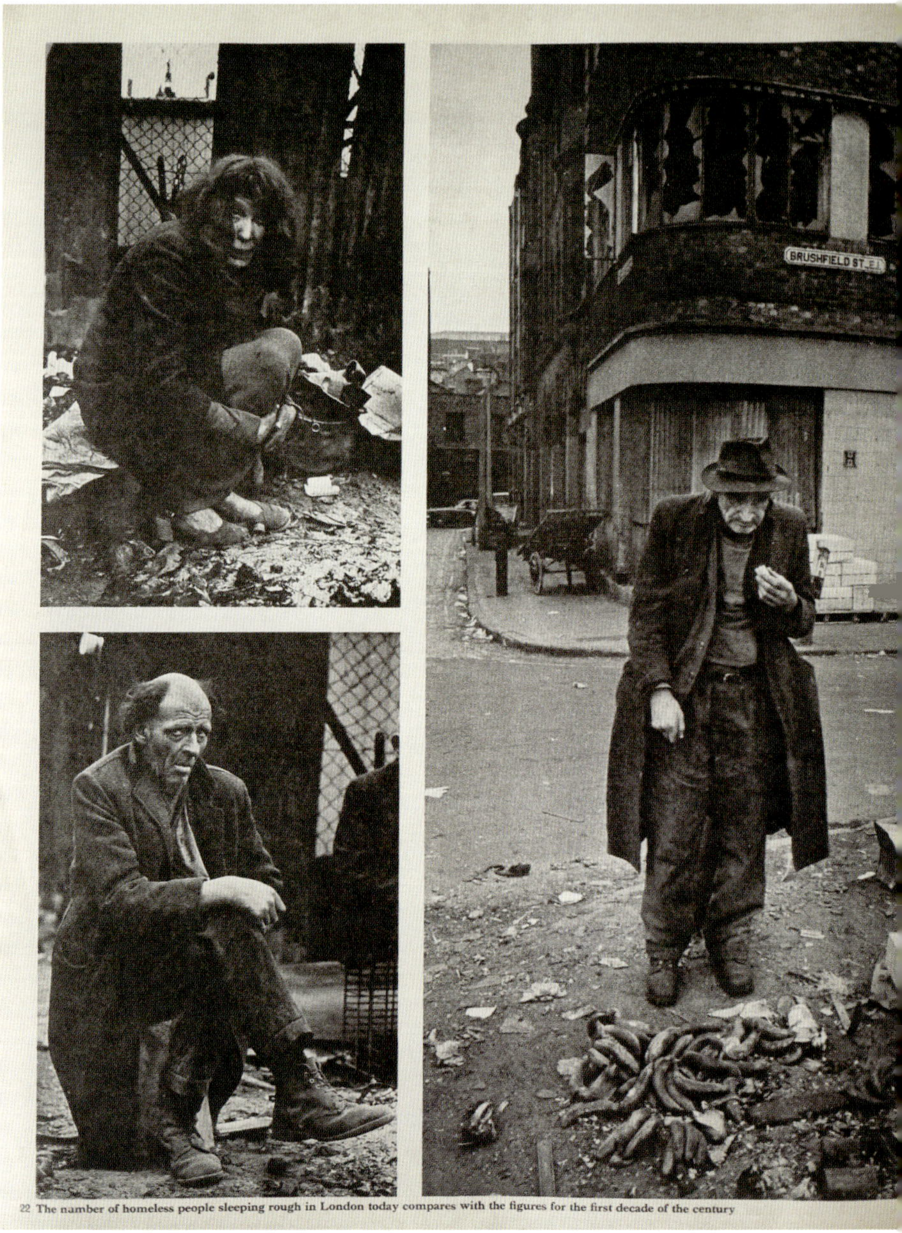

Figure 3.25 *The Sunday Times Magazine*, June 24, 1973, pp. 22–3. Photographs by Don McCullin.

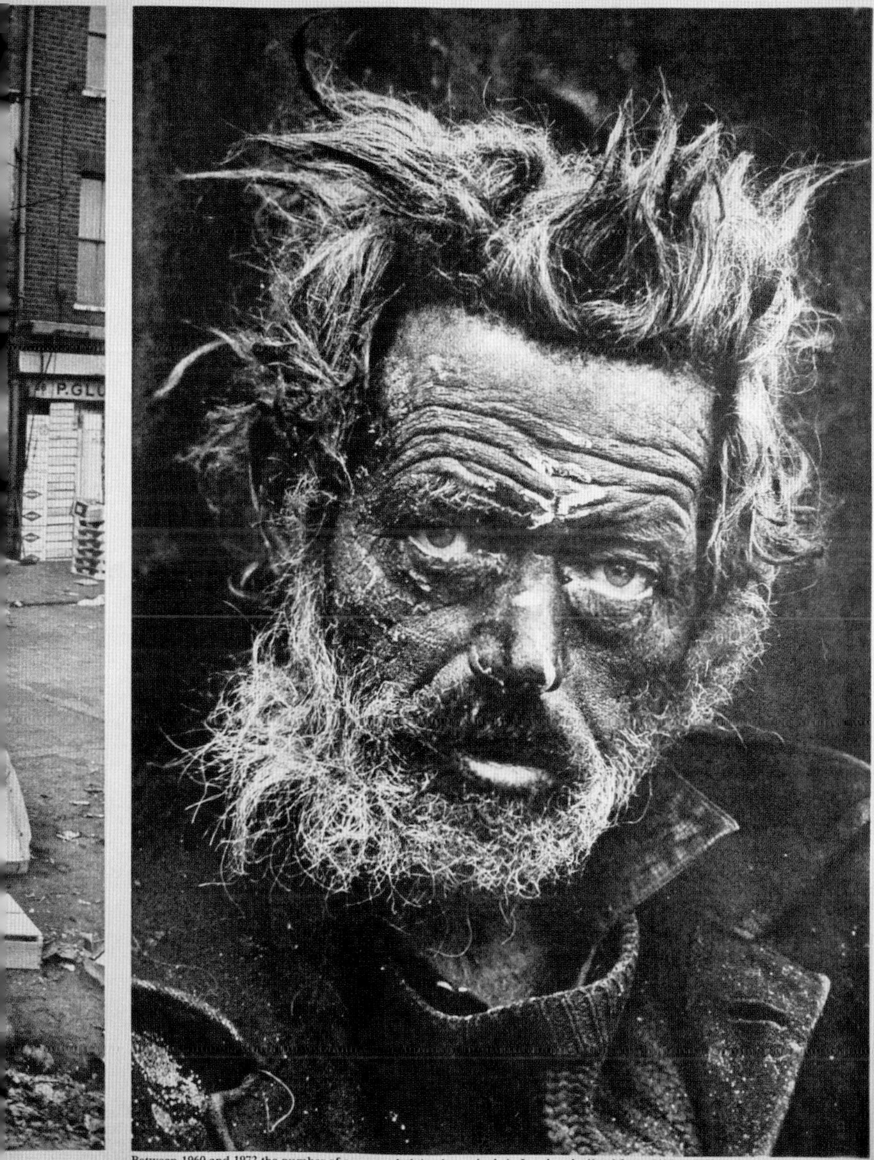

Between 1960 and 1972 the number of common lodging house beds in London declined from 6405 to 4708

23

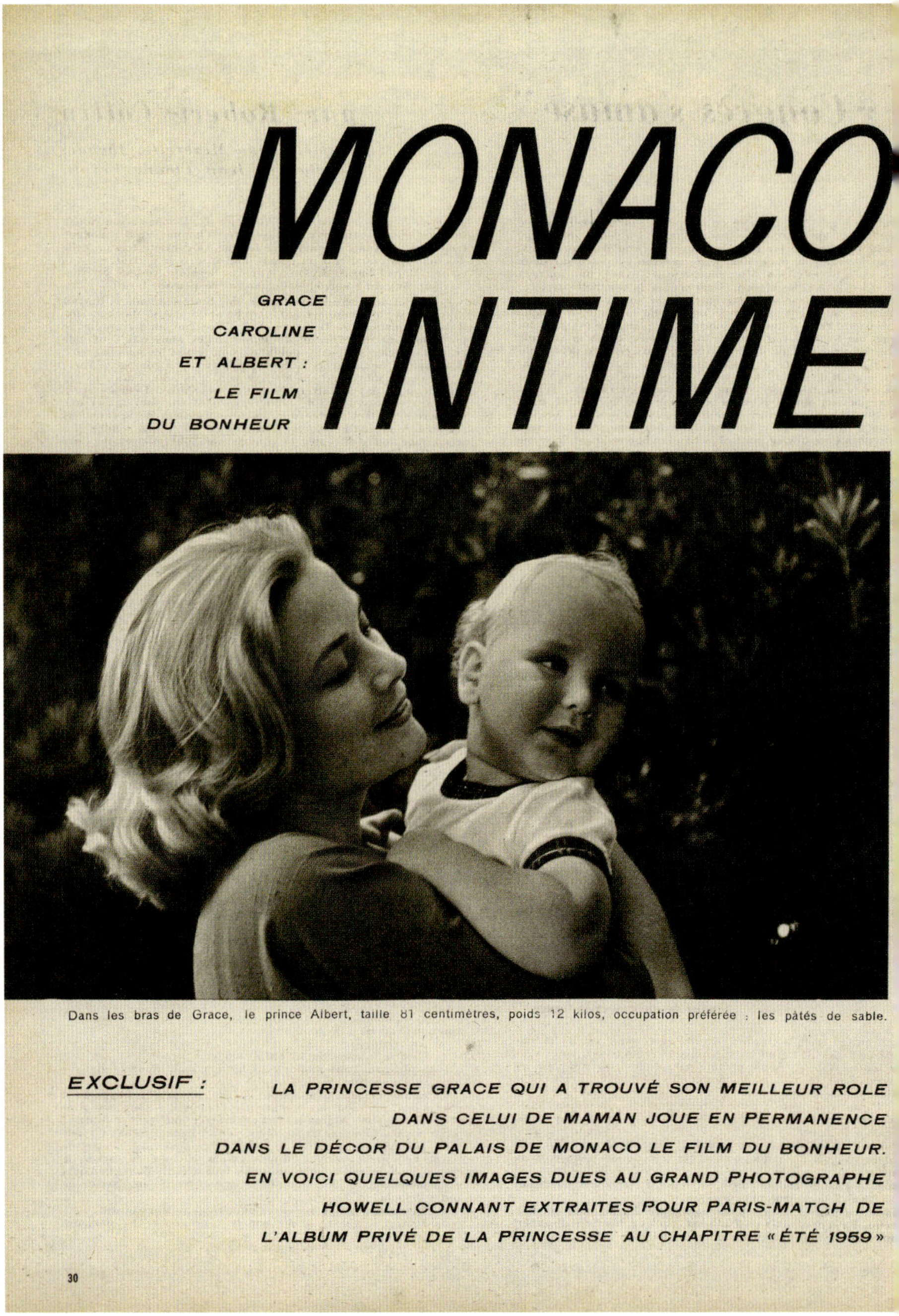

MONACO INTIME

GRACE
CAROLINE
ET ALBERT :
LE FILM
DU BONHEUR

Dans les bras de Grace, le prince Albert, taille 81 centimètres, poids 12 kilos, occupation préférée : les pâtés de sable.

EXCLUSIF : LA PRINCESSE GRACE QUI A TROUVÉ SON MEILLEUR ROLE DANS CELUI DE MAMAN JOUE EN PERMANENCE DANS LE DÉCOR DU PALAIS DE MONACO LE FILM DU BONHEUR. EN VOICI QUELQUES IMAGES DUES AU GRAND PHOTOGRAPHE HOWELL CONNANT EXTRAITES POUR PARIS-MATCH DE L'ALBUM PRIVÉ DE LA PRINCESSE AU CHAPITRE «ÉTÉ 1959»

30

Figure 3.26 *Paris Match*, August 29, 1959, pp. 30–1. Photographs by Howell Conant © Paris Match / Scoop.

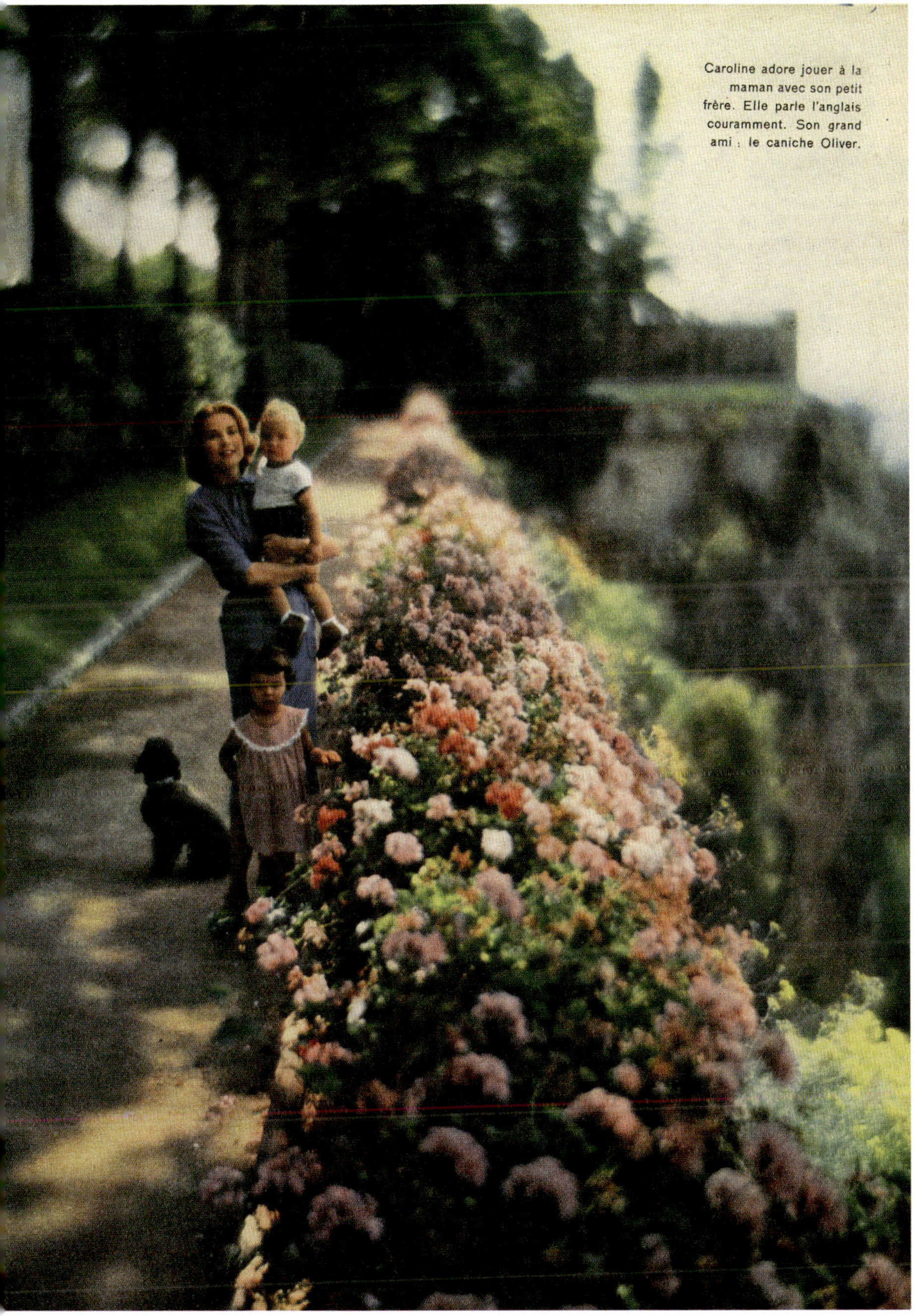
Caroline adore jouer à la maman avec son petit frère. Elle parle l'anglais couramment. Son grand ami : le caniche Oliver.

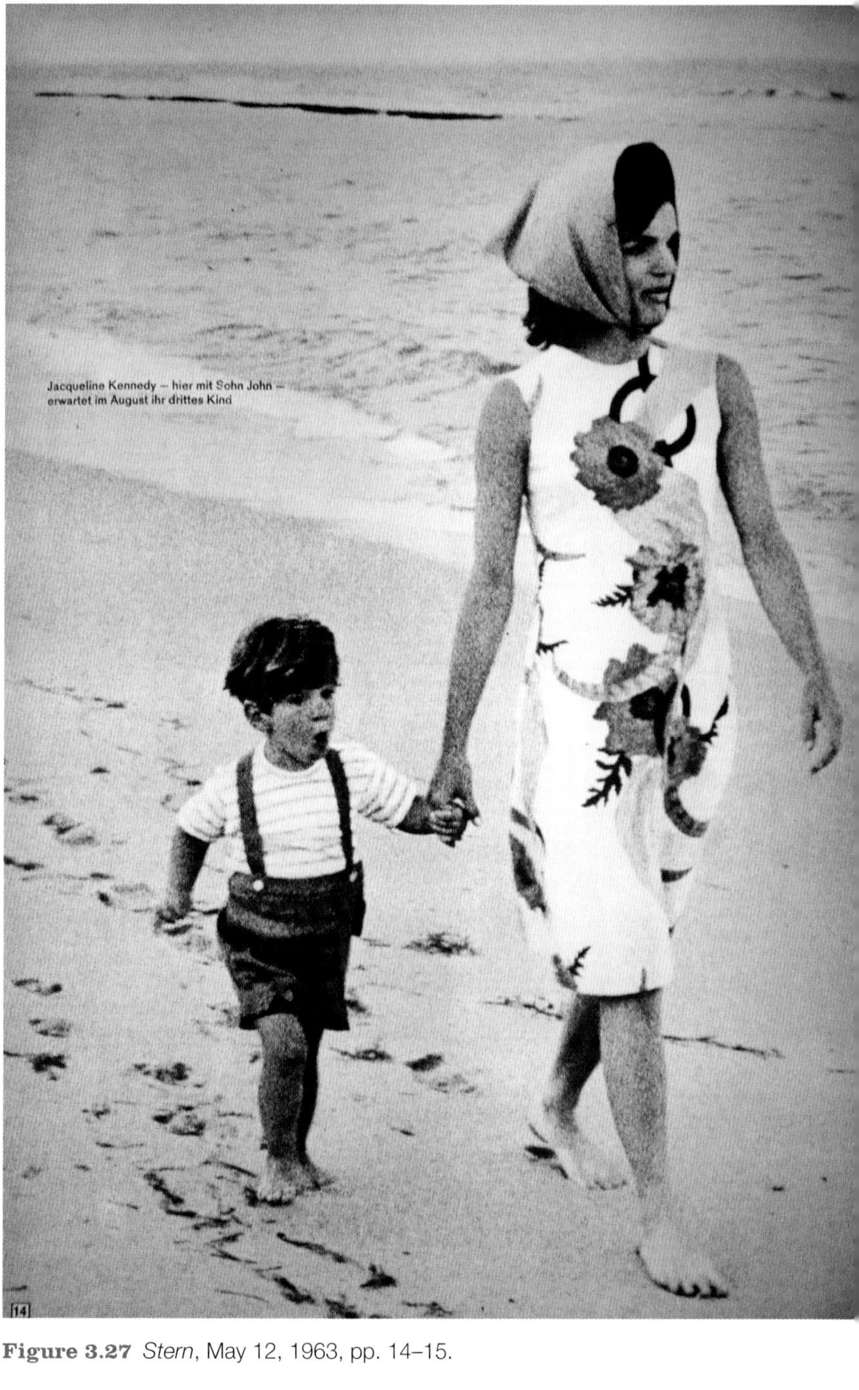

Figure 3.27 *Stern*, May 12, 1963, pp. 14–15.

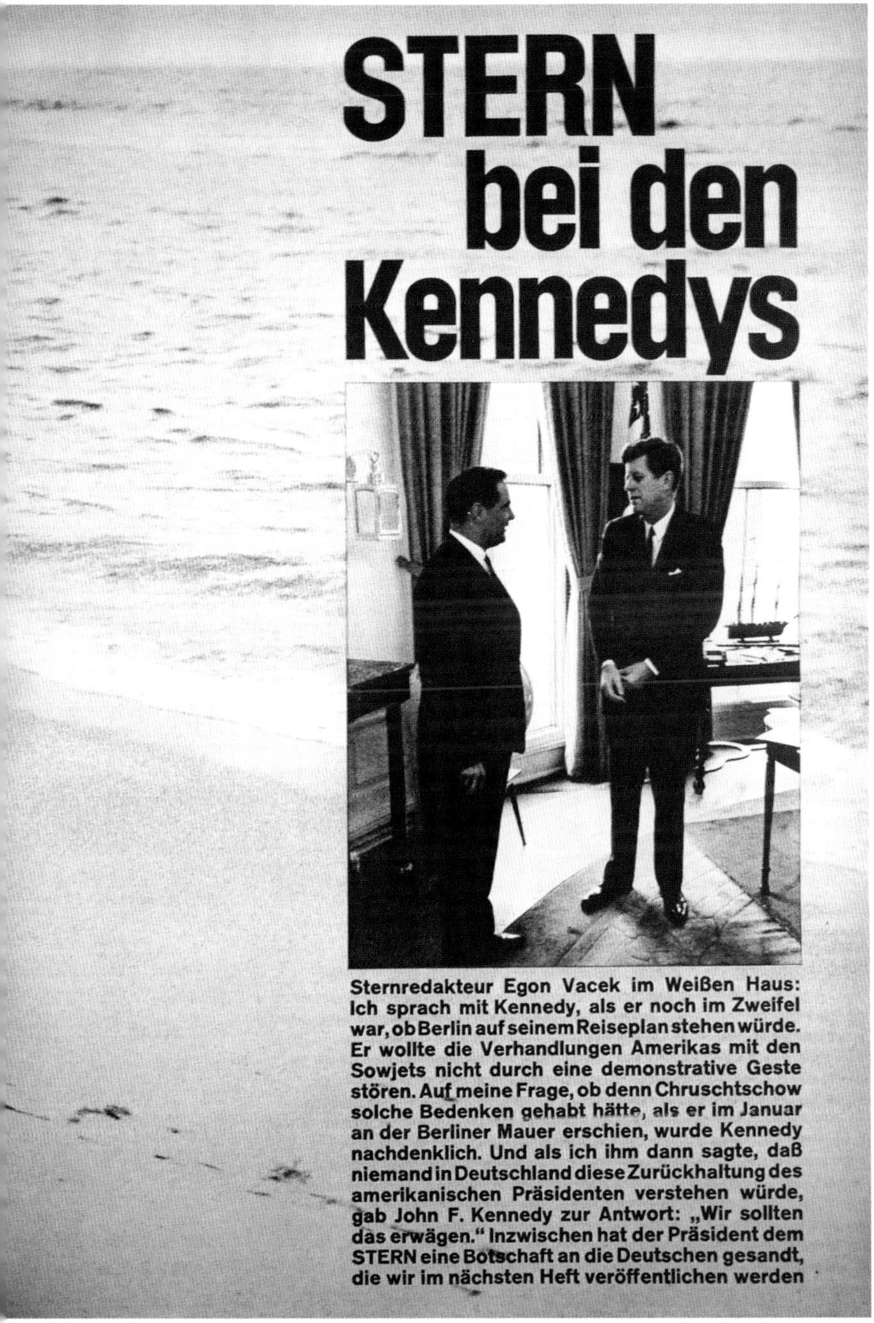

STERN bei den Kennedys

Sternredakteur Egon Vacek im Weißen Haus: Ich sprach mit Kennedy, als er noch im Zweifel war, ob Berlin auf seinem Reiseplan stehen würde. Er wollte die Verhandlungen Amerikas mit den Sowjets nicht durch eine demonstrative Geste stören. Auf meine Frage, ob denn Chruschtschow solche Bedenken gehabt hätte, als er im Januar an der Berliner Mauer erschien, wurde Kennedy nachdenklich. Und als ich ihm dann sagte, daß niemand in Deutschland diese Zurückhaltung des amerikanischen Präsidenten verstehen würde, gab John F. Kennedy zur Antwort: „Wir sollten das erwägen." Inzwischen hat der Präsident dem STERN eine Botschaft an die Deutschen gesandt, die wir im nächsten Heft veröffentlichen werden

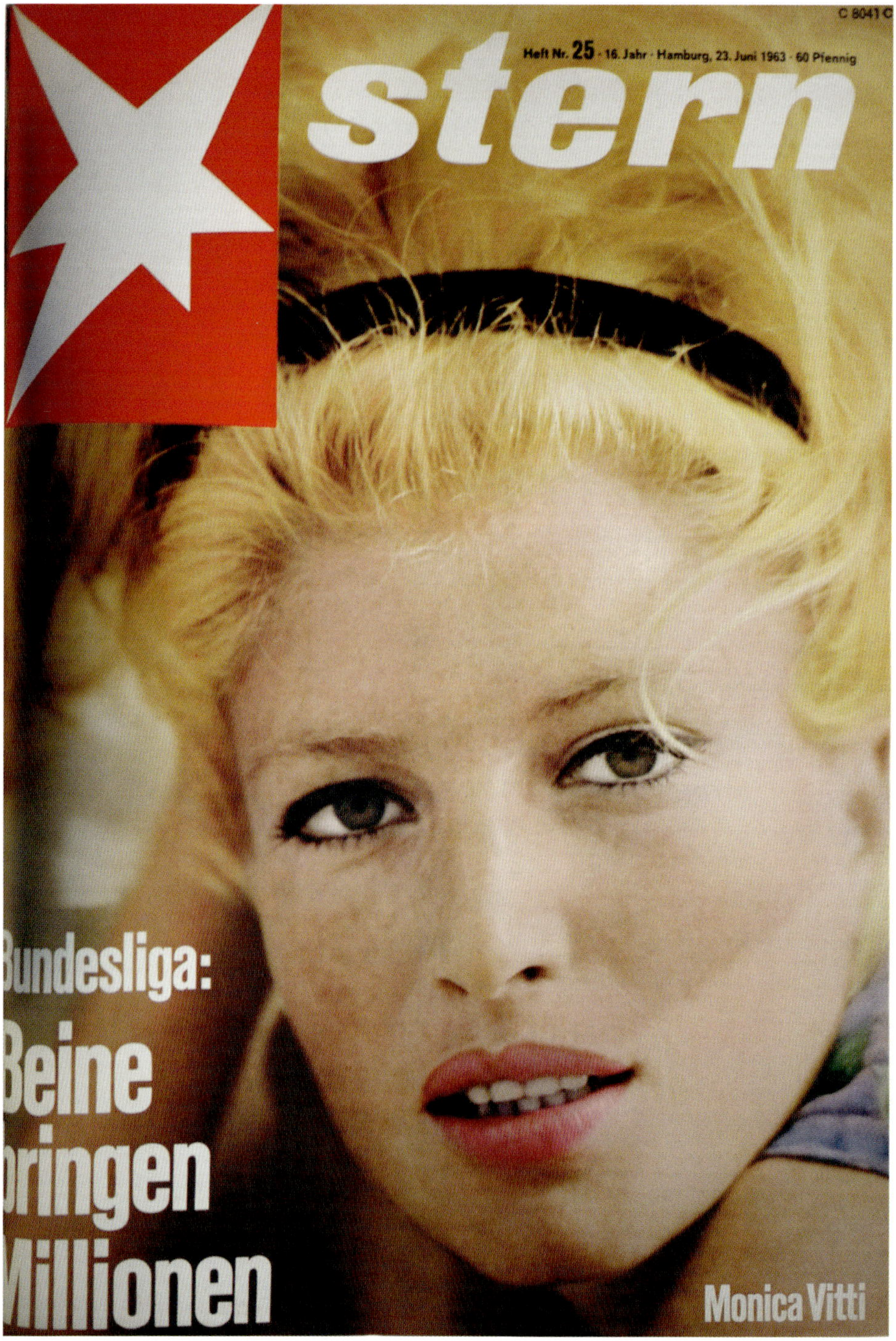

Figure 3.28 *Stern*, June 23, 1963, cover.

Roger Thérond in charge.[131] Beginning in 1976, as the choice of cover photographs indicates, stories about the aristocracy and the entertainment business prevailed over political and social news.[132] *Paris Match* is still considered a general news magazine by the OJD, the *Office de justification des tirages*, which classifies France's print and digital press and among other things certifies circulation figures; but the combination of *Paris Match*'s "classy celebrities"[133] emphasis and a sensationalism summed up by the 1978 slogan "Le poids des mots, le choc des photos" (The power of words and the pow! of photos) has brought its circulation back up to a steady 800,000 (see Figure 3.30).[134]

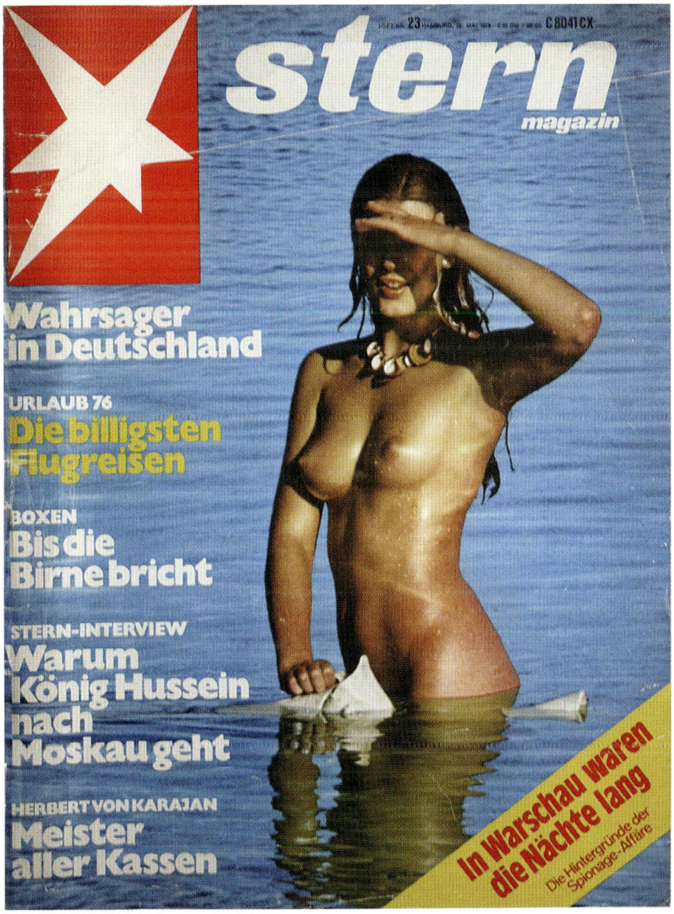

Figure 3.29 *Stern*, May 26, 1976, cover.

The period spanned by *Life* was unquestionably a vital one in the history of photojournalism. The circulation levels of general news magazines gave them a visibility and a cultural, political and commercial clout hitherto unheard of and never to be repeated. In this context photography's information value—especially in the case of snapshots, which minimized the presence of the photographer—was confirmed and the function of images in the news justified. The photographic essay as defined by *Life* emerged as a further stage in the recognition of the photographer as journalist and as such acquired mythic status within the profession. At the same time a comparison between discourse and actual use reveals that in fact the role of images and photographers was clearly demarcated by the editorial teams in charge of the magazines' layouts. The pigeonholing of Eugene Smith's essays as either "photographic" or "pictorial" is a salutary reminder that the photographer's style, as a means of expressing a point of view, was just as closely regulated. What must not be forgotten, either, is that these essays represented only a tiny part of any one issue of *Life*, half of which was already occupied by advertising and the rest largely given over to trivia. And while agencies like Magnum did their best to defend the creative status of their photographers, the handling of Cartier-Bresson's Russian material demonstrates that once sold to the press, images were forced into an editorial straitjacket. Rich in achievements, this period fueled photographers' hopes, but at the same time often left them frustrated and plagued by doubt. In the 1970s, when general news magazines were in crisis or actually disappearing, photographers had already begun to diversify the use of their images by publishing books; and the institutional recognition of photography that was then developing generated increased interest in reportages which had begun to circulate in various media. This groundswell facilitated the rise of a new figure in photography: the *auteur*, who symbolized accession to a status as creator and cultural producer that justified the movement of photographs from the press to the walls of galleries.

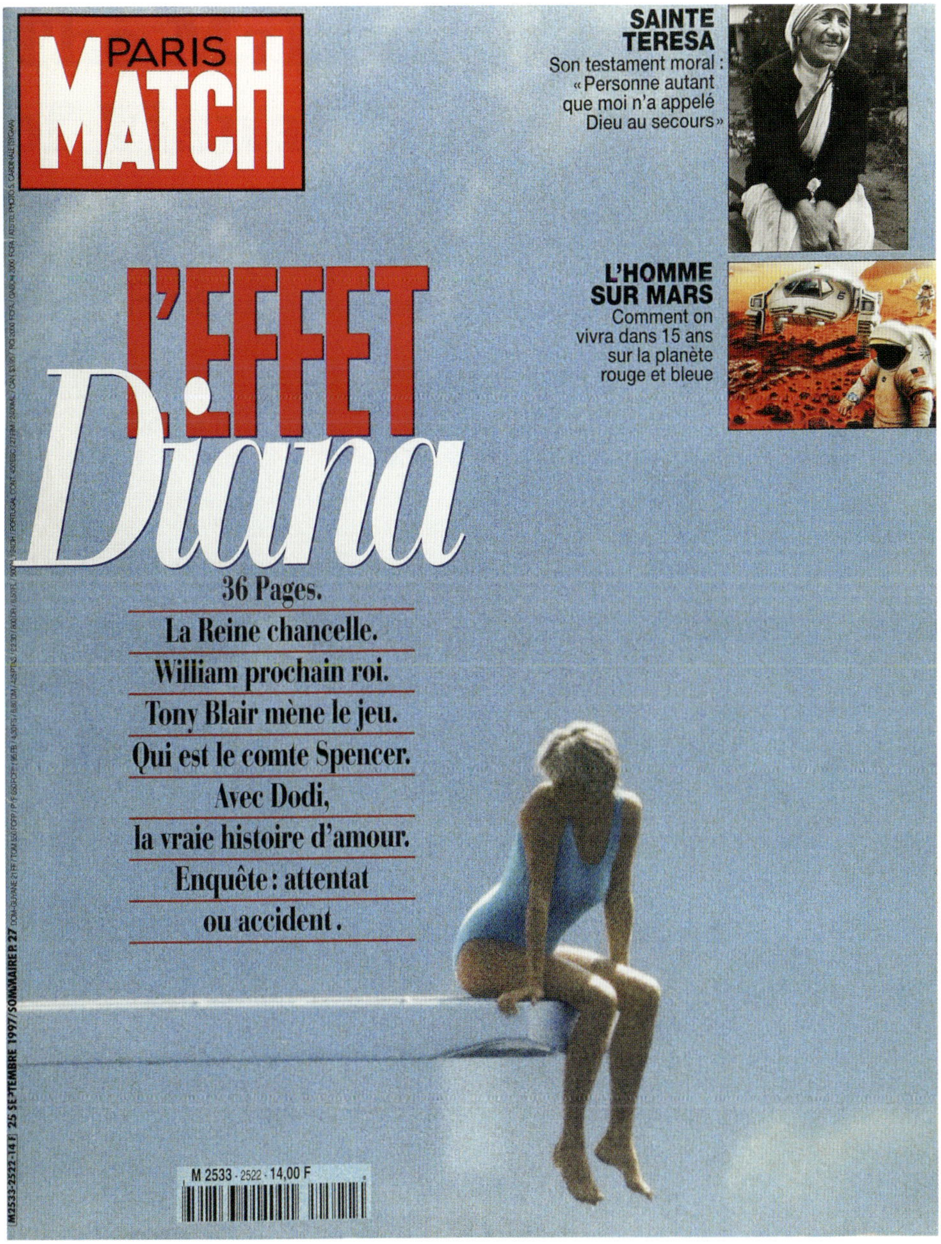

Figure 3.30 *Paris Match*, September 25, 1997, cover. Photograph by Stéphane Cardinale © Paris Match / Scoop.

Conclusion

Beginning in the 1970s, and concomitant with the economic decline of the illustrated press—itself notably due to the escalating influence of television and, later, the Internet—photojournalism was specifically affected by the overall artistic and cultural institutionalization of photography. The legitimation of the medium hinged in particular on acceptance or rejection of press images by museums. Photographers, whose images were already appearing in magazines, galleries and museums, were much in demand by art institutions: the Magnum agency, for example, was achieving ongoing recognition through showings of its members' work at the International Center of Photography (ICP) in New York, founded in 1974 by Robert Capa's brother Cornell. The main focus at ICP was on "concerned photographers," as would be the case at the Centre National de la Photographie when it opened in Paris in 1982.

During the 1980s and 1990s this emphasis on press photography came under considerable fire as an obstacle to artistic recognition of the medium. On a number of occasions the French critic Jean-François Chevrier spoke out urging the acquisition and exhibition of photography by museums on an equal footing with the other visual arts.[1] Stressing the need for the medium's integration into such legitimizing institutions as the Museum of Modern Art in New York and the Musée National d'Art Moderne in Paris, Chevrier inveighed against the creation of institutions specifically devoted to photographic usage and practices, and was especially opposed to the prominence given to photojournalism in France. Thus the arrival of press photography in museums was long seen as a belittling factor by the advocates of exclusively artistic recognition for the medium.

The specifically photographic institutions took the opposite point of view, and to justify their legitimation of photojournalism those concerned—photographers, publishers, directors of institutions—opted for joint vindication of a new figure, that of the photojournalist/*auteur*.[2]

Photojournalism and art

During the 1990s the American photographer and Magnum agency member James Nachtwey regularly covered the conflicts in the Balkans for *Time* magazine.[3] In black and white, his work was characterized by distinctive formal effects: the use of blur, the absence of frontality, and resort to deframing and optical distortion. These images were brought together in the book *Inferno*[4] (1999) and later shown in numerous institutions including ICP (2000), the Museum of Fine Arts in Leipzig (2004), and the Bibliothèque Nationale de France (2005). The prints are currently being sold by the Fahey/Klein Gallery in Los Angeles.

This emblematic example brings together all the factors symptomatic of the institutionalization of photojournalism: subjective involvement by the photographer, a specific aesthetic and the circulation of the images. This legitimation mechanism draws on the figure of the *auteur* as symbolizing the achievement of a status as creator and cultural producer whose pictures are henceforth disseminated in a variety of forms. The photographer is now an *auteur*: while not relinquishing the use value of his images, he aspires at the same time to cultural recognition by the traditional structures of legitimation, and thus subverts the habitual status of his photographs. This shift notably hinges on the photographer's personality and subjectivity. The concept of the *auteur*, already well embedded in the fields of literature and the cinema since the 1950s,[5] gradually found its way into the historiography of photography and, as Fred Ritchin writes, was used to legitimize a certain creative approach to photojournalism: "Many photographers are increasingly becoming the 'authors' of their own work, contextualizing its presentation themselves in books, audio-visual presentations, films, or exhibitions, or demanding a greater say in a publication's ultimate use of their material."[6]

The art of press photography

Institutional recognition of photojournalism also depends on identification and acceptance of a long tradition of appropriation of press images by artists. In 2005 modern art curator Hartwig Fischer shook up the museum world when he presented *Covering the Real: Art and the Press Picture, from Warhol to Tillmans* at the Kunstmuseum Basel.[7] Behind this exhibition lay a dual ambition: presentation of a historical panorama exploring the links between contemporary art and the press image since the 1960s, including painting, photography and video installations; and the embedding of this gambit in an innovative scenography notably associating the works on show with images arriving from a photographic agency in real time.[8] Utilization of press images with established use value makes possible projects capable of asserting their uniqueness in the artistic domain. It would seem, then, that this photographic practice, with its "anti-artistic products"[9]—and, often, its dismissal as devoid of all aesthetic implications—in fact constitutes an essential formal paradigm both in the field of artistic creation and that of its modes of display. Media images—attacked, analyzed, taken over, circumvented and/or assimilated—govern the aesthetic intentions of a significant part of today's artistic output. Artists are exploring the economic, aesthetic and moral rules of today's mass imagery through forms of assimilation that find their fulfillment as much in the visual arts generally as in the strictly photographic domain. A number of the artists on show in Basel—Malcolm Morley, Andy Warhol, Martha Rosler, Sarah Charlesworth, Arnulf Rainer, Wolfgang Tillmans—had in common the transformation of the utilitarian press image into artistic visual experience, and the

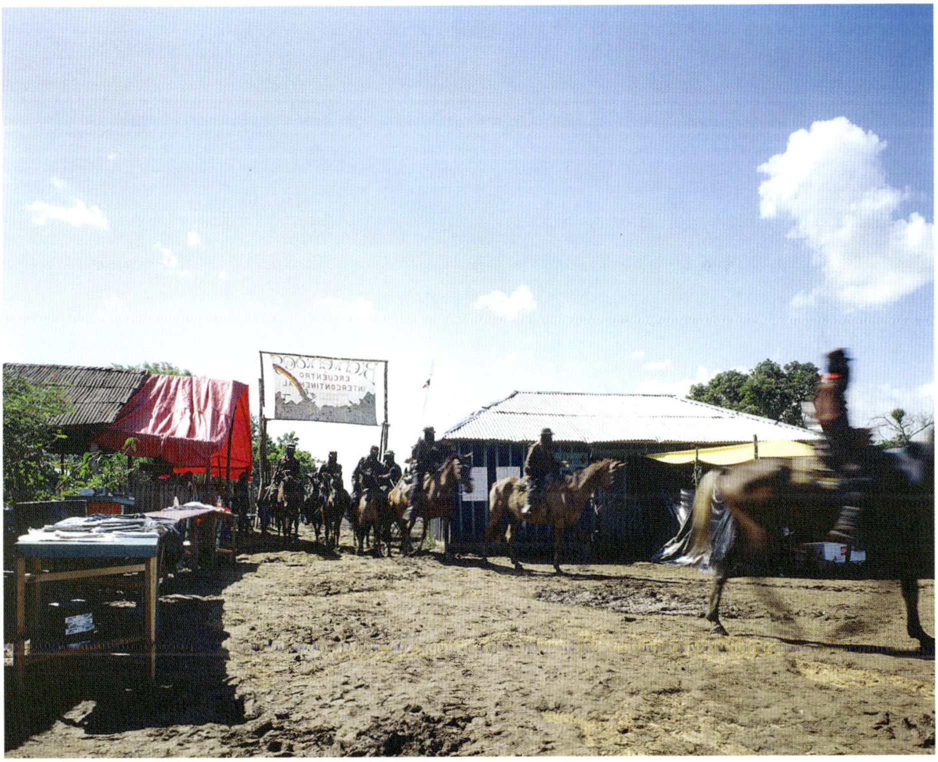

Figure 4.1 Bruno Serralongue, *The Arrival of Subcomandante Marcos and His Guard (Chiapas)*, *Encuentro* series, cibachrome print mounted on aluminium, 125 × 156 cm, 1996. Courtesy of the artist and Air de Paris, Paris.

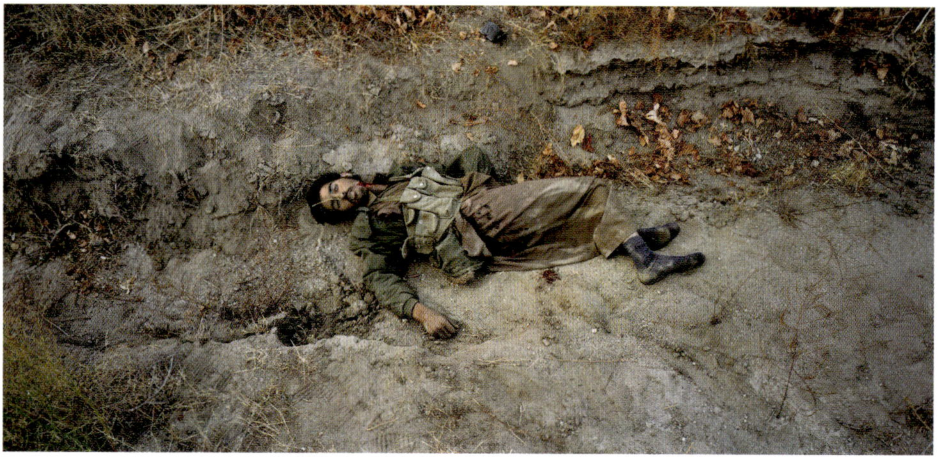

Figure 4.2 Luc Delahaye, *Taliban*, C-print, 111 × 237 cm, 2001. Courtesy of Galerie Nathalie Obadia, Paris / Brussels.

exhibition seemed to confirm Georges Didi-Huberman's assertion that "Contemporary art is more interested than ever in photojournalism."[10]

This novel inclusion of press images alongside works of art prompted one critic to describe the overall design of *Covering the Real* as a "groundbreaking interactive approach."[11] The works of the twenty-five participating artists were exhibited in the classical manner, but together with a large screen set up in the second-to-last room "so as to be visible throughout the visit, thanks to the aligned arrangement of the rooms."[12] Succeeding each other on the screen were photographs from the Keystone agency in Zurich, supplied by correspondents all over the world. As Hartwig Fischer put it, "for the first time ever, the world-wide flow of digital press pictures is presented to the public in real time;"[13] this screening, then, was a way of asserting a clear break with curatorial tradition.

These real-time photographs of events were tied in with cut-out newspaper images from different points in the past, deliberately shown caption-free in vitrines in the nine rooms. The result was an ambitiously atypical scenography focusing on the visual impact of press pictures and their relationship with the artworks. The captions for the screened images were available for consultation on a monitor at the entrance to the museum. Likewise, in the catalogue, the photographs originally taken for the press were interspersed among the artworks and all the captions were grouped together at the end. The curator's choice of works was universally hailed by the critics, but the screening was sometimes faulted as too mannered and conducive to a confusion of status between the press images and the artworks.[14] For Hartwig Fischer, "the 'public image' is indeed a challenging forum for artists to redefine the aesthetic autonomy and social significance of their own work."[15] This confrontation—press images and artworks brought together as part of the same event, and thus generating a new experience within an art institution—is now accepted practice, and despite certain contradictions of intent has come to be used by photojournalism institutions long refractory to this kind of challenge to the *métier*. In 2006 French photographer Éric Baudelaire showed a war scene at the Visa pour l'Image photojournalism festival in Perpignan. Commissioned by France's Centre National des Arts Plastiques, the diptych *The Dreadful Details* employs a form of realism to portray an imaginary moment from the war in Iraq. Working with professional actors, Baudelaire used a Hollywood TV series set—a kind of outdoor stage. The overall size of the prints (209 × 375 cm) and the diptych form combine to produce pictorial reminiscence, with the photographer seeking to integrate his work into the history of art and the visual tradition of representations of war. In two images Baudelaire groups various dramatic scenes of the kind preferred by the media and applies the war-image codes of the press and television. *The Dreadful Details* was shown in the former Dominican convent in Perpignan amid press images produced by other photographers working in a classical vein.

Photojournalism as formal paradigm

The confrontation between press images and artistic practices is also taking place on the terrain of contemporary photography.[16] For artists Roy Arden and Jeff Wall "the classic sense of art photography was defined by photographers who wanted their work not to be bound by photojournalism, but still to make some claim to be reportage. But photojournalism was, and is, such a dominant social institution that it seemed that everyone positioned themselves in relation to it."[17] Thus the need to tackle press images seems a decisive factor in the defining of art photography. Working in a documentary vein leads many photographers into the same territory as photojournalists and obliges them to work under the same conditions: Bruno Serralongue "regularly attends events that, for a few days, will be making waves in the media."[18] His trips to Chiapas (1996, see Figure 4.1) and the World Summit on the Information Society in Geneva (2003) were opportunities to explore the codes, procedures and formal approaches of press photography,[19] and the resulting works are notably intended as a response to the process of cultural and patrimonial legitimation impacting a photojournalism now anointed by numerous exhibitions and sundry attempts to build up a collectors' market.[20] For photography historian Michel Poivert this prestige boost for press images reflects the temptation of a "history photography" that would seem to be slotting photojournalism into the status niche left vacant by painting.[21] Similarly, in 2005 the Maison Rouge contemporary art foundation in Paris presented a selection of panoramic photographs by Luc Delahaye. Since 2001 this ex-Sipa and Magnum veteran has been travelling to the world's hotspots and returning with mostly frontal, wide angle, documentary-style images: the wars in Afghanistan (see Figure 4.2) and Iraq, the dismantling of the colonies in Palestine, Mass being celebrated by Pope John Paul II at St. Peter's in Rome, the Indonesian city of Meulaboh after the tsunami, all captured in panoramic format. Addressing high profile events with a cumbersome apparatus offering a limited number of shots per roll of film, Delahaye achieves a distance enhanced by his large-format view camera.[22] His aim is to differentiate his work from press photography while occupying the same media terrain as photojournalists. The implementation of this artistic project, contingent as it in on a tool that excludes any "snapshot" approach, has its roots in an emphasis on landscape and the importance of the out-of-frame.[23] The imposing format of his prints is suggestive more of a painterly than a photographic tradition, to the point where critic Michel Guerrin has even spoken of "historical tableaux."[24] But despite significant recognition on the international museum circuit, Delahaye also attracts critical flak: he has been accused, for instance, of a formal glamorizing of newsworthy subjects that induces "a more than dubious spectacularization of the event."[25]

Despite the insistence of critics resisting the inclusion of press photography in the museum, the press image/artwork nexus is becoming more common in the exhibition context. In 2014 the Centre Pompidou-Metz presented *Paparazzi! Photographers, Stars, Artists*,[26] curated by Clément Chéroux, then chief curator at the Musée National d'Art Moderne. Focusing on a practice widely disparaged—including in photojournalism circles—the project triggered something of a media storm with its mix of stealth photographs, magazine images, and artworks.[27] Its investigation of the aesthetics of news pictures drew considerable critical ire, mostly revolving around the habitual allegations of "moral offense."[28] And yet, without lumping artworks and press photographs together indiscriminately, these innovative institutional projects seem decisive in, finally, giving media images their place in a general history of forms and representations.

Notes

Introduction

1 See Chapter 1.

2 Dominique Kalifa, Philippe Régnier, Marie-Ève Thérenty and Alain Vaillant, "Scansions internes à l'histoire de la presse," in Dominique Kalifa, Philippe Régnier, Marie-Ève Thérenty and Alain Vaillant (eds), *La Civilisation du journal: histoire culturelle et littéraire de la presse française au XIXe siècle* (Paris: Nouveau Monde, 2011), 249–68.

3 "Préface," in *L'Illustration*, vol. 4, March 1, 1845.

4 Adolphe Joanne, "La Californie: San Francisco et Sacramento," in *L'Illustration*, no. 392, August 31, 1850, 135.

5 Thomas Grimm, "L'Art de vivre cent ans," in *Le Petit Journal*, no. 8649, August 31, 1886, 1.

6 "This Is War!," in *Picture Post*, vol. 1, no. 10, December 3, 1938, 14.

7 *La Vie au grand air*, no. 248, June 12, 1903, 386–7.

8 *Life*, vol. 5, no. 24, December 12, 1938, 28.

9 *Life*'s circulation was 5.8 million in 1956 and *Paris Match*'s circulation was 1.8 million in 1958. See Loudon Wainwright, *The Great American Magazine: an Inside History of Life* (New York: Knopf, 1986), 179 and Jean-Pierre Bacot, "Le Retard et le Rattrapage de *Paris Match*," in Karine Taveaux-Grandpierre and Joëlle Beurier (eds), *Le Photojournalisme des années 1930 à nos jours: structures, culture et public* (Rennes: Presses Universitaires de Rennes, 2014), 41.

10 Roland Barthes, "The Photographic Message," translated by Stephen Heath, in Vicki Goldberg (ed.), *Photography in Print: Writings from 1816 to the Present* (Albuquerque: University of New Mexico Press, 1988), 524.

11 Barthes. "The Photographic Message," 524.

12 Tim Gidal, *Modern Photojournalism: Origin and Evolution, 1910–1933* (New York: Collier Books, 1973); Gisèle Freund, *Photographie et Société* (Paris, Le Seuil, 1974); for the English translation, see Gisèle Freund, *Photography and Society* (Boston: David R. Godine, 1980). Mention should also be made of the chapter "Photography and the Pictorial Press" in Robert Taft, *Photography and the American Scene* (New York: Dover Publications, 1938), 419–50.

13 "I should like to take this opportunity to express heartfelt thanks to my friend and mentor Stefan Lorant—the motor force of modern photojournalism—for his invaluable information and

advice." Tim Gidal, *Modern Photojournalism*, 5; see also Michael Hallett, *Stefan Lorant, Godfather of Photojournalism* (Lanham, MD: Scarecrow Press, 2005).

14 Gisèle Freund, *La Photographie en France au XIXe siècle: essai de sociologie et d'esthétique* (Paris: A. Monnier, 1936). See also the facsimile edition published by Bourgois in 2011. For samples of her photography, see *VU*, no. 259, March 1, 1933, 325 and *Life*, vol. 8, no. 16, April 15, 1940, 49–50.

15 Tim Gidal, *Modern Photojournalism*, 6.

16 Gisèle Freund, *Photography and Society*, 103.

17 Tim Gidal, *Modern Photojournalism*, 6.

18 Gisèle Freund, *Photographie et société* (Paris: Le Seuil, 1974), 103–4 (translated by John Tittensor).

19 On this point see Vincent Lavoie, *Photojournalismes: revoir les canons de l'image de presse* (Vanves: Hazan, 2010).

20 "Une journée de combat entre Yen-Tai et le Cha-Ho photographiée heure par heure," in *L'Illustration*, no. 3224, December 10, 1904, 412–13; "The Greatest War-Photographer in the World: Robert Capa," in *Picture Post*, vol. 1, no. 10, December 3, 1938, 13; *Paris Match*, no. 1087, March 7, 1970, cover.

21 Clément Chéroux, "Mythologie du photographe de guerre," in Laurent Gervereau et al. (eds), *Voir / Ne pas voir la guerre: histoire des représentations photographiques de la guerre* (Paris: BDIC / Somogy, 2001), 310.

22 See Chapter 2.

23 "The Camera as Essayist," in *Life*, vol. 2, no. 17, April 26, 1937, 62–3; the "Photographic Essay" feature was launched in the *Life* issue dated August 30, 1937. See Chapter 3.

24 See for example Eugene Smith's "Spanish Village" in *Life*, vol. 30, no. 5, April 9, 1951, 120–9; and Henri Cartier-Bresson "Everything Goes On in the Piazza" in *Life*, vol. 35, no. 3, July 20, 1953, 71–9.

25 See Gaëlle Morel, *Le Photoreportage d'auteur: l'institution culturelle de la photographie en France depuis les années 1970* (Paris: CNRS, 2006).

26 Beaumont Newhall, "Photojournalism," in *The History of Photography: From 1839 to the Present* (New York: Museum of Modern Art, 1982, 248–67). In Michel Frizot (ed.), *A New History of Photography* (Cologne: Könemann, 1998), see Hubertus von Amelunxen, "The Century's Memorial," 130–47; Pierre Albert and Gilles Feyel, "Photography and the Media," 358–69; Michel Frizot, "Metamorphoses of the Image," 430–55; Françoise Ducros, "The Dream of Beauty," 534–53; Thomas Michael Gunther, "The Spread of Photography," 554–80; Fred Ritchin, "Close Witnesses," 590–611; and Jean-Claude Gautrand, "Looking at Others," 612–32.

27 Beaumont Newhall, "Photojournalism," *The History of Photography*, 623.

28 Jean-Claude Gautrand, "The Leica" in Michel Frizot, *A New History of Photography*, 596.

29 See Thierry Gervais and Gaëlle Morel, "Les Formes de l'information," in André Gunthert and Michel Poivert (eds), *L'Art de la photographie* (Paris, Citadelles / Mazenod, 2007), 302–55.

30 Wilson Hicks, *Words and Pictures: An Introduction to Photojournalism* (New York: Harper, 1952).

31 Hicks *Words and Pictures: An Introduction to Photojournalism*, 58.

32 Gisèle Freund, *Photography and Society*, 145.

33 John G. Morris, *Get the Picture: A Personal History of Photojournalism* (Chicago: Chicago University Press, 2002), 37.

34 Erika Doss (ed.), *Looking at* Life *Magazine* (Washington: Smithsonian Institution Press, 2001), 17.

35 Bodo von Dewitz and Robert Lebeck, *Kiosk: eine Geschichte der Fotoreportage* (Göttingen: Steidl, 2001); Mary Panzer and Christian Caujolle, *Things As They Are: Photojournalism in Context since 1955* (New York: Aperture Foundation / World Press Photo, 2005).

36 Jason E. Hill and Vanessa R. Schwartz (eds), *Getting the Picture: the Visual Culture of the News* (London: Bloomsbury, 2015). See also the articles in *Études photographiques*, no. 20: "La Trame des images: histoires de l'illustration photographique," June 2007; *Études photographiques*, no. 26: "Caught in the Act: Re-Thinking the History of Photojournalism," November 2010.

37 See Kevin Barnhurst and John Nerone, "Civic Picturing vs. Realist Photojournalism: the Regime of Illustrated News, 1856–1901," in *Design Issues*, vol. 16, no. 1, spring 2000, 59–79; and Thierry Gervais, "D'après photographie: premiers usages de la photographie dans le journal *L'Illustration*, 1843–1859," in *Études photographiques*, no. 13, July 2003, 56–85.

38 See Wendy Kozol, *Life's America* (Philadelphia: Temple University Press, 1994); Chris Vials, "The Popular Front in the American Century: *Life* Magazine, Margaret Bourke-White, and Consumer Realism, 1936–1941," in *American Periodicals: a Journal of History, Criticism, and Bibliography*, vol. 16, no. 1, 2006, 74–102.

39 We would like to thank Robert and Cordula Lebeck for allowing us access to their collection of nineteenth and twentieth-century periodicals. We are also grateful to François Cheval and Sylvain Besson of the Musée Nicéphore Niépce for permission to use the museum's sumptuous press photography and publications collections.

Chapter 1

1 Bodo von Dewitz and Robert Lebeck (2001), *Kiosk*.

2 Thierry Gervais (2003), "D'après photographie," 56–85; Kevin Barnhurst and John Nerone (2001), "Civic Picturing," 59–79.

3 *L'Illustration*, no. 26, August 26, 1843, 404.

4 *L'Illustration*, no. 279–80, July 1–8, 1848, 276.

5 See *The Illustrated London News*, no. 666, February 4, 1854, 88; no. 767, October 6, 1855, 405; no. 765, October 13, 1855, cover; no. 766, October 20, 1855, 472; no. 768, November 3, 1855, 520 524; no. 769, November 10, 1855, 557; no. 777, December 29, 1855, cover.

6 See for example *Harper's Weekly* (Brady), January 5, 1861, 1; *Harper's Weekly* (Gardner), July 2, 1864, 421; *Frank Leslie's Illustrated Newspaper* (Brady), August 9, 1862, 305; *Frank Leslie's Illustrated Newspaper* (Gardner), July 16, 1864, 257. See Kate Addleman-Frankel, "Photographic Engravings During the American Civil War," in Thierry Gervais (ed.), *Dispatch: War Photographs in Print, 1854–2008* (Toronto: Ryerson Image Centre, 2014), 65–73.

7 Olivier Ihl, "Dans l'œil du daguerréotype. La Rue du Faubourg-du-Temple, juin 1848," in *Études photographiques*, no. 34, spring 2016, 86–107.

8 Charles François Thibault, "The Barricade on Rue Saint-Maur-Popincourt After the Attack by General Lamoricière's Troops, Monday 26 June 1848," daguerreotype, 12.7 x 10.4 cm, *L'Illustration*, no. 279–80, July 1–8, 1848, 276. Now in the Musée d'Orsay, Paris.

9 Roger Fenton, "General Bosquet and Captain Dampierre," salted paper print, 18.3 x 15.2 cm, 1855, *The Illustrated London News*, October 6, 1855, 405. Now in the Musée d'Orsay, Paris.

10 See Thierry Gervais, "On Either Side of the 'Gatekeeper:' Technical Experimentation with Photography at *L'Illustration* (1880–1900)," in *Études photographiques*, no. 23, May 2009, 30–50.

11 See for example Reutlinger's photographic portrait of Madame Marie Magnier, extensively retouched before its publication in *L'Illustration*, no. 2598, December 10, 1892, 488.

12 See the photograph of the monument to Paul Baudry, unveiled in 1890, in which the background has been reworked by the illustrator to focus attention on the monument itself: *L'Illustration*, no. 2452, February 22, 1890, 164.

13 See *L'Illustration*, no. 2614, April 1, 1893, 249.

14 Nadar, Bibliothèque Nationale de France, Mss, N.a.f, fol. 55.

15 The term is used several times by Thomas Grimm in "L'Art de vivre cent ans," *Le Petit Journal*, no. 8649, August 31, 1886, 1.

16 "The Drawings in this Issue [were] Obtained Using Eastman Film that Provides the Image in Two Thousandths of a Second," *Le Journal illustré*, no. 36, September 5, 1886, 287.

17 Only Paul Nadar, several months after the interview, spoke—in very general terms—of the new illustrational possibilities it had generated. See "Sur les papiers positifs et négatifs Eastman: châssis à rouleaux et porte-membrane pour leur emploi," in *Bulletin de la Société française de photographie (BSFP)*, 2nd series, vol. III, February 1887, 49.

18 "Entrevue photographique," in *Le Figaro*, "Supplément littéraire," no. 47, November 23, 1889, 1–3.

19 Thierry Gervais, "La Similigravure: le récit d'une invention, 1878–1893," in *Nouvelles de l'estampe*, no. 229, March–April 2010, 2–29.

20 William Henry Fox Talbot, British Patent no. 565: "Patent for Improvements in the Art of Engraving," October 29, 1852: "The metallic plate is first coated or covered with a substance which is easily changed or altered by being exposed to the light of the sun or to day-light. Then by the methods which are employed in the art of photography an image or picture is formed . . . This being done, chemical substances are employed which have the property of etching or biting into the metallic plate in those places only which have been protected from the light or upon which the light has not acted strongly." Quoted in *The Repertory of Patent Inventions*

(London: Mackintosh, 1853), vol. 22, 58; Charles-Guillaume Petit, "Photo-typographie ou traduction d'un cliché en demi-teinte, d'après nature, en cliché au trait pouvant fournir un relief typographique," Institut National de la Propriété Indsutrielle (INPI), no. 126024, August 8, 1878; Stanislas Krakow, "Système d'obtention de planches typographiques avec hachures ou pointillés, au moyen de clichés photographiques ordinaires dit Photo-typographie," INPI, no. 163488, July 25, 1884; Frederic E. Ives, "Method of producing impression in line or stipple from photographic negatives," United States Patent Office, no. 237664, February 8, 1881; Georg Meisenbach, "Neuerungen in der Herstellung photographischer Platten für Hoch-und Tiefdruck-Clichés," Kaiserliches Patentamt, Patentschrift no. 22244, May 9, 1882.

21 William Gamble, "Écrans et diaphragme pour les épreuves tramées et trichromes," in *Le Moniteur de la photographie*, no. 17, 1902, 276.

22 Anonymous, "La Photogravure typographique," in *BSFP*, no. 4, April 4, 1884, 96.

23 See Petit in *Annuaire-almanach du commerce, de l'industrie, de la magistrature et de l'administration* (Paris: Firmin Didot Frères, 1887), 1776; and Robert S. Kahan, *The Antecedents of American Photojournalism*, doctoral dissertation, University of Wisconsin-Madison, 1969, 205.

24 *Illustrierte Zeitung*, no. 2616, August 19, 1893, cover.

25 See Thierry Gervais, "Photographies de presse? Le journal *L'Illustration* à l'ère de la similigravure," in *Études photographiques*, no. 16, May 2005, 166–81.

26 See for example "A Plague of Men: Scenes Among the Immigrants on the East Side of New York," in *The Illustrated American*, vol. 14, no. 187, September 16, 1893, 325.

27 Regarding the rise of amateur photography in the late nineteenth century, see Clément Chéroux, *Une généalogie des formes récréatives en photographie, 1890–1940*, doctoral dissertation, Université Paris-I, 2004; see also Denis Bernard and André Gunthert, *L'Instant rêvé: Albert Londe* (Nîmes/Laval: Jacqueline Chambon/Trois, 1993); Reese V. Jenkins, "Technology and the Market: George Eastman and the Origins of Mass Amateur Photography," in *Technology and Culture*, vol. 16, no. 1, January 1975, 1–19.

28 See Kevin Moore, *Jacques Henri Lartigue: The Invention of an Artist* (Princeton, NJ: Princeton University Press, 2004); Dominique de Font-Réaulx and Thierry Gervais (eds), *Léon Gimpel, 1873–1948: les audaces d'un photographe* (Paris: Musée d'Orsay/Éditions des Cinq Continents, 2008).

29 Kevin Moore (2012), *Jacques Henri Lartigue*.

30 *L'Illustration*, no. 3187, March 26, 1904, 195; *La Vie au grand air*, no. 290, March 31, 1904, 252; *La Vie illustrée*, no. 303, August 1, 1904.

31 Léon Gimpel, *Quarante Ans de reportages: souvenirs de Léon Gimpel, collaborateur à* L'Illustration, *1897–1932*, Domaine de Castellemont, Jurançon, manuscript (SFP collection), February 20, 1944, 7a.

32 "Le Roi et la Reine du Danemark," in *L'Illustration*, no. 3357, June 29, 1907, no page number; "La Grève des chemins de fer," in *L'Illustration*, no. 3529, October 15, 1910, 264; "La Phalange de Bétheny," in *L'Illustration*, no. 3471, September 4, 1909, 161–3, and *Le Matin*, September 4, 1909, 1.

33 Ernest Clair-Guyot, "Un demi-siècle à *L'Illustration*," in *L'Illustration*, no. 4713, July 1, 1933, no page number.

34 Lewis L. Gould and Richard Greffe, *Photojournalist: the Career of Jimmy Hare* (Austin: University of Texas Press, 1977); Thierry Gervais, "'The Greatest of War Photographer': Jimmy Hare, A Photojournalist at the Turn of the Twentieth Century," in *Études photographiques*, no. 26, November 2010, 35–49.

35 Cecil Carnes, *Jimmy Hare, News Photographer: Half a Century with a Camera* (New York: The Macmillan Company, 1940), 64.

36 Hélène Puiseux, *Les Figures de la guerre: représentations et sensibilités, 1839–1996* (Paris: Gallimard, 1997).

37 F.C. Yohn, "Final Charge of Chaffee's Brigade at El Caney," in *Collier's Weekly*, vol. 21, no. 15, July 16, 1898, no page number.

38 *Collier's Weekly*, vol. 21, no. 17, July 30, 1898, 4, 5, 8, 15, 20, 21.

39 See for example Hare's photographs in *Die Woche*, vol. 6, no. 24, June 11, 1904, 1045; *The Illustrated London News*, no. 3408, August 13, 1904, 229; *Le Matin*, no. 7493, August 31, 1904, 1. Regarding the treatment of the Russo–Japanese War in the French daily press, see Myriam Chermette, "La Guerre russo–japonaise, 1904–1905: début du reportage moderne ou fin d'une époque?," in *Donner à voir: la photographie dans Le Journal. Discours, pratiques, usages, 1892–1944*, doctoral dissertation, Université de Versailles–Saint-Quentin-en-Yvelines, 2009, 88–9.

40 See for example Adolphe Joanne, *L'Illustration*, August 31, 1850.

41 "La Photographie à la guerre," in *L'Illustration*, no. 3200, June 25, 1904, 422–3.

42 "Scènes de guerre," in *L'Illustration*, no. 3209, August 27, 1904, 136.

43 "Une journée de combat entre Yen-Tai et le Cha-Ho photographiée heure par heure," in *L'Illustration*, December 10, 1904, 412–13.

44 G.B. [Gustave Babin], "La Guerre vue par les photographes: Jimmy Hare," in *L'Illustration*, no. 3238, March 18, 1905, 167.

45 See Laurent Gervereau *et al.* (eds) (2001), *Voir / Ne pas voir la guerre*; Anne Tucker (ed.), *War / Photography: Images of Armed Conflict and its Aftermath* (Houston: Museum of Fine Arts, 2012).

46 See A.D. Harvey, "The Russo–Japanese War 1904–1905: Curtain Raiser for the Twentieth Century World Wars," in *The RUSI Journal*, vol. 148, no. 6, December 2003, 58–61.

47 "War Has Begun!," in *Collier's Weekly*, vol. 32, no. 20, February 13, 1904, no page numbers.

48 "James H. Hare, Greatest of War Photographers," in *Leslie's Weekly*, vol. 119, no. 3077, August 27, 1914, 195.

49 In 1898 a subscription to *L'Illustration* cost 36 francs, as against 15 francs for *La Vie illustrée*. Prices for single issues were 75 and 30 centimes respectively. In the same year an issue of *L'Illustration* contained an average of 28 images of all types, while the cover of *La Vie illustrée* regularly announced 50. See Thierry Gervais, "Dessins et Photographies publiés dans *L'Illustration* de 1897 à 1915," in *L'Illustration photographique: naissance du spectacle de l'information, 1843–1914*, doctoral dissertation, EHESS, 2007, 489–92.

50 The mention on the cover of the number of illustrations ended with the issue of January 26, 1899, three months after publication began.

51 See *La Vie illustrée* nos. 2, 25 and 30 of October 27, 1898, and April 6 and May 11, 1899.

52 See *La Vie illustrée* no. 299 of July 8, 1904.

53 The original image (8.5 x 14.3 cm) was by George Rogers and was included in a photographic album titled *Le Bioscope*, now part of the collection at the Archive of Modern Conflict in London.

54 Henri de Weindel and Lucien Métivet, "Bloc-Notes," in *La Vie illustrée*, no. 1, October 20, 1898, 2; The Editors, "À nos lecteurs," in *La Vie au grand air*, no. 59, October 29, 1899, 74.

55 *La Vie au grand air,* no. 21, February 4, 1899, 243–54. In issue no. 59, of October 29, 1899, the editors estimated that there were 60 "photogravures" in each issue ("À nos lecteurs," 74).

56 *La Vie au grand air*, no. 321, November 3, 1904, cover.

57 See Tom Gretton, "Différence et compétition: l'imitation et la reproduction des œuvres d'art dans un journal illustré du XIXe siècle," in Georges Roque (ed.), *Majeur ou mineur? Les hiérarchies en art* (Nîmes: Jacqueline Chambon, 2000), 105–43.

58 Fioravanti, "La Ceinture d'or," in *La Vie au grand air*, no. 276, December 24, 1903, 963.

59 "Les Jeux olympiques à Londres," in *La Vie au grand air*, no. 515, August 1, 1908, 88–9.

60 *La Vie au grand air*, no. 233, February 28, 1903, 136–7.

61 Regarding the context in which these new forms of spectacle arose and the reciprocation between different media during the Belle Époque, see Vanessa Schwartz, "Cinematic Spectatorship before the Apparatus: the Public Taste for Reality in Fin-de-Siècle Paris," in Leo Charney and Vanessa Schwartz (eds), *Cinema and the Invention of Modern Life* (Berkeley: University of California Press, 1995), 297–319; Vanessa Schwartz, *Spectacular Realities: Early Mass Culture in Fin-de-Siècle Paris* (Berkeley: University of California Press, 1998), 177–99.

62 *La Vie au grand air*, no. 197, June 21, 1902, 408–9.

63 See Marcel Huret, *Ciné Actualités: histoire de la presse filmée, 1895–1980* (Paris: Veyrier, 1984).

64 See Jacques Malthête and Laurent Mannoni (eds), *Méliès: magie et cinéma* (Paris: Paris Musées, 2002). See also Jean Mitry, "Le Montage dans les films de Méliès," in Madeleine Malthête-Méliès (ed.), *Méliès et la naissance du spectacle cinématographique* (Paris: Klincksieck, 1984), 149–55.

65 For everything relating to the history of screening venues in Paris before the First World War, see Jean-Jacques Meusy, *Paris-Palaces ou le Temps des cinémas, 1894–1918* (Paris: CNRS Éditions, 1995).

66 Pierre Lafitte, "Notre programme," in *Excelsior: journal illustré quotidien*, no. 1, November 16, 1910, 2.

67 René Jeanne and Charles Ford, *Le Cinéma et la Presse* (Paris: Armand Colin, 1961), 8.

68 Jean Selz, "Le Cinéma et la mise en pages," in *Presse-Publicité*, no. 3, March 28, 1937, 8, my italics.

69 Georges Roque, "Introduction," in Georges Roque (ed.), *Majeur ou mineur?* (Nîmes: Jacqueline Chambon, 2000), 20.

70 Tom Gunning, "The Cinema of Attractions: Early Film, Its Spectator and the Avant-Garde," in Thomas Elsaesser (ed.), *Early Cinema: Space, Frame, Narrative* (London: British Film Institute, 1990), 58.

71 See Thierry Gervais, "L'Invention du magazine: la photographie mise en page dans *La Vie au grand air*, 1898–1914," in *Études photographiques*, no. 20, June 2007, 50–67.

72 *Le Miroir*, no. 1, January 28, 1912.

73 See Jean-Pierre Bacot, *La Presse illustrée au XIX*[e] *siècle: une histoire oubliée* (Limoges: Presses universitaires de Limoges, 2005), 153.

74 See Joëlle Beurier, *Images et Violence, 1914–1918: quand* Le Miroir *racontait la Grande Guerre . . .* (Paris: Nouveau Monde Editions, 2007).

75 This appeal first appeared in the issue of August 16, 1914.

76 See Joëlle Beurier, "L'Apprentissage de l'événement: *Le Miroir* et la Grande Guerre," in *Études photographiques*, no. 20, June 2007, 68–83.

77 *Le Miroir*, vol. 5, no. 75, May 2, 1915, 8–9.

78 *Le Miroir*, vol. 6, no. 124, April 9, 1916, 2.

79 See for example the recommendations issued to amateurs in *Le Miroir*, vol. 5, no. 82, June 20, 1915, 3.

80 See for example *Le Miroir*, vol. 5, no. 65, February 21, 1915, 3.

Chapter 2

1 Tim Gidal, *Modern Photojournalism* (New York: Collier Books, 1973); Gisèle Freund, "The Birth of Photojournalism in Germany," in *Photography and Society*, 115–140; Beaumont Newhall (1982), *The History of Photography*; Mary Panzer and Christian Caujolle (1955), "Introduction," in *Things As They Are*, 8–33.

2 See Clément Chéroux (2001), "Mythologie du photographe de guerre," in Laurent Gervereau (eds) *et al.*, *Voir / Ne pas voir la guerre*, 306–11.

3 See André Gunthert, "Esthétique de l'occasion: naissance de la photographie instantanée comme genre," in *Études photographiques*, no. 9, May 2001, 64–87.

4 Vincent Lavoie (2010), "L'Instant actualisé," in *Photojournalismes* (Vanves: Hazan, 2010), 39–72.

5 See Hanno Hardt, "Pictures for the Masses: Photography and the Rise of Popular Magazines in Weimar Germany," in *Journal of Communication Inquiry*, vol. 13, no. 1, January 1989, 13.

6 Respectively the *Berliner Illustrirte Zeitung* covers for vol. 13, no. 36, September 4, 1904; vol. 15, no. 17, April 29, 1906; vol. 19, no. 24, June 12, 1910; vol. 13, no. 49, December 4, 1904.

7 *Berliner Illustrirte Zeitung*, vol. 13, no. 12, March 20, 1904, cover.

8 *Berliner Illustrirte Zeitung*, vol. 13, no. 20, May 15, 1904, cover.

9 *Berliner Illustrirte Zeitung*, vol. 20, no. 29, July 16, 1911, cover.

10 See Thierry Gervais, "L'Exploit mis en page: la médiatisation de la conquête de l'air à la Belle Époque," in Régis Durand and Michel Poivert (eds), *L'Événement: les images comme acteurs de l'histoire* (Paris: Hazan, 2007), 65–83.

11 The term was coined by Clément Vautel for the practitioners of this new photographic method, which left its mark on the Belle Époque: see his "Échos et Nouvelles," in *Bulletin du Photo-Club de Paris*, 1901, 67.

12 Respectively the covers of the *Berliner Illustrirte Zeitung*: vol. 19, no. 15, April 10, 1910, and vol. 19, no. 31, July 31, 1910.

13 *Berliner Illustrirte Zeitung*, vol. 19, no. 38, September 18, 1910, cover.

14 *Berliner Illustrirte Zeitung*, vol. 28, no. 34, August 24, 1919, cover.

15 See especially the use Hannah Höch immediately made of it in her montage *Dada-Rundschau* of 1919 (Berlinische Galerie Collection, Berlin).

16 Kurt Korff, "Die Berliner Illustrirte," in Max Osborn (ed.), *50 Jahre Ullstein*, 1877–1927 (Berlin: Ullstein Verlag, 1927), quoted in Anton Kaes *et al.* (eds), *The Weimar Republic Sourcebook* (Berkeley: University of California Press, 1995), 646 (revised translation).

17 See Chapter 1.

18 See Herman Ullstein, *The Rise and Fall of the House of Ullstein* (London: Nicholson & Watson, 1943), 78–9.

19 Herman Ullstein, *The Rise and Fall of the House of Ullstein* (London: Nicholson & Watson, 1943), 76–8.

20 See Winfried Lerg, "Media Culture of the Weimar Republic: a Historical Overview," in *Journal of Communication Inquiry*, vol. 13, no. 1, January 1989, 96; On the Weimar Germany see also Daniel H. Magilow, *The Photography of Crisis: The Photo Essay of Weimar Germany* (University Park, PA: Pennsylvania State University Press, 2012).

21 Martin Munkácsi and Albert Renger-Patzsch, "Halt mal still!," in *UHU*, no. 10, July 1929, 18–25.

22 "Photogramme," in *UHU*, no. 5, February 1928, 36–7.

23 Kurt Tucholsky, "Ein Bild sagt mehr als tausend Worte," in *UHU*, vol. 3, no. 2, November 1926, 75, quoted in Van Deren Coke, *Avant-garde Photography in Germany, 1919–1939* (New York: Pantheon, 1982), 45 (revised translation).

24 See Thierry Gervais, "D'après photographie," in *Études photographiques*, no. 13, July 2003, 56–85.

25 Kurt Korff, "Die Berliner Illustrirte," quoted in Anton Kaes *et al.* (eds), *The Weimar Republic Sourcebook* (Berkeley: University of California Press, 1995), 646.

26 Hanno Hardt, "Pictures for the Masses," in *Journal of Communication Inquiry*, January 1989, 13.

27 Winfried Lerg points out that at this time only the daily *Berliner Morgenpost* (also published by Ullstein) enjoyed a circulation of over 500,000. See "Media Culture of the Weimar Republic," in *Journal of Communication Inquiry*, January 1989, 96.

28 Hanno Hardt, "Pictures for the Masses," in *Journal of Communication Inquiry*, January 1989, 18.

29 See Klaus Pohl, *Ansichten der Ferne: Reisefotografie, 1850—heute* (Giessen: Anabas, 1983), 103.

30 Lorant's name appeared on the *Münchner Illustrierte Presse* masthead from August 6, 1928 (vol. 5, no. 32) to March 19, 1933 (vol. 10, no. 11). His status changed, but his duties remained the same. See Michael Hallett, *Stefan Lorant* (Lanham: Scarecrow Press, 2005), 32.

31 Kurt Korff, "Die Berliner Illustrirte," in Max Osborn (ed.), *50 Jahre Ullstein, 1877–1927* (Berlin: Ullstein Verlag, 1927); see Olivier Lugon, *La Photographie en Allemagne: anthologie de textes* (Nîmes: Jacqueline Chambon, 1997), 249–50.

32 See Chapter 1.

33 Pierre Lafitte, "Notre programme," in *Excelsior*, November 16, 1910, 2.

34 Kurt Korff, "Die Berliner Illustrirte," quoted in Anton Kaes *et al.* (eds), *The Weimar Republic Sourcebook* (Berkeley: University of California Press, 1995), 646.

35 See for example the double page 792–3, vol. 13, no. 49, December 4, 1904.

36 See for example vol. 13, no. 50, December 11, 1904; vol. 28, no. 34, August 24, 1919; vol. 40, no. 21, May 24, 1931.

37 *Berliner Illustrirte Zeitung*, vol. 38, no. 37, September 15, 1929, 1610–13.

38 Kurt Korff, "Die Berliner Illustrirte," quoted in Anton Kaes *et al.* (eds), *The Weimar Republic Sourcebook* (Berkeley: University of California Press, 1995), 646.

39 "Ein Tag auf der Forschungsreise" (photographs by Walter Bosshard), in *Berliner Illustrirte Zeitung*, vol. 38, no. 7, February 17, 1929, 275–7; "Das Haus des Schweigens" (photographs by André Kertész and Piermay), in *Berliner Illustrirte Zeitung*, vol. 38, no. 1, January 6, 1929, 35–7.

40 "Sous la règle de saint Benoît," in *VU*, no. 109, April 16, 1930, 336–40.

41 For a study of the different published versions of this reportage, and notably of the discussions between the photographers and *VU*'s management regarding image rights, see Michel Frizot and Annie-Laure Wanaverbecq, *André Kertész* (Paris: Jeu de Paume / Hazan, 2010), 186–8.

42 "Heute wie vor 5 000 Jahren" (photographs by Walter Bosshard), in *Münchner Illustrierte Presse*, vol. 9, no. 4, January 24, 1932, 78–9; "Das stille Königsberg," *in Münchner Illustrierte Presse*, vol. 9, no. 6, February 7, 1932, 148–9; "Schleswig-Holstein meerumschlungen" (photographs by Felix H. Man, Dephot), in *Münchner Illustrierte Presse*, vol. 9, no. 30, July 24, 1932, 797–9; "Im Elendsviertel von London" (photographs by Alfred Eisenstaedt), in *Münchner Illustrierte Presse,* vol. 9, no. 35, August 28, 1932, 940–1. About Stefan Lorant's layouts, see Hila Cooper, *Reading Magazines: Stefan Lorant and* Picture Post, *1939–1941*, masters thesis, Ryerson University, 2012.

43 See Charlotte Morton, "The *Arbeiter Illustrierte Zeitung* in Weimar Germany," in *Media, Culture & Society*, vol. 7, no. 2, April 1985, 187.

44 See Lugon, *La Photographie en Allemagne* (Nîmes: Jacqueline Chambon, 1997), 283.

45 See Heinz Willmann, *Geschichte der Arbeiter Illustrierten Zeitung, 1921–1938* (East Berlin: Dietz, 1975), 123.

46 Kurt Korff, "Die Berliner Illustrirte," quoted in Anton Kaes *et al.* (eds), *The Weimar Republic Sourcebook* (Berkeley: University of California Press, 1995), 646.

47 John Heartfield, "Fotomontage: ein Mittel des Klassenkampfes," retranslated here from Emmanuel Guigon and Franck Knoery (eds), *John Heartfield: photomontages politiques, 1930–1938* (Strasbourg: Musées de Strasbourg, 2006), 129.

48 John Heartfield, "Fotomontage: ein Mittel des Klassenkampfes," retranslated here from Emmanuel Guigon and Franck Knoery (eds), *John Heartfield: photomontages politiques, 1930–1938* (Strasbourg: Musées de Strasbourg, 2006), 129.

49 See Siegfried Kracauer, *The Past's Threshold: Essays on Photography*, translated by Conor Joyce (Chicago: University of Chicago Press, 2014); Walter Benjamin, "Small History of Photography," in Esther Leslie (ed./trans.), *On Photography: Walter Benjamin* (London: Reaktion, 2015); László Moholy-Nagy, *Painting, Photography, Film* (Boston: MIT Press, 1969).

50 See Emmanuel Guigon, "Tranchons-en !," in Emmanuel Guigon and Franck Knoery (eds), *John Heartfield* (Strasbourg: Musées de Strasbourg, 2006), 11; and Andrés Mario Zervigón, *John Heartfield and the Agitated Image: Photography, Persuasion, and the Rise of Avant-Garde Photomontage* (Chicago / London: University of Chicago Press, 2012).

51 *AIZ*, vol. 11, no. 48, November 27, 1932, cover.

52 Carlos Pérez, "John Heartfield: Dada, caricature politique et lutte des classes," in Emmanuel Guigon and Franck Knoery (eds), *John Heartfield* (Strasbourg: Musées de Strasbourg, 2006), 20.

53 See Andrés Mario Zervigón, "Persuading with the Unseen? Die Arbeiter-Illustrierte-Zeitung, Photography, and German Communism's Iconophobia," in *Visual Resources*, vol. 26, no. 2, 2010, 148.

54 "15 Jahre Sowjet-Macht," in *AIZ*, vol. 11, no. 47, November 20, 1932, 1124–25.

55 *AIZ*, vol. 14, no. 9, February 8, 1935, cover; *Regards*, vol. 4, no. 67, April 25, 1935, cover.

56 See Alexander Lavrentiev, *Alexander Rodchenko: Photography, 1924–1954* (Cologne: Könemann, 1995).

57 Bertolt Brecht, "An der Schwelle des 2. Jahrzehnts," in *AIZ*, vol. 10, no. 41, October 1931, 810, quoted in Siegfried Mews (ed./trans.), *A Bertolt Brecht Reference Companion* (Westport, CT: Greenwood Press, 1997), 143.

58 Tim Gidal, *Modern Photojournalism* (New York: Collier Books, 1973), 16–17.

59 Voir Peter Hunter-Salomon, *Erich Salomon: Portrait of an Age* (New York: Collier Books, 1967).

60 See Todd Gustavson, *Camera: a History of Photography from Daguerreotype to Digital* (New York: Sterling, 2009), 217.

61 Unknown author ("the editors"), "Notre but" (Our Goal) in *L'Illustration*, no. 1, March 4, 1843, 1.

62 "In Monte-Carlo," in *Berliner Illustrirte Zeitung*, vol. 38, no. 15, April 14, 1929, 643–4; "Erster Klasse auf dem Ozeanriesen," in *Berliner Illustrirte Zeitung*, vol. 38, no. 18, May 5, 1929, 748–9; "Vom Festbankett der Berliner Sezession," in *Die Dame*, no. 6, December 1929, 56; "Hinter den Kulissen der Lausanner Konferenz," in *Münchner Illustrierte Presse*, vol. 9, no. 30, July 24, 1932, 794–5.

63 See Sylvain Morand (ed.), *Erich Salomon: un photographe en smoking dans les années trente* (Strasbourg: Musées de Strasbourg, 2004); Peter Hunter-Salomon, *Erich Salomon* (New York: Collier Books, 1967), xiii; Tim Gidal, *Modern Photojournalism* (New York: Collier Books, 1973), 17.

64 Léon Gimpel, *Quarante ans de reportages* (1944), 61.

65 See Dominique de Font-Réaulx and Thierry Gervais (eds), *Léon Gimpel, 1873–1948* (Paris: Musée d'Orsay / Éditions des Cinq Continents, 2008).

66 For Felix H. Man, see *Berliner Illustrirte Zeitung*, vol. 38, no. 34, August 25, 1929, cover; and for Alfred Eisenstaedt, *Berliner Illustrirte Zeitung*, vol. 41, no. 7, February 21, 1932, 174.

67 "The Spanish sovereigns dining in the French restaurant at the Barcelona Exhibition," photograph by Jean Clair-Guyot. *L'Illustration*, no. 4500, June 1, 1929, 669.

68 See Clément Chéroux, *Henri Cartier-Bresson* (New York: Abrams, 2008), 29–30.

69 *Berliner Illustrirte Zeitung*, vol. 39, no. 25, June 22, 1930, cover.

70 Enno Kaufhold, "Photographic Heights: the Berlin Years, 1928–1934," in F.C. Gundlach (ed.), *Martin Munkácsi* (New York / Göttingen: ICP / Steidl, 2006), 215–16.

71 Quoted in Clément Chéroux, *Henri Cartier-Bresson* (New York: Abrams, 2008), 30.

72 *Berliner Illustrirte Zeitung*, "Der 21. März: die Staatsfeierlichkeiten bei der Reichstagseröffnung," special issue, March 1933.

73 *Berliner Illustrirte Zeitung*, vol. 38, no. 7, February 17, 1929, cover.

74 See Enno Kaufhold, in F.C. Gundlach (ed.), *Martin Munkácsi* (New York / Göttingen: ICP / Steidl, 2006), 206–7.

75 "Die Fieber-Division von Rio" (photograph by Martin Munkácsi), in *Berliner Illustrirte Zeitung*, vol. 41, no. 28, July 17, 1932, 906–7.

76 Martin Munkácsi and Albert Renger-Patzsch, "Halt mal still!," *UHU*, no. 10, July 1929, 18–25; "Photogramme," *UHU*, no. 5, February 1928, 36–7.

77 "Spanische Tänze," in *Die Dame*, no. 25, September 1, 1930, 11–13.

78 André Gunthert, "Esthétique de l'occasion," *Études photographiques*, 2001.

79 Gabriel Rongier, "Notre illustration: à la couverte," in *L'Amateur photographe*, vol. 5, no. 5, March 1, 1889, 88, quoted in André Gunthert, "Esthétique de l'occasion," *Études photographiques*, 2001, 76.

80 *Die Dame*, no. 9, January 1932 (2nd number), 4–9; *Le Miroir du monde*, no. 191, October 28, 1933, cover; *VU*, no. 313, March 14, 1934, 328; *Art et Médecine*, March 1934, 23.

81 *Berliner Illustrirte Zeitung*, vol. 39, no. 25, June 22, 1930, cover.

82 *Berliner Illustrirte Zeitung*, vol. 41, no. 17, April 30, 1932, cover.

83 See Felix H. Man, *Man with Camera: Photographs from Seven Decades* (New York: Schocken Books, 1983); Alfred Eisenstaedt, *Witness to Our Time* (New York: Penguin Books, 1980).

84 *Münchner Illustrierte Presse*, vol. 8, no. 19, March 1, 1931, 260–1; *Berliner Illustrirte Zeitung*, vol. 40, no. 11, March 15, 1931, 403; see Felix H. Man, "Journey in the Desert," in *Man with Camera* (New York: Schocken Books, 1983), no page number.

85 *Berliner Illustrirte Zeitung*, vol. 39, no. 37, September 14, 1930, cover.

86 Henry Luce, "Foreword," in Alfred Eisenstaedt, *Witness to Our Time* (New York: Penguin Books, 1980), 7.

87 Felix H. Man, "Introduction," in *Man with Camera* (New York: Shocken Books, 1983), no page number.

88 "Préface," in *L'Illustration*, September 1, 1843, no page number; Nadar, Bibliothèque Nationale de France, Mss, N.a.f, fol. 55.

89 See especially Vincent Lavoie, "Prestige de la News Value et quantification du mérite," in *Photojournalismes* (Vanves: Hazan, 2010), 152–73.

90 André Gaudreault, "L'Institutionnalisation comme effet de rupture," in *Cinéma et Attraction: pour une nouvelle histoire du cinématographe* (Paris: CNRS Editions, 2008), 74–5.

91 Lucien Vogel, "*VU*: remarques sur un nouveau journal illustré," in *VU*, no. 1, March 21, 1928, 11.

92 See Danielle Leenaerts, *Petite histoire du magazine* VU, *1928–1940: entre photographie d'information et photographie d'art* (Brussels: Peter Lang, 2010), 27.

93 Edmond Gréville (ed.), "Un grand journal illustré moderne," Pathé, 1928, 6′ 30″. Sixty-six stills are reproduced in Michel Frizot and Cédric de Veigy, VU: *le magazine photographique, 1928–1940* (Paris: La Martinière, 2009), 298–9.

94 See note 16.

95 "*VU*: remarques sur un nouveau journal illustré," in *VU*, no. 1, March 21, 1928.

96 See Françoise Denoyelle, "La Presse," in *La Lumière de Paris: les usages de la photographie, 1919–1939* (Paris: L'Harmattan, 1997), 19–148.

97 "VU dans le monde," in *VU*, no. 72, July 31, 1929, 615.

98 My thanks go to François Cheval and Sylvain Besson for having given me access both to these statistics and to their digitized versions of *VU*, *Voilà*, *Le Miroir*, *Art et Médecine*, *Paris Match* and *Réalités*.

99 Françoise Denoyelle, "Le Studio Keystone," in *La Lumière de Paris*, 86–8.

100 Carlo Rim, "Le Métier de journaliste," in *VU*, no. 249, December 21, 1932, 2065.

101 Jacques Berr, "Comment on fait *VU*," in *VU*, no. 54, March 27, 1929, 245–6.

102 Danielle Leenaerts, *Petite histoire du magazine* VU (Brussels: Peter Lang, 2010), 391.

103 "Sous la règle de saint Benoît," in *VU*, no. 109, April 16, 1930, 336–40.

104 Michel Frizot and Annie-Laure Wanaverbecq, *André Kertész* (Paris: Jeu de Paume / Hazan, 2010), 188, 193–5.

105 Michel Frizot and Annie-Laure Wanaverbecq, *André Kertész* (Paris: Jeu de Paume / Hazan, 2010), 190.

106 "Les Mystères de la vie chère," in *VU*, no. 245, November 23, 1932, 1846–56, comprises seven photographs by Kertész, five anonymous photographs and one from the Universal agency, one by Simon(?), one by "Z."(?), four photomontages by Marcel Ichac and one by Alexandre (Liberman). "Quartier Latin 1933," in *VU*, no. 297, February 22, 1933, 235–8, contains six photographs by Kertész, two anonymous photographs and one from the Aral agency.

107 "La Journée des enfants," in *VU*, no. 198, December 30, 1931, 2882–5.

108 Emmanuel Burl, "Les Ouvrières de Paris," in *VU*, no. 247, December 7, 1932, 1925–8 (twelve photographs by Krull); no. 248, December 14, 1932 (nine photographs by Krull), 2011–14; no. 249, December 21, 1932, 2047–51; no. 250, December 28, 1932 (three photographs by Krull), 2079–82; no. 251, January 4, 1933, 12–15; no. 252, January 11, 1933 (two photographs by Krull), 43–7.

109 Florent Fels, "Les Mystères de la foire aux puces" (photographs by Germaine Krull), in *VU*, no. 12, June 6, 1928, 306–7.

110 Jean Gallotti, "Au souffle du verrier," in *VU*, no. 36, November 21, 1928, 788–9.

111 See Michel Frizot and Annie-Laure Wanaverbecq, *André Kertész* (Paris: Jeu de Paume / Hazan, 2010), 188.

112 "Mussolini," in *VU*, no. 14, June 20, 1928, 352–3.

113 Alexander Liberman and Charles Churchward, *Then: Photographs, 1925–1995* (New York: Random House, 1995).

114 Michel Frizot and Cédric de Veigy, *VU* (Paris: La Martinière, 2009), 9–11.

115 Danielle Leenaerts, *Petite histoire du magazine* VU (Brussels: Peter Lang, 2010), 26.

116 "Un homme tombe dans la rue" (photographs by Brassaï), in *VU*, no. 228, July 27, 1932, 1222–3.

117 "Un illustre temple de la musique: la Scala de Milan," in *VU*, no. 309, February 14, 1934, 208–9.

118 "Je patine, tu patines, il patine," in *VU*, no. 203, February 3, 1932, 144–5; "Skis . . .," in *VU*, no. 208, March 9, 1932, 304–5; "On tuera en plaine," in *VU*, no. 338, September 5, 1934, 1127–8.

119 "La Naissance d'un navire" (photographs by Roger Schall), in *VU*, no. 343, October 10, 1934, 1268–9.

120 See for example the covers of *VU* no. 105 of March 19, 1930 and no. 115 of May 28, 1930.

121 "La Voix de la province," in *VU*, no. 310, February 21, 1934, cover; "Colonisation," in *VU*, special number, March 3, 1934, cover.

122 "Voici," in *Voilà*, no. 1, March 28, 1931, 4.

123 Florent Fels became director of *Voilà* in 1932. See Élisa Baitelli, *L'Image du fait divers dans la revue* Détective *de 1928 à 1940*, masters dissertation, Université Paris-1–Panthéon-Sorbonne, 2012, 8, 18.

124 "La présentation de ce numéro est de Pierre Laguarrigue" (This issue designed by Pierre Laguarrigue), *Voilà*, no. 1, March 28, 1931, 5.

125 See for example "Burlesque," in *Voilà*, no. 46, February 6, 1932, 12–13; "Danseuses nues," in *Voilà*, no. 47, February 13, 1932; "La Femme en URSS," in *Voilà*, no. 52, March 19, 1932, 5–6; and most of the back covers.

126 Léo Larguier, "La Cour des miracles" (photographs by Alfred Eisenstaedt), in *Voilà*, no. 103, March 11, 1933, 12–13.

127 Antoine Zischka, "Un nouvel empire du fer," in *Voilà*, no. 60, May 14, 1932, 8–9.

128 Georges Simenon, "Europe 33," in *Voilà* nos. 104–10, March 18 to April 29, 1933.

129 See Élisa Baitelli, *L'Image du fait divers dans la revue* Détective *de 1928 à 1940*, 15–16.

130 See for example "Chairs d'or," in *Voilà*, nos. 151–9, February 10 to April 7, 1934; and "Mes amies les bêtes," in *Voilà*, nos. 163–7, May 5 to June 2, 1934.

131 May Reeves, "Charlie Chaplin intime," in *Voilà*, nos 164–72, May 12 to July 7, 1934.

132 Pierre Scize, "La Mort blanche," in *Voilà*, nos. 181–3, September 8–22, 1934.

133 "*VU*: remarques sur un nouveau journal illustré," in *VU*, no. 1, March 21, 1928, 11.

134 "Voici," in *Voilà*, no. 1, March 28, 1931, 4.

135 "La Guerre civile en Espagne," in *VU*, September 23, 1936, 1106.

136 Lucien Vogel, "En manière de conclusion," in *VU*, special issue: "En Espagne: la défense de la République," August 29, 1936, 59.

137 See Danielle Leenaerts, *Petite histoire du magazine* VU (Brussels: Peter Lang, 2010), 338.

138 See Arnaud Mercier, "L'Institutionnalisation de la profession de journaliste," in *Hermès*, no. 13–14, 1994, 219–35.

139 See Arnaud Mercier, "L'Institutionnalisation de la profession de journaliste," in *Hermès*, no. 13–14, 1994, 223.

140 See Georges Bourdon, "Les Étapes de l'organisation du journalisme français," in *Cahier de la presse*, no. 1, January–March 1938, 23–30.

141 See Vincent Lavoie, *Photojournalismes*, 126–47.

142 Siegfried Kracauer, "Photography" (1927), in *The Mass Ornament: Weimar Essays*, translated by Thomas Y. Levin (Cambridge, MA: Harvard University Press, 2005), 58.

143 Walter Benjamin, "A Small History of Photography," in Esther Leslie (ed./trans.), *On Photography: Walter Benjamin* (London: Reaktion, 2015).

Chapter 3

1 Bodo von Dewitz and Robert Lebeck, *Kiosk* (Göttingen: Steidl, 2001), 274.

2 Mary Panzer and Christian Caujolle, *Things As They Are* (New York: Aperture Foundation / World Press Photo, 2005), 9.

3 See Chapter 1.

4 See Erika Doss (ed.), *Looking at Life Magazine* (Washington: Smithsonian Institution Press, 2001).

5 "The Camera as Essayist," in *Life*, vol. 2, no. 17, April 26, 1937, 62–3; see also Thomas Duquesnoy, "L'Essai photographique: histoire d'un genre au sein de la presse illustrée du xxe siècle," in *Revue de l'art*, no. 175, first quarter 2012, 37–41.

6 See Michael Schudson, *Discovering the News: A Social History of American Newspapers* (New York: Basic Books, 1978); Robert T. Elson, *Time Inc.: The Intimate History of a*

Publishing Enterprise, 1923–1941 (New York: Atheneum, 1968); Loudon Wainwright, *The Great American* Magazine (New York: Knopf, 1986); James L. Baughman, *Henry R. Luce and the Rise of the American News Media* (Baltimore: Johns Hopkins University Press, 2001); Jason Hill, "On the Efficacy of Artifice: PM, Radiophoto, and the Journalistic Discourse of Photographic Objectivity," in *Études photographiques*, no. 26, November 2010, 71–85.

7 See Chapters 1 and 2.

8 *Life*, vol. 61, no. 15, October 7, 1966, 100.

9 See the quotations by Gordon Parks in Erika Doss, "Visualizing Black America: Gordon Parks at *Life*, 1948–1971," in *Looking at* Life *Magazine* (Washington: Smithsonian Institution Press, 2001), 229–30.

10 Clare Boothe Brokaw, memo to Condé Nast, May 9, 1931, used as evidence in the lawsuit *Corcoran v. Time Inc.*, Supreme Court of the County of New York, quoted in Otha C. Spencer, *Twenty Years of* Life: *a Study of Time, Inc.'s Picture Magazine and its Contributions to Photojournalism*, doctoral dissertation, University of Missouri, 1958, 134–5. Condé Nast and Lucien Vogel first got to know each other in 1922, when Vogel was made art director of the French edition of *Vogue*. In 1923 Condé Nast bought *L'Illustration des modes*, which Vogel had launched in 1920, and turned it into *Jardin des modes*, which Vogel would direct until 1954. See Danielle Leenaerts, *Petite histoire du magazine* VU (Brussels: Peter Lang, 2010), 19–21.

11 See Loudon Wainwright, *The Great American Magazine* (New York: Knopf, 1986), 3.

12 "Purpose," in *Fortune*, no. 1, February 1930, 38.

13 See Vicki Goldberg, "Fortune and Men's Eyes," in *Margaret Bourke-White: a Biography* (New York: Harper & Row, 1986), 101–12.

14 "Tsaa-a Tsaa-a Tsaa-a," in *Fortune*, no. 1, February 1930, 54–62, 120, 124, 126.

15 See Michael Hallett, *Stefan Lorant, Godfather of Photojournalism* (Lanham: Scarecrow Press, 2005), 39, 49.

16 See C. Zoe Smith, "Germany's Kurt Korff: an Emigré's Influence on Early *Life*," in *Journalism & Mass Communication Quarterly*, vol. 65, no. 2, June 1988, 412–24.

17 Letter from Henry Luce to Kurt Safranski, December 5, 1956, private collection.

18 See Robert T. Elson, *Time Inc.* (New York: Atheneum, 1968), 272–3.

19 See C. Zoe Smith, "Germany's Kurt Korff," in *Journalism and Mass Communication Quarterly*, 414–18.

20 Kurt Korff, "Essential Outline for a New Illustrated Magazine," 1935, Time Inc. Archives, in C. Zoe Smith, *Émigré Photography in America: Contributions of German Photojournalism from Black Star Picture Agency to* Life *Magazine, 1933–1938*, doctoral dissertation, University of Iowa, 1983, 245.

21 See C. Zoe Smith, "Germany's Kurt Korff," in *Journalism and Mass Communication Quarterly*, vol. 65, no. 2, 419.

22 See Hendrik Neubauer, *Black Star: 60 Years of Photojournalism* (Cologne: Könemann, 1997).

23 See C. Zoe Smith, "Black Star Picture Agency: *Life*'s European Connection," in *Journalism History*, vol. 13, no. 1, spring 1986, 19–25.

24 Robert T. Elson, *Time Inc.* (New York: Atheneum, 1968), 291.

25 Robert T. Elson, Time Inc. (New York: Atheneum, 1968), 287–28 and 305; see also Wilson Hicks, *Words and Pictures* (New York: Harper, 1952).

26 "Speaking of Pictures," in *Life*, vol. 1, no. 2, November 30, 1936, 2–3.

27 "*VU*: remarques sur un nouveau journal illustré," in *VU*, art. cit., 11.

28 As calculated by the author, with the assistance of Elisa Gilmour and Paige Lindsay, on the basis of the first two issues of each year.

29 See Sally Stein, "The Graphic Ordering of Desire: Modernization of a Middle-Class Women's Magazine, 1919–1939," in Richard Bolton (ed.), *The Contest of Meaning: Critical Histories of Photography* (Cambridge, MA: MIT Press, 1989), 144–61.

30 *Life*, vol. 2, no. 1, January 4, 1937, 2–3. The magazine's circulation reached 1 million in 1937, exceeded 5 million in 1948 and was close to 8 million in the 1960s. Overall readership between 1936 and 1972 was estimated at 17–25 million. See James L. Baughman, "Who Reads *Life*? The Circulation of America's Favorite Magazine," in Erika Doss (ed.), *Looking at* Life *Magazine* (Washington: Smithsonian Institution Press, 2001), 40–51.

31 Wilson Hicks, *Words and Pictures* (New York: Harper, 1952), 42.

32 As calculated by the author, with the assistance of Elisa Gilmour and Paige Lindsay, on the basis of the first two issues of each year.

33 Wilson Hicks, *Words and Pictures* (New York: Harper, 1952), 43.

34 See for example the cover of *Picture Post*, vol. 1, no. 7, November 12, 1938 or of *Match*, no. 634, July 7, 1938.

35 Michael Hallett, *Stefan Lorant, Godfather of Photojournalism* (Lanham: Scarecrow Press, 2005), 73.

36 See Loudon Wainwright, *The Great American Magazine* (New York: Knopf, 1986), 17.

37 *Lilliput*, vol. 1, no. 6, December 1937, no page number.

38 *Lilliput*, vol. 3, no. 2, August 1938, 222–3.

39 See Michael Hallett, *Stefan Lorant, Godfather of Photojournalism* (Lanham, Scarecrow Press, 2005), 60–8.

40 See Michael Hallett, *Stefan Lorant, Godfather of Photojournalism* (Lanham, Scarecrow Press, 2005), 72.

41 "With the Candid Camera in the Café of Artists," in *Picture Post*, vol. 1, no. 7, November 12, 1938, 29–33.

42 As Hallett and Lorant tell it, no photographer was credited for fear of drawing the attention of the British authorities to the absence of work permits. See Michael Hallett, *Stefan Lorant, Godfather of Photojournalism* (Lanham, Scarecrow Press, 2005), 71.

43 For a structural analysis of the *Picture Post* of the early years, see Hila Cooper, *Reading Magazines: Stefan Lorant and* Picture Post, *1939–1941*, masters dissertation, Ryerson University, 2012.

44 See Richard Whelan, *This is War! Robert Capa at Work* (New York / Göttingen: ICP / Steidl, 2007), 134–205.

45 "La Victoire du rio Segre," in *Regards*, November 24, 1938, 11–15; "This Is War!," in *Picture Post*, December 3, 1938, 14–24; "*Life*'s Camera Gets Closer to Spanish War Than Any Camera Has Ever Got Before," in *Life*, vol. 5, no. 4, December 12, 1938, 28–9; "Une heure d'assaut," in *Match*, December 22, 1938, 21–7.

46 "This Is War!," in *Picture Post*, December 3, 1938, 14.

47 For both quotations: "The Greatest War Photographer in the World," in *Picture Post*, December 3, 1938, 13.

48 "James H. Hare, Greatest of War Photographers," in *Leslie's Weekly*, art. cit.

49 "Une journée de combat entre Yen–Tai et le Cha–Ho photographiée heure par heure," in *L'Illustration*, December 10, 1904, 412–13.

50 Image 15 in *Picture Post* corresponds to image 8 in *Match*, which captions it, "This wounded man can still walk with assistance." The *Picture Post* caption reads, "Bringing back a prisoner." The *Match* version fits with Capa's notes.

51 "Une heure d'assaut," in *Match*, December 22, 1938, 21.

52 See Chapter 1.

53 "La Photographie à la guerre," in *L'Illustration*, art. cit., 422–3.

54 "*Life*'s Camera Gets Closer to Spanish War Than Any Camera Has Ever Got Before," in *Life*, art. cit., 28.

55 "'Show me a man who thinks he's objective,' Luce said, 'and I'll show you a man who's deceiving himself.'" Michael Schudson, *Discovering the News* (New York: Basic Books, 1978), 149. See also the chapters devoted to *Time* in James L. Baughman, *Henry R. Luce and the Rise of the American News Media* (Baltimore: Johns Hopkins University Press, 2001), 37–61; Robert T. Elson, *Time Inc.* (New York: Atheneum, 1968), 58–118; and Alan Brinkley, *The Publisher: Henry Luce and His American Century* (New York: Vintage Books, 2010), 108–44.

56 There is an abundant literature on *Life* magazine: regarding its use of photography see, among others, Wendy Kozol, Life*'s America* (Philadelphia: Temple University Press, 1994); Chris Vials, "The Popular Front in the American Century," in *American Periodicals*, vol. 16, no. 1, 2006, 74–102; Jason Hill, "On the Efficacy of Artifice," in *Études photographiques*, no. 26, November 2010; and Thomas Duquesnoy, "L'Essai photographique," in *La Revue de l'art*, no. 175, first quarter 2012.

57 "The Camera as Essayist," in *Life*, vol. 2, no. 17, April 26, 1937, 62.

58 "The Camera as Essayist," in *Life*, vol. 2, no. 17, April 26, 1937, 62.

59 As calculated by the author with the assistance of Elisa Gilmour and Paige Lindsay.

60 "The Japanese: the World's Most Conventional People," in *Life*, vol. 3, no. 9, August 30, 1937, 40–50.

61 Print no. BS.2–005,071917/43–1887, Ryerson Image Centre Collection, Ryerson University, Toronto, Canada.

62 See for example the Yonosuke Natori bromide print "Army Recruiting and Training," 21.3 x 14 cm, c. 1940, no. BS.2005.074394/45–222, Ryerson Image Centre Collection, Ryerson University, Toronto, Canada.

63 As calculated by the author with the assistance of Elisa Gilmour and Paige Lindsay.

64 See Chapter 2.

65 "The Hairy Ainus: Japan's Aborigines Are Strange Relic of Primitive Man," in *Life*, vol. 20, no. 23, June 10, 1946, 109–17; "A Summer Resort in Winter," in *Life*, vol. 34, no. 4, January 26, 1953, 94–101; "Part Goddess, Part Imp, All Woman," in *Life*, vol. 51, no. 6, August 11, 1961, 50–64.

66 See for example Henri Cartier–Bresson, "Everything Goes On in the Piazza," in *Life*, vol. 35, no. 3, July 20, 1953, 71–9.

67 "Harlem Gang Leader," in *Life*, vol. 25, no. 18, November 1, 1948, 96–106. Regarding this reportage, see Russell Lord, *Gordon Parks: the Making of an Argument* (Göttingen / Pleasantville: Steidl / Gordon Parks Foundation, 2013).

68 "Freedom's Fearful Foe: Poverty," in *Life*, vol. 50, no. 24, June 16, 1961, 86–98. Concerning Gordon Parks, see Paul Roth, *Gordon Parks (Photofile)* (London: Thames & Hudson, 2014).

69 Quoted in Erika Doss, "Visualizing Black America," in *Looking at* Life (Washington: Smithsonian Institution Press, 2001), 229–30.

70 George Hunt, "To Gene Smith, Welcome Back," in *Life*, vol. 55, no. 9, August 30, 1963, 3.

71 "A Man of Mercy," in *Life*, vol. 37, no. 20, November 15, 1954, 161–72.

72 See Glenn G. Willumson, "A Man of Mercy," in *W. Eugene Smith and the Photographic Essay* (Cambridge / New York: Cambridge University Press, 1992), 179–82.

73 *Life*, vol. 18, no. 17, April 23, 1945, 11.

74 "The Last Round" (photographs by Robert Capa) and "The Battlefield of Iwo" (photographs by Eugene Smith), in *Life*, vol. 18, no. 15, April 9, 1945, 27–37 and 93–101.

75 See Glenn G. Willumson, "Photojournalistic Practice," in *W. Eugene Smith and the Photographic Essay* (Cambridge / New York: Cambridge University Press, 1992), 233–59.

76 "Country Doctor" (Eugene Smith), in *Life*, vol. 25, no. 12, September 20, 1948, 115–25.

77 "Hard Times on Broadway," in *Life*, vol. 26, no. 7, February 14, 1949, 87–95.

78 "Nurse Midwife," in *Life*, vol. 31, no. 19, November 5, 1951, 134–45.

79 "Spanish Village: Photographed for *Life* by Eugene Smith," in *Life*, vol. 30, no. 15, April 9, 1951, 120–9; Maitland Edey, "Spanish Village," in *Great Photographic Essays from Life* (Boston: New York Graphic Society, 1978), 105–15.

80 Maitland Edey, "Spanish Village," in *Great Photographic Essays from Life* (Boston: New York Graphic Society, 1978), 105.

81 Maitland Edey, "Spanish Village," in *Great Photographic Essays from Life* (Boston: New York Graphic Society, 1978), 105; see also John G. Morris, *Get the Picture: A Personal History of Photojournalism* (Chicago and London: The Chicago University Press, 2002), 181.

82 A *Life* in-house report on reader reaction to Smith's essay, in Glenn G. Willumson, *W. Eugene Smith and the Photographic Essay* (Cambridge / New York: Cambridge University Press, 1992), 127.

83 For these two quotations: "The History of Western Culture," in *Life*, vol. 22, no. 9, March 3, 1947, 69.

84 See Marie-Laure Aurenche, "La Presse de vulgarisation ou la Médiation des saviors," in Dominique Kalifa, Philippe Régnier, Marie-Ève Thérenty and Alain Vaillant (eds), *La Civilisation du journal* (Paris: Nouveau Monde Éditions, 2011), 383–416.

85 "The Book of Hours," in *Life*, vol. 24, no. 1, January 5, 1948, 38–50; "Life of the Chinook," in *Life*, vol. 29, no. 10, September 4, 1950, 48–57; "Geography of the Universe," in *Life*, vol. 29, no. 15, October 9, 1950, 94–108.

86 "Odd Partners Found in Nature," in *Life*, April 28, 1958, 86–98; "Helicopter Safari on Africa" (photographs by Howard Sochurek), in *Life*, vol. 42, no. 23, June 10, 1957, 80–93.

87 Letter from Edward K. Thompson to W. Eugene Smith, December 2, 1954, quoted in Glenn G. Willumson, *W. Eugene Smith and the Photographic Essay* (Cambridge / New York: Cambridge University Press, 1992), 228.

88 "The People of Russia, Part One: Moscow," in *Life*, vol. 30, no. 3, January 17, 1955, 15–30; "The People of Russia, Part Two: Travel in the USSR," in *Life*, vol. 38, no. 5, January 31, 1955, 83–91.

89 As calculated by the author with the assistance of Elisa Gilmour and Paige Lindsay. See "What We Hope You Will Like," in *Life*, vol. 50, no. 22, June 2, 1961, 2 and *Life*, vol. 50, no. 23, June 9, 1961, 2; in this regard see also Thomas Duquesnoy, "L'Essai photographique," *La Revue de l'art*, no. 175, first quarter 2012.

90 "This Is Castro's Cuba Seen Face to Face" (Henri Cartier-Bresson), in *Life*, vol. 54, no. 11, March 15, 1963, 28–43; "On Ride with Yankee Papa 13" (Larry Burrows), in *Life*, vol. 58, no. 15, April 16, 1965, 24–33; "Khe Sanh" (David Douglas Duncan), in *Life*, vol. 64, no. 8, February 23, 1968, 20–31; "Death-Flow from a Pipe" (Eugene Smith), in *Life*, vol. 72, no. 21, June 2, 1972, 74–81.

91 Wendy Kozol, "Photographic Realism and Cultural Politics," in *Life's America*, 6–11.

92 See Chris Vials, "The Popular Front in the American Century," in *American Periodicals*, vol. 16, no. 1, 2006.

93 See Gaëlle Morel, "L'Agence de photographes Magnum," in *Le Photoreportage d'auteur*, 21–3.

94 See Françoise Denoyelle, La *Lumière de Paris*, 91–5.

95 Jean Lacouture, William Manchester and Fred Ritchin, *In Our Time: The World As Seen by Magnum Photographers* (New York: W.W. Norton & Co., 1989), 430.

96 See John G. Morris, *Get the Picture,* 148.

97 "Women and Children in the USSR," in *Ladies' Home Journal,* February 1948, 44–59; "Scènes de la vie quotidienne en Russie soviétique," in *Réalités*, no. 25, February 1948, 49–68; "People of the Soviet," in *Illustrated*, May 1, 1948, 5–21.

98 John Steinbeck and Robert Capa, *A Russian Journal* (New York: Viking Press, 1948), 8.

99 Robert Capa, *Death in the Making* (New York: Covici-Friede Publishers, 1938); Robert Capa, *Slightly Out of Focus* (New York: Henry Holt, 1947).

100 "Israel's First Year," in *Illustrated*, August 27, 1949, 9–17; "Israel Reborn," in *Look*, vol. 13, no. 23, November 8, 1949, 25–33.

101 Irwin Shaw and Robert Capa, *Report on Israel* (New York: Simon and Schuster, 1950), 8.

102 See Jean-Pierre Montier, "Henri Cartier-Bresson, 'Public Intellectual'?," in *Études photographiques*, no. 25, May 2010, 167–79.

103 See Clément Chéroux, "La Reconfiguration du monde," in *Henri Cartier-Bresson* (Paris: Centre Pompidou, 2013), 218–35.

104 See John G. Morris, *Get the Picture*, 202.

105 "Le Peuple russe," in *Paris Match*, no. 304, January 29, 1955, 44–67; "Le Peuple russe," in *Paris Match*, no. 305, February 5, 1955, 46–63.

106 *Life*, vol. 38, no. 3, January 17, 1955, 16; *Paris Match*, no. 304, January 29, 1955, 44.

107 "Uniformed Children, Glorified Elders," in *Life*, vol. 38, no. 3, January 17, 1955, 24–5; "Uniform compulsory for Russian schoolchildren," in *Paris Match*, no. 304, January 29, 1955, 62–3.

108 Roland Barthes, "The Photographic Message," translated by Stephen Heath, in Vicki Goldberg (ed.), *Photography in Print: Writings from 1816 to the Present* (Albuquerque: University of New Mexico Press, 1988), 522.

109 For the cropped image, see "Hôtel Ukraine à l'heure de la pause: le fox-trot des ouvriers," in *Paris Match*, no. 304, January 29, 1955, 60–1, and compare with Henri Cartier-Bresson, *The People of Moscow. Photographed and Introduced by Henri Cartier-Bresson* (London: Thames & Hudson, 1955), illustration 53. For the reversed image see "A Western Sightseer's View of Plain Georgians," in *Life*, vol. 38, no. 5, January 31, 1955, 86–7, and "Prix d'excellence des ouvriers: la Riviera de la mer Noire," in *Paris Match*, no. 305, February 5, 1955, 56–7.

110 Regarding the editorial strategies practiced at *Paris Match*, see Audrey Leblanc, "The Color of May 1968: *Paris Match* and the Events of May and June 1968," in *Études photographiques*, no. 26, November 2010, 179–89.

111 *The People of Moscow. Photographed and Introduced by Henri Cartier-Bresson* (London: Thames and Hudson, 1955), no page numbers [4].

112 Jean-Pierre Montier, "Henri Cartier-Bresson, 'Public Intellectual'?," in *Études photographiques*, 173.

113 *Henri Cartier-Bresson: photographies, 1930–1955*, Musée des Arts décoratifs, Paris, October–November 1955.

114 "Khe Sanh," in *Life*, 23 February 1968, 20–31.

115 David Douglas Duncan, *I Protest!* (New York: Signet Books, 1968).

116 Philip Jones Griffiths, *Vietnam Inc.* (New York: Collier Books; London: Collier-Macmillan, 1971), 4.

117 See Gaëlle Morel, "Gilles Caron, auteur photographe dans les années 1960?," in *Revue de l'art*, no. 175, first quarter 2012, 59–66; and Michel Poivert, *Gilles Caron: le conflit intérieur* (Arles: Photosynthèses, 2013), 46–89.

118 See Gaëlle Morel, "Les Agences de presse: Gamma, Sygma, Sipa," in *Le Photoreportage d'auteur*, 23–5.

119 "Quatre Jours de guerre: le canal!," in *Paris Match*, no. 949, June 17, 1967, 46–89.

120 Interview with Jean-Claude Gautrand in Michel Poivert, *Gilles Caron* (Arles: Photosynthèses, 2013), 23.

121 "Une journée de combat entre Yen-Tai et le Cha-Ho photographiée heure par heure," in *L'Illustration*, December 10, 1904, 412–13.

122 Michel Poivert, "La conscience malheureuse du photographe," in *Gilles Caron* (Arles: Photosynthèses, 2013), 358–411.

123 "Liste des reportages de Gilles Caron," Gilles Caron Foundation. Our thanks to the foundation for providing this information.

124 Alain Chenu, "Des sentiers de la gloire aux boulevards de la célébrité: sociologie des couvertures de *Paris Match*, 1949–2005," in *Revue française de sociologie*, vol. 49, no. 1, 2008, 3–52.

125 Alain Chenu, "Des sentiers de la gloire aux boulevards de la célébrité: sociologie des couvertures de *Paris Match*, 1949–2005," in *Revue française de sociologie*, vol. 49, no. 1, 2008, 24.

126 "Monaco intime" (photographs by Howell Conant), in *Paris Match*, no. 542, August 29, 1959, 30–7.

127 "Stern bei den Kennedys," in *Stern*, vol. 16, no. 19, May 12, 1963, 14–17.

128 Covers of *Paris Match*, no. 736, May 18, 1963 and *Stern*, vol. 16, no. 25, June 23, 1963.

129 Cover of *Stern*, vol. 29, no. 23, May 26, 1976.

130 See Marie-Françoise Lévy (ed.), *La Télévision dans la République: les années 1950* (Brussels / Paris: Éditions Complexe / IHTP-CNRS, 1999); Patrick Eveno, "La Publicité," in *L'Argent de la presse française des années 1820 à nos jours* (Paris: Éditions du CTHS, 2003), 158–61.

131 See Jean-Pierre Bacot, "Le Retard et le Rattrapage de *Paris Match*," in Karine Taveaux-Grandpierre and Joëlle Beurier (eds), *Le photojournalisme des années 1930 à nos jours* (Rennes: Presses Universitaires de Rennes, 2014), 37–45.

132 See Alain Chenu, "Des sentiers de la gloire aux boulevards de la célébrité," in *Revue française de sociologie*, vol. 49, no. 1, 2008, 30.

133 Hubert Henrotte, "Roger Thérond, le géant de *Paris Match*," in *Le Monde dans les yeux: Gamma-Sygma, l'âge d'or du photojournalisme* (Paris: Hachette, 2005,) 79.

134 For details of the OJD see www.ojd.com/Support/paris-match. In 2013 *Paris Match*'s certified circulation was 781,672.

Conclusion

1 Jean-François Chevrier, "Entre l'actualité et l'histoire," in Philippe Néagu (ed.), *La Photographie: dix ans d'enrichissement des collections publiques* (Paris: RMN, 1992), 6–15.

2 Voir Gaëlle Morel, *Le Photoreportage d'auteur* (Paris: CNRS, 2006), and Gaëlle Morel, "La Figure de l'auteur: l'accueil du photoreporter dans le champ culturel français, 1981–1985," in *Études photographiques,* no. 13, July 2003, 35–55.

3 For examples see James Nachtwey, "Death As a Way of Life," in *Time*, vol. 141, no. 24, June 14, 1993, 42–5; and "Outside Kosovo," in *Time*, vol. 153, no. 22, June 7, 1999, 48–53.

4 James Nachtwey, *Inferno* (London: Phaidon, 1999).

5 See for example Antoine de Baecque (ed.), *La Politique des* auteurs (Paris: Cahiers du Cinéma, 2001); Michel Foucault, "What is an Author?," in James D. Faubion (ed.), *Michel Foucault: Aesthetics, Method and Epistemology*, translated by Robert Hurley *et al.* (New York: The New Press, 1998), vol. 2, 205–22.

6 Fred Ritchin, "Close Witnesses," in Michel Frizot (ed.), *New History of Photography* (Paris, A. Biro / Bordas, 1994), 610–11.

7 Hartwig Fischer (ed.), *Covering the Real: Art and the Press Picture, from Warhol to Tillmans* (Cologne: DuMont, 2005).

8 See Garance Chabert, "Covering the Real: entretien avec Hartwig Fischer," in Gaëlle Morel (ed.), *Photojournalisme et Art contemporain: les derniers tableaux* (Paris: Éditions des Archives contemporaines, 2008), 13–24.

9 Michel Poivert, "Photojournalism as Cultural Object," in *art press*, no. 306, November 2004, 23.

10 Georges Didi-Huberman, "Emotion Does Not Say 'I': Ten Fragments on Aesthetic Freedom," in Nicole Schweizer (ed.), *Alfredo Jaar: The Politics of Images* (Zurich / Lausanne: J.R.P. Ringier / Musée cantonal des Beaux-Arts, 2007), 65.

11 Michel Guerrin, "L'Actualité en images confrontée à des œuvres d'art," in *Le Monde*, July 29, 2005, 18.

12 See Garance Chabert, "Covering the Real: entretien avec Hartwig Fischer," in Gaëlle Morel (ed.), *Photojournalisme et Art contemporain* (Paris: Éditions des Archives contemporaines, 2008), 18.

13 Hartwig Fischer and Bernhard Mendes Bürgi, "Preface," in *Covering the Real* (Cologne: DuMont, 2005), 6.

14 See Garance Chabert, "Covering the Real: entretien avec Hartwig Fischer," in Gaëlle Morel (ed.), *Photojournalisme et Art contemporain* (Paris: Éditions des Archives contemporaines, 2008), 17–19.

15 Hartwig Fischer and Bernhard Mendes Bürgi, "Preface," in *Covering the Real* (Cologne: DuMont, 2005), 6.

16 For a definition of contemporary photography, see Michel Poivert, *La Photographie contemporaine* (Paris: Flammarion, 2002).

17 Jeff Wall and Roy Arden, "The Dignity of the Photograph," in *art press*, no. 251, November 1999, 17.

18 Pascal Beausse, "Photography versus the Image," *art press*, no. 251, November 1999, 46.

19 See Bruno Serralongue, "Droit de regard," in Gaëlle Morel (ed.), *Photojournalisme et Art contemporain* (Paris: Éditions des Archives contemporaines, 2008), 45–55.

20 See Michel Poivert, "Le Photojournalisme érigé en objet culturel," in *art press*, no. 306, November 2004, 21–4.

21 Michel Poivert, "La Tentation d'une photographie d'histoire," in Laurent Gervereau *et al.* (eds), *Voir / Ne pas voir la guerre* (Paris, BDIC / Somogy, 2001), 337–40.

22 See Gaëlle Morel, "Esthétique de l'auteur: signes subjectifs ou retrait documentaire?," in *Études photographiques*, no. 20, June 2007, 134–47.

23 For a study of this series, see in particular Quentin Bajac, "Le Regard élargi: les photographies panoramiques de Luc Delahaye," in *Les Cahiers du MNAM*, no. 92, summer 2005, 30.

24 Michel Guerrin, "Les 'tableaux d'histoire' contemplatifs de Luc Delahaye," *Le Monde*, March 2, 2003, 17.

25 Dominique Baqué, "Reasons for a Lack of Focus," *art press*, no. 319, January 2006, 89. Georges Didi-Huberman reacts to this accusation in "Emotion Does Not Say 'I': Ten Fragments on Aesthetic Freedom," in Nicole Schweizer (ed.), *Alfredo Jaar* (Zurich / Lausanne: J.R.P. Ringier / Musée cantonal des Beaux-Arts, 2007), 64–5.

26 See Clément Chéroux (ed.), *Paparazzi! Photographers, Stars, Artists* (Paris: Flammarion, 2014).

27 See Claire Guillot, "Le Joli Coup du Centre Pompidou-Metz," in *Le Monde*, February 28, 2014, consulted on line.

28 Georges Didi-Huberman, "Emotion Does Not Say 'I': Ten Fragments on Aesthetic Freedom," in Nicole Schweizer (ed.), *Alfredo Jaar* (Zurich / Lausanne: J.R.P. Ringier / Musée cantonal des Beaux-Arts, 2007), 64.

Bibliography

Primary Sources

Anonymous ('la rédaction'), "Notre but," in *L'Illustration*, no. 1, March 4, 1843, 1.
Babin, Gustave, "La Guerre vue par les photographes: Jimmy Hare," in *L'Illustration*, no. 3238, March 18, 1905, 167.
Baum, Vicki, *Grand Hotel*, translated by Basil Creighton, London: Geoffrey Bles, 1930.
Baum, Vicki, *Helene*, translated by Felice Bashford, London: Geoffrey Bles, 1932.
Berr, Jacques, "Comment on fait," in *VU*, March 27, 1929, 245–6.
Capa, Robert, *Death in the Making*, New York: Covici-Friede Publishers, 1938.
Capa, Robert, *Slightly Out of Focus*, New York: Henry Holt, 1947.
Clair-Guyot, Ernest, "Un demi-siècle à *L'Illustration*," in *L'Illustration*, no. 4713, July 1, 1933, n.p.
Duncan, David Douglas, *I Protest!*, New York: Signet Books, 1968.
Gimpel, Léon, *Quarante ans de reportages: souvenirs de Léon Gimpel, collaborateur à* L'Illustration, *1897–1932*, Domaine de Castellemont, Jurançon, manuscrit (collection SFP), February 20, 1944.
Griffiths, Philip Jones, *Vietnam Inc.* (1971), Paris: Phaidon, 2001.
Grimm, Thomas, "L'Art de vivre cent ans," in *Le Petit Journal*, no. 8649, August 31, 1886, 1.
Hicks, Wilson, *Words and Pictures: An Introduction to Photojournalism*, New York: Harper, 1952.
Joanne, Adolphe, "La Californie: San Francisco et Sacramento," in *L'Illustration*, no. 392, August 31, 1850, 135–8.
La Direction, "À nos lecteurs," in *La Vie au grand air*, no. 59, October 29, 1899, 74.
Lafitte, Pierre, "Notre programme," in *Excelsior: journal illustré quotidien*, no. 1, November 16, 1910, 2.
Rim, Carlo, "Le Métier de journaliste," in *VU*, no. 249, December 21, 1932, 2065.
Selz, Jean, "Le Cinéma et la mise en pages," in *Presse-Publicité*, no. 3, March 28, 1937, 8.
Shaw, Irwin, and Robert Capa, *Report on Israel*, New York, Simon and Schuster, 1950.
Steinbeck, John and Robert Capa, *A Russian Journal*, New York: Viking Press, 1948.
Vautel, Clément, "Échos et Nouvelles," in *Bulletin du Photo-Club de Paris*, 1901, 66–8.
Vogel, Lucien, "En manière de conclusion," in *VU*, special issue: "En Espagne: la défense de la République," August 29, 1936, 59.
de Weindel, Henri and Lucien Métivet, "Bloc-Notes," in *La Vie illustrée*, no. 1, October 20, 1898, 2.

Secondary Sources

Albert, Pierre and Gilles Feyel, "Photographie et Médias," in Michel Frizot (ed.), *Nouvelle histoire de la photographie*, Paris: A. Biro / Bordas, 1994, 358–69.

von Amelunxen, Hubertus, "Le Mémorial du siècle," in Michel Frizot (ed.), *Nouvelle histoire de la photographie*, Paris: A. Biro / Bordas, 1994, 130–47.

Aurenche, Marie-Laure, "La Presse de vulgarisation ou la Médiation des savoirs," in Dominique Kalifa, Philippe Régnier, Marie-Ève Thérenty and Alain Vaillant (eds), *La Civilisation du journal: histoire culturelle et littéraire de la presse française au XIXe siècle*, Paris: Nouveau Monde Éditions, 2011, 383–416.

Bacot, Jean-Pierre, *La Presse illustrée au XIXe siècle: une histoire oubliée*, Limoges: Presses universitaires de Limoges, 2005.

Bacot, Jean-Pierre, "Le Retard et le rattrapage de *Paris Match*," in Karine Taveaux-Grandpierre and Joëlle Beurier (eds), *Le Photojournalisme des années 1930 à nos jours: structures, culture et public*, Rennes: Presses Universitaires de Rennes, 2014, 37–45.

Barnhurst, Kevin and John Nerone, "Civic Picturing vs. Realist Photojournalism: the Regime of Illustrated News, 1856–1901," in *Design Issues*, vol. 16, no. 1, spring 2000, 56–79.

Barnhurst, Kevin and John Nerone, *The Form of News: a History*, New York: Guilford Press, 2001.

Barthes, Roland, "Le Message photographique," in *Communication*s, no. 1, 1961, 127–38.

Barthes, Roland, *La Chambre claire: note sure la photographie*, Paris: Gallimard, 1981.

Barthes, Roland, *Mythologies* (1957), Paris: Le Seuil, 2010.

Baughman, James L., *Henry R. Luce and the Rise of the American News Media*, Baltimore, Johns Hopkins University Press, 2001.

Baughman, James L., "Who Reads *Life*? The Circulation of America's Favorite Magazine," in Erika Doss (ed.), *Looking at* Life *Magazine*, Washington: Smithsonian Institution Press, 2001, 40–51.

Bellanger, Claude, Jacques Godechot, Pierre Guiral and Fernand Terrou (eds), *Histoire générale de la presse française*, t. III: *De 1871 à 1940*, Paris: Puf, 1972.

Benjamin, Walter, "Petite histoire de la photographie" (1931), in *Études photographiques*, no. 1, November 1996, 6–39.

Benjamin, Walter, "The Work of Art in the Age of Mechanical Reproduction" (1936), in Hannah Arendt (ed.), *Walter Benjamin: Illuminations*, New York: Schoken Books,1968, 217-251.

Bernard, Denis and André Gunthert, *L'Instant rêvé:* Albert Londe, Nîmes / Laval: Jacqueline Chambon / Trois, 1993.

Bernière, Vincent and Marie Primois (eds), Actuel: *les belles histoires*, Paris: Actuel / La Martinière, 2011.

Beurier, Joëlle, *Images et Violence, 1914–1918: quand* Le Miroir *racontait la Grande Guerre . . .*, Paris: Nouveau Monde Éditions, 2007.

Beurier, Joëlle, "L'Apprentissage de l'événement: *Le Miroir* et la Grande Guerre," in *Études photographiques*, no. 20, June 2007, 68–83.

Bouqueret, Christian, *Des années folles aux années noires: la Nouvelle Vision photographique en France, 1920–1940*, Paris: Marval, 1997.

Bourdon, Georges, "Les Étapes de l'organisation du journalisme français," in *Cahier de la presse*, no. 1, January–March 1938, 23–30.

Brinkeley, Alan, *The Publisher: Henry Luce and His American Century*, New York: Vintage Books, 2010.
Campany, David, "Recalcitrant Intervention: Walker Evans's Pages," in *Études photographiques*, no. 27, May 2011, 111–123.
Campany, David, *Walker Evans: the Magazine Work*, Göttingen: Steidl, 2014.
Carnes, Cecil, *Jimmy Hare, News Photographer: Half a Century with a Camera*, New York: The Macmillan Company, 1940.
Chenu, Alain, "Des sentiers de la gloire aux boulevards de la célébrité: sociologie des couvertures de *Paris Match*, 1949–2005," in *Revue française de sociologie*, vol. 49, no. 1, 2008, 3–52.
Chéroux, Clément, "Mythologie du photographe de guerre," in Laurent Gervereau *et al.* (eds), *Voir / Ne pas voir la guerre: histoire des représentations photographiques de la guerre*, Paris: BDIC / Somogy, 2001, 306–11.
Chéroux, Clément, *Henri Cartier-Bresson: le tir photographique*, Paris: Gallimard, 2008.
Chéroux, Clément, *Henri Cartier-Bresson*, Paris: Centre Pompidou, 2013.
Chéroux, Clément (ed.), *Paparazzi! Photographes, stars et artistes*, Paris / Metz: Flammarion / Centre Pompidou-Metz, 2014.
Cox, Aurianne, "Le Journal *Signal*: presse illustrée et propagande allemande en France," in Agnès Calu, Patrick Eveno and Hervé Joly (eds), *Culture et médias sous l'Occupation: des entreprises dans la France de Vichy*, Paris: CTHS, 2009, 187–216.
Deleu, Christophe, "Le Monde selon *Le Nouveau Détective*: quand le fait divers renonce au réel," in *Les Cahiers du journalisme*, no. 14, spring–summer 2005, 76–92.
Denoyelle, Françoise, "La Presse," in *La Lumière de Paris: les usages de la photographie, 1919–1939*, Paris: L'Harmattan, 1997, 19–148.
von Dewitz, Bodo and Robert Lebeck, *Kiosk: eine Geschichte der Fotoreportage*, Göttingen: Steidl, 2001.
Didi-Huberman, Georges, "L'Émotion ne dit pas 'je': dix fragments sur la liberté esthétique," in *Alfredo Jaar: la politique des images*, Zurich / Lausanne: JRP Ringier / musée cantonal des Beaux-Arts, 2007, 57–69.
Didi-Huberman, Georges, *Quand les images prennent position. L'Oeil de l'histoire, 1*, Paris: Minuit, 2009.
Doss, Erika (ed.), *Looking at* Life *Magazine*, Washington: Smithsonian Institution Press, 2001.
Ducros, Françoise, "L'Imaginaire de la beauté," in Michel Frizot (ed.), *Nouvelle histoire de la photographie*, Paris: A. Biro / Bordas, 1994, 534–53.
Duquesnoy, Thomas, "L'Essai photographique: histoire d'un genre au sein de la presse illustrée du XXe siècle," in *Revue de l'art*, no. 175, premier trimestre 2012, 37–41.
Edey, Maitland, "Spanish Village," in *Great Photographic Essays from* Life, Boston: New York Graphic Society, 1978, 105–15.
Eisenstaedt, Alfred, *Witness to Our Time* (1966), New York: Penguin Books, 1980.
Elson, Robert T., *Time Inc.: the Intimate History of a Publishing Enterprise, 1923–1941*, New York: Atheneum, 1968.
Études photographiques, no. 20: "La Trame des images: histoires de l'illustration photographique," June 2007.
Études photographiques, no. 26: "Caught in the Act: Re-Thinking the History of Photojournalism," November 2010.

Eveno, "La Publicité," in *L'Argent de la presse française des années 1820 à nos jours*, Paris: Éditions du CTHS, 2003, 158–61.
de Font-Réaulx, Dominique, and Thierry Gervais (eds), *Léon Gimpel, 1873–1948: les audaces d'un photographe*, Paris: Musée d'Orsay / Éditions des Cinq Continents, 2008.
Freund, Gisèle, *La Photographie en France au XIXe siècle*: *essai de sociologie et d'esthétique* (1936), Paris: Bourgois, 2011.
Frizot, Michel, "Les Métamorphoses de l'image," in Michel Frizot (ed.), *Nouvelle histoire de la photographie*, Paris: A. Biro / Bordas, 1994, 430–55.
Frizot, Michel and Cédric de Veigy, *VU: le magazine photographique, 1928–1940*, Paris: La Martinière, 2009.
Frizot, Michel and Annie-Laure Wanaverbecq, *André Kertész*, Paris: Jeu de Paume / Hazan, 2010.
Gaudreault, André, *Cinéma et Attraction: pour une nouvelle histoire du cinématographe*, Paris: CNRS Éditions, 2008.
Gautrand, Jean-Claude, "Le Regard des autres," in Michel Frizot (ed.), *Nouvelle histoire de la photographie*, Paris: A. Biro / Bordas, 1994, 612–33.
Geers, Alexie, "L'Invention médiatique de la beauté," *Hypothèses / L'appareil des apparences*, October 25, 2011, http://apparences.hypotheses.org/684.
Geers, Alexie, "*Marie-Claire*, une rhétorique des savoirs utiles," *Hypothèses / L'appareil des apparences*, March 12, 2013, http://apparences.hypotheses.org/tag/rhetorique/684.
Gervais, Thierry, "D'après photographie: premiers usages de la photographie dans le journal *L'Illustration*, 1843–1859," in *Études photographiques*, no. 13, July 2003, 56–85.
Gervais, Thierry, "Photographies de presse? Le journal *L'Illustration* à l'ère de la similigravure," in *Études photographiques*, no. 16, May 2005, 166–81.
Gervais, Thierry, "L'Exploit mis en page: la médiatisation de la conquête de l'air à la Belle Époque," in Régis Durand and Michel Poivert (eds), *L'Événement: les images comme acteurs de l'histoire*, Paris: Hazan, 2007, 60–83.
Gervais, Thierry, "L'Invention du magazine: la photographie mise en page dans *La Vie au grand air*, 1898–1914," in *Études photographiques*, no. 20, June 2007, 50–67.
Gervais, Thierry, "On Either Side of the 'Gatekeeper:' Technical Experimentation with Photography at *L'Illustration* (1880–1900)," in *Études photographiques*, no. 23, May 2009, 51–63.
Gervais, Thierry, "La Similigravure: le récit d'une invention, 1878–1893," in *Nouvelles de l'estampe*, no. 229, March–April 2010, 2–29.
Gervais, Thierry, "'The Greatest of War Photographers:' Jimmy Hare, A Photojournalist at the Turn of the Twentieth Century," in *Études photographiques*, no. 26, 2010, 35–49.
Gervais, Thierry and Gaëlle Morel, "Les Formes de l'information," in André Gunthert and Michel Poivert (eds), *L'Art de la photographie*, Paris: Citadelles et Mazenod, 2007, 302–55.
Gervereau, Laurent *et al.* (eds), *Voir / Ne pas voir la guerre: histoire des représentations photographiques de la guerre*, Paris: BDIC / Somogy, 2001.
Gidal, Tim, *Modern Photojournalism: Origin and Evolution, 1910–1933*, New York: Collier Books, 1973.
Gould, Lewis L. and Richard Greffe, *Photojournalist: The Career of Jimmy Hare*, Austin: University of Texas Press, 1977.
Gretton, Tom, "Différence et compétition: l'imitation et la reproduction des œuvres d'art dans un journal illustré du XIXe siècle," in Georges Roque (ed.), *Majeur ou mineur? Les hiérarchies en art*, Nîmes: Jacqueline Chambon, 2000, 105–43.

Gretton, Tom, “Le Statut subalterne de la photographie: étude de la présentation des images dans les hebdomadaires illustrés (Londres, Paris, 1885–1910),” in *Études photographiques*, no. 20, June 2007, 34–49.
Gretton, Tom, “The Pragmatics of Page Design in Nineteenth-Century General-Interest Weekly Illustrated News Magazines in London and Paris,” in *Art History*, vol. 33, no. 4, September 2010, 680–709.
Guerrin, Michel, *Profession photoreporter: vingt ans d’images d’actualité*, Paris: Centre Georges-Pompidou / Gallimard, 1988.
Guerrin, Michel, “Le Marché des images de paparazzi,” in Clément Chéroux (ed.), *Paparazzi! Photographes, stars et artistes*, Paris / Metz: Flammarion / Centre Pompidou-Metz, 2014, 51–9.
Gundlach, F.C. (ed.), *Martin Munkácsi*, New York / Göttingen: ICP / Steidl, 2006.
Gunther, Thomas Michael, “La Diffusion de la photographie,” in Michel Frizot (ed.), *Nouvelle histoire de la photographie*, Paris: A. Biro / Bordas, 1994, 554–80.
Gunthert, André, “Un laboratoire de communication de masse. Le spectacle du sport et l’illustration photographique,” in Laurent Véray and Pierre Simonet (eds), *Montrer le sport: photographie, cinéma, télévision*, Paris: INSEP, 2000, 29–35.
Gunthert, André, “Esthétique de l’occasion: naissance de la photographie instantanée comme genre,” in *Études photographiques*, no. 9, May 2001, 64–87.
Gunthert, André, “L’Image parasite: après le journalisme citoyen,” in *Études photographiques*, no. 20, June 2007, 174–86.
Gustavson, Todd, *Camera: A History of Photography from Daguerreotype to Digital*, New York: Sterling, 2009.
Hallett, Michael, *Stefan Lorant, Godfather of Photojournalism*, Lanham: Scarecrow Press, 2005.
Hardt, Hanno, “Pictures for the Masses: Photography and the Rise of Popular Magazines in Weimar Germany,” in *Journal of Communication Inquiry*, vol. 13, no. 1, January 1989, 7–29.
Henrotte, Hubert *Le Monde dans les yeux: Gamma-Sygma, l’âge d’or du photojournalisme*, Paris: Hachette, 2005.
Herschdorfer, Nathalie, *Papier glacé: un siècle de photographie de mode chez Condé Nast*, Paris: Thames & Hudson, 2012.
Hill, Jason, “On the Efficacy of Artifice: *PM*, Radiophoto, and the Journalistic Discourse of Photographic Objectivity,” in *Études photographiques*, no. 26, November 2010, 71–85.
Hill, Jason E. and Vanessa R. Schwartz (eds), *Getting the Picture: The Visual Culture of the News*, London: Bloomsbury, 2015.
Huret, Marcel, *Ciné actualités: histoire de la presse filmée, 1895–1980*, Paris: Veyrier, 1984.
Ihl, Olivier, “Dans l’œil du daguerréotype. La rue du Faubourg-du-Temple, juin 1848,” in *Études photographiques*, no. 34, spring 2016, 86–107
Jeanne, René, and Charles Ford, *Le Cinéma et la presse*, Paris: Armand Colin, 1961.
Kalifa, Dominique, Philippe Régnier, Marie-Ève Thérenty and Alain Vaillant (eds), *La Civilisation du journal: histoire culturelle et littéraire de la presse française au XIX*[e] *siècle*, Paris: Nouveau Monde Éditions, 2011.
Korff, Kurt, “Die Berliner Illustrirte,” in Max Osborn (ed.), *50 Jahre Ullstein, 1877–1927*, Berlin: Ullstein Verlag, 1927, French translation by Olivier Lugon, *La Photographie en Allemagne: anthologie de textes, 1919–1939*, Nîmes: Jacqueline Chambon, 1997, 249–50.
Kozol, Wendy, Life’s *America*, Philadelphia: Temple University Press, 1994.

Kracauer, Siegfried, "Photography" (1927), in *The Mass Ornament: Weimar Essays*, translated by Thomas Y. Levin (Cambridge, MA: Harvard University Press, 2005), 47–64.

Lacouture, Jean, William Manchester and Fred Ritchin, *Magnum: 50 ans de photographies*, Paris: La Martinière, 1995.

Lavoie, Vincent, *L'Instant-monument: du fait divers à l'humanitaire*, Montréal: Dazibao, 2001.

Lavoie, Vincent, "Le Mérite photojournalistique: une incertitude critériologique," in *Études photographiques*, no. 20, June 2007, 120–33.

Lavoie, Vincent, *Photojournalismes: revoir les canons de l'image de presse*, Vanves: Hazan, 2010.

Lavoie, Vincent, "Photojournalistic Integrity: Codes of Conduct, Professional Ethics, and the Moral Definition of Press Photography," in *Études photographiques*, no. 26, November 2010, 190–212.

Lavoie, Vincent, "War and the iPhone: New Fronts for Photojournalism," in *Études photographiques*, no. 29, May 2012, 229–241.

Lavrentiev, Alexander, *Alexander Rodchenko: Photography, 1924–1954*, Cologne: Könemann, 1995.

Leblanc, Audrey, "The Color of May 1968: *Paris Match* and the Event of May and June 1968," in *Études photographiques*, no. 26, November 2010, 179–89.

Leenaerts, Danielle, *Petite histoire du magazine* VU, *1928–1940: entre photographie d'information et photographie d'art*, Brussels: Peter Lang, 2010.

Lerg, Winfried, "Media Culture of the Weimar Republic: a Historical Overview," in *Journal of Communication Inquiry*, vol. 13, no. 1, January 1989, 94–110.

Lévy, Marie-Françoise (ed.), *La Télévision dans la République: les années 50*, Brussels / Paris: Éditions Complexe / IHTP-CNRS, 1999.

Liberman, Alexander and Charles Churchward, *Then: Photographs, 1925–1995*, New York: Random House, 1995.

Lord, Russell, *Gordon Parks: The Making of an Argument*, Göttingen / Pleasantville: Steidl / Gordon Parks Foundation, 2013.

Lugon, Olivier, *La Photographie en Allemagne: anthologie de textes, 1919–1939*, Nîmes: Jacqueline Chambon, 1997.

Magilow, Daniel H., *The Photography of Crisis: The Photo Essay of Weimar Germany*, University Park, PA: Pennsylvania State University Press, 2012.

Malthête, Jacques, and Laurent Mannoni (eds), *Méliès: magie et cinéma*, Paris: Paris Musées, 2002.

Man, Felix H., *Man with Camera: Photographs from Seven Decades*, New York: Schocken Books, 1983.

Mercier, Arnaud, "L'Institutionnalisation de la profession de journaliste," in *Hermès*, no. 13–14, 1994, 219–35.

Meusy, Jean-Jacques, *Paris-Palaces ou le temps des cinémas, 1894–1918*, Paris: CNRS Éditions, 1995.

Mitry, Jean, "Le Montage dans les films de Méliès," in Madeleine Malthête-Méliès (ed.), *Méliès et la naissance du spectacle cinématographique*, Paris: Klincksieck, 1984, 149–55.

de Mondenard, Anne, and Michel Guerrin, Réalités: *un mensuel français illustré, 1946–1978*, Arles / Paris: Actes Sud / Maison européenne de la photographie, 2008.

Montier, Jean-Pierre, "Henri Cartier-Bresson, 'Public Intellectual'?," in *Études photographiques*, no. 25, May 2010, 167–79.

Moore, Kevin, *Jacques Henri Lartigue: the Invention of an Artist*, Princeton: Princeton University Press, 2004.

Morand, Sylvain (ed.), *Erich Salomon: un photographe en smoking dans les années trente*, Strasbourg: musées de Strasbourg, 2004.

Morel, Gaëlle, "Du peuple au populisme: les couvertures du magazine communiste *Regards*, 1932–1939," in *Études photographiques*, no. 9, May 2001, 44–63.

Morel, Gaëlle, "La Figure de l'auteur: l'accueil du photoreporter dans le champ culturel français, 1981–1985," in *Études photographiques*, no. 13, July 2003, 35–55.

Morel, Gaëlle, "Entre art et culture: politique institutionnelle et photographie en France, 1976–1996," in *Études photographiques*, no. 16, May 2005, 32–40.

Morel, Gaëlle, "Les Agences d'auteurs et la légitimation de la photographie en France, 1972–2001," in *Histoire et Sociétés: revue européenne d'histoire sociale*, no. 14, May 2005, 98–112.

Morel, Gaëlle, *Le Photoreportage d'auteur: l'institution culturelle de la photographie en France depuis les années 1970*, Paris: CNRS, 2006.

Morel, Gaëlle, "Esthétique de l'auteur: signes subjectifs ou retrait documentaire?," in *Études photographiques*, no. 20, June 2007, 134–47.

Morel, Gaëlle (ed.), *Photojournalisme et art contemporain: les derniers tableaux*, Paris: Éditions des Archives contemporaines, 2008.

Morel, Gaëlle, "Gilles Caron, auteur photographe dans les années 1960?," in *Revue de l'art*, no. 175, premier trimestre 2012, 59–66.

Morel, Gaëlle, "Photojournalism: A Formal Paradigm for Contemporary Art," in Jason E. Hill and Vanessa R. Schwartz (eds), *Getting the Picture: The Visual Culture of the News*, London: Bloomsbury, 2015, 266–71.

Morris, John G., *Get the Picture: A Personal History of Photojournalism*, Chicago and London: The Chicago University Press, 2002.

Morton, Charlotte, "The *Arbeiter Illustrierte Zeitung* in Weimar Germany," in *Media, Culture & Society*, vol. 7, no. 2, April 1985, 187–203.

Neubauer, Hendrik, *Black Star: 60 Years of Photojournalism*, Cologne: Könemann, 1997.

Newhall, Beaumont, "Photojournalism," in *The History of Photography: from 1839 to the Present*, New York: Museum of Modern Art, 1982, 248–67.

Panzer, Mary and Christian Caujolle, *Things As They Are: Photojournalism in Context since 1955*, New York: Aperture Foundation / World Press Photo, 2005.

Poivert, Michel, *La Photographie contemporaine*, Paris: Flammarion, 2002.

Poivert, Michel, "Le Photojournalisme érigé en objet culturel," in *art press*, no. 306, November 2004, 21–6.

Poivert, Michel, *Gilles Caron: le conflit intérieur*, Arles: Photosynthèses, 2013.

Puiseux, Hélène, *Les Figures de la guerre: représentations et sensibilités, 1839–1996*, Paris: Gallimard, 1997.

Ritchin, Fred "La Proximité du témoignage," in Michel Frizot (ed.), *Nouvelle histoire de la photographie*, Paris: A. Biro / Bordas, 1994, 590–611.

Roque, Georges "Introduction," in Georges Roque (ed.), *Majeur ou mineur? Les hiérarchies en art*, Nîmes: Jacqueline Chambon, 2000, 7–29.

Roth, Paul, *Gordon Parks*, London: Thames & Hudson, 2014.

Schudson, Michael, *Discovering the News: a Social History of American Newspapers*, New York: Basic Books, 1978.

Schwartz, Vanessa, "Cinematic Spectatorship before the Apparatus: The Public Taste for Reality in *Fin-de-Siècle* Paris," in Leo Charney and Vanessa Schwartz (eds), *Cinema and the Invention of Modern Life*, Berkeley: University of California Press, 1995, 297–319.

Schwartz, Vanessa, *Spectacular Realities: Early Mass Culture in* Fin-de-Siècle *Paris*, Berkeley: University of California Press, 1998.

Schwartz, Vanessa, "Wide Angle at the Beach: The Origins of the Paparazzi and the Cannes Film Festival," in *Études photographiques*, no. 26, November 2010, 151–61.

Sekula, Allan, "Paparazzo Notes," in *Photography Against the Grain: Essays and Photo Works, 1973–1983*, Halifax: Press of Nova Scotia College of Art and Design, 1984.

Smith, C. Zoe, "Black Star Picture Agency: *Life*'s European Connection," in *Journalism History*, vol. 13, no. 1, spring 1986, 19–25.

Smith, C. Zoe, "Germany's Kurt Korff: an Emigré's Influence on Early *Life*," in *Journalism & Mass Communication Quarterly*, vol. 65, no. 2, June 1988, 412–24.

Stein, Sally, "The Graphic Ordering of Desire: Modernization of a Middle-Class Women's Magazine, 1919–1939," in Richard Bolton (ed.), *The Contest of Meaning: Critical Histories of Photography*, Cambridge: MIT Press, 1989, 144–61.

Straw, Will, "Formal Strategies in the True Crime Photograph," in *Études photographiques*, no. 26, November 2010, 107–19.

Taft, Robert, "Photography and the Pictorial Press," in *Photography and the American Scene*, New York: Dover Publications, 1938, 419–50.

Taveaux-Grandpierre, Karine and Joëlle Beurier (eds), *Le Photojournalisme des années 1930 à nos jours: structures, culture et public*, Rennes: Presses Universitaires de Rennes, 2014.

Tucker, Anne (ed.), *War / Photography: Images of Armed Conflict and its Aftermath*, Houston: Museum of Fine Arts, 2012.

Ullstein, Herman, *The Rise and Fall of the House of Ullstein*, London: Nicholson & Watson, 1943.

Vials, Chris, "The Popular Front in the American Century: *Life* Magazine, Margaret Bourke-White, and Consumer Realism, 1936–1941," in *American Periodicals: A Journal of History, Criticism, and Bibliography*, vol. 16, no.1, 2006, 74–102.

Wainwright, Loudon, *The Great American Magazine: An Inside History of* Life, New York: Knopf, 1986.

Whelan, Richard, *This is War! Robert Capa at Work*, New York / Göttingen, ICP / Steidl, 2007.

Willmann, Heinz, *Geschichte der* Arbeiter-Illustrierten Zeitung*, 1921–1938*, Berlin-Est: Dietz, 1975.

Willumson, Glenn G., *W. Eugene Smith and the Photographic Essay*, Cambridge / New York: Cambridge University Press, 1992.

Wolf, Erika, "When Photographs Speak, to Whom Do They Talk? The Origins and Audience of *SSSR na stroike* (*USSR in Construction*)," in *Left History*, vol. 6, no. 2, 1999, 53–82.

Wolf, Erika, "'As at the Filippovs:' The Foreign Origins of the Soviet Narrative Photographic Essay," in Jorge Ribalta (ed.), *The Worker Photography Movement, 1926–1939: Essays and Documents*, Madrid: Museo Nacional Centro de Arte Reina Sofía, 2011, 124–30.

Zervigón, Andrés Mario, "Persuading with the Unseen? *Die Arbeiter-Illustrierte-Zeitung*, Photography, and German Communism's Iconophobia," in *Visual Resources*, vol. 26, no. 2, 2010, 147–64.

Zervigón, Andrés Mario, *John Heartfield and the Agitated Image: Photography, Persuasion, and the Rise of Avant-Garde Photomontage*, Chicago / London: University of Chicago Press, 2012.

Academic Dissertations

Baitelli, Élisa, *L'Image du fait divers dans la revue* Détective *de 1928 à 1940*, masters dissertation, Université Paris-1–Panthéon-Sorbonne, 2012.

Chermette, Myriam, "La Guerre russo–japonaise, 1904–1905: début du reportage moderne ou fin d'une époque?," in *Donner à voir: la photographie dans* Le Journal *– discours, pratiques, usages, 1892–1944*, doctoral dissertation, université de Versailles–Saint-Quentin-en-Yvelines, 2009.

Chéroux, Clément, *Une généalogie des formes récréatives en photographie, 1890–1940*, doctoral dissertation, Université Paris-I–Panthéon-Sorbonne, 2004.

Cooper, Hila, *Reading Magazines: Stefan Lorant and* Picture Post*, 1939–1941*, masters dissertation, Ryerson University, 2012.

Fossard, Aurore, *Paparazzi à l'écran: présence et disparition d'un personnage photographe dans la fiction cinématographique et télévisée occidentale, 1940–2008*, doctoral dissertation, université Lumière-Lyon 2, 2013.

Gervais, Thierry, *L'Illustration photographique: naissance du spectacle de l'information, 1843–1914*, doctoral dissertation, EHESS, 2007.

Gunthert, André, *La Conquête de l'instantané: archéologie de l'imaginaire photographique en France, 1841–1895*, doctoral dissertation, EHESS, 1999.

Kahan, Robert S., *The Antecedents of American Photojournalism*, doctoral dissertation, University of Wisconsin-Madison, 1969.

Smith, C. Zoe, *Émigré Photography in America: Contributions of German Photojournalism from Black Star Picture Agency to* Life *Magazine, 1933–1938*, doctoral dissertation, University of Iowa, 1983.

Spencer, Otha C., *Twenty Years of* Life*: a Study of Time, Inc.'s Picture Magazine and its Contributions to Photojournalism*, doctoral dissertation, University of Missouri, 1958.

Index

Page numbers in **bold** refer to figures.